CRITICAL INSIGHTS

The Grapes of Wrath

by John Steinbeck

Editor
Keith Newlin
University of North Carolina Wilmington

Salem Press
Pasadena, California   Hackensack, New Jersey

Cover photo: Library of Congress

Published by Salem Press

© 2011 by EBSCO Publishing
Editor's text © 2011 by Keith Newlin
"The *Paris Review* Perspective" © 2011 by Ha Jin for *The Paris Review*

∞ The paper used in these volumes conforms to the American National
Standard for Permanence of Paper for Printed Library Materials, Z39.48-1992
(R1997).

Library of Congress Cataloging-in-Publication Data
The grapes of wrath, by John Steinbeck / editor, Keith Newlin.
   p. cm. — (Critical insights)
Includes bibliographical references and index.
ISBN 978-1-58765-715-3 (alk. paper)
1. Steinbeck, John, 1902-1968. Grapes of wrath. I. Newlin, Keith.
PS3537.T3234G8525 2010
813'.52—dc22
                                      2010029214

PRINTED IN CANADA

Contents

The Book and Author

Critical Contexts

Critical Readings

Resources

About This Volume

Keith Newlin

This collection of essays contains a diverse selection of criticism on *The Grapes of Wrath*, the novel that catapulted John Steinbeck to the top of the best-seller lists and that is central to an understanding of the nature of his artistic achievement. The volume is divided into two main parts. The first, "Critical Contexts," provides a series of essays specifically commissioned for this collection; these present an overview of the critical history of *The Grapes of Wrath* as well as discussions of the context in which Steinbeck composed the novel and the work's influence. The second main section, "Critical Readings," consists of reprinted essays that, in addition to being interesting and revealing in their own right, reflect the trajectory of criticism of the novel over the years. Preceding the "Critical Contexts" section are a brief biography of Steinbeck by Joseph R. Millichap and a perspective from *The Paris Review* by Ha Jin. I also supply an introduction that provides a brief account of actual Dust Bowl migrants' responses to the novel. Following the "Critical Readings" section, the volume concludes with a chronology of Steinbeck's life, a list of his works, and a bibliography.

In the "Critical Contexts" section, Jennifer Banach examines *The Grapes of Wrath* as part of the tradition of protest literature, which "invokes faith and justice in the pursuit of social reform." Matthew J. Bolton places the novel in the context of the social protest novel as the genre grappled with the legacy of modernism. Steinbeck, he writes, "manages to synthesize the two strands, putting modernist themes, techniques, and tropes to work for a social cause." Michael Wentworth argues that the novel is a classic road novel in the tradition of the migration narrative central to America's founding. Camille-Yvette Welsch closes the section with a survey of the shifting trends in the scholarship devoted to the novel.

The essays reprinted in the "Critical Readings" section offer a representative selection of a variety of critical perspectives, beginning with a series of influential essays concerning the status of *The Grapes of Wrath* as a work of art. Reflecting the aesthetic ideologies of the times, early critics were preoccupied with the coherence of the novel's structure, themes, characters, and language. In an important essay about the philosophy of the novel, Frederic I. Carpenter argues that *The Grapes of Wrath* provides an "imaginative realization . . . in new and concrete forms" of Ralph Waldo Emerson's transcendentalism, Walt Whitman's democratic principles, and William James's and John Dewey's pragmatic philosophies, which in the novel "coalesce into an organic whole." Martin Shockley suggests that Jim Casy "represents a contemporary adaptation of the Christ image . . . in which the meaning of the book is revealed through a sequence of Christian symbols." Eric W. Carlson offers a rebuttal to Shockley, arguing that while "a few loose Biblical analogies may be identified," they are not central to the novel, and to suggest that the novel is a Christian parable "is to distort Steinbeck's intention and its primary framework of non-Christian symbolism."

Peter Lisca provides the section's first examination of the novel in terms of its fictional art, focusing on the novel's integration of interchapters, biblical and thematic symbols, and development of character. Warren Motley applies anthropologist Robert Briffault's theory of matriarchal societies to the novel and finds that Ma Joad becomes a "cohesive rather than a fragmenting force" and "a source of communal strength sheltering human dignity from the antisocial effects of individualism." Howard Levant contends that "*The Grapes of Wrath* is an attempted prose epic" and examines the coherence of its structure, themes, characters, and symbols; he concludes that while the first three-quarters are "masterful," the last quarter represents a decline, the result of Steinbeck's structural decision "to apply allegory to character, metaphor, and theme." Donald Pizer reads the novel in terms of literary naturalism, in which the Joads are "primitives" and are "close to the natural processes and rhythms of life." In his examination of the structure and themes of the novel and the role of profanity and language in the work, John H. Timmerman concludes that "Ma Joad and her dream of 'the fambly of man'" are a "clear response to the ongoing tension between the individual and the Group Man, freedom and restraint."

During more recent years, critics have been less concerned with the novel's aesthetic integrity and more interested in assessing its continued relevance for contemporary readers. With Steinbeck's papers and letters available, Robert DeMott provides a detailed discussion of the novel's composition and the effect of its publication on the writer. Keith Windschuttle counters the perception that Steinbeck's fictional portrayal of the Okie migration is accurate by discussing the work's exaggerations and distortions. Charles Cunningham assesses the politics of the novel, finding that "*The Grapes of Wrath* in effect wrestles with the contradiction between a radical class politics and American racial nationalism." Vivyan C. Adair connects the novel's feminine archetype to Steinbeck's metaphorical depiction of the land "as feminized, maternal space" that presents the "poor mother and wife as willing midwife to her own oppression . . . as she labors only to re-empower man."

THE BOOK AND AUTHOR

On *The Grapes of Wrath*

Keith Newlin

The publication of *The Grapes of Wrath* in 1939 was the media event of the year: reviewers were ecstatic, with Clifton Fadiman of *The New Yorke*r accurately predicting:

> A lot of readers and critics are going to abandon themselves to orgies of ohing and ahing over Steinbeck's impressive literary qualities, happy to blink at the simple fact that fundamentally his book is a social novel exposing social injustice and calling, though never explicitly, for social redress. It's going to be a great and deserved best-seller; it'll be read and praised by everyone; it will almost certainly win the Pulitzer Prize; it will be filmed and dramatized and radio-acted—but, gentle reader, amid all the excitement let's try to keep in mind what "The Grapes of Wrath" is about: to wit, the slow murder of half a million innocent and worthy American citizens. (140)

The novel quickly shot to the top of the best-seller lists, with more than 400,000 hardcover copies selling within a year. Steinbeck received the Pulitzer Prize in 1940. Movie rights were quickly negotiated, and Paramount released the film version starring Henry Fonda in 1940. Cultural commentators praised the book for its portrayal of what was emerging as a national calamity, while in Oklahoma and California, citizens and, especially, political leaders were outraged at Steinbeck's depiction of corrupt governments and heartless farm owners who treat migrant workers as dispensable cogs in the machinery of agricultural harvest. The novel received its most effective publicity when it was banned by the public library in Kern County, California, as well as by the public libraries in East St. Louis and Kansas City. Congressman Lyle Boren of Oklahoma denounced the novel from the floor of the U.S. House of Representatives on January 24, 1940: "I stand before this body as a son of a tenant farmer, labeled by John Steinbeck as an 'Okie.' . . . I say to you, and to every honest, square-minded reader in America, that the painting Steinbeck made in this book is a lie, a black, infernal creation of a twisted, distorted mind" (qtd. in Shockley 358).

Since the novel's publication, much has been written about how Steinbeck came to write it, of its genesis in his investigation of the conditions of migrant workers that led to the publication of a seven-part series of newspaper articles titled "The Harvest Gypsies." With the passage of years and the more objective perspective of historians, a number of articles and books have traced Steinbeck's distortion of facts and his careful structuring of events to elicit sympathy for the plight of the displaced migrant farmer. *The Grapes of Wrath* remains perhaps the most distinguished example of the proletarian novel to emerge from the 1930s. It is one of the true classic American novels.

How did the migrants themselves respond to the novel's depiction of their migration? Did the incidents of the novel and Steinbeck's depiction of the conditions of their lives and the reaction of native Californians to them reflect the reality of their experience?

From 1980 through 1982, a number of migrants were interviewed about their experiences as part of the California Odyssey Project, a National Endowment for the Humanities-funded effort to record the oral histories of fifty-seven individuals who migrated to California in the 1930s from Oklahoma, Texas, Missouri, Kansas, Arkansas, and other states. The interviews, which have been transcribed and are available in the Dust Bowl Migration Digital Archives on the Web site of the Walter W. Stiern Library, California State University, Bakersfield, provide a rich resource for determining the texture of the migrants' pre-emigration lives, their experiences en route to California, their responses to California, the conditions of farm life, and the reactions of Californians to the migrants. Of considerable interest are the migrants' responses to *The Grapes of Wrath* as a novel documenting their experiences and to the word "Okie," a term freighted with meaning. In the novel, the Joads first encounter the word when a back-trailing migrant warns them that the promised land holds little hope of alleviating their misery, that native Californians deeply resent their arrival. "You ain't never been called 'Okie' yet," the traveler tells Tom Joad. "Okie use' ta mean you was from Oklahoma. Now it means you're a dirty son-of-a-bitch. Okie means you're scum. Don't mean nothing itself, it's the way they say it" (280). After the Joads pass through a service station, one attendant tells another, "Them goddamn Okies got no sense and no feeling. They ain't human. A human being wouldn't live like they do. A human being couldn't stand it to be so dirty and miserable. They ain't a hell of a lot better than gorillas" (301).

In interview after interview, migrants recalled how hearing the term affected their self-esteem. Arkansas native Hazel Fay Mitchell said that she felt degraded by the term, that many Californians used "Okie" to refer to all migrants and that the term meant "trash, I guess—and I didn't feel like I was trash" (22). Loye Holmes remembered that "I had had two or three fights over people slurring me about being an Okie. That was what most of the people fights was over when we first came here. They'd call us all kinds of things." Children especially were the targets of much teasing. One mother refused to let Holmes's children in her house. "My children came home and I asked them what happened. They said that the woman told them to go home and that so-and-so couldn't play with us because we were Okies and might have lice." Even after the passage of more than forty years, the memory still angered Holmes. "'You have humiliated my children,'" she told the mother. "'I don't care what you say to me if you think you can get by with it. You call me one right now.' She began to back off and said, 'I'm sorry. I didn't know you knew.' I slapped her right beside the head. I slapped her so hard that my husband said I'd probably get arrested. I said, 'I don't care. It would be worth going to jail for'" (33-34). Vera Criswell remembered that, while her family was living in tents, her children were harassed at school: "They said that Okies ate worms or something. Just things that kids would think of and naturally, no kid with any self respect is going to take that all day. They're going to fight back" (36).

Elizabeth Day, who emigrated from Nebraska and whose father was a laborer for the Works Progress Administration rather than a field worker, related how she was careful to distinguish her own people from the Okies:

> We set ourselves apart because my mother was scrupulously clean. . . . In our minds the Okies were dirty and lacking in morals. This was an objective view of course because we didn't have any friends amongst the grape picker migrants and I'm sure we did them a disservice in our minds but there was the distinction. They also followed the crops which we didn't. We might have been better off had we done so. We were a step above them in our own minds. (18)

Day said that one could recognize an Okie "by a certain look about the eyes, defeatism, perhaps, and, of course, their Okie grammar when they spoke. . . . They had that twang in their talk, that midwest Okie twang and it's very likely that there were some Okies who were clean and just like we were. We just didn't recognize them or didn't put them in that class" (21). In retrospect, Day recognized that the stereotype was unkind, but prejudices die hard. "We laughed at them," she remembered:

> We thought they were the scum of the earth. They were no better than pigs. I think that was prevalent. There was no charity as I think back. I don't think I'm just drawing on my own lack of charity in my nature. I think we didn't want them there or if they were there we just looked at them with ridicule and that type of thing. We were very uncharitable. (21)

Not all migrants, however, were offended by the term "Okie." To James Lambert, the word signified the strength of will it took to survive in harsh economic times. He recalled:

To a lot of people "Okie" means a dirty word. Back years and years ago, back in the 1920s and 1930s "Okie" was trash. But "Okie" meaning to me is that you are one hell of a man or a woman or a child whichever one you might have been at that time. You worked hard, you lived hard and you played hard. There was nobody else to do the work same as your "Arkies," your "Texan" people, they were the same. (17)

Clara Davis, proud of her Oklahoma heritage, pointed out that there are two meanings to the word "Okie" and that Okies themselves use the term both as a point of pride and to point to the stereotype:

Some people just want to call the Okies trashy Okies. That's all they want. That's the way some people look at them. . . . Now there's one family I met from Oklahoma and they were Okies. They had eight kids and honest to goodness that woman and those kids never took a bath. We lived on a ranch and they moved on it. They never took a bath and they never combed their hair. They used to call them typical Okies because they were the typical people that came from Oklahoma that had the trashy name. Their kids are all grown and married now. They still live the way their mother raised them. And their mother's dead but they still live that same way. And you know there's no reason for anybody to live that way nowadays because a bar of soap don't cost much and they could go to the river and take a bath if there was no other way. (32-33)

When it comes to Steinbeck's depiction of Okies in *The Grapes of Wrath*, the real-life migrants who were interviewed for the most part took offense at the novel's portrayal of their lives, though many based their responses on the film version. Nebraskan Elizabeth Day, who throughout her interview displayed a lingering prejudice, thought the novel was "very, very accurate, yes. I think from what I had seen and heard I think he hit it right on the head. I think it was an excellent representation. . . . I think he hit the nail right on the head from what I saw of the 1940 Okies in Buttonwillow" (22). Most interviewees, however, saw the novel as an exaggeration. Dorothy Rose, a native of Arkansas, remembered that "I read the book and I liked the book as a story but we didn't like it. Everyone who spoke about it just said that he didn't know what he was talking about. It wasn't like that and so forth. I feel a lot of that was like that but I feel a lot of it wasn't like that" (34). Like other migrants, she blamed the novel for perpetuating the Okie stereotype when it was published and only later did she recognize Steinbeck's effort to elicit sympathy for the plight of the migrants:

> At the time the book came out the people from the dust bowl were having such difficult times anyway and they were a proud people they didn't want their misery emphasized. I think that it was hard for them to look at the book and feel that he was showing great compassion for these people. It took a few years to re-read the book to see that's what he was doing, that's what he did in reality. I know in discussing the book during that time I can't remember anyone who had any relatives or anybody who came out here who'd served time for murder like the main character in the book. (35)

Oklahoman Martha Jackson remembered, "I just didn't think it was really true to life. It was kind of making fun in a way. I don't think it was like that at all. At least it wasn't in this area. But it was a good movie and I enjoyed it. I just don't think it truly represented the people" (23). She, like other interviewees, credited some of the scenes in the book and movie with creating a false sense of Okie morality: "The part that I felt so bad about at the time was when the grandmother died and they buried her along the road. I just can't believe that they would really do that. I just don't believe that they did those things" (24). Texan Vera Criswell "thought it didn't coincide with any experience I'd ever had." What particularly rankled was the scene in the Weedpatch camp in which Ruthie and Winfield are introduced to flush toilets:

What made my daughter so mad was when the little children flushed the toilet and it scared them. They were girls nearly as old as she was. Oh, that made her so mad. She said that he would have you believe that we didn't even know what flush toilets were. . . . He took a little circumstance or condition that maybe happened to one person, maybe happened in a minor way, and he blew it into a great big thing and had it happening to everybody. I can't say that that kind of thing didn't happen to one or two people because I don't know what happened to all these other people but I think that he took an experience and built on it and exaggerated it and made it encompass more people. (45)

One constant in most of the interviews is the inability of interviewees to recognize the purpose of Steinbeck's documentary narrative strategy. Like all writers of fiction, Steinbeck selects key events to represent larger emotional truths, with the scenes serving to elicit compassion for his characters. Criswell, like most of the other interviewees, tended to see the scenes as "facts" without recognizing their fictional purpose. Juanita Price faulted the novel for its exaggeration: "It was stretched till some of the points were just outrageous" (26). Referring to the novel's closing scene, in which Rose of Sharon gives her breast to a starving man, Price complained, "An old man got real sick and they put a young girl in the bed with him to keep him warm. That's a myth. All that kind of stuff didn't happen. It's almost like teaching the little girl to be a prostitute before she got out of the baby stage putting her to bed with a man. I don't think people were that crazy" (27). Another example is Price's reaction to Ma Joad's taking charge of the family: "Then there was an old lady that would see after all of the food that was bought. The woman was kind of the boss over everybody. I don't believe that either" (27). Vera Criswell also believed Steinbeck's depiction of the Joads as a representative Okie family strained credulity:

They had every baser thing in human nature all combined in one family. They would have you believe that was the norm for those people that came from back there. Sure, they had things that would make you sympathetic to them. You couldn't help but be sympathetic to some of the things. At the same time they had this suggestion of immorality. They used language that was never used in my family. I really feel like he did a disservice with that book. He could have written an interesting book without all that. (46)

Clara Davis took particular offense at the characters' swearing:

Back in the thirties people didn't use language then like they do now. They just didn't say anything at all. My husband seldom ever said a word and if I ever said a word more than darn when I was a child growing up, my parents got me. Steinbeck was writing this and I think he exaggerated there about the language. (34)

Another constant in the interviews is the migrants' belief that *The Grapes of Wrath* is a kind of betrayal of the Okies—that, in the short run, the novel perpetuated stereotypes and insulted the very people for whom Steinbeck hoped to arouse sympathy. "Had the book not been written I don't think it would have been nearly as strong a feeling" against Okies (34), stated Dorothy Rose. "I think he did a disservice to an awful lot of people," agreed Vera Criswell. "He took a little grain of truth and made it into a mountain" (45). Native Oklahoman and retired schoolteacher Frank Manies offered a more balanced assessment of the novel's accuracy: "In some respects it was quite accurate. The economic situation was accurate. I'm sure John Steinbeck did a tremendous amount of research in the preparation of his book. There's no question in my mind that he was well versed in the things that he wanted to write about. The economic situations were quite accurate." The characters' language, however, particularly "the vile language," offended Manies: "It simply wasn't like that to any great degree—you would find some of it but it just wasn't like that and I resented John

Steinbeck using that kind of language. I didn't use it. I still don't and I know many of my friends and relatives did not" (29).

Loye Holmes stated her belief that the anti-Okie feeling never subsided until "after the war when our boys—the Okies and Arkies and Texans and Missourians—help[ed] win the war. We became equal" (34). Ernest Martin agreed that as the Okies settled into Californian culture and established roots, the anti-Okie sentiment subsided: "I think that we won. By that I mean, we took over. We were the outcasts in a certain sense at first. . . . we won—we took over. This is why you don't really hear so much of Okies anymore in the area—you might but it's only a nostalgic term—it's something that's not really derogatory anymore" (32-33).

Dorothy Rose, who emigrated from Arkansas and went on to become a published poet, captured the response of many of the migrants to the depiction of their experience in *The Grapes of Wrath* in her poem "Salinas" (1939), which she read to her interviewer:

> I hate him I hate him Charlcia said
> His book is a bunch of lies
> Dirty filthy nasty lies Mary Elizabeth said
> Steinbeck sells our hearts
> Our guts our pride Royce said
> He makes things worse
> For all the Okies in California Louise said
> Better to leave it alone
> Unwritten untold Grandma said
> It should be banned Gerald Ray said
>
> Daddy everyone is reading the book
> How can we go to school tomorrow I said
>
> With your heads held high Mamma said
>
> (34)

Though the migrants resented the novel for perpetuating anti-Okie prejudice, reviewers persisted in viewing the novel as a realistic and artful exposé of one of America's less shining moments, epic in scale and inspiring in effect. As Sterling North noted for the *Chicago Daily News*:

> Around a typical family of "Okies," the Joads, [Steinbeck] has written a novel which is tough and tender, religious and obscene, hard-hitting, magnificently realistic and unselfconsciously beautiful. . . . It is not sacrilegious to compare this novel to Homer and the old prophets. Filled with suffering, prophecy and enduring courage, it is the story not alone of our time and people—it is the story of the human race. (148)

Works Cited

Criswell, Vera. Interview by Stacy Jagels. 24 Feb. 1981. Oildale, CA. *Dust Bowl Migration Digital Archives*. 8 Jan. 2010. http://www.csub.edu/library/special/dustbowl/interviews/Criswell114.pdf.

Davis, Clara. Interview by Stacy Jagels. 29 Jan. 1981. Bakersfield, CA. *Dust Bowl Migration Digital Archives*. 8 Jan. 2010. http://www.csub.edu/library/special/dustbowl/interviews/Davis106.pdf

Day, Elizabeth. Interview by Stacy Jagels. 2 May 1981. Oakhurst, CA. *Dust Bowl Migration Digital Archives*. 8 Jan. 2010. http://www.csub.edu/library/special/dustbowl/interviews/Day132.pdf.

Dust Bowl Migration Digital Archives. California Odyssey Project's Oral History Program. Special Collections, Walter W. Stiern Library, California State University, Bakersfield. 8 Jan. 2010. http://www.csub.edu/library/special/dustbowl/dustbowl.shtml.

Fadiman, Clifton. "Highway 66—a Tale of Five Cities." *The New Yorker* 15 Apr. 1939: 81-82. Rpt. in Ray Lewis White, "*The Grapes of Wrath* and the Critics of 1939." *Resources for American Literary Study* 13 (1983): 134-64.

Holmes, Loye. Interview by Stacy Jagels. 12 Jan. 1981. Bakersfield, CA. *Dust Bowl Migration Digital Archives*. 8 Jan. 2010. http://www.csub.edu/library/special/dustbowl/interviews/Holmes113.pdf.

Jackson, Martha. Interview by Stacy Jagels. 10 Mar. 1981. Clovis, CA. *Dust Bowl Migration Digital Archives*. 8 Jan. 2010. http://www.csub.edu/library/special/dustbowl/interviews/Jackson118.pdf.

Lambert, James. Interview by Michael Neely. 10 Feb. 1981. Oildale, CA. *Dust Bowl Migration Digital Archives*. 8 Jan. 2010. http://www.csub.edu/library/special/dustbowl/interviews/Lambert109.pdf.

Manies, Frank. Interview by Stacy Jagels. 18 Feb. 1981. Tulare, CA. *Dust Bowl Migration Digital Archives*. 8 Jan. 2010. http://www.csub.edu/library/special/dustbowl/interviews/Manies110.pdf.

Martin, Ernest. Interview by Judith Gannon. 5 Apr. 1981. Pasadena, CA. *Dust Bowl Migration Digital Archives*. 8 Jan. 2010. http://www.csub.edu/library/special/dustbowl/interviews/Martin127abc.pdf.

Mitchell, Hazel Fay. Interview by Michael Neely. 29 May 1981. Arvin, CA. *Dust Bowl Migration Digital Archives*. 8 Jan. 2010. http://www.csub.edu/library/special/dustbowl/interviews/Mitchell137.pdf.

North, Sterling. "Book of the Week." *Chicago Daily News* 19 Apr. 1939: 26. Rpt. in Ray Lewis White, *"The Grapes of Wrath* and the Critics of 1939." *Resources for American Literary Study* 13 (1983): 134-64.

Price, Juanita. Interview by Stacy Jagels. 26 Jan. 1981. Bakersfield, CA. *Dust Bowl Migration Digital Archives*. 8 Jan. 2010. http://www.csub.edu/library/special/dustbowl/interviews/Price105.pdf.

Rose, Dorothy. Interview by Stacy Jagels. 7 Apr. 1981. Northridge, CA. *Dust Bowl Migration Digital Archives*. 8 Jan. 2010. http://www.csub.edu/library/special/dustbowl/interviews/Rose128.pdf.

Shockley, Martin. "The Reception of *The Grapes of Wrath* in Oklahoma." *American Literature* 15 (1944): 351-61.

Steinbeck, John. *"The Grapes of Wrath": Text and Criticism*. Ed. Peter Lisca. New York: Penguin, 1977.

Biography of John Steinbeck_____

Joseph R. Millichap

John Ernst Steinbeck was born on February 27, 1902, in Salinas, California. The time and place of his birth are important because Steinbeck matured as an artist in his early thirties and during the darkest days of the Depression, and his most important fictions are set in his beloved Salinas Valley. In one sense, Steinbeck's location in time and place may have made him a particularly American artist. Born just after the closing of the frontier, Steinbeck grew up with a frustrated modern America and witnessed the most notable failure of the American Dream with the Great Depression. He was a writer who inherited the great tradition of the American Renaissance of the nineteenth century and who was forced to reshape it in terms of the historical and literary imperatives of twentieth century modernism.

Steinbeck's family background evidences this strongly American identity. His paternal grandfather, John Adolph Steinbeck, emigrated from Germany, settling in California after serving in the Civil War. His mother's father, Samuel Hamilton, sailed around Cape Horn from northern Ireland, finally immigrating to the Salinas Valley. John Ernst Steinbeck and Olive Hamilton were the first-generation descendants of sturdy, successful, and Americanized immigrant farm families. They met and married in 1890 and settled in Salinas, where John Steinbeck, Sr., became prominent in local business and government, and Olive stayed home to rear their four children—three daughters and a son, the third child, who was named for his father. The Steinbecks were refined, intelligent, and ambitious people who lived a quiet middle-class life in the small agricultural service town of Salinas.

Steinbeck seems to have enjoyed a happy childhood, and, in fact, he often asserted that he did. His father made enough money to indulge him in small ways, even to buy him a red pony. His mother encouraged him to read and to write and provided him with the classics of English and American literature. At school, he proved a popular and successful student and was elected president of his senior class.

After graduation from Salinas High School in 1919, Steinbeck enrolled at Stanford University. His subsequent life belies the picture of the happy, normal young man he presented while in high school. He was soon in academic difficulties and dropped out of college several times to work on ranches in the Salinas Valley and observe "real life." His interests were varied, but he settled on novel writing as his ambition, despite his family's insistence that he prepare for a more prosaic career. This traumatic rejection of middle-class values would prove a major force in shaping Steinbeck's fiction, both his social protest novels and his lighter entertainments such as *Cannery Row*.

Leaving Stanford without a degree in 1925, Steinbeck sojourned in New York for several months, where he worked as a laborer, a newspaper reporter, and a freelance writer. Disillusioned in all his abortive pursuits, Steinbeck returned to California, where a job as winter caretaker of a lodge at Lake Tahoe provided the time to finish his first novel, *Cup of Gold*. The novel, a romance concerning the Caribbean pirate Henry Morgan, was published by a small press directly before the stock market crash of 1929, and it earned the young writer little recognition and even less money. In 1930, he married Carol Henning and moved with her to Los Angeles and later to Pacific Grove, a seaside resort near Monterey, where he lived in his parents' summer house. Still supported by his family and his wife, the ambitious young writer produced the manuscripts of several novels.

A friend, Edward F. Ricketts, a marine biologist trained at the University of Chicago, encouraged Steinbeck to treat his material more objectively. Under Ricketts's influence, Steinbeck modified his earlier commitment to satire, allegory, and romanticism and turned to modern accounts of the Salinas Valley. Steinbeck set his next two novels, *The Pastures of Heaven* and *To a God Unknown*, in the Valley, but both were still marked by excessive sentimentality and symbolism. Both were virtually ignored by the public and the critics. Steinbeck's short fiction, however, began to receive recognition; for example, his story "The Murder" was selected as an O. Henry Prize story in 1934.

Tortilla Flat, a droll tale of Monterey's Mexican quarter, established Steinbeck as a popular and critical success in 1935. (Unfortunately, his parents died just before he achieved this first real success.) The novel's sales provided enough money for Steinbeck to pay his debts, travel to Mexico, and continue writing seriously. His next novel, *In Dubious Battle*, established him as a serious literary artist and began the period of his greatest success, both critical and popular. This harshly realistic strike novel followed directions Steinbeck had established in earlier stories such as "The Raid" and was influenced by the realistic impulse of American literature in the 1930's. Succeeding publications quickly confirmed this development in his fiction. His short novels *The Red Pony* and *Of Mice and Men* followed in 1937, his story collection *The Long Valley* in 1938, and his epic of the "Okie" migration to California, *The Grapes of Wrath*, in 1939. His own play version of *Of Mice and Men* won the Drama Critics' Circle Award in 1938, and *The Grapes of Wrath* received the Pulitzer Prize in 1940. Steinbeck had become one of the most popular and respected writers in the United States, a spokesman for an entire culture.

In 1941, the Japanese attack on Pearl Harbor changed the direction of American culture and of John Steinbeck's literary development. During the war years, Steinbeck seemed to be in a holding pattern, trying to adjust to his phenomenal success while absorbing the cataclysmic events around him. His career stalled for many reasons. He left the California subjects and realistic style of his finest novels, and he was unable to come to terms with a world at war, though he served for a few months as a frontline news correspondent. Personal developments in Steinbeck's life paralleled these literary ones. He divorced his first wife and married Gwyndolyn Conger, a young Hollywood starlet; no doubt she influenced his decision to move from California to New York. Steinbeck began to write with an eye on Broadway and Hollywood.

Steinbeck was forty-three years old when World War II ended in 1945;

he died in 1968 at the age of sixty-six. Over those twenty-three years, he was extremely productive and won considerable acclaim—most notably, the Nobel Prize in Literature in 1962. Yet the most important part of his career was finished. The war had changed the direction of his artistic development, and Steinbeck seemed powerless to reverse his decline.

Again, his personal life mirrored his literary difficulties. Although Gwyn Conger presented him with his only children—Tom, born in 1944, and John, born in 1946—they divorced in 1948. Like his first divorce, this one was bitter and expensive. In the same year, his mentor, Ed Ricketts, was killed in a car accident. Steinbeck traveled extensively, devoting himself to film and nonfiction projects. In 1950, he married Elaine Scott, establishing a supportive relationship that allowed him to finish his epic Salinas Valley novel *East of Eden*.

Steinbeck tried again and again to write his way back to the artistic success of his earlier years, notably in *The Wayward Bus*, but his commercial success kept getting in the way. *East of Eden*, his major postwar novel, was an attempt at another California epic to match the grandeur of *The Grapes of Wrath*. Although the book was a blockbuster best seller, it was an artistic and critical failure. Steinbeck himself seemed to recognize his own decline, and in his last years he virtually abandoned fiction for journalism.

Of his last novels, only *The Winter of Our Discontent* transcends mere entertainment, and it does not have the literary structure necessary to support its serious themes. Despite the popularity of Steinbeck's nonfiction, such as *Travels with Charley*, despite awards such as the Nobel Prize and the Presidential Medal of Freedom, and despite his personal friendship with President Lyndon Johnson as a supporter of the U.S. war effort in Vietnam, Steinbeck was only the shell of the great writer he had been during the 1930's. He died in New York City on December 20, 1968.

From *Critical Survey of Long Fiction*. 4th ed. Edited by Carl Rollyson. Pasadena, CA: Salem Press, 2010.

Bibliography

Astro, Richard, and Tetsumaro Hayashi, eds. *Steinbeck: The Man and His Work.* Corvallis: Oregon State University Press, 1971. One of the first full-length works published after Steinbeck's death; the essays in this superb collection present Steinbeck as everything from a mere proletarian novelist to an artist with a deep vision of humans' essential dignity.

Benson, Jackson J. *The True Adventures of John Steinbeck, Writer.* New York: Viking Press, 1984. This biography emphasizes Steinbeck's rebellion against critical conventions and his attempts to keep his private life separate from his role as public figure. Benson sees Steinbeck as a critical anomaly, embarrassed and frustrated by his growing critical and popular success.

DeMott, Robert. *Steinbeck's Typewriter: Essays on His Art.* Troy, N.Y.: Whitston, 1996. Presents in-depth criticism of Steinbeck's work. Includes bibliographical references and an index.

Fontenrose, Joseph. *John Steinbeck: An Introduction and Interpretation.* New York: Holt, Rinehart and Winston, 1963. A good introduction, this book discusses some of the symbolism inherent in much of Steinbeck's fiction and contains some insightful observations on Steinbeck's concept of the "group-man"— that is, the individual as a unit in the larger sociobiological organism.

French, Warren. *John Steinbeck's Fiction Revisited.* New York: Twayne, 1994. The chapter on *The Long Valley* in this revision of French's earlier Twayne book on Steinbeck provides brief discussions of the major stories, including "Flight" and "Chrysanthemums."

George, Stephen K., ed. *John Steinbeck: A Centennial Tribute.* New York: Praeger, 2002. A collection of reminiscences from Steinbeck's family and friends as well as wide-ranging critical assessments of his works.

Hayashi, Tetsumaro, ed. *Steinbeck's Short Stories in "The Long Valley": Essays in Criticism.* Muncie, Ind.: Steinbeck Research Institution, 1991. A collection of new critical essays on the stories in *The Long Valley* (excluding *The Red Pony*), from a variety of critical perspectives.

Hughes, R. S. *John Steinbeck: A Study of the Short Fiction.* New York: Twayne, 1989. A general introduction to Steinbeck's short fiction, focusing primarily on the critical reception to the stories. Also includes some autobiographical statements on short-story writing, as well as four essays on Steinbeck's stories by other critics.

Johnson, Claudia Durst, ed. *Understanding "Of Mice and Men," "The Red Pony," and "The Pearl": A Student Casebook to Issues, Sources, and Historical Documents.* Westport, Conn.: Greenwood Press, 1997. This casebook contains historical, social, and political materials as a context for Steinbeck's three novellas. Contexts included are California and the West, landownership, the male worker, homelessness, and oppression of the poor in Mexico.

McCarthy, Paul. *John Steinbeck.* New York: Frederick Ungar, 1980. Though much of this study is a recapitulation of earlier critical views, the book has the virtues of clarity and brevity and contains a fairly thorough bibliography.

McElrath, Joseph R., Jr., Jesse S. Crisler, and Susan Shillinglaw, eds. *John Steinbeck: The Contemporary Reviews*. New York: Cambridge University Press, 1996. A fine selection of reviews of Steinbeck's work.

Noble, Donald R. *The Steinbeck Question: New Essays in Criticism*. Troy, N.Y.: Whitston, 1993. A collection of essays on most of Steinbeck's work; most important for a study of the short story is the essay by Robert S. Hughes, Jr., are "The Art of Story Writing," Charlotte Hadella's "Steinbeck's Cloistered Women," and Michael J. Meyer's "The Snake."

Parini, Jay. *John Steinbeck: A Biography*. New York: Henry Holt, 1995. This biography suggests psychological interpretations of the effect of Steinbeck's childhood and sociological interpretations of his fiction. Criticizes Steinbeck for his politically incorrect gender and social views; also takes Steinbeck to task to what he calls his blindness to the political reality of the Vietnam War.

Steinbeck, Elaine, and Robert Wallsten. *Steinbeck: A Life in Letters*. New York: Viking Press, 1975. An indispensable source for the Steinbeck scholar, this collection of letters written by Steinbeck between 1929 and his death forty years later shows a writer both well read and well disciplined. Those letters to his friend and publisher Pascal Covici shed light on the writer's working methods and are particularly revealing.

Timmerman, John H. *The Dramatic Landscape of Steinbeck's Short Stories*. Norman: University of Oklahoma Press, 1990. A formalist interpretation of Steinbeck's stories, focusing on style, tone, imagery, and character. Provides close readings of such frequently anthologized stories as "The Chrysanthemums" and "Flight," as well as such stories as "Johnny Bear" and "The Short-Short Story of Mankind."

the PARIS REVIEW

The *Paris Review* Perspective_____

Ha Jin for *The Paris Review*

Among the great American novels, *The Grapes of Wrath* stands out for its absolute sincerity and earnest social concern. Seven decades after its publication, it is still relevant to our time and still challenges some fundamental assumptions of our society. The eminent position of the novel in American literature is already indisputable, and yet its artistic achievement might still need appraising.

Steinbeck wrote the book in roughly one hundred days, from late May to late August 1938, though he had ruminated on it for several years. The writing process was so intense and agonizing that he often got disheartened and even despaired in his journal, "I am not a writer." In fact, he was not only a seasoned novelist but working at the peak of his powers. Prior to *The Grapes of Wrath*, he had written eight books of fiction, including the small masterpieces *Tortilla Flat* (1935), *The Red Pony* (1937), and *Of Mice and Men* (1937). But *The Grapes of Wrath* must have stretched his art to its limit—he had to strain every nerve to meet the demands of the novel's creation.

Before writing the book, Steinbeck had never been to Oklahoma and had no firsthand experience with the place where the "Okies" came from. Yet the beginning of the novel conveys an intimate knowledge about the Dust Bowl and its inhabitants. This illusion of authenticity is accomplished through a focus on the dust storm and the damaged crop. (Corn is described in practically every paragraph in the first chapter.) Through his art, the author strove hard to make up for his lack of firsthand experience. As a matter of fact, the entire novel is largely based on secondhand experiences. Steinbeck's friend Tom Collins had worked as a manager in several migrant camps, and, as an amateur sociologist of sorts, he kept files on the migrants' manners of speech, activities, songs, customs and habits, and economic conditions. Later Collins gave Steinbeck all of his files for the author to use as material for his novel. That is why originally the book had the dedication, "To Carol who willed it. To Tom who lived it."

Carol was Steinbeck's first wife, who typed the manuscript twice and also suggested the title. Steinbeck grabbed that title; he understood that the phrase "the grapes of wrath," from the "Battle Hymn of the Republic," would set the novel strictly within the American context, both in its intellectual and spiritual heritage and in the migrant experience that the book depicts. Later on, the title would help deflect some accusations that the novel propagated socialist sentiments.

The moral spokesman of the novel is the self-defrocked preacher Jim Casy, who also announces the book's artistic principle: "Gonna cuss an' swear an' hear the poetry of folks talkin'" (94). The book often reads like a chorus, yet one in which every voice is distinct. The characters' voices are rustic, passionate, and forceful. In them we hear a kind of poetry articulated by the have-nots, about their hunger, bitterness, goodness, prejudices, hopes. It is a poetry one rarely encounters in modern fiction. Steinbeck had used similar dialects in rendering his characters' speeches in his earlier works, such as the language spoken by Lennie and George in *Of Mice and Men*, but in *The Grapes of Wrath* we have a whole symphony of voices, which oscillate from the earthy to the sublime and between the angry and the joyous. Together they make the novel a quintessential text of polyphonic narrative.

In the midst of that symphony appears the motif of the Joads' story. This plotline, in fact, is rather simple and could even be considered shabby, if it were not for the interchapters, which give the novel its unique structure and uplift the narrative to real artistic achievement. It is in these sixteen interchapters that Steinbeck shows his genius. In essence, each of these chapters is a big poem: a land turtle's perilous trek told from the animal's point of view; a yardful of jalopies being fobbed off on the uprooted who need vehicles to migrate to California, the promised land; a condemnation of ruthless capitalism delivered in a biblical style; the cotton pickers' joy of work. Besides the technique of newsreel and a variety of prose styles, the most striking feature in these interchapters is the collage of voices, most of which are created with virtuosity. For example, the crook of a car dealer in chapter 7 speaks secretively and boisterously, his voice shifting between monologue and dialogue. It changes according to the roles of the interlocutors, and, as a result, his voice is chameleonic and vibrant, full of nuances and drama. It might not be difficult to write one of these interchapters, but it takes a master to make sixteen of them without repetition. Moreover, these chapters are carefully placed among the plot chapters, providing a social and dramatic backdrop for the main line of drama. Steinbeck was meticulous in arranging these poetic pieces and with them wove a spectacular tapestry for the Joads' story.

That meticulousness is displayed everywhere in the novel, even in the controversial final episode, wherein Rose of Sharon gives the breast to a man dying of hunger. Steinbeck's editor at the Viking Press, Pascal Covici, raised doubts about this scene and suggested revision, but Steinbeck replied:

I am sorry but I cannot change that ending. It is casual—there is no fruity climax, it is not more important than any other part of the book—if there is a symbol, it is a survival symbol not a love symbol, it must be an accident, it must be a stranger, and it must be quick. To build this stranger into the structure of the book would be to warp the whole meaning of the book. The fact that the Joads don't know him, don't care about him, have no ties to him—that is the emphasis. The giving of the breast has no more sentiment than the giving of a piece of bread. I'm sorry if that doesn't get over. It will maybe. I've been on this design and balance for a long time and I think I know how I want it. And if I'm wrong, I'm alone in my wrongness. . . . You know that I have never been touchy about changes, but I have too many thousands of hours on this book, every incident has been too carefully chosen and its weight judged and fitted. The balance is there. One other thing—I am not writing a satisfying story. I've done my damndest to rip a reader's nerves to rags, I don't want him satisfied. (178)

Steinbeck's words reveal both his confidence and vision and the way he worked. The design of the novel, every part of it, does give a sense of care and balance. Steinbeck is a supreme artist, and the more we read this novel, the more intricate and magnificent it grows as a work of art.

Works Cited

Steinbeck, John. *The Grapes of Wrath*. 1939. New York: Penguin, 2006.
_____. "To Pascal Covici." 16 Jan. 1939. *Steinbeck: A Life in Letters*. Ed. Elaine Steinbeck and Robert Wallsten. 1975. New York: Penguin, 1989. 178-79.

CRITICAL
CONTEXTS

The Grapes of Wrath:
Faith and Justice in "Our Own Revolutionary Tradition"

Jennifer Banach

When John Steinbeck set out to title to his 1939 novel about an impoverished family of sharecroppers who migrate to California in the hope of finding a better life, he ultimately chose a phrase from Julia Ward Howe's 1861 poem "Battle Hymn of the Republic." His choice was significant and highly symbolic. Though Steinbeck wrote *The Grapes of Wrath* for an America that was dramatically different from Howe's, like Howe he was deeply concerned with the country's future and the plight of the oppressed. In the 1930s, the United States was faced not with a civil war but with economic disasters of the Great Depression and the Dust Bowl, a postwar disillusionment in God and country, labor strife, and fears about the incursion of communism. Given these conditions, Steinbeck could easily have written an unremitting condemnation of agribusiness's exploitation of migrant workers and of American capitalism at large. He could have issued an unambiguous call for a radical, leftist revolution. Instead, by choosing as his title a phrase from Howe's poem, Steinbeck did not align his novel and himself with the period's radicals; rather, he embedded the work within an American tradition, one that invokes faith and justice in the pursuit of social reform.

Howe composed her poem with the marching songs of the Civil War in mind. While visiting a Union Army camp near Washington, D.C., in 1861, she overhead soldiers singing Thomas Bishop's "John Brown's Body," one of many Union marching songs that took as its subject a soldier's assurance of life after death. Lines in the first stanza, for instance, proclaim, "John Brown's body lies a-mouldering in the grave;/ His soul's marching on!" Bishop's own lyrics had first been laid over another song, "Say, Brothers, Will You Meet Us?" This work, a spiritual composed by William Steffe in 1855, asks, "Say, brothers, will you meet us on Canaan's happy shore?" The tunes and their themes of un-failing faith and sure justice were incredibly popular during the war, but Howe's lyrics were and remain the most popular of all. They create a vivid portrait of unswerving and inescapable divine justice, as the familiar first stanza illustrates:

> Mine eyes have seen the glory of the coming of the Lord:
> He is trampling out the vintage where the grapes of wrath are stored;
> He hath loosed the fateful lightning of His terrible swift sword:
> His truth is marching on.

As it does in the twenty-first century, the "Battle Hymn of the Republic" remained in Steinbeck's time a symbol of the American spirit; the work was sung and quoted not only during times of war but also at political conventions, inaugurations of elected officials, and labor strikes. About a quarter century after Steinbeck wrote his famous novel, the Reverend Martin Luther King, Jr., quoted the song in a few of his speeches.

Although today many Americans view the song simply as patriotic, when we examine it within the context of the Civil War, we can also see that it participates in the tradition of protest literature. The hymn was sung by Union soldiers who believed that their cause—abolition—was just and of vital importance to the country's future. Though they were fighting against their countrymen, their protest was patriotic, for it was born out of a love for their country, a desire to make the nation more just by bringing freedom to the oppressed and enslaved. So convinced were they of the rightness of their cause that they believed they were carrying out the very will of God by fighting in the war, an idea captured succinctly in this passage from *Unto a Good Land: A History of the American People*:

> Many Union soldiers went off to war with the full blessings of their families and churches, confident they were doing God's will and sure of suc-

cess. Individual Union soldiers often expected to be protected by Providence from danger and death. . . . Early defeats strained this confidence in Union victory and personal safety, but in the final year of the war northern ministers returned to the theme of providential purpose as they sought to reconcile the terrible costs in deaths with the concept of a just God. (Harrell et al. 499)

Thus the "fateful lightning" that Howe describes in the "Battle Hymn" is not simply an act of God that will strike the country; rather, the soldiers themselves become the lightning as they carry out God's will.

When Steinbeck set out to draft his novel in 1938, the United States, as it was during the 1860s, was embroiled in social unrest, and people at both ends of the political spectrum were calling out for justice and seeking a way to accomplish it. Slavery had been abolished more than seventy years before, but in the intervening period the rise of industrialism and its technological advancements had widely stratified the classes. A small number of agriculturalists, industrialists, and financiers had amassed incredible wealth while more and more workers, many of them immigrants who had come to the United States in search of a better life, had slid into poverty.

The death and destruction of World War I had also left a sort of spiritual malaise hanging over the country. The "lost generation," the young men and women who had fought in and grown up during the war, and whom Ernest Hemingway and F. Scott Fitzgerald so vividly captured in works such as *The Sun Also Rises*, *In Our Time*, *The Great Gatsby*, and *Tender Is the Night*, seemed to have little to believe in. Modern warfare—with its protracted, tedious battles and large-scale, seemingly senseless carnage—had proven to be a decidedly unromantic venture, and many of these men and women could find no reason to believe in their country or God, or to subscribe to any sort of traditional morality.

Shortly after the war, the first Red Scare—nationwide fear that communists, socialists, anarchists, and other radicals were preparing to overthrow the U.S. government—took place. It likely began as a result of demobilization and the slowdown in production after the war: when workers in war industries were let go at the same time that soldiers were returning home from Europe, widespread unemployment, under-employment, and labor unrest followed. At first the brunt of the hostility toward radicals was felt by the Socialist Party, whose platform advocated for workers, and the International Workers of the World, a prominent labor union. The leader of the Socialist Party, Eugene Debs, was tried (and imprisoned) under the Espionage Act of 1917 for attempting to incite treason and mutiny, and the power of the IWW was systematically curtailed by legislation. When a series of strikes and riots ensued across the country in 1919 and multiple bomb plots were uncovered, fear reached the level of hysteria; citizens and government intelligence agencies set about rounding up and arresting or deporting anyone suspected of having communist ties or sympathies. The furor subsided in 1920 as, out of concern that the "Red hunters" were over-zealously pursuing suspected communists and violating civil rights in the process, public opinion turned against them, but the memory of the panic was slow to die out.

When the Great Depression hit after the stock market crash of 1929, further disillusionment and social unrest ensued. As stock values on the New York Stock Exchange declined to one-fifth of what they had been in 1929, more and more businesses, banks, and factories closed. With less income, businesses and families spent less, thus accelerating the economy's downward spiral. At the height of the Depression, nearly one-fourth of the U.S. workforce was unemployed, and it would not be until the outbreak of World War II that the country's economy would begin to recover.

The Dust Bowl, an ecological disaster brought on by overcultivation and an extended drought, only exacerbated the economic turmoil. Throughout the previous decades, overcultivation had left the soil susceptible to erosion, and when a regional drought hit in the early 1930s, large regions of farmland in Oklahoma, Texas, New Mexico, Colorado, and Kansas were rendered unusable as the soil dried up and was blown away as far as the East Coast in enormous dust clouds. With no means to support themselves, farmers and their families were, like Steinbeck's Joads, forced to abandon their homes and migrate to areas in other states where work was rumored to be more plentiful, such as Steinbeck's Salinas Valley in California.

The journeys these families undertook were difficult, and once they arrived at their destinations, many found far less than they had hoped for. The sudden influx of migrant workers in California meant further job shortages, and migrants often found themselves living in slums with poor sanitation and little protection from the elements. Those migrants who did find work were often exploited by their wealthy employers, who took advantage of their employees' desperation by offering little pay and denying basic labor rights. Rather than realizing their dreams of owning land and homes, as the Joads hope to do in the opening chapters of *The Grapes of Wrath*, many migrants, like the Joads and the people around them, faced malnutrition, starvation, and even death.

The Depression, which many leftists took as a sign of capitalism's inherent instability, also helped swell the ranks of the American Communist Party and the Socialist Party at the same time that it pushed the right to embrace more and more conservative politics. As the conservative Liberty League was creating propaganda that cast President Franklin Delano Roosevelt and his New Deal as socialist, actual socialists, communists, and other leftists were claiming that, because Roosevelt's initiatives were less than a complete overhaul of the American economy and political system, they were simply not enough. As the Depression wore on, workers became more and more frustrated with their lot. With the help of the 1933 National Industrial Recovery Act and the 1935 National Labor Relations Act, which together gave workers the right to join unions and engage in collective bargaining, they began to band together to demand better wages and improved working conditions. Between 1933 and 1939 alone, union membership more than doubled in the United states, from 3 million to roughly 6.5 million. Strikes, too, became more common and, occasionally, violent.

As a longtime resident of the Salinas Valley in California—a prosperous agricultural area that achieved an almost mythical reputation during the Dust Bowl as a place where the American Dream was not a dream but a promise—John Steinbeck observed all of these national and regional disturbances with acute interest, concern, and trepidation. While working on local ranches as a young man during the early 1920s, Steinbeck had witnessed firsthand the harsh conditions under which migrant workers labored, and though many at the time blamed the migrants themselves for the squalor in which they lived, as Rick Wartzman explains in *Obscene in the Extreme: The Burning and Banning of John Steinbeck's "The Grapes of Wrath,"* Steinbeck took another view:

> This one laid the blame for the migrants' deprivation at the door of California agriculture, an industry that since the late nineteenth century had been defined by one main thing: its enormity. The state's giant landowners had made a travesty of the Jeffersonian ideal of 160 acres, assembling dominions that ballooned to one thousand times or more that size. . . . This wasn't family farming; it was agribusiness. And with it came a caste system in which relatively few got rich while many remained mired in the worst sort of poverty. (5)

Many people aside from Steinbeck were outraged by the injustices of the agribusiness industry, but, as Wartzman writes, Steinbeck was "the most articulate and powerful of the finger-pointers" (5).

Steinbeck was already thoroughly familiar with the conditions of the lives of migrant workers when he set about writing *The Grapes of Wrath* in 1938. He had spent the previous year writing a series of articles, titled "The Harvest Gypsies," on the Dust Bowl migration for the *San Francisco News,* and in the course of writing the articles he had visited the agricultural areas where migrant workers were employed and the settlements where their families lived in tents and makeshift shelters. As he had during his days on the ranches, he witnessed deep poverty, poor sanitation, illness, and malnutrition, and the articles he wrote paint a tragic portrait of the fate of migrant workers at the hands of the modern agribusiness.

Despite his experience, however, Steinbeck had a great deal of difficulty writing a novel about the migrants. In December of 1937, he began writing "L'Affaire Lettuceberg," a satire about displaced workers in California, but he eventually scrapped this work because, as he wrote to his agent, he believed it was "a bad book because it isn't honest":

> Oh! these incidents all happened but—I'm not telling as much of the truth about them as I know.... I know that a great many people would think they liked the book. I myself have built up a hole-proof argument on how and why I liked it. I can't beat the argument but I don't like the book. ... My whole work drive has been aimed at making people understand each other and then I deliberately write this book the aim of which is to cause hatred through partial understanding. My father would have called it a smart-alec book. It was full of tricks to make people ridiculous. (qtd. in DeMott, "Introduction," *Working Days* xl)

Beginning work on *The Grapes of Wrath*, he fretted that he would replicate the mistakes of "Lettuceberg." A journal entry from the first month of the novel's composition reveals that Steinbeck's main goal for himself was "honesty":

> If I can keep an honesty it is all I can expect of my poor brain—never temper a word to a reader's prejudice, but bend it like putty for his understanding. If I can do that it will be all my lack of genius can produce. (qtd. in DeMott, "'This Book'" 150)

What sort of truth was Steinbeck searching for?

Like the characters of other protest novels of the period, the characters in *The Grapes of Wrath* suffer largely at the hands of their fellow human beings. The Dust Bowl, for instance, though a natural disaster, was instigated by the unsustainable agricultural practices of people. The Joads and the other migrants they meet are exploited by landowners, banks, and unscrupulous used-car salesmen. The young, pregnant Rose of Sharon is abandoned by her husband, and Noah Joad also abandons his family. The problems created by human beings, the novel suggests, can equal or even exceed those inflicted by nature. Unlike Howe, who makes people the mere servants of God's will, Steinbeck, by granting such great power to people, makes it clear that only people will be able to execute justice.

Steinbeck's purpose, and the truth he was seeking, can be found in the treatment of character in the novel. As he did with "Lettuceberg," Steinberg wanted *The Grapes of Wrath* to be a true novel, and to some extent it can be read as a sort of representative, although fictional, account of the very real migrant problem in California and the general plight of the worker in the United States. The characters represent not only the people Steinbeck encountered in his own life in Salinas Valley but also, more generally, all of the tired, downtrodden, exploited, and oppressed. Consequently, the novel is not about any particular one of the Joads, and no single family member is more important than any of the others. As Cynthia Burkhead explains: "The thematic emphasis of *The Grapes of Wrath* is on the importance of the group rather than the individual and is mirrored by Steinbeck's treatment of characters in the novel. There is no one character that is the story's hero" (70).

Despite this emphasis on the power of people, Steinbeck takes care to make each of his characters vivid, fully developed, and dynamic. He takes care to make all the characters understandable to the average reader, and, to avoid prejudicing the reader, he makes them neither entirely saintly nor entirely villainous. Each is simply human, and the transformation each undergoes suggests that justice is not simply a political matter but also one of personal growth and reform.

Tom Joad, a convict paroled from prison, is introduced as a selfish, out-of-control man with shallow desires. However, as he lives in community with his family and, later, other migrants and workers, he becomes more responsible and increasingly selfless. When the Joads encounter the Wilsons, for instance, it is Tom who, with the help of Al, repairs the Wilsons' car, and it is Tom who takes revenge on the man who kills Casy and then goes into hiding to protect his family. Still, in line with Steinbeck's communitarian vision, Tom's development is not wholly his own; rather, it is tethered, from the very start of the book, to that of another character, the Reverend Jim Casy. It is perhaps the fallen Casy who speaks most deeply of the two cornerstones for reform in the American tradition: faith and justice. Casy, who no longer holds his post as a preacher because of his repeated sexual relations with the women of his parish, reflects the lost faith and decline in traditional American morality that Hemingway and Fitzgerald captured during the 1920s. Although he is aware of his failings, he is unable to overcome them and live a Christian life. Still, although he is unable to maintain his congregation, Casy does maintain a belief in the importance of community, as can be seen when he says: "Why do we got to hang it on God or Jesus? Maybe . . . it's all men an' all women we love; maybe that's the Holy Sperit—the human sperit—the whole shebang. Maybe all men got one big soul ever'body's a part of" (24). By the end of the novel, Tom has adopted Casy's view. When he returns from hiding, he tells his mother that "a fella ain't no good alone" (570) and that, if he is killed, he'll live on "in the way guys yell when they're mad an'—I'll be in the way kids laugh when they're hungry" (572). Through his personal reformation, he becomes a symbol for political reformation. As Burkhead notes:

> From the beginning, Tom represents justice, but initially it is a justice for self. . . . When he is hiding from the law for killing Casy's murderer, however, Tom experiences an epiphany; indeed, he comes to understand that fighting against unjust oppressors is the greatest type of justice. (71)

Through Casy and Tom, Steinbeck seems to suggest that, although traditional religious beliefs are no longer tenable, faith has not disappeared altogether. As Burkhead explains, "Disconnected theories of souls and sin have congealed into solid ideas about justice and about how collective action is necessary to achieve this justice" (72).

The development of Ma Joad and the other characters supports Casy's and, eventually, Tom's notion of community. While at the novel's beginning Ma is devoted to her blood family, by the end she counts other migrants, even if they are strangers, as part of her family. She is more than just an individual; in her hardship she takes on a leadership role, at first within her family and then within the larger community. Finally, like Ma, Casy, and Tom, Rose of Sharon undergoes a similar transformation in the face of tragedy. After being abandoned by her husband, Connie, and giving birth to a stillborn child, she is still able to put aside her own misfortunes and help a man dying of starvation by offering him milk from her breast. As R. Baird Shuman writes:

> The Joads survive their hardships by sticking together as a family. At the same time, they come to appreciate that thousands of other people share their hardships. By the end of the novel, they see their plight not only as a family struggle but also a struggle to win dignity for all people. (1462)

Unlike during the nineteenth century, in which a writer like Howe could believably claim that God has guaranteed justice, the disillusionment that resulted from World War I meant that reform had to be undertaken in the absence of a sure faith in God and country. Steinbeck finds this faith in humankind. So, although the callousness of one person or an entire group of people can do great harm—as when Connie abandons Rose of Sharon and vigilantes kill Casy—we also find in *The Grapes of Wrath* evidence of the redemptive powers of community. The Wilsons and the Joads offer one another mutual assistance, Casy willingly dies for a cause he believes in, and Rose of Sharon breastfeeds a starving stranger. All of these acts demonstrate that, although there may be no divine justice, people can realize their own justice through selflessness, camaraderie, and understanding. In his introduction to *Working Days: The Journals of "The Grapes of Wrath," 1938-1941*, Robert DeMott explains: "*The Grapes of Wrath* . . . advances a belief in the essential goodness and forbearance of the 'common people,' and prophesies a fundamental change to produce equitable social conditions" (xxii).

Reading Steinbeck's 1962 Nobel Prize acceptance speech, we can see that, twenty years after *The Grapes of Wrath* was published, the author's vision of humankind's power and responsibility was undimmed:

> We have usurped many of the powers we once ascribed to God. . . . Having taken Godlike power, we must seek in ourselves for the responsibility and the wisdom we once prayed some deity might have. Man himself has become our greatest hazard and our only hope.

In his introduction to the 2006 Penguin edition of *The Grapes of Wrath*, DeMott explains that Steinbeck chose his novel's title because the phrase belonged to a march, an anthem even, and he meant his book to be the same: an anthem in "our own revolutionary tradition" (x). This is not, however, the revolution that the conservatives of the 1930s feared and for which their leftist counterparts longed. As we can see from the way Steinbeck worried about writing an "honest" book and from the manner in which he developed his characters, he meant his novel to be a thoroughly American and patriotic one—one that, like Howe's poem, would make social reform not a political matter but a matter of nonpartisan justice and personal reform. Like Howe, Steinbeck was concerned not with political problems so much as with epidemic injustices and the country's need for some sort of faith to see it through those injustices and work toward correcting them.

Despite all of his care, however, Steinbeck's conservative critics viewed the novel with suspicion, especially its treatment of labor issues. With the panic of the Red Scare still fresh in their minds and sometimes

---

violent labor strikes regularly in the news, more than a few reviewers saw the novel as an unpatriotic condemnation of American capitalism. Just as in *The Grapes of Wrath* the Californians are wary of a united uprising of hungry migrant workers, so the novel, with its depictions of the power of united workers, raised fears in some readers. At one extreme, the book was accused of being a call to arms and communist propaganda, and it was banned and censored in more than a few U.S. states.

In spite of complaints from conservatives and leftists that the *The Grapes of Wrath* is socialist or not socialist enough, the revolution that Steinbeck calls for, built upon a demand for dignity and justice for all, ultimately resists classification. As David Minter remarks: "To read Steinbeck as a realist, a naturalist, or a proletarian novelist is to misread him. . . . He values social movements, including strikes and protests in the name of social justice, but he values them even more in the name of loyalty to life" (233-35). Steinbeck's understanding of faith and justice encompasses both the political and the personal realms, and upon close inspection *The Grapes of Wrath* is revealed to be a remarkably balanced novel: for every character who abandons someone, there is another who holds a family together. For every person who loses faith, there is another who reclaims it. It is perhaps for these reasons that *The Grapes of Wrath* ultimately triumphed over its detractors, winning the Pulitzer Prize in 1940 and playing a large role in Steinbeck's receiving the Nobel Prize in Literature in 1962. If any doubt still remains, there is also Steinbeck's own denial that "the novel was ever intended as a social record or a work of protest . . . its focus was 'streams in man more profound and dark and strong than the libido of Freud'" (Ruland and Bradbury 282).

Works Cited

Burkhead, Cynthia. *Student Companion to John Steinbeck*. Westport, CT: Greenwood Press, 2002.

DeMott, Robert. Introduction. *The Grapes of Wrath*. By John Steinbeck. 1939. New York: Penguin, 2006.

_____. Introduction. *Working Days: The Journals of "The Grapes of Wrath," 1938-1941*. By John Steinbeck. New York: Penguin, 1990.

_____. "'This Book Is My Life': Creating *The Grapes of Wrath*." *Steinbeck's Typewriter: Essays on His Art*. Troy, NY: Whitston, 1996. 146-205.

Harrell, David Edwin, Jr., et al. *Unto a Good Land: A History of the American People*. Vol. 1. *To 1900*. Grand Rapids, MI: Wm. B. Eerdmans, 2005.

Minter, David. "The Search for Shared Purpose: Struggles on the Left." *The Cambridge History of American Literature*. Vol. 6. Ed. Sacvan Bercovitch. New York: Cambridge UP, 2002.

Ruland, Richard, and Malcolm Bradbury. *From Puritanism to Postmodernism: A History of American Literature*. London: Routledge, 1991.

Shuman, R. Baird, ed. *Great American Writers: Twentieth Century*. Vol. 11. Tarrytown, NY: Marshall Cavendish, 2002.

Steinbeck, John. *The Grapes of Wrath*. 1939. New York: Penguin, 2006.

_____. Nobel Prize Banquet Speech. *Nobel Lectures, Literature 1901-1967*. Ed. Horst Frenz. Amsterdam: Elsevier, 1969. 6 Jan. 2010. http://nobelprize.org/nobel_prizes/literature/laureates/1962/steinbeck-speech.html.

Wartzman, Rick. *Obscene in the Extreme: The Burning and Banning of John Steinbeck's "The Grapes of Wrath."* New York: PublicAffairs, 2008.

A Minstrel and a Scrivener:
Steinbeck, the Protest Novel, and Modernism_____

Matthew J. Bolton

At the start of his career, not yet having published a novel, John Steinbeck wrote a letter to a Stanford classmate in which he laid out his emerging manifesto: "I have no interest in the printed word. . . . I put my words down for a matter of memory. They are more to be spoken than read. I have the instincts of a minstrel rather than those of a scrivener" (*Letters* 19). The twenty-seven-year-old Steinbeck made this declaration in 1929, the last year of the decade in which modernism reached its apex. Steinbeck was launching his literary career in the wake of T. S. Eliot's *The Waste Land* (1922), James Joyce's *Ulysses* (1922), F. Scott Fitzgerald's *The Great Gatsby* (1925), Virginia Woolf's *Mrs. Dalloway* (1925) and *To the Lighthouse* (1927), Ernest Hemingway's *The Sun Also Rises* (1926) and *A Farewell to Arms* (1929), and William Faulkner's *The Sound and the Fury* (1929). Given such predecessors, it is no wonder that the novice author chose to distance himself from "the printed word." With such a declaration, Steinbeck attempted to clear the ground for his own work by allying himself with oral and folk traditions rather than with the literary traditions out of which the formidable novels of 1920s modernism had grown. As a self-proclaimed minstrel, he sought to draw on the language and culture of the common people and thereby remain uninfluenced by the work of his immediate predecessors. Steinbeck's relationship to modernism is more complex than he would have it appear, however, for whether he is courting or rejecting comparisons between his own work and that of the great modernists, these authors never seem to be far from his mind.

Nowhere is Steinbeck's conflicted relationship with modernism more apparent than in *The Grapes of Wrath* (1939), his undisputed masterpiece. The novel draws on two literary traditions, the longstanding one of the American protest novel and the emerging one of the

---

modernist novel. At his best, Steinbeck manages to synthesize the two strands, putting modernist themes, techniques, and tropes to work for a social cause.

One might study *The Grapes of Wrath* by first locating it solidly in the tradition of the social protest novel, identifying those aspects of it that are most calculated to advance a social or political position. Steinbeck's readiness to sacrifice characterization in favor of argumentation, as well as his moments of didacticism and oratory, make *The Grapes of Wrath* an inheritor to Harriet Beecher Stowe's *Uncle Tom's Cabin* (1852), Upton Sinclair's *The Jungle* (1906), and other socially engaged novels. Other aspects of the novel, however, show Steinbeck grappling with the legacy of modernism. His experimentation with form and language can seem positively Joycean, while his interest in contrasting literary and vernacular language is reminiscent of Faulkner. After establishing some of these broad connections to modernism, one might focus on the author's bravura use of a single word across the opening chapters of *The Grapes of Wrath*. Through his obsessive repetition of the word "dust"—which appears some two dozen times in the first one hundred pages of the novel—Steinbeck not only establishes his setting and dramatizes the plight of the Oklahoma farmers but also engages in a subtle competition with Eliot, Fitzgerald, Hemingway, and other great modernists. In weaving this word so tightly into the fabric of his novel, Steinbeck appropriates and redeploys a modernist trope that figures in so many of the important novels and poems of the 1920s. To borrow the title of an early Faulkner novel, Steinbeck plants his own "flags in the dust," as if to announce that he is both a social critic and a literary innovator, both a minstrel and a modernist.

Upton Sinclair, whose 1906 novel *The Jungle* exposed the deplorable working conditions of the Chicago slaughterhouses, was tremendously impressed by *The Grapes of Wrath*. Soon after the novel was released, Sinclair declared: "I have come to the age where I know I won't be writing forever. I remember reading how Elijah put his mantle on the shoulders of Elisha. John Steinbeck can have my old mantle if he has any use for it" (Rev. 3). An author could not ask for a better endorsement than this. Sinclair was perhaps the greatest living exemplar of the tradition of muckraking, in which the novelist writes for the express purpose of bringing to light social, economic, or political injustices. Morris Dickstein terms Sinclair "a one-man reform movement and radical crusader" (vi), an author who brought his literary success to bear on a series of causes and movements. Sinclair ushers Steinbeck into the fold, declaring him heir to Stephen Crane, Frank Norris, Theodore Dreiser, and Sinclair himself. Nor was Upton Sinclair the only reader to place *The Grapes of Wrath* in the tradition of the social protest novel. Granville Hicks praised the book in a 1939 article in the Marxist journal *The New Masses*, terming it a "proletariat novel" and claiming that Steinbeck's "insight into capitalism illuminates every chapter of the book" (23).

Other critics made the point that *The Grapes of Wrath* succeeded primarily as a political work, rather than as a literary one. A review in *Time* magazine asserted that the passages in which Steinbeck's narrator directly addresses the plight of migrant farmers are "not a successful fiction experiment. In them a 'social awareness' outruns artistic skill" ("Okies" 87). Perhaps the most telling commentary came from Edmund Wilson, whose monumental 1930 critical survey *Axel's Castle: A Study in the Imaginative Literature of 1870-1930* was pivotal in building the canon of modernism and in positioning Yeats, Eliot, Proust, and Joyce at the center of it. In discussing Steinbeck, Wilson drew a distinction between the craft necessary to write a good novel and the genius necessary to write a great one. In a 1940 article, Wilson wrote: "Mr. Steinbeck has invention, observation, a certain color of style which for some reason does not possess what is called magic" ("Californians" 785). A decade later, in his survey of 1940s literature, Wilson expanded on this argument: "The characters in *The Grapes of Wrath* are animated and put through their paces rather than brought to life; they are like excellent character actors giving very conscientious performances in a fairly well written play" (*Classics* 42). Wilson maintained that *The Grapes of Wrath* is "a propaganda novel, full of preachments and sociological interludes" (36). Wilson might be thought of as the gatekeeper of modernism, and in his treatment of *The Grapes of Wrath* he seemed to be turning Steinbeck away. From its first reviews, then, *The Grapes of Wrath* was read largely through the lens of the social issues it raised rather than through that of literary modernism.

It is certainly fair to identify *The Grapes of Wrath* as a social protest novel in the tradition of Stowe's *Uncle Tom's Cabin*, Crane's *Maggie: A Girl of the Streets* (1893), or Sinclair's *The Jungle*. Like these earlier novels, Steinbeck's work takes an ethnographic interest in the lives of the American poor. Steinbeck may write *of* socially marginalized characters, but he is writing *for* a mainstream audience. The book therefore has a reformist slant, in that it dramatizes the lives of the powerless so that the powerful might be compelled to ameliorate their condition. As a result, the characters tend to drift inevitably toward caricature. Steinbeck is not of the same social milieu as the Joad family and their contemporaries, and his literary representation of their patterns of speech and social behavior is an act of mimicry. In this respect, Steinbeck does have "the instincts of a minstrel," and one might go so far as to compare some of the broad humor in his representations of the Oklahoma dialect and culture to the blatantly racist tradition of blackface minstrel shows, in which white actors portrayed cartoonish African American stereotypes. Steinbeck's Joad family members are rounded and sympathetic in a way in which minstrel-show characters were not, but mixed with Steinbeck's sympathy is an element of condescension. Take this description of Granma Joad as she makes her first appearance in the novel:

Behind him hobbled Granma, who had survived only because she was as mean as her husband. . . . Once, after a meeting, while she was still speaking in tongues, she fired both barrels of a shotgun at her husband, ripping one of his buttocks nearly off, and after that he admired her and did not try to torture her as children torture bugs. As she walked she hiked her Mother Hubbard up to her knees, and she bleated her shrill terrible war cry: "Puraise Gawd fur vittory." (78)

In scenes such as this one, Steinbeck's representation of the Joads feels less like mimicry than like mockery. The author may have great sympathy for the plight of these people, but he is also ready to present them in a comic light for the amusement of the reader. Passages such as these can be jarring, for they underscore the distance between the author or narrator and his characters. As a point of reference, Faulkner's *As I Lay Dying* (1930) centers on a rural family, the Bundrens, whose mores and language are, like those of the Joads, often mined for laughs. Yet the absence of a central narrator and of a social cause eliminates in Faulkner's novel the sense of narratorial distance that can make Steinbeck's portrayal of the Joads feel condescending. It is precisely because *The Grapes of Wrath* is a protest novel that the reader may take umbrage at some of Steinbeck's caricatures of his protagonists.

In other passages of *The Grapes of Wrath*, one feels a distance between the author and his characters that is part and parcel of Steinbeck's larger social and political agenda. This is perhaps most apparent when Steinbeck uses a character as a mouthpiece for mounting an ideological argument. Some of the Reverend Jim Casy's meditations, for example, feel like thinly veiled socialist agitprop. In his speech about his loss of faith, he explains: "I figgered, 'Why do we got to hang it on God or Jesus? Maybe,' I figgered, 'maybe it's all men an' all women we love; maybe that's the Holy Sperit—the human sperit— the whole shebang. Maybe all men got one big soul ever'body's a part of'" (24). In the world of the novel, the preacher has arrived at his concept of a proletariat ("one big soul ever'body's a part of") through his own "figger"-ing. The reader, however, may feel that this concept has been handed to Casy by the author. One can sense the author behind the character, recasting the tenets of Marxism or collectivism into the preacher's vernacular. In having his characters articulate political or societal positions, Steinbeck strikes a hard bargain: he mounts an ideological argument at the expense of organic characterization.

Casy can be compared to Joyce's Leopold Bloom, who, like the preacher, is full of ideas about how society might be run more progressively. At a funeral, for example, Bloom finds himself thinking about how well the mourners would be served were a tramline laid down from the city to the cemetery (81). This is an eminently sensible idea, yet there is no sense that Bloom is speaking on behalf of Joyce himself or propounding an idea that Joyce subscribes to outside of the context of his novel. One might make the same argument regarding Hemingway's Jake Barnes, Faulkner's Quentin Compson, and Woolf's Mr. Ramsey: each has a coherent worldview, and one can assume that the author sympathizes with that view to one extent or another, but the expression of the character's viewpoint in the context of the novel serves no didactic purpose. The triumph of modernism lies in its depiction of the human mind at work, and its major innovations, such as stream-of-consciousness narration, all work to create psychological verisimilitude. Steinbeck is willing to sacrifice some of this verisimilitude in order to advance a social and political argument.

The passages in which the reader is most aware of Steinbeck's presence as a narrator and of the ideas and positions animating *The Grapes of Wrath* are found in the interchapters, in which the author speaks directly to the reader. These passages have great power, in part because Steinbeck breaks out of the dialect of his protagonists. Their power is more than rhetorical, however; there is force to the author's analysis itself. He frames the struggle of the Joads against the larger backdrop of banking regulations, agricultural policy, demographic patterns, supply-and-demand market dynamics, and capitalism as a whole. In the best of these interchapters, Steinbeck marshals the indignation of a preacher or a prophet railing against the failings of his people. Meditating on the agribusiness policy of destroying produce and livestock to keep down prices, for example, Steinbeck writes:

There is a crime here that goes beyond denunciation. There is a sorrow here that weeping cannot symbolize. There is a failure here that topples all our success. The fertile earth, the straight tree rows, the sturdy trunks, and the ripe fruit. And children dying of pellagra must die because a profit cannot be taken from an orange. And coroners must fill in the certificates—died of malnutrition—because the food must rot, must be forced to rot. (349)

This is a powerful argument that challenges some of the basic assumptions of free market capitalism; it shows the human cost of decisions that are made on purely economic grounds. Reading the interchapters, one can see why Steinbeck's contemporaries tended to focus on the social cause that he advocates rather than on the literary techniques that he uses. The social agenda that runs throughout the novel and this sort of impassioned argumentation is not found in Joyce, Woolf, Fitzgerald, or Faulkner, and none of their novels have the didactic intent that marks *The Grapes of Wrath*.

The term "didactic" has become a pejorative one, particularly when it is referring to literature. The twenty-first-century reader views didacticism suspiciously, as he or she might a piece of propaganda or an advertisement. In literary circles, modernism itself was a powerful force in marginalizing didactic literature. The modernist novel or poem places a premium on aesthetics rather than on social utility, and, as a result, *The Grapes of Wrath* is in some ways more akin to novels written before the 1920s than to those written after. However, given that it is important to read a work of literature on its own ground, it may be worth reexamining assumptions about the value of didacticism. Novelist and theologian C. S. Lewis mounted several impassioned defenses of it. In *The Personal Heresy*, he argued that "the poet is not a man who asks me to look at him; he is a man who says 'look at that' and points" (11). This is a good model for what Steinbeck is doing in *The Grapes of Wrath*: pointing at an American injustice and saying "look at that." By this definition, the novel is a stunning success.

Indeed, comparing *The Grapes of Wrath* with a work of high modernism, such as Faulkner's *The Sound and the Fury*, might prompt one to reconsider how a "great novel" is defined. Most readers and critics would agree that Faulkner's novel is greater by purely literary standards; it surpasses Steinbeck's best work in its language, depth of characterization, layered complexity, and mix of comedy and tragedy. To take up Edmund Wilson's point, Faulkner may have a genius or a "magic" that Steinbeck does not. Yet, read through a political and a social lens, Steinbeck's novel may surpass Faulkner's. One can imagine a person of great power—say, a senator, a banker, or the head of a corporation—reading *The Grapes of Wrath* and being moved or shamed into using his or her political or economic power to improve the terrible situations Steinbeck describes. In point of fact, Eleanor Roosevelt was one such powerful figure who took direct action after reading *The Grapes of Wrath*, visiting a migrant camp in 1940 and afterward remarking "I have never thought *The Grapes of Wrath* was exaggerated" (qtd. in DeMott xl). Steinbeck's novel calls for a practical response in a way that Faulkner's work does not, and if it seems unlikely that a novel could move its readers to take dramatic political action, one should remember the words that Abraham Lincoln is reported to have said to Harriet Beecher Stowe, author of *Uncle Tom's Cabin*: "So you're the little woman who wrote the book that started this great war!" The protest novel, at its core, attempts to be a catalyst for larger social or political change. Its value therefore should be measured not on purely aesthetic grounds but with regard to the effect it has on its readers and on the world outside the novel.

Steinbeck succeeded in writing not merely a social protest novel but a book that bears comparison to the work of Joyce, Eliot, Fitzgerald, Hemingway, and other modernists of the 1920s and 1930s. Steinbeck freely adopted and adapted techniques from many of these authors, and as such *The Grapes of Wrath* can be read as an engagement with and continuation of the modernist tradition.

What most clearly allies Steinbeck's novel with the modernist canon is his interest in language itself. He structures the novel around a clash of voices: the dialect of the Joads and their contemporaries, the lyrical observations of the third-person narrator, and the prophetic, biblical voice that thunders across the interchapters. In this respect, Steinbeck's novel bears comparison to the work of Faulkner and Joyce. Like these two predecessors, Steinbeck allows the form of his novel to change radically in response to its content. The chapter in which the Joads buy a used car, for example, opens with a description of the used-car lots on the edge of town but almost immediately modulates into the language of the signs lining the road:

> In the towns, on the edges of the towns, in fields, in vacant lots, the used-car yards, the wreckers' yards, the garages with blazoned signs Used Cars, Good Used Cars. Cheap transportation, three trailers. '27 Ford, clean. Checked cars, guaranteed cars. Free radio. Car with 100 gallons of gas free. Come in and look. Used Cars. No overhead. (61)

Later in the chapter, the language of the signs gives way to the staccato patter of the salesmen. Writing in this experimental, Joycean mode allows Steinbeck to replicate for the reader the sense of confusion and uncertainty that the Joads themselves face in trying to negotiate a decent price for a used car. The reader is as overwhelmed by the salesmen's patter as are the characters. This is an extremely effective way for Steinbeck to ally the reader's sympathies more closely with the migrant family; the reader not only identifies them but also identifies *with* them. Moreover, this chapter gives Steinbeck a chance to perform, for he shows not only that he can convincingly adopt a voice and language that is far from his own but also that he can experiment boldly with novelistic form in the manner of Joyce. The car lot chapter is one of several instances in which Steinbeck's experimentation with modernist techniques works both to advance his social cause and to burnish his own credentials as a literary modernist.

Steinbeck engages with modernist traditions in more subtle ways as well. One way to examine Steinbeck's modernist qualities is to analyze his use of the "dust" motif within the first several chapters of the novel. Of course, *The Grapes of Wrath* is set during the Dust Bowl of the 1930s in Oklahoma, and so it is only natural that the word "dust" should appear with great frequency. For his novel to succeed, Steinbeck must convey the gravity of the situation facing the Oklahoma farmers. In Steinbeck's hands, however, the word "dust" speaks not only to the reality of life on the Great Plains during the 1930s but also to the modernist tradition itself. Steinbeck's dust imagery effectively links the novel to some of the touchstones of the previous twenty years of poetry and fiction.

A generation before the Joad family and their contemporaries arrived, the Great Plains were grasslands inhabited by herds of buffalo and by Native Americans whose nomadic way of life was built around hunting these animals. The plains of Oklahoma and the surrounding states had always been buffeted by high winds, but the grass that blanketed them held the soil in place. The plains, in short, were a delicate ecosystem. In his recent best seller *The Worst Hard Time: The Untold Story of Those Who Survived the Great American Dust Bowl*, Timothy Egan details the series of economic and political decisions that led to the utter devastation of these grasslands. The buffalo were systematically eradicated, the Native Americans relocated to reservations, and the land itself parceled out and sold to ranchers and farmers. In the 1920s, a decade that saw high levels of rainfall, the future of the Great Plains seemed bright. The new farms produced record amounts of wheat and other staples, turning the plains into a new American breadbasket. The Oklahoma farms were not sustainable, however: when the wet 1920s gave way to the droughts of the 1930s, the exposed soil was prey to the high plains winds. The stage had been set for a human-made ecological disaster.

The Grapes of Wrath opens with a description of "the last rains" to settle on the Oklahoma plains. The rains are not heavy enough to break through the hard crust of the dry ground, and after those last rain clouds move through, the barren earth lies exposed to the sun. The crops dry up and the ground grows hard and then, under the weight of wagon wheels and automobile tires and the shoes of human beings, the dry earth turns to airborne dust:

> In the roads where the teams moved, where the wheels milled the ground and the hooves of the horses beat the ground, the dirt crust broke and the dust formed. Every moving thing lifted the dust into the air: a walking man lifted a thin layer as high as his waist, and a wagon lifted the dust as high as the fence tops, and an automobile boiled a cloud behind it. The dust was long in settling back again. (2)

Over the course of the novel's next several chapters, Steinbeck uses dust imagery to create a wholly convincing portrait of life in drought-ridden Oklahoma. His descriptions are more than journalistic report-age; instead, they gesture toward the mythic and the archetypal, as in the conclusion of the first chapter: "As the day went forward the sun became less red. It flared down on the dust-blanketed land. The men sat in the doorways of their houses; their hands were busy with sticks and little rocks. The men sat still—thinking—figuring" (4). This descrip-tion is concrete and objective, yet it is also shot through with symbolic overtones; there is a sense of gravity and timelessness in the landscape and in the plight of its inhabitants.

The "dust-blanketed land" that Steinbeck evokes owes something to the landscapes of T. S. Eliot's *The Waste Land* (1922) and "The Hollow Men" (1925), two poems in which dust and the desert stand as symbols of humankind's spiritual aridity. In the former poem, an unidentified speaker with the cadences of an Old Testament prophet describes a stony land and says:

> There is shadow under this red rock
> (Come in under the shadow of this red rock),
> And I will show you something different from either

> Your shadow at morning striding behind you
> Or your shadow at evening rising to meet you;
> I will show you fear in a handful of dust.
>
> (25-30)

The handful of dust is fearful because it is a reminder of human mortality, as in the lines from Genesis that serve as a liturgical refrain on Ash Wednesday: "Dust you are, and to dust you shall return" (3:19). Steinbeck's characters fear the dust in a way that is far more literal and immediate, yet the "dust-blanketed land" in which they find themselves is akin to that of Eliot's poem. Eliot's wasteland has also seen its last rains; it is now a place of "no water but only rock/ Rock and no water and the sandy road" (331-32). In the last section of the poem, the reader encounters people who have much in common with Steinbeck's farmers:

> There is not even silence in the mountains
> But dry sterile thunder without rain
> There is not even solitude in the mountains
> But red sullen faces sneer and snarl
> From doors of mudcracked houses
>
> (341-45)

Steinbeck's landscape effectively dramatizes the plight of the Oklahoma farmers, but it also moves that plight to the same plain as Eliot's poem. His farmers squatting in the dust inhabit a wasteland that partakes of the mythic and the symbolic. Steinbeck's powerful language and his evocation of Eliot both write large the desolation facing the farmers and draw his novel into the orbit of the modernist tradition.

One might compare Steinbeck's dust imagery to imagery in several other works by his modernist forerunners. In *The Great Gatsby*, Fitzgerald makes a similar raid on Eliot's imagery in writing of the valley of ashes that lies between New York City and the north shore of Long

---

Island. The trains and automobiles passing from the city to the gentri-fied shoreline must pass through this placeless place, a modern waste-land of ash and dust:

> This is a valley of ashes—a fantastic farm where ashes grow like wheat into ridges and hills and grotesque gardens; where ashes take the form of houses and chimneys and rising smoke and, finally, with a transcendent ef-fort, of men who move dimly and already crumbling through the powdery air. Occasionally, a line of gray cars crawls along an invisible track, gives out a ghastly creak, and comes to rest, and immediately the ash-gray men swarm up with leaden spades and stir up an impenetrable cloud, which screens their obscure operations from your sight. (23)

Fitzgerald creates a landscape that perfectly symbolizes the nihilism and spiritual deadness underlying the gilded world that Nick, Tom, Daisy, and Jay Gatsby inhabit. The city and the countryside alike have relationships to the valley of ashes, for the lifestyles of both places are grounded in the refuse of this industrial landscape. It is fitting that an encounter in the valley of ashes will doom Gatsby. Of course, the name echoes a place described in the book of Psalms: the valley of the shadow of death. As in Eliot's poem—and in Steinbeck's later novel—a modern landscape takes on prophetic and mythic overtones.

Steinbeck's repetition of a single, simple word in long descriptions of a landscape also feels distinctly Hemingwayesque. In fact, some of Steinbeck's greatest passages describing the Dust Bowl seem to echo the magisterial opening of Hemingway's *A Farewell to Arms*. Heming-way's narrator, Frederic Henry, describes the Italian countryside on the brink of World War I:

> In the late summer of that year we lived in a house in a village that looked across the river and the plain to the mountains. In the bed of the river there were pebbles and boulders, dry and white in the sun, and the water was clear and swiftly moving and blue in the channels. Troops went by the

house and down the road and the dust they raised powdered the leaves of the trees. The trunks of the trees too were dusty and the leaves fell early that year and we saw the troops marching along the road and the dust rising and leaves, stirred by the breeze, falling and the soldiers marching and afterward the road bare and white except for the leaves. (3)

Hemingway is a master of the compound sentence, using "and" to string together simple phrases that create a powerful whole. The sense of movement and transformation in this paragraph is undeniable; this is not a static description of a landscape but rather a moving picture of a landscape in flux, for the soldiers raise dust that settles back on the trees around them.

Steinbeck shares Hemingway's interest in creating through words a fair and true representation of the natural world, and many of the passages in *The Grapes of Wrath* describing the landscape of the Dust Bowl show the author animating a scene through Hemingwayesque repetition and rephrasing. Like Hemingway, Steinbeck uses polysyndeton; the simple conjunction "and" produces long compound sentences that create the illusion of motion:

The dust from the roads fluffed up and spread out and fell on the weeds beside the fields, and fell into the fields a little way. Now the wind grew strong and hard and it worked at the rain crust in the corn fields. Little by little the sky was darkened by the mixing dust, and the wind felt over the earth, loosened the dust, and carried it away. (2)

Passages such as this show Steinbeck reveling in his own abilities as a writer rather than advancing an argument or a cause. His descriptions of the movement of dust are brilliant and bear comparison to Faulkner's descriptions of horses and dogs in *Spotted Horses* and of floodwaters in *Old Man*. Like a painter choosing a particularly challenging subject to depict and then putting his or her stamp on it—the way, say, Monet makes water lilies his own or Turner brilliantly captures a certain kind of seascape—Steinbeck sets himself a task that showcases his own virtuosity.

The Grapes of Wrath is one of the great American novels on account of both the gravity of its subject matter and the surety and inventiveness of its author's prose. Had Steinbeck placed himself wholly in either the tradition of the social protest novel or that of the modernist novel, his book would no doubt be a lesser achievement. As it is, the author's fusion of these two strands of American literature allowed him to bring all of his talents to fruition in a powerful, hybrid novel. *The Grapes of Wrath* is therefore a singular achievement: the most literary of protest novels and the most socially engaged of modernist ones.

Works Cited

DeMott, Robert. Introduction. *The Grapes of Wrath*. By John Steinbeck. 1939. New York: Penguin, 2006.

Dickstein, Morris. Introduction. *The Jungle*. By Upton Sinclair. 1906. New York: Bantam, 1981. v-xvii.

Egan, Timothy. *The Worst Hard Time: The Untold Story of Those Who Survived the Great American Dust Bowl*. New York: Houghton Mifflin, 2005.

Eliot, T. S. *The Complete Poems and Plays, 1909-1950*. New York: Harcourt, Brace & World, 1962.

Faulkner, William. *As I Lay Dying*. 1930. New York: Random House, 1990.

_____. *The Sound and the Fury*. 1929. New York: Random House, 1990.

Fitzgerald, F. Scott. *The Great Gatsby*. New York: Charles Scribner's Sons, 1925.

Hemingway, Ernest. *A Farewell to Arms*. New York: Charles Scribner's Sons, 1929.

_____. *The Sun Also Rises*. New York: Charles Scribner's Sons, 1926.

Hicks, Granville. "Steinbeck's Powerful New Novel." *The New Masses* 31.6 (2 May 1939): 22-23.

Joyce, James. *Ulysses*. 1922. New York: Vintage, 1986.

Lewis, C. S., and E. M. W. Tillyard. *The Personal Heresy: A Controversy*. London: Oxford UP, 1939.

"Okies." *Time* 17 Apr. 1939: 87.

Sinclair, Upton. *The Jungle*. 1906. New York: Bantam, 1981.

_____. Rev. of *The Grapes of Wrath*, by John Steinbeck. *Common Sense* 8.5 (May 1939): 23.

Steinbeck, John. *The Grapes of Wrath*. 1939. New York: Penguin Books, 1997.

_____. *Steinbeck: A Life in Letters*. Ed. Elaine Steinbeck and Robert Wallsten. New York: Penguin Books, 1975.

Stowe, Harriet Beecher. *Uncle Tom's Cabin*. 1852. New York: Bantam, 1982.

Wilson, Edmund. "The Californians: Storm and Steinbeck." *New Republic* 103 (9 Dec. 1940): 784-87.

_____. *Classics and Commercials: A Literary Chronicle of the Forties*. New York: Farrar, Straus and Giroux, 1950.

Woolf, Virginia. *Mrs. Dalloway*. New York: Harcourt, Brace, 1925.

_____. *To the Lighthouse*. New York: Harcourt, Brace, 1927.

The Great American Joad Trip:
On the Road in John Steinbeck's
*The Grapes of Wrath*_____

Michael Wentworth

"You ought to be out on 66. Cars from all over the country. All headin' west. Never seen so many before."

–The Grapes of Wrath

"This Land Is Your Land"

John Ditsky asserts that "the American road provides the major theme of American literature." Focusing more directly on John Steinbeck's *The Grapes of Wrath*, he proposes that "four decades after its creation [the novel] begs recognition as the sort of book it really is: a classic of undiminished power that is fundamentally a romantic epic of the U.S. highway" (215). Together with Mark Twain's *Adventures of Huckleberry Finn*, Herman Melville's *Moby Dick*, Harriet Beecher Stowe's *Uncle Tom's Cabin*, and Jack Kerouac's *On the Road*, *The Grapes of Wrath* is, in fact, one of America's classic road novels, tracking the epic cross-country journey of the Joad family during the height of the Great Depression in 1938 as they travel along Route 66 in a customized Hudson Super-Six from their small tenant farm outside of Sallisaw, Oklahoma, to California, where they hope to discover a better life than the one they have left behind.

At the same time, Steinbeck's novel is one of the most enduring and memorable migration narratives in American cultural history. The story of America is very much a story of migration across an expansive and often physically daunting landscape. The very foundation of the United States itself is grounded in early group migrations, one of the most notable of which is that of the Pilgrims, a group of religious nonconformists who separated from the Church of England and, led by William Bradford, in 1620 set sail from Holland for America on the now legendary *Mayflower* and established the Plymouth Plantation in Massachusetts. Equally notable is a radical group of Puritan dissidents led by John Winthrop, who, as part of the Great Migration of disaffected Puritans during the 1630s, set sail for America in 1630 and, following landfall, like Bradford's Pilgrims, established residence in Massachusetts. The Pilgrim and Puritan migrations both originated in religious, social, political, and economic persecution and, thus, were motivationally *reactive* as a matter of expediency. Both migratory ventures, however, were further motivated by the groups' visions of freedom, self-governance, and a fresh start and, as such, were idealistically *proactive*. Thus Bradford likened the Pilgrims to the Israelites searching for the promised land in the Old Testament, and Winthrop envisioned the Puritan settlement in America in distinctly millenarian terms, as a "citty upon a hill."

Like the Pilgrims and the Puritans, the Joads and the displaced legions of other migrants who lost their farms to drought, crop failures, and bank foreclosures were exiled from the land. Not unlike the Pilgrims and the Puritans, the Joads and other refugees from the southern Great Plains imagined a better life and a fresh start in another land—California, culturally the most magical and golden of all American settings. Thus, for the Joads and other migrant families, California, "as it had been since the nineteenth century . . . was the frontier, the new Eden, the last outpost of the old American dream of opportunity and the good life" (Dettelbach 69). Beyond recalling earlier migration chapters in American history, several critics, looking even further back, have identified a revealing parallel between the three-part structure of the Joads' narrative and the Bible, most notably the exodus story of the Old Testament. Thus Paul McCarthy compares the journey of the twelve Joads to the journey of the twelve tribes of Israel: all "engaged in their own archetypal quest for a better way of life" (79). More specifically:

Like the Jews in Egypt under Pharaoh, the Joads in Oklahoma are oppressed by landowners and banks. When dust, drought, and oppression
prove to be too much, the Joads begin their exodus and years of wandering.
Like the Jews, the Joads must face down detractors and enemies to reach
California, or Canaan, "the promised land." There they must remain off the
land unless the growers need them for work. (68)

Unique to the Joads' migratory narrative are the combined circumstances of agricultural change and catastrophic climatic conditions that
in the 1930s led to one of the most memorable, sustained, and, to that
point in time, unprecedented migratory road trips in American history.
Equally unique is the fact that, in contrast to travelers of the century before, who rode in Conestoga wagons, or "prairie schooners," the Joads
undertook their epic westward trek in what Cynthia Golomb Dettelbach describes as "a new messiah for the masses—the automobile"
(70), though in the case of the Joads and other migrants such a "messiah" would cut a decidedly unpromising profile and would require of
them a good deal of patience, mechanical ingenuity, and financial ex-
penditure.

"Dust Bowl Blues"

A primary cause of the Joads' flight from the land is the ever-shifting
dust that covers the landscape, the result of the persistent drought and
unremitting dust storms that devastated the Great Plains during the
1930s and that led to what would eventually become known as the
Dust Bowl, the heart of which covered nearly 100 million acres in Colorado, Nebraska, Kansas, Oklahoma, Texas, and New Mexico.[1] Such
acreage had originally been grassland, the thick turf of which the early
westering pioneers had used to build sod houses a century before. This
grassland was ideally suited for grazing, but with a boom in wheat
prices in the 1880s, wheat farming became "the main agricultural activity," and by the end of the century, "the keys of the cattle kingdom

had faded into the past, and steam engines had often replaced horses in front of the plow as well as powered threshing machines" (Hurt 8). Whether it was to compensate for a drop in wheat prices or to capitalize on a rise, over the ensuing three decades more and more sod was broken, a process facilitated by the introduction of tractor technology and one-way disk plows. Ominously, as R. Douglas Hurt explains,

in the wake of the plows, the roots of the sod lay exposed to the wind and the sun. Five to six million acres of that newly broken soil were submarginal—that is, land not fit for cultivation given the current price of wheat. That land was easily windblown, and it should have been left in the protective hold of the grass. Yet across the southern plains, farmers plowed acre after acre and transformed rangeland to breadbasket. (9)

Indeed, "between 1925 and 1931, wheat acreage doubled on the southern plains, and in some counties it expanded ten-fold" (Hurt 9). Following a decline in the early 1920s, the price of wheat peaked once again later in the decade, at which point, in and around Cimarron County, Oklahoma, as elsewhere, "you could put 25 percent down on grassland that cost as little as $15 an acre. You could 'break it out' with a plow, hope to raise 20 bushels of wheat per acre, sell each bushel for a dollar and pay off the land in a single season" (Parfit 47). However, with the stock market crash in 1929, the price of wheat dropped from one dollar a bushel to twenty-five cents (Parfit 48). Later, in spite of a record wheat crop in 1931 that yielded 50 bushels an acre, the stage was set for the human-made and natural catastrophe of the Dust Bowl.

Beginning in 1932 and continuing through 1936, regional rainfall levels dropped dramatically below the annual average. As Hurt explains: "When the rains stopped and the protective winter snows stopped falling, the wheat died, leaving the land exposed to the relentless winds. . . . by 1932 the soil was dry, pulverized, and easily lifted by the wind" (11). Widespread soil erosion was further exacerbated by the appearance of the first dust storms, or "black blizzards," in 1932; such storms continued until the end of the decade. The worst storm of the period hit on April 14, 1935, a date that would become known as Black Sunday; this event is memorably recounted in Woody Guthrie's ballads "Dust Bowl Disaster" and "So Long, It's Been Good to Know You." According to Timothy Egan: "The storm carried twice as much dirt as was dug out of the earth to create the Panama Canal. The canal took seven years to dig; the storm lasted a single afternoon. More than 300,000 tons of Great Plains topsoil was airborne that day" (8). In a feature story on the storm that appeared the next day in the Washington, D.C., *Evening Star*, journalist Robert Geiger remarked, "Three little words—achingly familiar on a Western farmer's tongue—rule life in the dust bowl of the continent—'If it rains'" (qtd. in Parfit 46). Two of Geiger's own words would later be adopted by a nation seeking a name for the phenomenon: Dust Bowl (Parfit 46). As Lawrence Svobida notes in *Farming the Dust Bowl: A First-Hand Account from Kansas*, its effects extended as far east as Washington, D.C., over which "floated . . . black cloud formations" (118). Egan reports that "American meteorologists [have] rated the Dust Bowl the number one weather event of the twentieth century. . . . historians say it was the nation's worst prolonged environmental disaster" (6).

It is in this setting that, in chapter 2 of Steinbeck's novel, Tom Joad finds himself as he walks down the road to his family's farm, stirring dust in his wake. Sentenced to prison on a homicide charge four years before and just recently paroled, Tom encounters Jim Casy, a preacher who had baptized Tom in his youth. Unable to reconcile his ministry with his fornication in the fields with the very women he has "saved" just moments before, Casy has renounced his calling and has been away for some time, wandering alone in the hills. Upon reaching the Joad place, Tom and Casy find the farm deserted and soon after are approached by neighbor and displaced farmer Muley Graves, who informs them that Tom's family members have been evicted from the farm and are "'gonna buy a car and shove on west where it's easy livin'"" (63). Muley's own family have relocated in the West, but he remains, wandering the barren landscape "'like a damn ol' graveyard ghos'"" (69).

For Muley, the Joads, and other tenant farmers, it is not only a matter of drought and dust that leads to their eventual flight from their native ground—a mismanagement of the land and a shift from an agrarian to a technological mode of agricultural production play a no less instrumental role in their departure. Thus, at one point, Muley, with an insightful conservationist awareness, observes, "'I know this land ain't much good 'cept for grazin'. Never should a broke her up. An' now she's cottoned damn near to death'" (64).[2] Yet, after his farm has been tractored out, Muley defiantly refuses to comply with an order to pack up and leave. Such defiance is, in part, a measure of Muley's independence and stubbornness, but in a larger sense it is grounded, both figuratively and literally, in the land itself, however worthless and unproductive it might be, for the land is invested with community, tradition, and ritualistic cycles of family history. Thus Muley has "'been goin' aroun' the places where stuff happened'": the site of his first sexual encounter, "'the place down by the barn where Pa got gored to death by a bull,'" and the room where his son Joe was born (69-70). Such a personal and social investment in the land transcends legalistically constructed, and ultimately artificial, notions of ownership and possession. Muley protests:

"Cause what'd they get when they tractored folks off the lan'? What'd they get so their 'margin a profit' was safe? They got Pa dyin' on the groun', an' Joe yellin' his first breath, an' me jerkin' like a billy goat under a bush in the night. What'd they get? God knows the lan' ain't no good. Nobody been able to make a crop for years. But them sons-a-bitches at their desks, they jus' chopped folks in two for their margin a profit. They jus' cut 'em in two." (70-71)

Such a "margin a profit" is achieved by "tractoring out" small farms to open up the land to a more expansive, efficient, and profitable system of tractor farming. Indeed, "by 1929, 42 percent of America's farmers were tenants rather than owners" (Kelly and Scott 37). Beyond enforced mortgage foreclosures then, Muley's and the Joads' powerlessness is directly related to their indentured status as tenant farmers. Thus, as a tractor driver informs a typical displaced farmer in chapter 5, "'Times are changing, mister, don't you know? Can't make a living on the land unless you've got two, five, ten thousand acres and a tractor. Crop land isn't for little guys like us any more'" (50).

Anticipating the Joads' own eventual plight on the road, Muley observes, "'[The migrants] ain't whole, out lonely on the road in a piled-up car. They ain't alive no more. Them sons-a-bitches killed 'em'" (71). With a sudden and renewed sense of vocation, Casy later reiterates Muley's concern over the migrants' fugitive existence: "'Maybe I can preach again. Folks out lonely on the road, with no lan', no home to go to. They got to have some kind of home'" (76). For Muley, however, the road is not an option any more than is the promise of a fresh start in California. As a foil to the Joads, Muley, true to his name, remains stubbornly entrenched on the land, a casualty to circumstances he cannot comprehend, doomed by his own futile resignation to repeat unviable rituals of family, community, and the land. Still, for the Joads and others, no less than Muley, the small farms from which they have been evicted remain "part of themselves—the locus of their family and history," as a result of which "they wonder if, in abandoning them, they are not doing grave injury to the very essence of their existence" (Cook 172).

Sam Bluefarb, in *The Escape Motif in the American Novel*, regards *The Grapes of Wrath*, like *Huckleberry Finn*, as

> not only a book of travel but a novel of escape—as in Tom Joad's instance, from the consequences of his acts; as in the instance of the Joad family, from the conditions and economics of the land; as in the instance of Preacher Casy, from an untenable past with its irreconcilable split between what the preacher is (or becomes) and the tenets he has long preached but now no longer believes in. (95)

Unlike the featured "escapers" in earlier American escape novels, however, such as *Huckleberry Finn*, Harold Frederic's *The Damnation of Theron Ware*, and Sherwood Anderson's *Winesburg, Ohio*, in all of whom "one senses a strong desire to be off—to be anywhere but where they happen to be," in the case of the Joads

> there is almost a sense of nostalgia for the land that has served them as home for generations. For the Joads differ from the other escapers in that, for the most part, when the time comes for them to leave, *they do not want to go*; this cannot be stressed enough. (107)

When Tom and Casy arrive at Uncle John's farm, where the Joads have taken up temporary residence, they discover the family hurriedly preparing to leave for California. Their vehicle is a used Hudson Super-Six sedan, which Al, Tom's younger brother and a skilled and knowledgeable mechanic, has purchased for seventy-five dollars and, together with his father, has converted into "a strange truck, for while the front of it was a sedan, the top had been cut off in the middle and the truck bed fitted on" (95). It is Al who, throughout the novel, is primarily responsible for driving and repairing the Hudson and eventually, in fact, "become[s] the [very] soul of the car" (167). Thus, even Pa, the head of the family, "would hold a wrench and take orders from Al" (132).

For the Joads, the "ancient Hudson" will serve as "the new hearth, the living center of the family; half passenger car and half truck, high-sided and clumsy" (136). Thus, prior to their departure, "the family met at the most important place, near the truck. The house was dead, and the fields were dead; but this truck was the active thing, the living principle" (128). Joseph Interrante observes, in this regard:

> A migrant family's car was not only a means of consumption, it was also the necessary basis for the migrant household's survival as a unit. As migrant labor reorganized around automobile movement, it became neces-

sary to use the car to find work and reach that work as a family unit. The automobile thus dominated the lives of migrant families in a unique and deliberate way. (103)

For McCarthy, the car anticipates the mobile home of the future while recalling the covered wagons of the previous century's westward great migration (77). Dettelbach likewise views the car, which has aptly "usurped the name of Hudson, a major American explorer, and taken over his pioneering role," as "the Conestoga wagon of the twentieth century" (71-72, 75). Thematically, Dettelbach adds that the car is also "emblematic of the pursuit of opportunity and the hope for a new life. As a dream image, the car promises social and economic liberation, a way out of Egypt and into the promised land" (75).

Such a sanguine view is voiced by various family members following Tom's arrival. Ma imagines how nice it will be in California with "'fruit ever' place, an' people just bein' in the nicest places, little white houses in among the orange trees. I wonder—that is, if we all get jobs an' all work—maybe we can get one of them little white houses'" (124). Tom's father likewise imagines California as a halcyon contrast to Oklahoma—"'plenty work, an' ever'thing nice an' green, an' little white houses an' oranges growin' aroun'"" (149). Grampa's anticipation is more specifically focused: "'Know what I'm a-gonna do? I'm gonna pick me a wash tub full of grapes, an I'm gonna set in 'em, an' scrooge aroun', an' let the juice run down my pants'" (126).

Metaphorically, however, as announced by the novel's titular allusion to the biblical "grapes of wrath" and the "Battle Hymn of the Republic," what the Joads discover in California are grapes of a far different vintage.[3] Ma herself voices a qualifying measure of skepticism: "'I'm scared of stuff so nice. I ain't got faith. I'm scared somepin ain't so nice about it'" (123). And when it comes time to leave, Grampa, recalling Muley and in words similar to Muley's, loses his enthusiasm and stubbornly refuses to leave:

"Me—I'm stayin'. . . . this here's my country. I b'long here. An' I don't give a goddamn if they's oranges an' grapes crowdin' a fella out of bed even. I ain't a goin'. This country ain't no good, but it's my country. No, you all go ahead. I'll jus' stay right here where I b'long." (152)

After drinking a cup of coffee dosed with "soothin' syrup," however, he falls asleep and is loaded onto the truck just prior to the family's departure. Ma—unlike Muley, whose presence is rooted in the enduring legacy of the land and the past—privately and stoically burns treasured personal and family memorabilia and keepsakes from the past, retaining only a ring, a watch charm, one gold cuff link, and a pair of earrings, which she later gives to her pregnant daughter Rose of Sharon.

As they prepare to leave, Ma asks Tom how long it will take to get to California, and Tom calculates, "'Two weeks, maybe ten days if we get luck'" (123). It is Al who actually comes closer to the truth, however, when, upon leaving, he remarks, "'Chr-ist, what a load. We ain't makin' no time on this trip'" (156). Over the course of their journey, the Joads, like so many migrants before them, will discover that life on the road carries a far different set of challenges than did the more certain, if no less daunting, life they leave behind. As Bluefarb observes, "The flight of the migrants westward is like a huge and disastrous military defeat; but unlike a retreat in conventional warfare, what lies away from the battle zone may be even more disastrous than what lies behind, in it" (110).

"Hard Travelin'"

In chapter 12, one of the most memorable interchapters in the novel, Steinbeck describes Route 66 as "the main migrant road . . . the long concrete path across the country . . . the path of a people in flight, refugees from dust and shrinking land, from the thunder of tractors, and shrinking ownership. . . . 66 is the mother road, the road of flight" (151). Cultural geographer Arthur Krim describes it as "biblical, leading the hopeful from the confines of an Eastern culture to the promised land of the unlimited West" and remarks that in *The Grapes of Wrath* Steinbeck means to "to capture the meaning of Route 66 as a metaphor of democratic determination on the open highway" (206).

It is just this sense of "democratic determination"—accompanied by a notable degree of resourcefulness, self-reliance, stamina, and what Steinbeck describes as the migrants' "terrible faith"—that enables the Joads to withstand and endure the series of challenges, hardships, and setbacks they encounter in flight along the "mother road." The precarious conditions they leave behind are replaced by a new and equally precarious set of challenges on the road, not the least of which is the challenge of adapting to unfamiliar and alien environments. Three days into their journey, finding the land "too huge for them," the Joads, in stark contrast to Muley, "settled into a new technique of living; the highway became their home and movement their medium of expression. Little by little they settled into the new life" (222). This "new life" eventually leads to a change in "social life" and social organization and an accompanying shift in focus, priorities, and survival skills. The Joads, no less than other fugitive families on the road,

were not farm men any more, but migrant men. And the thought, the planning, the long staring silence that had gone out to the fields, went now to the roads, to the distance, to the West. That man whose mind had been bound with acres lived with narrow concrete miles. (267-68)

Likewise, the migrants' previous concerns "with rainfall, with wind and dust, with the thrust of crops" have been replaced by an anxious preoccupation with their broken-down jalopies, "limping along 66 like wounded things, panting and struggling" (165), and the ever-present threat of tire punctures, overheated radiators, broken bearings, and other assorted mechanical problems. Thus, as the people in flight streamed out on 66 . . . ancient leaky radiators sent up columns of steam, loose connecting rods hammered and pounded. And the men driving the trucks and overloaded cars listened apprehensively. How far between towns? It is a terror between towns. If something breaks— well, if something breaks we camp right here while Jim walks to town and gets a part and walks back—and how much food we got? (161)

In the event that something does break, the migrants, lacking any other options, are forced to deal with opportunistic repair dealers who inflate the price of what turns out to be defective merchandise. Such is the case when a typical migrant family finds it necessary to replace a worn tire: "'We got to get a tire, but, Jesus, they want a lot for a ol' tire. They look a fella over. They know he can't wait and the price goes up'" (162). And despite the salesman's assurance that the tire is "good," it turns out to have a "'busted casing,'" as, of course, the salesman had known all along.

The already impaired efficiency and reliability of the second- and third-hand jalopies is further exacerbated by the severity of the terrain, which ranges from prohibitive mountain ascents to the searing heat of the desert, where "the water grew scarce" and, once again, on the basis of a ruthless economy of supply and demand, "was to be bought, five cents, ten cents, fifteen cents a gallon" (274).

For the Joads, as for other migrant families, "the car [becomes] a stern taskmaster. At the expense of its human cargo, the car (like its predecessor, the Conestoga wagon) must be fed and tended first" (Dettelbach 75). Thus "the wills [of the migrants] thrust westward ahead of them, and fears that had once apprehended drought or flood now lingered with anything that might stop the westward crawling" (268).[4]

Uprooted from the stabilizing influences of their native homes and of the social, cultural, and religious values shared by their communities, the Joads and their fellow fugitives are forced to manage not only the hardships incurred by the prohibitive conditions of the road itself but also the special challenges presented by life off the road. Not the least of these challenges, as Christopher L. Salter explains in "John Steinbeck's *The Grapes of Wrath* as a Primer for Cultural Geography," is "finding a few physical elements deemed necessary for a nighttime haven—water, a little firewood, and perhaps a nearby dump for scavenging" (146). Without the original "hearth place," housing becomes improvised, mutable, and temporary. Thus, "as the families moved westward, the technique of building up a home in the evening and tearing it down with the morning light became fixed" (267).

Such an improvised adaptation leads to an equally improvised social contract, the basis of which is a sense of common purpose, solidarity, mutual generosity, and self-governance, which anticipates the ethic of the federal government camp at Arvin, California, later in the novel. Thus, "in the evening a strange thing happened: the twenty families became one family, the children were the children of all. The loss of home became one loss, and the golden time in the West was one dream" (264). Displaced from the familiar provincial circumference of their local communities, the migrants evolve into a larger community that respects, but democratically transcends, geographic origins and thereby anticipates the progressive, but as yet inchoate, evolution of Steinbeck's concept of "Manself." Introduced and explained in chapter 14, it is the means whereby the oppressed eventually organize to protest and ultimately revolt against the institutions and agencies responsible for their oppression. Over time, such a sense of democratic enfranchisement leads to the development of intuitive and unspoken social protocols and laws, which recalls a parallel development in the Israelites' migratory flight, as recorded in the book of Deuteronomy. As Peter Lisca explains, "It is this context which makes of the Joads' journey 'out west' an archetype of mass migration" (*Wide World* 71).

What is true of the migrants in a general sense is more specifically modeled in the case of the Joads' interactions with Ivy and Sairy Wilson, refugees from Galena, Kansas, whose 1925 Dodge touring car has broken down, immobilizing them along the side of the road outside Bethany, Oklahoma. Like so many other migrants, Ivy has been duped into buying a barely functional jalopy. As Ivy explains to Tom, his situation is further complicated by the fact that, unlike Al, "'I don' know nothin' about cars'" (200). Prior to leaving Galena, in fact, Ivy had never driven a car; nor had his brother Will, who wrecks his own newly purchased car and becomes so enraged that he refuses to leave.

When the Joads and Wilsons first meet, Tom is looking to pull over to a campsite occupied by the Wilsons. As a matter of deference, and sensitive to matters of occupancy and the land, Tom requests permission to pull over and explains, "'You got a right to say if you wan' neighbors or not'" (183). For Ivy Wilson, "the appeal to hospitality had an instant effect. . . . 'Why, sure, come on off the road. Proud to have ya'" (183). The Joads and Wilsons quickly forge a genuine and affectionate alliance, which—in contrast to the insensitivity and disregard of the landowners, banks, and finance companies, and the ruthless and proprietary self-interest of the used-car salesmen, automotive parts dealers, and junk dealers—is informed by mutual respect and a spontaneous sense of generosity. When Grampa takes ill, Sairy Wilson, who herself is secretly terminally ill, arranges a mattress and quilt in the Wilsons' tent so he can rest. When he dies of a stroke shortly afterward, she comforts Granma, gets supper for the two families, and helps prepare the body for burial. Tom and Al, in turn, volunteer to repair the Wilsons' car and then propose that the two families pool their resources for their journey to California, a proposal immediately and decisively confirmed by Ma: "'Each'll help each, an' we'll all git to California. Sairy Wilson he'ped lay Grampa out'" (202). Eventually, however, Sairy's physical condition reaches the point where she is "'jus' pain covered with skin'" (298), and the two families part, but not before Pa leaves the Wilsons some pork and potatoes and two one-dollar bills.

Pa's financial generosity is particularly notable since the Joad family's finances, which amounted to a mere $154 when the family left Oklahoma, have been seriously depleted by expenses on the road and the fact that mechanical breakdowns and the challenging terrain of the mountains and the Mojave Desert still ahead will make it unlikely that, contrary to Tom's original calculation, they will reach California in ten to fourteen days. Moreover, whatever the selfless and communitarian social contract forged by the migrant families in flight, various developments threaten their prospects of even reaching California.

Especially ominous in this regard is the fact that native Californians are hostile to the ever-burgeoning influx of migrants. Sylvia Jenkins Cook observes in this regard that "the expansion of the Okies' experience from parochial and provincial to national . . . is paralleled by the shrinking of tolerance for them among the Californians" (176). As a gas station attendant in the novel informs a typical migrant family, drawing a revealing dichotomy that stands in direct contrast to the migrants' undifferentiated notion of class, "'There ain't room enough for you an' me, for your kind an' my kind, for rich an poor together all in one country. . . . Whyn't you go back where you come from?'" (163). To discourage the influx of migrants, he further explains, border patrols have been set up on the California state line, in direct violation of constitutional law, to turn back any migrants who cannot prove they possess sufficient funds to buy real estate.

Ma experiences such aggressive hostility firsthand at a makeshift campground on the California side of the Colorado River when she is harassed by a cop who informs her, "'We don't want none of you settlin' down here'" and then adds, "'You're in California, an' we don't want you goddamn Okies settlin' down'" (291). Shortly before, Tom—during an exchange with a father and son who, discouraged by the uninviting and hostile social climate in California, are actually returning home—had his first encounter with the term "Okies," which, as his informant explains, no longer means a person from Oklahoma: "'Now it means you're a dirty son-of-a-bitch. Okie means you're scum. Don't mean nothing itself, it's the way they say it'" (280).

The Californians' hostility runs counter to the handbills the migrants have seen that advertise to tenant farmers and small independent farmers who have been evicted and "tractored out" an abundance of jobs in the orchards and fields of California and the lucrative promise of a fresh start. It is the large corporate farmers and farm associations that circulate these handbills, and, as the Joads and other migrants soon find out, they are no less unscrupulous and exploitative than the landowners, banks, and finance companies in the Midwest and Southwest. Like Pa Joad, Ivy Wilson has seen a handbill soliciting workers to pick fruit and vegetables, and he, too, imagines a fresh start that includes more than enough to eat and "good wages," and he even predicts, "'Why, hell, in a couple years I bet a fella could have a place of his own'" (201). The handbills, however, are deliberately misleading—the possibility of which Tom himself considers even before leaving Oklahoma. He informs his mother that he had met "a fella from California" who told him, "'They's too many folks lookin' for work right there now. An' he says the folks that pick the fruit live in dirty ol' camps an' don't hardly get enough to eat. He says wages is low an' hard to get any'" (124). When Ma counters with the fact that Tom's father has seen a handbill "'tellin' how they need folks to work'" and that "'they wouldn't go to that trouble if they wasn't plenty work,'" Tom responds, "'I don't know, Ma. It's kinda hard to think why they done it'" (124).

The rationale for "why they done it" is sounded on several occasions on the road: the bottom line is the corporate farmers' self-serving, profit-driven exploitation of the migrants, who have been driven to desperation by the landowners, banks, and finance companies of their home states.[5] At one point, Tom, Al, Pa, and Casy encounter a "ragged man" who describes the supply-and-demand economics directly: "'This fella wants eight hundred men. So he prints up five thousand of them things an' maybe twenty thousan' people sees 'em. An' maybe three thousan' folks get movin' account of this han'bill. Folks that's crazy with worry'" (259). Such worry and the surplus of labor provide the farm owners with the leverage to reduce the original contracted wage. As the ragged man goes on to explain:

"Maybe he needs two hundred men, so he talks to five hundred, an' they tell other folks an' when you get to the place, they's a thousan' men. This here fella says, 'I'm payin' twenty cents an hour.' An' maybe half the men walk off. But they's still five hundred that's so goddamn hungry they'll work for nothin' but biscuits." (259)

As for the ragged man, who has lost a wife and two children, he is returning home: "'I'm goin' back to starve. I ruther starve all over at oncet'" (257). Once the ragged man leaves, Pa asks Casy, "'S'pose he's tellin' the truth—that fella?'" and Casy responds, "'He's tellin' the truth awright. The truth for him. He wasn't makin' nothin' up'" (261). Then, when Tom demands, "'Is that the truth for us?'" Casy and Pa answer in unison, "'I don't know'" (261). The "truth" of the immediate situation is that they have little choice but to move on to a future that remains distant and uncertain. This "truth" has already been articulated by Casy, who, in response to a service station owner's bewilderment over "'what the country's comin' to,'" says:

"Seems to me we never come to nothin'. Always on the way. Always goin' and goin'.... They's movement now. People moving. We know why, an' we know how. Movin' 'cause they got to. That's why folks always move. Movin' 'cause they want somepin better'n what they got. An' that's the on'y way they'll ever git it. Wantin' it an' needin' it, they'll go out an' git it." (173)

Perhaps the greatest challenge confronting the Joads on the road is that of sustaining the family unit. Not counting Casy, the original family totals twelve members, but on the road this figure is depleted by a number of deaths and defections. Removed from his native ground, Grampa dies from a stroke just outside of Bethany, Oklahoma, although, as Casy explains, "'He died the minute you took 'im off the place'" (199). Given the daunting expense of a funeral, Grampa receives not the more proper and formal "home burial" he would have had "on the land" but rather is buried in a makeshift grave along the highway, yet another improvised adaptation of the Joads to life "on the road." Granma dies during the night the family crosses the Mojave Desert. When they reach Bakersfield, California, the family arranges a town burial, at a cost of forty dollars, which further depletes their already precarious financial resources. Prior to crossing the desert, Noah, the firstborn, leaves the family, explaining to Tom, "'I'm sad, but I can't he'p it. I got to go'" (284).

When, at one point, Tom proposes that the family continue west in the family truck while he and Casy remain behind to repair the Wilsons' car, Ma grabs a jack handle and threatens, "'I'm a goin' cat-wild with this here piece of bar-arn if my own folks busts up'"; she declares, "'All we got is the family unbroken. . . . I ain't scairt while we're all here, all that's alive, but I ain't gonna see us bust up'" (231). For the moment, Ma, whose "tone was cold and final," carries the day, but when Tom informs her of Noah's departure even she, the controlling and unifying force in the family, reveals the strain of circumstance: "'Family's fallin' apart. I don't know. Seems like I can't think no more. I jus' can't think. They's too much'" (294). Ma's resilience, stamina, and faith will be further tested in California, where "the truth" of the ragged man's experience becomes her and her family's own truth and where the family unit is further compromised.

"Pastures of Plenty"

In his autobiography, *Bound for Glory*, folk musician Woody Guthrie describes how, on arriving in California for the first time after leaving his home in Pampa, Texas, in 1937, he was struck equally by the vibrant colors and fecundity of the landscape and by the fruit rotting on the ground, which could feed "every hungry kid from Maine to Florida, and from there to Seattle" (223). (In one of the more powerful interchapters in *The Grapes of Wrath*, Steinbeck regards this waste as "a crime . . . that goes beyond denunciation" as children die of malnutrition "because the food must rot, must be forced to rot" [477].) Shortly after his arrival in California, Guthrie was harassed and threatened by a cop who suspected that Guthrie might be "one of them labor boys," "one of them trouble causers" (237). As he traveled around the state, Guthrie came into contact with migrant workers who, like himself, had left the Dust Bowl in search of work and a better life only to experience hunger, disease, homelessness, and exploitation.

The Joads' experiences in California closely parallel Guthrie's. Driving through Tehachapi in the early morning, they suddenly discover the "great valley below them. . . . The vineyards, the orchards, the great flat valley, green and beautiful, the trees set in rows, and the farm houses" (309-10). Pa, observing "the peach trees and the walnut groves, and the dark green patches of oranges," reflects, "'I never knowed they was anything like her'" (310), and, no less moved, Ruthie and Winfield stand "silent and awestruck, embarrassed before the great valley" (310). Such an edenic setting, in direct contrast to the parched, desolate landscape back home and the challenging topography along Highway 66, would seem to confirm the Joads' original idealistic perception of California. Far from giving the Joads a new beginning, however, California merely extends their improvised and makeshift life on Route 66. Upon reaching California, they, like the other migrant families who have been brutalized by the landowners, banks, and finance companies of the Great Plains, discover that they have a "new boss," who, as it turns out, is "the same as the old boss." In California, the selfsame institutional oppression just assumes a new face—that of corporate agribusiness, which enforces its profit-driven agenda in collusion with official and vigilante law enforcement groups, residential and absentee landowners, and, once again, banks and finance companies. Collectively, they constitute a monolithic system of control and intimidation that would seem to preclude, at least for the moment, any sort of protest and resistance.

Financially destitute, and thus forced to travel in search of work, the Joads find that their life in California is no less transitory and nomadic than was life on the road. Moving from a Hooverville to the Hooper ranch and then to a boxcar camp, the Joads discover for themselves the demoralizing scenario described by the ragged man and others who have witnessed the dispiriting conditions firsthand. Thus, as Bluefarb explains, the Joads

> are forever forced . . . to flee from one place to another, always on the move, always searching for a way out of their plight. Eventually, the westward flight of the Joads turns inward upon itself; and after their arrival in California, it is no longer a flight west but simply a flight, chronic and labyrinthine, down the road, to the next government camp, to another ranch, to a hundred and one dead ends of hope. The flight of the Joads thus becomes a chronic mode of existence. (109)

The Joads find their single respite at the Weedpatch camp, a government-run migrant camp near Arvin, California, where they discover decent living conditions and a sense of community and, thereby, rediscover their dignity and self-respect. They are unable to find work, however, and, after a little more than a month, are forced to leave and resume their life on the road, where they experience further losses within the family unit and a series of additional reversals.[6]

By the end of the novel, beyond demoralizing economic circumstances and continuing privations, the Joad family unit has been devastated. Connie, increasingly disgruntled with life on the road and regretful that he did not remain back home and "'stud[y] nights 'bout tractors'" (343)—ironically, the very cause of the Joads' displacement—eventually walks off and abandons his pregnant wife Rose of Sharon, who, as it turns out, is the only family member to regret his defection. As Bluefarb observes, Connie's desertion stands in "strong contrast to the pioneer husbands . . . who, for the most part, were supposed to have stuck by their womenfolk and protected them" (105). More seriously, Casy is jailed when he kicks a deputy who has shown up at a squatters' camp in search of labor union agitators and accidentally shoots a defenseless woman. Upon his release, Casy, who by now is fully committed to the labor cause, is tracked down and killed by a vigilante. Tom retaliates by killing Casy's assailant and is consequently forced to go into hiding. Eventually, he leaves the family for their own benefit.

Their will and faith broken, Pa and Uncle John become increasingly discouraged. Uncle John "'can't think nothing out. Don't seem like I'm hardly awake no more,'" and Pa likewise observes, "'I ain't no good any more. Spen' all my time thinkin' how it use' ta be. Spen' all my time thinkin' of home, an' I ain't never gonna see it no more'" (576-77). Rose of Sharon, worn down by an insufficient diet and physical exhaustion, loses her baby. Al, still restless and resentful of the responsibility that ties him to the family, makes plans to leave with his fiancée; however, following Tom's departure, he more selflessly assumes a greater leadership role as the man of the family, a role essentially forfeited by Pa and Uncle John.

Given the failure of their original expectations and ever-worsening circumstances, the remaining Joads face a future that would seem to hold little relief or promise, and it does not appear likely that they will find any means of remediation or that social, economic, or political reform will take place. More than a means of transit, however, the road, as in so many road and migration narratives, can be experientially, socially, and morally transformative, facilitating a higher consciousness and understanding. As Stephen Railton observes, "Thematically, Route 66 and the various state highways in California that the Joads travel along all run parallel to the road to Damascus that Saul takes in Acts, or to the Way taken by Bunyan's Christian in *Pilgrim's Progress*" (29). Thus, for Railton, the Joads' journey, like that of Bunyan's Christian, is an "inward one" and "a pilgrimage toward the prospect of a new consciousness" (32). In a more expansive vein, Peter Lisca asserts that

The Grapes of Wrath moves not along route 66, east to west, like some delayed Wagon Wheels adventure, but along the unmapped roads of social change, from an old concept of community based on sociological conditions breaking up under an economic upheaval, to a new and very different sense of community formulating itself gradually on the new social realities. ("Dynamics" 128)

For Railton, Jim Casy is instrumental in modeling this "inward journey" toward a "new consciousness," and for Lisca, Casy is no less crucial in articulating Steinbeck's revisionary concept of community.

Early in the novel, when Casy meets Tom after his release from prison, he explains that he has been "'in the hills, thinkin', almost you might say like Jesus went into the wilderness to think His way out of a mess of troubles'" (109). Though he fails to recover his ministerial vocation, Casy does manage to discover a number of insights, such as the notion that "'there ain't no sin and there ain't no virtue. There's just stuff people do'" (32). Even more radical are Casy's speculations on "the human sperit," which recall Emerson's notion of the "oversoul":

> "I figgered about the Holy Sperit and the Jesus road. I figgered, 'Why do we got to hang it on God or Jesus? Maybe,' I figgered, 'maybe it's all men an' all women we love; maybe that's the Holy Sperit—the human sperit— the whole shebang. Maybe all men got one big soul ever'body's a part of.' Now I sat there thinkin' it, an' all of a suddent—I knew it. I knew it so deep down that it was true, and I still know it." (32-33)[7]

Shortly thereafter, before leaving Oklahoma, Casy, intoning Walt Whitman's fraternal and egalitarian impulses, announces:

"I ain't gonna baptize. I'm gonna work in the fiels, in the green fiel's, an' I'm gonna be near to folks. I ain't gonna try to teach 'em nothin'. I'm gonna try to learn. . . . Gonna lay in the grass, open an' honest with anybody that'll have me. Gonna cuss an' swear an' hear the poetry of folks talkin'. All that's holy, all that's what I didn' understan'. All them things is good things." (127-28)

Though he doesn't recognize it at the time, Casy has already "learned" a great deal, most notably his reconfiguration of the "Holy Sperit" (the third part of the divine trinity) as the "human sperit," in which "all men got one big soul ever'body's a part of" (33). His experiences on the road progressively vindicate what was originally a generously inclusive, though abstract, concept. For Casy, such a concept manifests itself throughout the novel in repeated acts of charity and in a commitment to a collective vision that transcends the individual ego. It is more expansively demonstrated in the social organization of the typical migrant camp (in chapter 17) and the government camp at Arvin. Thus Casy's death, however regrettable, is merely an incidental setback, as Casy himself presciently explains shortly before his murder, as he recalls a "'fella in jail'" who, not unlike Henry David Thoreau in "Resistance to Civil Government," had said,

"'Anyways, you do what you can. An',' he says, 'the on'y thing you got to look at is that ever' time they's a little step fo'ward, she may slip back a little, but she never slips clear back. You can prove that,' he says, 'an' that makes the whole thing right. An' that means they wasn't no waste even if it seemed like they was.'" (525)

When Casy first announces his Emersonian notion of a larger, comprehensive "oversoul," Tom responds, "'You can't hold no church with ideas like that. People would drive you out of the country with ideas like that'" (33). But such "ideas" eventually provide the formative basis for Casy's more fully articulated social activism and the higher transcendental consciousness that evolves over the course of the novel; they culminate in Casy's martyrdom for a cause and a concept greater than himself.

After avenging Casy's murder, Tom, as a matter of expediency, hides in a makeshift cave to avoid arrest. As a pragmatist who is at first disinclined toward thoughtful reflection, Tom is initially focused on the immediate here and now, but over the course of the novel he gradually assimilates and assumes Casy's convictions. During his withdrawal, Tom has the opportunity to think about Casy, and, as he later explains to his mother, he adopts Casy's concepts:

> "I been thinkin' what he [Casy] said, an' I can remember—all of it. Says one time he went out in the wilderness to find his own soul, an' he foun' he didn' have no soul that was his'n. Says he foun' he jus' got a little piece of a great big soul. Says a wilderness ain't no good, 'cause his little piece of a soul wasn't no good 'less it was with the rest, an' was whole. Funny how I remember. Didn' think I was even listenin'. But I know now a fella ain't no good alone." (570)

When Tom announces that he is leaving, Ma expresses her fear that he might be killed, and Tom responds with an oracular eloquence reminiscent of Casy himself:

> "Then it don' matter. Then I'll be all aroun' in the dark. I'll be ever'where—wherever you look. . . . If Casy knowed, why, I'll be in the way guys yell when they're mad an'—I'll be in the way kids laugh when they're hungry an' they know supper's ready. . . . See? God, I'm talkin' like Casy. Comes of thinkin' about him so much. Seems like I can see him sometimes." (572)

Significantly, the focus of Tom's protean-activist manifesto is not his immediate biological family but rather the larger human family, the "whole shebang," as Casy would say. As Railton observes:

On the Road in *The Grapes of Wrath*   **79**

Wherever the people are—that is Tom's new home. All the boundaries around his self have dissolved. In this communion with the world soul, Tom finds a freedom that merely being paroled could never provide, and a meaning that living for himself or for his family could never have bestowed upon his acts. (37)

Still, Tom's own family is a component of this larger, extended family and no less the beneficiary of Tom's projected social activism than the Wilsons or any other oppressed family. Ma herself voices such a collectivist perspective earlier in the novel, when, in a discussion about the greed and self-interest of their oppressors, she assures Tom that "'us people will go on livin' when all them people is gone. Why, Tom, we're the people that live. They ain't gonna' wipe us out. Why we're the people—we go on'" (383). Such an expansive populist affirmation is reiterated later in the novel when she observes, "'Use' ta be the fambly was fust. It ain't so now. It's anybody. Worse off we get, the more we got to do'" (606). Though she never directly says as much, this survival is ensured by Casy's and eventually Tom's notion of the one big soul, or extended family, that born of the love and generosity that the Joads and other migrant families enact throughout the novel and that is most memorably demonstrated in the novel's concluding scene.

Near the end of the novel, the boxcar camp and the Joads' truck are flooded out, as a result of which the family members, with the exception of Al, who remains behind with the truck, set off on foot in search of higher ground. They eventually take shelter in a barn occupied by a young boy and his father, who is dying of hunger. Recognizing the man's desperate condition, Rose of Sharon nurses him with the breast milk that would have fed her baby. No less than any of Casy's or Tom's acts of generosity, Rose of Sharon's nurturing and life-giving gesture extends beyond her immediate family unit to sustain the survival of the larger human family. Thus, as Railton observes:

Thematically, the novel's last scene is perfect. It is the moment of Rose of Sharon's conversion. Out of the violent loss of her baby . . . comes a new self-less sense of self. When she breastfeeds the starving stranger who would otherwise die, a new boundary-less definition of family is born. Rose of Sharon's act is devoutly socialistic: from each according to ability, to each according to need. (43)

For Warren French, *The Grapes of Wrath* "is not about the [Joad] family's finding security; it is about their education" or, more specifically, "the education of the heart," which "results in a change from the family's proudly isolating itself as part of a self-important clan to its accepting a role as part of one vast human family that, in Casy's words, shares 'one big soul ever'body's a part of'" (77). The final scene thus "complete[s] their education by transcending familial prejudices. What happens now to them—to anyone—depends on the ability of the rest of society to learn what the Joads have learned" (81).

Steinbeck had seen firsthand all of the hardships, disappointments, and failed dreams the Joads experience following their arrival in California in the summer of 1936, when he was commissioned by the *San Francisco News* to write a series of articles on the migrant labor crisis in California. He took to the road himself and visited squatters' camps, labor camps, and, most notably, the federally sponsored Weedpatch camp near Arvin, California. In the seventh, and final, installment of his newspaper articles, Steinbeck made a number of recommendations regarding ways to alleviate the crisis, including the establishment of government-funded subsistence farms to be located "in regions which require an abundance of harvest labor" as well near schools, "so that the children can be educated" (*Harvest Gypsies* 59). He further recommended the establishment of a statewide network of migratory labor boards to eliminate the exploitative hiring practices of "the shipper-grower, the speculative farmer, and the corporation farm" along with the "vigilante terrorism" that enforced such practices (60, 61).

However, these recommendations, along with the protest and call for reform sounded in *The Grapes of Wrath*, were muted by the nation's increasing preoccupation with the political and militaristic developments that led to America's entry into World War II. Thus, as Charles Wollenberg notes, "by the end of 1940, reporter Ernie Pyle noted that the Okies no longer made headlines: 'people sort of forgot them'" (xvi). In fact, a year later, "the labor surplus of the Depression had been transformed into an extraordinary wartime shortage of workers. Migrants who were not subject to military service found employment in California's booming shipyards, aircraft factories and other defense plants" (xvi). Ironically, "the Joads and their fellow Okies ultimately found economic salvation, not in the small farms they dreamed of owning, but in urban industry fueled by billions of federal defense dollars" (xvi).

Though *The Grapes of Wrath* may fail to anticipate the Okies' eventual "economic salvation," it is true to the paradigm of reactive expediency and proactive idealism that informs so many notable migration narratives in America's cultural history, perhaps most notably William Bradford's Pilgrims and John Winthrop's Puritans, both of whom established the foundations for the nascent American republic and provided a model for subsequent American migratory movements. Thus, as a migrant appropriately observes in *The Grapes of Wrath*, "'We ain't foreign. Seven generations back Americans, and beyond that Irish, Scotch, English, German. One of our folks in the Revolution, an' they was lots of our folks in the Civil War—both sides. Americans'" (317-18). No less proudly, Ma Joad at one point boasts, "'We're Joads. We don't look up to nobody. Grampa's grampa, he fit in the Revolution'" (420). Finally, then, *The Grapes of Wrath* continues to retain its timelessness as a classic American migration narrative and as an equally classic American road novel. No less significantly, it reaches beyond any specific cultural and nationalistic affiliation to become an affirmation of what Jim Casy describes as the "human sperit." As Ma Joad would say, it "goes on" and ultimately transcends the mutable circumstances of time and place.

Notes

1. Technically, Sallisaw, Oklahoma, the town nearest the Joad farm, lay outside the epicenter of the Dust Bowl. Thus, in situating Sallisaw in the Dust Bowl, Steinbeck is geographically "off the mark." As Timothy Egan explains, unlike the actual "Exo-dusters" from the southern plains, "Steinbeck's exiles were from eastern Oklahoma, near Arkansas—mostly tenant farmers ruined by the collapse of the economy. The families in the heart of the black blizzards were further west, in towns like Guymon and Boise City in Oklahoma, or Dalhart and Follett in Texas, or Rolla and Kismet in Kansas" (9). Walter J. Stein likewise explains that "though Americans came to see the 'dust bowl' as synonymous with 'drought region,' it was not. The actual dust bowl was but a part of the drought region and most of the Okies came neither from the dust bowl nor from the areas of worst distress in the drought region. That Okies did come from the dust bowl is true; that the average Okie in California was a dust-bowl refugee is false" (15). In fact, as James N. Gregory reports in *American Exodus: The Dust Bowl and Okie Culture in California*, of the 315,000-400,000 southwesterners who moved west during the 1930s, fewer than "16,000 from the Dust Bowl proper ended up in Cal-ifornia, barely 6 percent of the total from the Southwestern states" (11). Moreover, as Gregory notes, of the 116,000 migrant families who settled in California in the 1930s, "most were not farmers, but rather had come from . . . cities and towns," and "only 43 percent had engaged in agricultural pursuits immediately prior to migration" (15). Equally notable is the fact that, in contrast to those farmers who did leave the Dust Bowl, the Joads were not wheat farmers but cotton farmers. Thus, when informed of a call for cotton pickers following the Joads' departure from the Hooper ranch, Pa says, "'By God, I'd like to get my hands on some cotton! There's work, I un'erstan'"" (551). The prospect of picking cotton did attract many "Okies" to California, and Arizona as well, as Marsha L. Weisiger discusses in *Land of Plenty: Oklahomans in the Cotton Fields of Arizona, 1933-1942*.

2. While, according to Louis Owens, Steinbeck "makes it clear that the sharecrop-pers are victimized by an inhuman economic monster that tears at the roots of Jef-fersonian agrarianism," he also "emphasize[s] the migrants' culpability, their re-sponsibility," as Muley suggests, "for what has happened to the land and themselves" (111).

3. For a concise but illuminating analysis of the thematic and symbolic significance of grapes in the novel, see Peter Lisca's *The Wide World of John Steinbeck* (169-70).

4. Contrary to the Joads' and other migrants' setbacks traveling to California, Greg-ory asserts that "in their desire to dramatize the migrant experience, novelists, journal-ists, and even historians have exaggerated the hardships of the journey to California" (31-32). Without discounting the difficulties encountered by many migrants in transit—automotive breakdowns and depletion of funds that required temporary employment off the road—Gregory claims that "the actual trip west posed few problems for most migrants" (32). In fact, "in a good car families could make it to California in as little as three days. Nights were spent either in auto courts or camping by the roadside" (33). Moreover, in contrast to the Joads—who viewed their displacement from the land as permanent—many migrants left their homes and farms in the Southwest on a far more

provisional and, in some cases, intentionally temporary basis, as they set out "to explore work projects," to engage in seasonal labor circuits, to visit relatives who had moved west, or simply to experience the romance and attractions of the open road. Thus, as Gregory explains, "many of the 1930s migrants were neither destitute nor the dirt farmers of popular paradigm, and even those who fit the image responded to many of the same kinds of attractions and dreams—'pulls'—which had traditionally been the chief basis for migration to California" (10). For those with no intention of returning, the journey to California was, according to Gregory, far less challenging than the prohibitive and dispiriting conditions they encountered upon their arrival (34-35).

5. Drawing on Farm Security Administration archives, Walter J. Stein reports in *California and the Dust Bowl Migration* that "many of the Okies themselves claimed to have chosen California in response to advertisements, in which 'the various Chambers of Commerces were advising agricultural laborers of the Dust Bowl areas that California was in need of thousands of cotton pickers. Any man that could pick cotton could make four dollars a day'" (19). Stein further states that one Okie referred to "circulars all over the county, crying for help in the beautiful state of California" (19). Thus, for the Okies, as Cynthia Golomb Dettelbach observes, California "was a state whose largely vanished past was perpetuated, especially by enterprising salesmen and landowners, in a golden flow of present tense verbs. And hungrily, if apprehensively, the people listened and got moving" (69).

6. For detailed accounts of migrant labor conditions in California during the 1930s, see Walter J. Stein's *California and the Dust Bowl Migration*, James N. Gregory's *American Exodus*, Cletus E. Daniel's *Bitter Harvest: A History of California Farmworkers, 1870-1941*, and Carey McWilliams's classic study *Factories in the Field*, published in 1939, the same year as *The Grapes of Wrath*.

7. Frederic I. Carpenter provides an illuminating assessment of Casy's notion of the "human sperit" in relation to Emerson's concept of the "transcendental oversoul" in his illuminating and frequently anthologized essay "The Philosophical Joads" (reprinted in this volume) and also cites Walt Whitman's "religion of the love of all men and his mass democracy" and "the realistic philosophy of pragmatism and its emphasis on effective action" as further influences in the formative development of Casy's (and, by implication, Steinbeck's) social philosophy.

Works Cited

Bluefarb, Sam. *The Escape Motif in the American Novel: Mark Twain to Richard Wright*. Columbus: Ohio State UP, 1972.

Carpenter, Frederic I. "The Philosophical Joads." *College English* 2.4 (1941): 315-25.

Cook, Sylvia Jenkins. *From Tobacco Road to Route 66: The Southern Poor White in Fiction*. Chapel Hill: U of North Carolina P, 1976.

Daniel, Cletus E. *Bitter Harvest: A History of California Farmworkers, 1870-1941*. Ithaca, NY: Cornell UP, 1981.

Dettelbach, Cynthia Golomb. *In the Driver's Seat: The Automobile in American Literature and Popular Culture*. Westport, CT: Greenwood Press, 1976.

Ditsky, John. "*The Grapes of Wrath*: A Reconsideration." *Southern Humanities Review* 13 (1979): 215-20.

Egan, Timothy. *The Worst Hard Time: The Untold Story of Those Who Survived the Great American Dust Bowl*. Boston: Houghton Mifflin, 2006.

French, Warren. *John Steinbeck's Fiction Revisited*. New York: Twayne, 1994.

Gregory, James N. *American Exodus: The Dust Bowl Migration and Okie Culture in California*. New York: Oxford UP, 1989.

Guthrie, Woody. *Bound for Glory*. 1943. New York: New American Library, 1983.

Hurt, R. Douglas. Foreword. *Farming the Dust Bowl: A First-Hand Account from Kansas*. By Lawrence Svobida. Lawrence: UP of Kansas, 1986. 7-32.

Interrante, Joseph. "The Road to Autopia: The Automobile and the Spatial Transformation of American Culture." *The Automobile and American Culture*. Ed. David L. Lewis and Laurence Goldstein. Ann Arbor: U of Michigan P, 1983. 89-104.

Kelly, Susan Croce, and Quinta Scott. *Route 66: The Highway and Its People*. Norman: U of Oklahoma P, 1988.

Krim, Arthur. "Mapping Route 66: A Cultural Cartography." *Roadside America: The Automobile in Design and Culture*. Ed. Jan Jennings. Ames: Iowa State UP, 1990. 198-208.

Lisca, Peter. "The Dynamics of Community in *The Grapes of Wrath*." *From Irving to Steinbeck: Studies in American Literature in Honor of Harry R. Warfel*. Ed. Motley Deakin and Peter Lisca. Gainesville: U of Florida P, 1972. 127-40.

––––––––––. *The Wide World of John Steinbeck*. 1958. New York: Gordian Press, 1981.

McCarthy, Paul. *John Steinbeck*. New York: Frederick Ungar, 1980.

McWilliams, Carey. *Factories in the Field: The Story of Migratory Farm Labor in California*. Boston: Little, Brown, 1939.

Owens, Louis. "The Culpable Joads: Desentimentalizing *The Grapes of Wrath*." *Critical Essays on Steinbeck's "The Grapes of Wrath."* Ed. John Ditsky. Boston: G. K. Hall, 1989. 108-16.

Parfit, Michael. "The Dust Bowl." *Smithsonian* June 1989: 45-55.

Railton, Stephen. "Pilgrims' Politics: Steinbeck's Art of Conversion." *New Essays on "The Grapes of Wrath."* Ed. David Wyatt. New York: Cambridge UP, 1990. 27-46.

Salter, Christopher L. "John Steinbeck's *The Grapes of Wrath* as a Primer for Cultural Geography." *Critical Essays on Steinbeck's "The Grapes of Wrath."* Ed. John Ditsky. Boston: G. K. Hall, 1989. 138-52.

Stein, Walter J. *California and the Dust Bowl Migration*. Westport, CT: Greenwood Press, 1973.

Steinbeck, John. *The Grapes of Wrath*. New York: Viking Press, 1939.

––––––––––. *The Harvest Gypsies: On the Road to "The Grapes of Wrath."* Ed. Charles Wollenberg. Berkeley, CA: Heyday Books, 1988.

Svobida, Lawrence. *Farming the Dust Bowl: A First-Hand Account from Kansas.* 1940 (as *Empire of Dust*). Lawrence: UP of Kansas, 1986.

Weisiger, Marsha L. *Land of Plenty: Oklahomans in the Cotton Fields of Arizona, 1933-1942.* Norman: U of Oklahoma P, 1995.

Wollenberg, Charles. Introduction. *The Harvest Gypsies: On the Road to "The Grapes of Wrath."* By John Steinbeck. Berkeley, CA: Heyday Books, 1988. v-xvii.

The Critical Reception of John Steinbeck's
*The Grapes of Wrath*_____
Camille-Yvette Welsch

To understand the initial critical responses to John Steinbeck's *The Grapes of Wrath*, one must begin with an understanding of the social and political climate in which the novel was published. When Steinbeck published his best seller in 1939, the United States was nearing the end of what had been one of its most tumultuous decades. Ten years before, the country's economy had been toppled by the stock market crash of 1929; just a year after the crash, the Dust Bowl began, rendering useless about 100 million acres of farmland in northern Texas, western Oklahoma and Kansas, and eastern New Mexico and Colorado. Years of uninterrupted grain farming had left the soil susceptible to erosion, and when a drought hit the region in the early 1930s, the dry, exposed soil was simply swept away by the wind. In November of 1933, one of the first dust clouds was reported to be stretching from Texas to South Dakota and even reaching up to Milwaukee, Wisconsin, at one of its outer points. This cloud was initially thought to be a meteorological anomaly, but scientists and farmers alike quickly realized that other dust clouds were extending across Texas, Oklahoma, Kansas, eastern Colorado, Wyoming, New Mexico, Missouri, Iowa, and Arkansas. The clouds wreaked havoc on the region. They swept across the Great Plains and gathered into storms that could suffocate anyone caught walking in one, take the paint off a car, or cause the sky to drop balls of mud, which were formed when the dust, at long last, made contact with moisture. Surrounding states, from Michigan to the northeast, Tennessee to the east, and Louisiana to the south, also felt the effects of the dust storms (French, *Companion* 4).

The Dust Bowl made farming impossible in the region, and many farmers, left without crops and income, went bankrupt. Banks foreclosed on properties, and California, which years before had embraced farming as agribusiness and pushed out many small, family-owned farms, began to lure displaced workers west with promises of high wages and the chance to have farms of their own. Hundreds of thousands heeded the call, packed their possessions into old jalopies, and made their way west across Route 66. However, many Californians did not welcome the sudden influx of poor farmers, derisively calling the immigrants Okies. At the same time, because labor was so plentiful, the agribusiness owners were able to drive down wages and, by allowing crops to rot, to inflate crop prices.

Steinbeck, a native Californian, watched these developments with growing horror, as did many other Americans. The decade of the 1930s, with all of its domestic and economic troubles, made the country uneasy about the need for and the advent of sweeping national changes, and among a small percentage of Americans, communism was finding a firm footing. Writers responded to the turmoil by producing protest novels that advocated the rights of women, of African Americans, and of workers. Artists, too, joined in to document and protest the conditions in which migrant workers lived. Photographers such as Dorothea Lange and Walker Evans, working for what would eventually be known as the Farm Security Administration, documented the Dust Bowl, and their photos made the faces of the disaster national news. John Steinbeck gave these faces stories in a series of works for which he has received nearly equal praise and criticism.

Steinbeck began his advocacy for the displaced workers in California with his 1936 novel *In Dubious Battle*, which tells the story of the leaders of a strike by fruit pickers in California. It was received well by critics, but Communist Party organizers were upset with the novel's negative depictions of the party. *Life* magazine offered Steinbeck a job covering the migrant scene later that year, but he refused it, saying that he did not want to "'cash in' on the misery of these people" (qtd. in French, *Companion* 153). Instead, he wrote a series of seven articles for the *San Francisco News* titled "The Harvest Gypsies," and in 1937 he went on the road with some migrant workers, living side by side with them in migrant camps. He wrote another article reflecting this experience and in 1938 collected all of these articles in a pamphlet ti-tled *Their Blood Is Strong*. Its publication went unnoticed during the period of upheaval leading up to World War II, but this work clearly il-lustrates the depth of compassion Steinbeck felt toward the migrant workers.

In December 1937, he started work on "The Oklahomans," which was to be a novel about displaced workers, but he shelved it and began "L'Affaire Lettuceberg," a satirical treatment of the violence following a lettuce strike in Salinas, California. He completed the latter work, but then destroyed the 700,000-word manuscript. In a 1938 letter to his agent, Elizabeth Otis, he explained:

> This book is finished and it is a bad book and I must get rid of it. It can't be printed. It is bad because it isn't honest. Oh! these incidents all happened but—I'm not telling as much of the truth about them as I know. In satire you have to restrict the picture and I just can't do satire. . . . My whole work drive has been aimed at making people understand each other and then I deliberately write this book the aim of which is to cause hatred through par-tial understanding. My father would have called it a smart-alec book. (qtd. in DeMott xl)

However, Steinbeck quickly recovered from this disappointment and started what would become *The Grapes of Wrath*, a title suggested by his wife, Carol. The book was a culmination of the work he had done on the newspaper articles, of the vestiges of the poisoned "L'Affaire," and of the inspiration he found in the "Battle Hymn of the Republic." After five months of intensive writing, he completed the novel in October 1938.

From the very beginning, critics' opinions of *The Grapes of Wrath* have been divided. Some have marked it as mere sentimental propa-ganda, whereas others have called it a literary masterpiece; some have seen Christian themes in the novel, while others have argued that its primary faith is in the natural order. Regardless of the decade, Stein-beck's novel has stratified the critics between those who believe it to be a sociologically interesting, populist romance and those who believe it to be literature and worthy of extended study. For the first decade or so after its publication, responses to the work were largely emotional. People either wanted to believe in the plight of the Okies or they desperately wanted to discredit Steinbeck. Many were angry at his portrayal of the Okies and of the class struggle in California. Critics charged the book with being overly sentimental propaganda or coarse sensationalism. Though some early critics lauded *The Grapes of Wrath* as the "great American novel," many were in dissent. The next decade and a half brought a different approach to the novel. By this point, the novel had entered the canon, and scholars were eager to prove its literary merit through the study of its technical and allusory aspects. In the past two decades, critical responses to the novel have largely been guided by particular theories and contexts within literature—feminism, Marxism, deconstructionism, New Historicism. Many of these approaches embrace the potential interdisciplinary opportunities within the novel, including biocritique, philosophy, and science. This trend will likely continue.

Publicity for *The Grapes of Wrath* began on the last day of 1938, in *Publishers Weekly*, a scant two and a half months before publication, but with the country so fascinated by the drama taking place in California, the book was the top seller of 1939, and in 1940 it won the Pulitzer Prize, a precursor to the Nobel Prize in Literature that Steinbeck was awarded in 1962, largely because of *The Grapes of Wrath*. When the book crossed the desks of reviewers, their responses tended to fall along two lines. Conservative reviewers thought the novel too graphic, its language too coarse, and its action too scatological. The swearing and spitting characters in the novel were simply too much for them. Many of these same reviewers also charged the novel with sentimentality and accused Steinbeck of creating a stereotypical migrant family to drum up sympathy for the migrating farmers. *Newsweek* critic Burton Rascoe, for instance, asserted that the book's point is "that 'there are no frontiers left and no place to go'" (38). Critics as influential as Malcolm Cowley and Louis Kronenberger were also dissatisfied with the novel; Cowley, for instance, felt that the work and its author were unworthy of such contemporary company as Ernest Hemingway, John Dos Passos, and F. Scott Fitzgerald. Other critics were less circumspect in expressing their negative opinions and wrote more explosive and much more incendiary reviews. Philip Rahv, for instance, remarked:

> The novel is far too didactic and long-winded. In addition to the defects that are peculiar to his own manner, Mr. Steinbeck has assembled in this one book, all the familiar faults of the 'proletarian' novel. There are the usual idealized portraits and customary conversions, psychologically false and schematic as ever, to militant principles. Moreover, the technical cleverness of *Of Mice and Men* is lacking in this novel. . . . Its unconscionable length is out of all proportion to its substance; the ornery dialect spoken by its farmers impresses one as being less a form of human speech than a facile convention of the local-color schools; and as to problems of characterization, Mr. Steinbeck does not so much create character as ape it. (qtd. in White 152)

In *Newsweek*, Burton Rascoe wrote:

> It was a terrific disappointment to me that a prose artist, so careful, conscientious, wise, compassionate, disenchanted and impersonal as John Steinbeck hitherto has been, should fall into the mess of silly propaganda, superficial observation, careless infidelity to the proper use of idiom, tasteless pornographical and scatological talk (dragged into the text by the heels) and into more serious faults. (qtd. in White 153)

More appreciative critics praised the novel for its powerful call for unity, compassion, and justice. Joseph Henry Jackson, a reviewer for the *New York Herald-Tribune*, wrote, "It is easy to grow lyrical about *The Grapes of Wrath*, to become excited about it, to be stirred to the shouting point by it" (115). The *Boston Herald* critic compared Steinbeck to Harriet Beecher Stowe and Charles Dickens. The American

Booksellers Association named *The Grapes of Wrath* its favorite novel of 1939, and the novel received the first annual award bestowed by the publication *Social Work Today*. Finally, beyond all of these literary, political, religious voices, was the voice of one very powerful woman who, championing the book in her newspaper column on June 28, 1939, caused sales to soar. First Lady Eleanor Roosevelt ringingly endorsed *The Grapes of Wrath* when she wrote:

> The book is coarse in spots, but life is coarse in spots, and the story is very beautiful in spots just as life is. . . . Even from life's sorrow some good must come. What could be a better illustration than the closing chapter of this book? (131)

Among general readers, the novel also sparked controversy. As Martin Shockley revealed in his 1944 article "The Reception of *The Grapes of Wrath* in Oklahoma," many Oklahoma residents took exception to Steinbeck's treatment of their lives. The Associated Farmers of Kern Country, California, for instance, called "the book 'obscene sensationalism' and 'propaganda in its vilest form'" (231), and libraries in Oklahoma, Missouri, California, and Missouri banned the book—actions that only increased sales across the region. Others, ignoring the fact that the book is fiction, attempted to discredit the novel by questioning its veracity or tried to discredit Steinbeck himself by challenging his claim that he had traveled with migrant families and lived with them in migrant camps. Lyle Boren, a congressman from Oklahoma, took his ire to the floor of the House of Representatives, saying:

> I cannot find it possible to let this dirty, lying, filthy manuscript go heralded before the public without a word of challenge or protest. . . . For myself, for my dad and my mother, whose hair is silvery in the service of building the state of Oklahoma, I say to you, and to every honest, square-minded reader in America, that the painting Steinbeck made in his book is a lie, a black, infernal creation of a twisted, distorted mind. (139)

Certain religious leaders found the book, and its fictional preacher, Jim Casy, objectionable for a number of reasons, among them Casy's sexual relations with his parishioners, his condoning of coarse language, and his espousal of what the Reverend W. Lee Rector of Ardmore, Oklahoma, called "communism." The novel, he said, is "heaven-shaming and Christ-insulting" (qtd. in Shockley, "Reception" 238). Similarly, in the first book-length study of Steinbeck's novels, published in 1939, Harry Thornton Moore claimed that the story of *The Grapes of Wrath* presents no central conflict and is little more than merely atmospheric.

After the initial firestorm of criticism, the novel seemed to drift out of public consciousness as the United States became embroiled in World War II. Between 1940 and 1954, very little was written about it, though there are a few notable exceptions. In 1941, Frederic I. Carpenter pioneered what has become one of the perennial interests for critics of *The Grapes of Wrath*: its philosophical lineage. Rather than arguing for the novel's narrative virtues, as so many earlier critics had done, Carpenter assumed them to be well established and began his discussion by identifying three veins of American thought that converge in the novel: "the mystical transcendentalism of Emerson . . . the earthy democracy of Whitman . . . and the pragmatic instrumentalism of William James and John Dewey" (563). In Carpenter's reading, what makes the book so engrossing is that, in Steinbeck's hands, the ideas of great American thinkers are transformed from intangible philosophy into lived fact. In 1947, critic Chester E. Eisinger added a fourth thinker to the triumvirate by naming Jeffersonian agrarianism as an integral part of the novel. Both Steinbeck and Jefferson, Eisinger wrote, believe that the loss of land entails the loss of an individual's dignity. Still, Eisinger questioned whether this belief ought to be upheld, and, in the process, he also questioned the value of the novel.

Also of note is Woodburn O. Ross's 1949 article "John Steinbeck: Naturalism's Priest." Ross turned attention toward the novelist's relations with science and nature and established a vein of criticism that focuses on Steinbeck as an inheritor of the naturalist tradition. Rather than relying on religion to order and provide meaning to the world, Ross argued, Steinbeck takes his cues from science and the natural world; however, he is no bleak naturalist like Theodore Dreiser or Frank Norris, whose characters act in strict accordance with the natural law. Instead, Steinbeck creates an amalgamation of the naturalistic imperative to survive and a mystical altruism, examples of which can be found in Jim Casy's view of the world and in the novel's final, and very controversial, scene, in which Rose of Sharon gives milk from her breast to a starving man.

In 1956, Martin Shockley reentered the critical discussion with an influential examination of Steinbeck's use of Christian symbols. Rebutting the claims of novelist Alan Paton and theologian Liston Pope, who argued that a Christ without a shred of divinity is no Christ at all, Shockley asserted that Jim Casy is indeed a Christ figure, although a much more modern one than the two critics might have expected. He also likened Steinbeck's prose style to that of the King James Version of the Bible, compared Tom Joad to the disciples of Christ, and drew parallels between Rose of Sharon's final act of mercy, in which she gives of her body and—by extension—her life, and Christ's own sacrifice on the cross.

Shockley's essay set off a flurry of critical activity. Eric W. Carlson spoke out directly against Shockley in 1958, arguing that the novel is humanistic rather than Christian. Shockley's central thesis, he contended, does not explain Casy's Unitarian tendencies or the complete absence from the novel of the Christian virtues of humility and resignation. Further, Steinbeck's own comments show that the novel was inspired not by a particular religious idea but by the people with whom Steinbeck traveled and lived. As the debate continued, other critics found the novel to be completely un-Christian, while still others unearthed more biblical parallels and allusions. Collin G. Matton, for instance, wrote about the work's biblical water and flood imagery. Joseph Fontenrose studied the rise of agribusiness and compared the industry to the Bible's Leviathan and the Joads to Judah. Intertwining myth and biology, he wrote that the family is an organism, a "democratic union," that is caught in conflict with the agribusiness monsters. Peter Lisca compared Tom Joad to Moses and Saint Paul and likened Rose of Sharon's breast-feeding to the image of Madonna and child (*Nature and Myth* 104-10).

Warren French, who would go on to champion Steinbeck's work for decades and offer many more valuable insights, entered the fray in 1955 with an attack on Bernard Bowron's assertion that *The Grapes of Wrath*'s appeal could be attributed to its similarity to the traditional "Wagons West" romance. The journey motif that Bowron had identified as a key element of the Western novel is much older than the genre, French wrote, and he went on to trace it back to much more august company, such as *Pilgrim's Progress*, the *Odyssey*, and the Bible's book of Exodus ("Another Look" 217).

In 1958, another influential and prolific Steinbeck critic, Peter Lisca, published his first book on the author, *The Wide World of John Steinbeck*. As French would many years later in *John Steinbeck's Fiction Revisited* (1994), Lisca provided an overview of the publishing history of *The Grapes of Wrath*; however, he deepened his discussion by offering some valuable insights into the symbolic significance of the turtle crossing the street and the intercalary chapters, and he also added to the biblical comparisons by noting the similarities in structure, plotting, prose style, and character development between the novel and the Scriptures. Lisca further drew parallels between the journey of the Joads and the Israelites' flight from Egypt and their wanderings in the wilderness before they arrive in Canaan. As time has passed, literary scholars and critics have built on and broadened all of the work noted above, finding other, non-Judeo-Christian, religious meanings in *The Grapes of Wrath*. In "Fermenting *The Grapes of Wrath*: From Violent Anger Distilling Sweet Concord," for instance, Michael Meyer (2000) explores the influence and presence of Daoism in the text, citing a variety of animal symbols, tropes, parallel characters, historical events, and plot points that invoke the Dao.

Lisca also laid the groundwork for comparative studies in a 1969 article, "Steinbeck and Hemingway: Suggestions for a Comparative Study," which compared the two authors and named them literary kin to the naturalistic tradition. For both authors, Lisca noted, nonfiction is central to the fiction, as are certain autobiographical details. Both had backgrounds in journalism, and, though their styles differ, both embrace in their work that which is animalistic in human beings.

Much more comparative study was to come. In 1971, John Ditsky, in comparing William Faulkner's and Steinbeck's uses of settings, noted that Steinbeck uses California as a sort of prototype to talk about natural and spiritual universal truths. Steinbeck's settings, he concluded, may be overly sentimental, and the author's works, which rely heavily and ineffectively on repetition to support their stories, certainly lack the strong central ideas that Faulkner uses to unify the disparate motifs of his novels. Some twenty years later, Abby H. P. Werlock would return to Faulkner with a comparison of the characters of *The Grapes of Wrath* and the downtrodden Snopeses, paying special attention to retaliation, aberration, and their similarities as journeying families. Another comparative study of note is that published in 1990 by Barry G. Maine, which traces Steinbeck's interchapters to John Dos Passos's *U.S.A.* and sees similarities between the two authors in their use of colloquial diction and multiple voices. Maine also likens the two novelists to proletarian writers.

Further comparative analyses can be found in three notable essay collections. The first, *Steinbeck's Literary Dimension: A Guide to Comparative Studies* (1973), edited by Tetsumaro Hayashi, considers an assortment of writers, including Charles Dickens, Faulkner, Nikos Kazantzakis, D. H. Lawrence, Émile Zola, Robert Penn Warren, John Milton, J. D. Salinger, and Daniel Mainwaring, and the stylistic and moral traits these writers share with Steinbeck as in *The Grapes of Wrath*. The second, *Beyond Boundaries: Rereading John Steinbeck*

(2002), edited by Susan Shillinglaw and Kevin Hearle, features essays compiled from presentations given during the 1997 Fourth International Steinbeck Conference. The volume is divided into four primary sections: "Beyond Boundaries," "Steinbeck as World Citizen," "Rereading Steinbeck's Women," and "Science and Ethics." This collection is also of interest because it does not limit the comparisons of Steinbeck to writers; here, one can find Gavin Cologne-Brooks's essay on the influence of *The Grapes of Wrath* on popular music, particularly Bruce Springsteen's in his album *The Ghost of Tom Joad*. Cologne-Brooks likens the theme and style of the album to Steinbeck's writing, paying close attention to Springsteen's artistic development as his songs' subjects shift from individuals to communities. This collection also features Warren French's essay on the self as character, "Steinbeck's 'Self-Characters' as 1930s Underdogs." The more recent *John Steinbeck and His Contemporaries* (2007), edited by Stephen K. George and Barbara A. Heavilin, opens up still more comparative angles with studies of Steinbeck in light of a diverse list of writers, including Sarah Orne Jewett, Hemingway, Faulkner, Willa Cather, Zora Neale Hurston, Toni Morrison, Charles Johnson, and Munshi Premchand. Finally, George Bluestone's chapter on *The Grapes of Wrath* in his *Novels into Film* discusses how the novel was adapted to film and offers yet another way to examine the novel's effect on popular culture.

Another prevalent strand of criticism attempts to identify and understand how social and historical circumstances shaped *The Grapes of Wrath* and its author. George Henderson argues that the book derives the majority of its power from real-life tensions between social and geographical relationships, which illuminate the larger battle between those who have power and those who do not, those who possess knowledge and those who do not. Susan Shillinglaw makes sense of the campaign to defame Steinbeck following the publication of the book in "California Answers *The Grapes of Wrath*," and Robert Murray Davis offers a comprehensive review of the real-world route the Joads would have taken in "The World of John Steinbeck's Joads." Kevin Hearle, in

"These Are American People," examines the role eugenics may have played in Steinbeck's composition of *Their Blood Is Strong* and shows how Steinbeck revises the idea in *The Grapes of Wrath* by grouping his immigrants according to their shared humanity rather than their race.

In "Changing Perceptions of Homelessness: John Steinbeck, Carey McWilliams, and California During the 1930s," Christina Sheehan Gold examines the rhetorical strategies of Steinbeck and Carey McWilliams, the author of a 1939 exposé of California agribusiness, *Factories in the Field*, and compares these strategies to those used by advocates for the homeless of the time. She begins with a discussion of Steinbeck's association with Tom Collins, a manager of one of the government migrant camps, and makes the case that the author may have learned some of his techniques from Collins and, like Collins, used them to create empathy for the displaced and downtrodden. Both Steinbeck and McWilliams, Gold writes, use a series of strategies. First, they compare the migrants to the pioneers of the nineteenth century, claiming for them their forefathers' strength of conviction and stalwart hearts as well as their desperation. Second, they invoke the brave Jeffersonian farmer, whose loss of land steals from him both his livelihood and his identity. Third, they make a conscious effort to characterize their migrants as true Americans searching for the American Dream promised to every hardworking person. Fourth, they show that the migrants want to work but, through no fault of their own, are caught up in circumstances that keep them from finding steady jobs. Finally, Steinbeck takes pains to show that his and the migrants' viewpoint is not a radical one that would destroy home and hearth; rather, theirs is a commitment to family and to helping one's fellow human beings. Whatever radicalism Steinbeck's migrants might evince is born of absolute desperation and injustice. All of these tactics, Gold concludes, help Steinbeck to evoke public compassion, at least in part, toward the migrant workers and their families.

The publication of McWilliams's book coincided with the publication of *The Grapes of Wrath*, and its visceral reportage of the conditions in which migrant farmers were living helped to bolster Steinbeck's claims that his depictions of the migrants were accurate. It, too, climbed to the top of the best-seller lists, and it was instrumental in encouraging the American public to acknowledge the problem and urge their government to take action. Biographical critic Jackson J. Benson took pains to prove that, while Steinbeck certainly conducted research at a California camp, he did not travel with a family from Oklahoma ("To Tom"). Benson's exhaustive investigation of Steinbeck's life has helped put to rest any lingering doubts, in the minds of the public and the critics, about the veracity of Steinbeck's details.

Peter Valenti has found other forces at work in the development of Steinbeck's technique. In a 1997 article, he argues that the intercalary chapters in *The Grapes of Wrath* were influenced by the ecological writings of conservationist Aldo Leopold, the stark photographs of migrant farmers published by the Farm Security Administration, and the high-romance tradition, which enabled Steinbeck to use the Joads as illustrations of the migrants' real-life plight. In the end, Valenti argues, *The Grapes of Wrath* is a kind of documentary, a novel that dramatizes explanation with example.

In recent years, critics have returned to examining Steinbeck's intellectual lineage, and a number of fascinating studies have continued the line of inquiry initiated in the 1940s by Frederic I. Carpenter and Woodburn O. Ross. Brian E. Railsback asserts that, though the novel demonstrates a definite Darwinist vision, it still offers a message of hope. The workers, whom Railsback casts as a species struggling to survive in a capitalist society, will prevail, for capitalism (and the agribusiness that is part of it) is a perversion of the natural order that will eventually topple. Barbara A. Heavilin links Steinbeck to Jean-Jacques Rousseau and William Wordsworth through their common belief that feeling precedes thought. The perspective of *The Grapes of Wrath*, she argues, shifts from the subjective to the objective, hence from feeling to thought. She also investigates Steinbeck's conceptions of good and evil, finding that, for him, hospitality is one of the greatest goods and disregard for the land is one of the worst evils. Richard Astro considers the influence on Steinbeck of naturalist Ed Ricketts and his non-teleological mode of thinking, while Dennis Prindle locates the novel within Steinbeck's larger interest in linking allegory and mythology, particularly the Arthurian legends, to the naturalist tradition. He sees the character of Jim Casy, with his broad faith, as a conduit between tradition and experience.

Michael G. Barry looks at the influence of science on the novel, examining the ways in which, through comparisons with the animal world, Steinbeck elevates humankind. Because humans can use nature—for example, through farming—they stand in a special relation to the nature. Nature serves as a metaphor by which the individual can understand the self; without it, human beings are lost, victims of a language that is divorced from the nature that humans intuitively comprehend. David N. Cassuto offers an interdisciplinary view of one of the natural elements in the novel: water. He sees it as both a commodity and a symbol that Steinbeck uses in a very literal way to show that whoever controls it controls the land and, by extension, the economy. Steinbeck, Cassuto argues, uses water to offer a critique of agribusiness as well as to debunk the notion of the West as an American Eden into which anyone might stumble and find salvation. Instead, for Steinbeck, only those with money can realize the dream promised by the frontier myth.

Adding to the philosophical views, Jackson Benson spent at least fifteen years of his career delving deeply into biographical criticism. His exhaustive eleven-hundred-page biography of Steinbeck, *The True Adventures of John Steinbeck, Writer*, uses unpublished letters and rare interviews to plumb the depths of the relatively shy Steinbeck. The volume offers a great deal of literary interpretation and helps to impress upon the reader Steinbeck's literary influences and the ways in which his work as an amateur naturalist and professional journalist influenced the philosophy inherent in his writing as well as his research techniques. Benson also carefully traces what he sees as Steinbeck's literary lineage. On a more literal level, Benson, in numerous articles as well as in his biography and his book *Looking for Steinbeck's Ghost*, provides factual evidence of Steinbeck's sources. For instance, in his 1976 article "To Tom, Who Lived It: John Steinbeck and the Man from Weedpatch," Benson dispels the myth that Steinbeck traveled with a family from Oklahoma and instead traces Steinbeck's actual relationship with Tom Collins, a camp director for the Farm Security Administration. He shows how that relationship and the reports that Collins shared with Steinbeck shaped particular instances in the novel. Benson also looks at science and the naturalistic tradition in "Steinbeck: Novelist as Scientist," in which he asserts that the naturalistic tradition is actually at odds with Steinbeck's technique in *The Grapes of Wrath*, creating a duality of form rather than coherence.

In addition to these diverse views of Steinbeck's philosophical foundations, one strand of criticism has been particularly influential: pioneered by Joseph Fontenrose in 1963, it examines the Joad family's growth as it develops from an isolated nuclear family into part of a universal human family. In the 1971 essay "Escape and Commitment: Two Poles of the Steinbeck Hero," Peter Lisca examines this polarity of individualism and communitarianism within the whole of Steinbeck's oeuvre before narrowing his discussion to Tom Joad. In Lisca's estimation, the Steinbeck hero is either completely dedicated to his individual pursuits—and, as a result, flouts his duties—or absolutely committed to a grand series of goals that benefit the community at large. One of the primary tensions in Steinbeck's work, Lisca notes, is the individual's struggle to grow and become capable of taking on societal responsibilities. He cites Tom Joad as a prime example of the Steinbeck hero: he begins the story completely concerned with his own life and his own family, only to become a spokesman for other disenfranchised migrants.

Sunita Jain discusses this same process but uses Rose of Sharon as a focal point. Jain finds that all the Joads are a kind of life force, and Rose of Sharon in particular grows from a self-involved, jilted woman into a very literal giver of life when she offers her breast to the starving man in the barn. Edwin T. Bowden, focusing on the theme of isolation in the novel, notes that *The Grapes of Wrath* differs from nineteenth-century novels in that it portrays the isolation not of a single character but of a whole group of people. Blending together this concern for community with a consideration of Steinbeck's naturalism, Charles Shively considers the relationship between the individual and the community and concludes that the novel marries social doctrine with a holistic vision. For Steinbeck, he notes, both the idealist and the naturalist are necessary to make sense of the vision; in this way, Steinbeck validates the necessity of extending oneself beyond the self-centered unit to become part of the greater communal whole.

French's *John Steinbeck's Fiction Revisited* is also a valuable resource in this vein of criticism for its discussion of Jim Casy as a catalyst for Tom's transformation from a selfish individual and family member into the leader of a universal struggle. Linking this struggle to Emerson's concept of the oversoul, French argues that the novel's conclusion is not vulgar or coarse, as many others have thought, but a fitting end, as it illustrates the end of the family's journey. Whereas the Joads once acknowledged and protected only their blood family, now they recognize themselves as part of what French calls "the human family," the larger, universal family to which they are bonded by universal need and dignity. In the 2002 article "Steinbeck's 'Self-Characters' as 1930s Underdogs," French expands on this view, arguing that Tom Joad is psychologically similar to Steinbeck and represents the author's view. Reviewing Steinbeck's novels, from *Tortilla Flat* to *Of Mice and Men* to *In Dubious Battle* and finally culminating in the national sensation of *The Grapes of Wrath*, French shows how, over the course of his career, Steinbeck, like Joad, grows from an "underdog failure" to become a leader.

Feminist critics have also examined the characterization of women within *The Grapes of Wrath*, particularly Ma Joad and Rose of Sharon. John H. Timmerman, in *John Steinbeck's Fiction: The Aesthetics of the Road Taken*, asserts that, from the very beginning, Ma Joad is one of the book's most enlightened characters. She is the character who dreams of a "'fambly of man,'" and she is the one who moves most quickly toward universal hospitality and love. As the book ends at the barn, it is Ma Joad who urges Rose of Sharon to offer her breast to the starving man. Timmerman also sees the characters' realism and their profanity as Steinbeck's aesthetic response to censorship. In a later essay, "The Squatter's Circle in *The Grapes of Wrath*," Timmerman offers a feminist examination of the family's change in leadership. Initially, Pa is the leader of the circle, but as time passes leadership slowly cedes to the more adaptable Ma Joad. This shift from a hierarchical and patriarchal system to a more unified and communal one, Timmerman states, reflects the larger changes in the family's ideology.

In "Beyond the Boundaries of Sexism: The Archetypal Feminine Versus Anima Women in Steinbeck's Novels," Lorelei Cederstrom expands the discussion of women in the novel, arguing that rather than simply adhering to the archetypal dichotomy of Madonna/whore, Steinbeck's women represent broader values, such as wholeness, relatedness, and a symbiosis with nature. Ultimately, she concludes that Steinbeck espouses the value and necessity of these traditional "women's values." Cederstrom continues her exploration of Steinbeck's women with "The 'Great Mother' in *The Grapes of Wrath*," in which she again finds women's values—family, caring, and harmony—in opposition to those of men, who, she writes, have metaphorically raped the land and now must pay the price. It is the women and their adherence to the pagan values associated with the Great Mother who help to save the clan, as Rose of Sharon does when, rather than support an exclusionary hierarchy, she adopts a pagan inclusiveness by nursing the dying man. Cederstrom sees this act as not Christian but pagan, an iconography built on all of the Great Mother images that precede it.

With the advent of ecocriticism, recent years have also seen a resurgence of interest in the philosophical and spiritual beliefs Steinbeck articulates in *The Grapes of Wrath*. Many critics read Steinbeck's embrace of nature as a kind of new faith and link the interconnectedness of humankind and nature in the novel back to transcendentalism. In "How Green Was John Steinbeck?" (1997), Warren French offers a fresh perspective by asking whether Steinbeck can rightly be called a "green" author. He notes that while Steinbeck did want Americans to live in harmony with nature and was optimistic about their potential to take better control of environmental management, he offered no substantive suggestions as to how this might be accomplished. Roy Simmonds asserts that Jim Casy functions as a mouthpiece through which Steinbeck preaches conservation. These types of ecocritical approaches seem to be a growing trend in Steinbeck criticism and are likely to continue providing fresh perspectives on *The Grapes of Wrath* in years to come.

Still, after more than seventy years of critical evaluation, the fight to validate *The Grapes of Wrath* and its place within the canon of American literature is not over. Accordingly, many critics have recently turned their attention to the question of why Steinbeck has been reviled in the academy and underused in college classrooms. Nicholas Visser describes how changing critical and political tides have caused scholars to overlook, misinterpret, and even disparage the novel, and he attempts to answer a question that has long plagued critics: Can a book that has such a broad mass appeal really be radical? Chris Kocela argues that part of the reason for the novel's tenuous status in the teaching of American literature lies in the fact that it has been mislabeled; he argues that it is a postmodern novel and draws comparisons between Steinbeck and Thomas Pynchon. The intercalary chapters, he writes, function as "frame-breakers": they force readers out of the fabric of the story to acknowledge the problems of history and politics. The biblical and mythical allusions, in turn, work to undermine history.

Jackson J. Benson, in "John Steinbeck: The Favorite Author We Love to Hate," claims that the dislike of Steinbeck is part fashion, part snobbery. He alleges that the academy is prejudiced against authors who are from Western backgrounds, popular with the general public, comedic, sentimental, and political in their work. On the other hand,

R. W. B. Lewis claims that Steinbeck is too superficial and that he never moves beyond political posturing long enough to master the techniques necessary for writing a successful novel. Mary M. Brown asserts that *The Grapes of Wrath* is dated, too sentimental, and too long for collegiate audiences. In direct opposition, Kenneth Swan argues that college students can still connect to Steinbeck because of his use of allusive images, his focus on uniquely American issues and social criticism, and his masterful integration of theme and structure. Modern students, Swan concludes, respond to *The Grapes of Wrath* because it is both dramatic and cinematic.

Louis Owens and Hector Torres argue that the novel's strength lies in the fact that it forces the reader to engage with the Joads and their journey. Steinbeck wants readers to experience the novel, they maintain, rather than simply read it. John Seelye looks again at the charge of sentimentality and finds that while some parts of the novel are sentimental, it does not end on an uplifting note as the typical sentimental novel does. Because the Joads' dream never comes to fruition, because all they have at the close of the novel is the instinct to survive, the novel cannot rightly be called sentimental. Rather than likening the novel to *Uncle Tom's Cabin*, as so many other critics have done, Seelye suggests that the *Iliad*, with its fruitless battles and unhappy conclusion, is a more apt comparison.

Despite its spotted critical history, *The Grapes of Wrath* endures within the psyche and culture of America. The face and plight of the migrant worker—whether manifested in Henry Fonda's impassioned film performance as Tom Joad or in Bruce Springsteen's music or in a passing allusion in an episode of *The Simpsons*—will be forever associated with Steinbeck's novel.

Works Cited

Astro, Richard. "Intimations of a Wasteland." *John Steinbeck and Edward F. Ricketts: The Shaping of a Novelist*. Minneapolis: University of Minnesota

Press, 1973. 158-77. Rpt. in *John Steinbeck*. Ed. Harold Bloom. New York: Chelsea House, 1987. 19-34.

Barry, Michael G. "Degrees of Mediation and Their Political Value in *The Grapes of Wrath*." *The Steinbeck Question: New Essays in Criticism*. Ed. Donald R. Noble. Troy, NY: Whitston, 1993. 108-24.

Benson, Jackson J. "John Steinbeck: The Favorite Author We Love to Hate." *The Steinbeck Question: New Essays in Criticism*. Ed. Donald R. Noble. Troy, NY: Whitston, 1993. 8-22.

_____. *Looking for Steinbeck's Ghost*. 1988. Reno: University of Nevada Press, 2002.

_____. "Steinbeck: Novelist as Scientist." *Novel: A Forum on Fiction* 10.3 (Spring 1977): 248-64. Rpt. in *John Steinbeck*. Ed. Harold Bloom. New York: Chelsea House, 1987. 103-24.

_____. "To Tom, Who Lived It: John Steinbeck and the Man from Weedpatch." *Journal of Modern Literature* 5.2 (Apr. 1976): 151-210.

_____. *The True Adventures of John Steinbeck, Writer*. New York: Viking Press, 1984.

Bluestone, George. "The Grapes of Wrath." *Novels into Film*. Baltimore: Johns Hopkins UP, 1957.

Boren, Lyle H. "*The Grapes of Wrath*." *Congressional Record* 10 Jan. 1940, Part 13: 139-40.

Bowden, Edwin T. "The Commonplace and the Grotesque." *The Dungeon of the Human Heart: Human Isolation and the American Novel*. New York: Macmillan, 1961. 138-49. Rpt. in *"The Grapes of Wrath": A Collection of Critical Essays*. Ed. Robert Con Davis. Englewood Cliffs, NJ: Prentice Hall, 1982. 15-23.

Bowron, Bernard. "*The Grapes of Wrath*: A 'Wagons West' Romance." *Colorado Quarterly* 3 (1954): 83-91. Rpt. in *A Companion to "The Grapes of Wrath."* Ed. Warren French. Clifton, NJ: Augustus M. Kelley, 1972. 208-17.

Brown, Mary M. "*The Grapes of Wrath* and the Literary Canon of American Universities in the Nineties." *The Critical Response to John Steinbeck's "The Grapes of Wrath."* Ed. Barbara A. Heavilin. Westport, CT: Greenwood Press, 2000. 285-98.

Carlson, Eric W. "Rebuttal: Symbolism in *The Grapes of Wrath*." *College English* 19.4 (Jan. 1958): 172-75.

Carpenter, Frederic I. "The Philosophical Joads." *College English* 2.4 (Jan. 1941): 315-25. Rpt. in *"The Grapes of Wrath": Text and Criticism*. By John Steinbeck. 2nd ed. Ed. Peter Lisca with Kevin Hearle. New York: Penguin Books, 1997. 562-71.

Cassuto, David N. "Turning Wine into Water: Water as Privileged Signifier in *The Grapes of Wrath*." *Papers on Language and Literature* 29.1 (Winter 1993): 67-95. Rpt. in *Steinbeck and the Environment: Interdisciplinary Approaches*. Ed. Susan F. Beegel, Susan Shillinglaw, and Wesley N. Tiffney, Jr. Tuscaloosa: U of Alabama P, 1997. 55-75.

Cederstrom, Lorelei. "Beyond the Boundaries of Sexism: The Archetypal Feminine Versus Anima Women in Steinbeck's Novels." *Beyond Boundaries: Re-reading John Steinbeck*. Ed. Susan Shillinglaw and Kevin Hearle. Tuscaloosa: U of Alabama P, 2002. 189-204.

_____. "The 'Great Mother' in *The Grapes of Wrath*." *Steinbeck and the Environment: Interdisciplinary Approaches*. Ed. Susan F. Beegel, Susan Shillinglaw, and Wesley N. Tiffney, Jr. Tuscaloosa: U of Alabama P, 1997. 76-91.

Cologne-Brooks, Gavin. "*The Ghost of Tom Joad*: Steinbeck's Legacy in the Songs of Bruce Springsteen." *Beyond Boundaries: Rereading John Steinbeck*. Ed. Susan Shillinglaw and Kevin Hearle. Tuscaloosa: U of Alabama P, 2002. 34-46.

Davis, Robert Murray. "The World of John Steinbeck's Joads." *World Literature Today* 64.3 (1990): 401-44. Rpt. in *The Critical Response to John Steinbeck's "The Grapes of Wrath."* Ed. Barbara A. Heavilin. Westport, CT: Greenwood Press, 2000. 163-70.

DeMott, Robert. Introduction. *Working Days: The Journals of "The Grapes of Wrath," 1938-1941*. By John Steinbeck. New York: Viking Penguin, 1989. xxi-lvii.

Ditsky, John. "Faulkner Land and Steinbeck Country." *Steinbeck: The Man and His Work*. Ed. Richard Astro and Tetsumaro Hayashi. Corvallis: Oregon State UP, 1971. 11-24.

Eisinger, Chester E. "Jeffersonian Agrarianism in *The Grapes of Wrath*." *University of Kansas City Review* 14 (Winter 1947): 149-54.

Fontenrose, Joseph. "*The Grapes of Wrath*." *John Steinbeck: An Introduction and Interpretation*. New York: Holt, Rinehart and Winston, 1963. 67-83.

French, Warren. "Another Look at *The Grapes of Wrath*." *Colorado Quarterly* 3 (Winter 1955): 337-43. Rpt. in *A Companion to "The Grapes of Wrath."* Ed. Warren French. Clifton, NJ: Augustus M. Kelley, 1972. 217-24.

_____. "How Green Was Steinbeck?" *Steinbeck and the Environment: Interdisciplinary Approaches*. Ed. Susan F. Beegel, Susan Shillinglaw, and Wesley N. Tiffney, Jr. Tuscaloosa: U of Alabama P, 1997. 281-92.

_____. *John Steinbeck's Fiction Revisited*. New York: Twayne,1994.

_____. "Steinbeck's 'Self-Characters' as 1930s Underdogs." *Beyond Boundaries: Rereading John Steinbeck*. Ed. Susan Shillinglaw and Kevin Hearle. Tuscaloosa: U of Alabama P, 2002. 66-76.

_____, ed. *A Companion to "The Grapes of Wrath."* Clifton, NJ: Augustus M. Kelley, 1972.

George, Stephen K., and Barbara A. Heavilin, eds. *John Steinbeck and His Contemporaries*. Lanham, MD: Scarecrow Press, 2007.

Gold, Christina Sheehan. "Changing Perceptions of Homelessness: John Steinbeck, Carey McWilliams, and California During the 1930s." *Beyond Boundaries: Rereading John Steinbeck*. Ed. Susan Shillinglaw and Kevin Hearle. Tuscaloosa: U of Alabama P, 2002. 47-65.

Hayashi, Tetsumaro, ed. *Steinbeck's Literary Dimension: A Guide to Comparative Studies*. Metuchen, NJ: Scarecrow Press, 1973.

Hearle, Kevin. "These Are American People: The Spectre of Eugenics in *Their*

Blood Is Strong and *The Grapes of Wrath.*" *Beyond Boundaries: Rereading John Steinbeck.* Ed. Susan Shillinglaw and Kevin Hearle. Tuscaloosa: U of Alabama P, 2002. 243-54.

Heavilin, Barbara A. "Judge, Observer, Prophet: The American Cain and Steinbeck's Shifting Perspective." *The Critical Response to John Steinbeck's "The Grapes of Wrath."* Ed. Barbara A. Heavilin. Westport, CT: Greenwood Press, 2000. 233-46.

Henderson, George. "John Steinbeck's Spatial Imagination in *The Grapes of Wrath.*" *California History* 68.4 (Winter 1989-90): 210-23. Rpt. in *The Critical Response to John Steinbeck's "The Grapes of Wrath."* Ed. Barbara A. Heavilin. Westport, CT: Greenwood Press, 2000. 99-118.

Jackson, Joseph Henry. "The Finest Book John Steinbeck Has Written." Rev. of *The Grapes of Wrath. New York Herald Tribune Books* 16 Apr. 1939: 3. Rpt. in *A Companion to "The Grapes of Wrath."* Ed. Warren French. Clifton, NJ: Augustus M. Kelley, 1972. 115.

Jain, Sunita. *John Steinbeck's Concept of Man: A Critical Study of His Novels.* New Delhi: New Statesman, 1979.

Kocela, Chris. "A Postmodern Steinbeck, or Rose of Sharon Meets Oedipa Maas." *The Critical Response to John Steinbeck's "The Grapes of Wrath."* Ed. Barbara A. Heavilin. Westport, CT: Greenwood Press, 2000. 247-67.

Lewis, R. W. B. "John Steinbeck: The Fitful Daemon." *The Young Rebel in American Literature.* New York: Frederick A. Praeger, 1959. 119-41. Rpt. in *Steinbeck: A Collection of Critical Essays.* Ed. Robert Murray Davis. Englewood Cliffs, NJ: Prentice Hall, 1972. 163-75.

Lisca, Peter. "Escape and Commitment: Two Poles of the Steinbeck Hero." *Steinbeck: The Man and His Work.* Ed. Richard Astro and Tetsumaro Hayashi. Corvallis: Oregon State UP, 1971. 75-88.

_____. *John Steinbeck: Nature and Myth.* New York: Crowell, 1978.

_____. "Steinbeck and Hemingway: Suggestions for a Comparative Study." *Steinbeck's Literary Dimension: A Guide to Comparative Studies.* Ed. Tetsumaro Hayashi. Metuchen, NJ: Scarecrow Press, 1973. Rpt. in *The Critical Response to John Steinbeck's "The Grapes of Wrath."* Ed. Barbara A. Heavilin. Westport, CT: Greenwood Press, 2000. 87-94.

_____. *The Wide World of John Steinbeck.* New Brunswick, NJ: Rutgers UP, 1958.

Maine, Barry G. "Steinbeck's Debt to Dos Passos." *Steinbeck Quarterly* 23.1 (Winter/Spring 1990): 17-27. Rpt. in *The Critical Response to John Steinbeck's "The Grapes of Wrath."* Ed. Barbara A. Heavilin. Westport, CT: Greenwood Press, 2000. 151-62.

Matton, Collin G. "Water Imagery and the Conclusion to *The Grapes of Wrath.*" *Northeast Modern Language Association Newsletter* 2 (1970): 44-47. Rpt. in *The Critical Response to John Steinbeck's "The Grapes of Wrath."* Ed. Barbara A. Heavilin. Westport, CT: Greenwood Press, 2000. 95-98.

Meyer, Michael. "Fermenting *The Grapes of Wrath:* From Violent Anger Distilling Sweet Concord." Rpt. in *The Critical Response to John Steinbeck's "The*

Grapes of Wrath." Ed. Barbara A. Heavilin. Westport, CT: Greenwood Press, 2000. 327-40.

Moore, Harry Thornton. *The Novels of John Steinbeck: A First Critical Study.* Chicago: Normandie House, 1939.

Owens, Louis, and Hector Torres. "Dialogic Structure and Levels of Discourse in Steinbeck's *The Grapes of Wrath."* *Arizona Quarterly* 45.4 (1989): 75-94. Rpt. in *The Critical Response to John Steinbeck's "The Grapes of Wrath."* Ed. Barbara A. Heavilin. Westport, CT: Greenwood Press, 2000. 119-36.

Paton, Alan, and Liston Pope. "The Novelist and Christ." *Saturday Review* 4 Dec. 1954: 15-16, 56-59.

Prindle, Dennis. "The Pretexts of Romance: Steinbeck's Allegorical Naturalism from *Cup of Gold* to *Tortilla Flat."* *The Steinbeck Question: New Essays in Criticism.* Ed. Donald R. Noble. Troy, NY: Whitston, 1993. 23-36.

Railsback, Brian E. "The Darwinian *Grapes of Wrath." Parallel Expeditions: Charles Darwin and the Art of John Steinbeck.* Moscow: U of Idaho P, 1995. 129-39. Rpt. in *The Critical Response to John Steinbeck's "The Grapes of Wrath."* Ed. Barbara A. Heavilin. Westport, CT: Greenwood Press, 2000. 221-32.

Rascoe, Burton. "Excuse It, Please." Rev. of *The Grapes of Wrath. Newsweek* 1 May 1939: 38.

Roosevelt, Eleanor. "My Day: June 28, 1939." Rpt. in *A Companion to "The Grapes of Wrath."* Ed. Warren French. Clifton, NJ: Augustus M. Kelley, 1972. 131.

Ross, Woodburn O. "John Steinbeck: Naturalism's Priest." *College English* 10.8 (May 1949): 432-38. Rpt. in *The Critical Response to John Steinbeck's "The Grapes of Wrath."* Ed. Barbara A. Heavilin. Westport, CT: Greenwood Press, 2000. 57-66.

Seelye, John. "Come Back to the Boxcar, Leslie Honey; Or, Don't Cry for Me, Madonna, Just Pass the Milk: Steinbeck and Sentimentality." *Beyond Boundaries: Rereading John Steinbeck.* Ed. Susan Shillinglaw and Kevin Hearle. Tuscaloosa: U of Alabama P, 2002. 11-13.

Shillinglaw, Susan. "California Answers *The Grapes of Wrath." John Steinbeck: The Years of Greatness, 1936-1939.* Ed. Tetsumaro Hayashi. Tuscaloosa: U of Alabama P, 1993. Rpt. in *The Critical Response to John Steinbeck's "The Grapes of Wrath."* Ed. Barbara A. Heavilin. Westport, CT: Greenwood Press, 2000. 183-200.

Shillinglaw, Susan, and Kevin Hearle, eds. *Beyond Boundaries: Rereading John Steinbeck.* Tuscaloosa: U of Alabama P, 2002.

Shively, Charles. "John Steinbeck: From the Tide Pool to the Loyal Community." *Steinbeck: The Man and His Work.* Ed. Richard Astro and Tetsumaro Hayashi. Corvallis: Oregon State UP, 1971. 25-34.

Shockley, Martin. "Christian Symbolism in *The Grapes of Wrath." College English* 18 (1956): 87-90. Rpt. in *Steinbeck and His Critics: A Record of Twenty-five Years.* Ed. E. W. Tedlock, Jr., and C. V. Wicker. Albuquerque: U of New Mexico P, 1957. 266-74.

_____. "The Reception of *The Grapes of Wrath* in Oklahoma." *American Literature* 15.4 (Jan. 1944): 351-61. Rpt. in *Steinbeck and His Critics: A Record of Twenty-five Years.* Ed. E. W. Tedlock, Jr., and C. V. Wicker. Albuquerque: U of New Mexico P, 1957. 231-40.

Simmonds, Roy. "A World to Be Cherished: Steinbeck as Conservationist and Ecological Prophet." *Steinbeck and the Environment: Interdisciplinary Approaches.* Ed. Susan F. Beegel, Susan Shillinglaw, and Wesley N. Tiffney, Jr. Tuscaloosa: U of Alabama P, 1997. 323-34.

Steinbeck, John. *"The Grapes of Wrath": Text and Criticism.* 2nd ed. Ed. Peter Lisca with Kevin Hearle. New York: Penguin Books, 1997.

_____. "The Harvest Gypsies." *San Francisco News* 5-12 Oct. 1936.

_____. *In Dubious Battle.* New York: Collier, 1936.

_____. *Their Blood Is Strong.* San Francisco: Simon J. Lubin Society of California, 1938.

Swan, Kenneth. "The Enduring Values of John Steinbeck's Fiction: The University Student and *The Grapes of Wrath*." *The Critical Response to John Steinbeck's "The Grapes of Wrath."* Ed. Barbara A. Heavilin. Westport, CT: Greenwood Press, 2000. 299-308.

Timmerman, John H. *John Steinbeck's Fiction: The Aesthetics of the Road Taken.* Norman: U of Oklahoma P, 1986.

_____. "The Squatter's Circle in *The Grapes of Wrath*." *Studies in American Fiction* 17.2 (Autumn 1989): 203-11. Rpt. in *The Critical Response to John Steinbeck's "The Grapes of Wrath."* Ed. Barbara A. Heavilin. Westport, CT: Greenwood Press, 2000. 137-50.

Valenti, Peter. "Steinbeck's Ecological Polemic: Human Sympathy and Visual Documentary in the Intercalary Chapters of *The Grapes of Wrath*." *Steinbeck and the Environment: Interdisciplinary Approaches.* Ed. Susan F. Beegel, Susan Shillinglaw, and Wesley N. Tiffney, Jr. Tuscaloosa: U of Alabama P, 1997. 92-112.

Visser, Nicholas. "Audience and Closure in *The Grapes of Wrath*." *Studies in American Fiction* 22.1 (Spring 1994): 19-36. Rpt. in *The Critical Response to John Steinbeck's "The Grapes of Wrath."* Ed. Barbara A. Heavilin. Westport, CT: Greenwood Press, 2000. 201-20.

Werlock, Abby H. P. "Poor Whites: Joads and Snopeses." *San Jose Studies* 18.1 (Winter 1992): 61-72. Rpt. in *The Critical Response to John Steinbeck's "The Grapes of Wrath."* Ed. Barbara A. Heavilin. Westport, CT: Greenwood Press, 2000. 171-81.

White, Ray Lewis. "The Grapes of Wrath and the Critics of 1939." *Resources for American Literary Study* 13.2 (1983): 134-64.

CRITICAL
READINGS

The Philosophical Joads_____

Frederic I. Carpenter

A popular heresy has it that a novelist should not discuss ideas—especially not abstract ideas. Even the best contemporary reviewers concern themselves with the entertainment value of a book (will it please their readers?), and with the impression of immediate reality which it creates. *The Grapes of Wrath*, for instance, was praised for its swift action and for the moving sincerity of its characters. But its mystical ideas and the moralizing interpretations intruded by the author between the narrative chapters were condemned. Presumably the book became a best seller in spite of these; its art was great enough to overcome its philosophy.

But in the course of time a book is also judged by other standards. Aristotle once argued that poetry should be more "philosophical" than history; and all books are eventually weighed for their content of wisdom. Novels that have become classics do more than tell a story and describe characters; they offer insight into men's motives and point to the springs of action. Together with the moving picture, they offer the criticism of life.

Although this theory of art may seem classical, all important modern novels—especially American novels—have clearly suggested an abstract idea of life. *The Scarlet Letter* symbolized "sin," *Moby Dick* offered an allegory of evil. *Huck Finn* described the revolt of the "natural individual" against "civilization," and *Babbitt* (like Emerson's "Self-reliance") denounced the narrow conventions of "society." Now *The Grapes of Wrath* goes beyond these to preach a positive philosophy of life and to damn that blind conservatism which fears ideas.

I shall take for granted the narrative power of the book and the vivid reality of its characters: modern critics, both professional and popular, have borne witness to these. The novel is a best seller. But it also has ideas. These appear abstractly and obviously in the interpretative interchapters. But more important is Steinbeck's creation of Jim Casy, "the preacher," to interpret and to embody the philosophy of the novel. And consummate is the skill with which Jim Casy's philosophy has been integrated with the action of the story, until it motivates and gives significance to the lives of Tom Joad, and Ma, and Rose of Sharon. It is not too much to say that Jim Casy's ideas determine and direct the Joads' actions.

Beside and beyond their function in the story, the ideas of John Steinbeck and Jim Casy possess a significance of their own. They continue, develop, integrate, and realize the thought of the great writers of American history. Here the mystical transcendentalism of Emerson reappears, and the earthy democracy of Whitman, and the pragmatic instrumentalism of William James and John Dewey. And these old philosophies grow and change in the book until they become new. They coalesce into an organic whole. And, finally, they find embodiment in character and action, so that they seem no longer ideas, but facts. The enduring greatness of *The Grapes of Wrath* consists in its imaginative realization of these old ideas in new and concrete forms. Jim Casy translates American philosophy into words of one syllable, and the Joads translate it into action.

"Ever know a guy that said big words like that?" asks the truck driver in the first narrative chapter of *The Grapes of Wrath*. "Preacher," replies Tom Joad. "Well, it makes you mad to hear a guy use big words. Course with a preacher it's all right because nobody would fool around with a preacher anyway." But soon afterward Tom meets Jim Casy and finds him changed. "I was a preacher," said the man seriously, "but not no more." Because Casy has ceased to be an orthodox minister and no longer uses big words, Tom Joad plays around with him. And the story results.

But although he is no longer a minister, Jim Casy continues to preach. His words have become simple and his ideas unorthodox. "Just

Jim Casy now. Ain't got the call no more. Got a lot of sinful idears—but they seem kinda sensible." A century before, this same experience and essentially these same ideas had occurred to another preacher: Ralph Waldo Emerson had given up the ministry because of his unorthodoxy. But Emerson had kept on using big words. Now Casy translates them: "Why do we got to hang it on God or Jesus? Maybe it's all men an' all women we love; maybe that's the Holy Sperit—the human sperit—the whole shebang. Maybe all men got one big soul ever'body's a part of." And so the Emersonian oversoul comes to earth in Oklahoma.

Unorthodox Jim Casy went into the Oklahoma wilderness to save his soul. And in the wilderness he experienced the religious feeling of identity with nature which has always been the heart of transcendental mysticism: "There was the hills, an' there was me, an' we wasn't sepa-rate no more. We was one thing. An' that one thing was holy." Like Emerson, Casy came to the conviction that holiness, or goodness, re-sults from this feeling of unity: "I got to thinkin' how we was holy when we was one thing, an' mankin' was holy when it was one thing."

Thus far Jim Casy's transcendentalism has remained vague and ap-parently insignificant. But the corollary of this mystical philosophy is that any man's self-seeking destroys the unity or "holiness" of nature: "An' it [this one thing] on'y got unholy when one mis'able little fella got the bit in his teeth, an' run off his own way. . . . Fella like that bust the holiness." Or, as Emerson phrased it, while discussing Nature: "The world lacks unity because man is disunited with himself. . . . Love is its demand." So Jim Casy preaches the religion of love.

He finds that this transcendental religion alters the old standards: "Here's me that used to give all my fight against the devil 'cause I fig-ured the devil was the enemy. But they's somepin worse'n the devil got hold a the country." Now, like Emerson, he almost welcomes "the dear old devil." Now he fears not the lusts of the flesh but rather the lusts of the spirit. For the abstract lust of possession isolates a man from his fel-lows and destroys the unity of nature and the love of man. As Steinbeck writes: "The quality of owning freezes you forever into 'I,' and cuts you off forever from the 'we.'" Or, as the Concord farmers in Emerson's poem "Hamatreya" had exclaimed: "'Tis mine, my children's and my name's," only to have "their avarice cooled like lust in the chill of the grave." To a preacher of the oversoul, possessive egotism may become the unpardonable sin.

If a society has adopted "the quality of owning" (as typified by absentee ownership) as its social norm, then Protestant nonconformity may become the highest virtue, and even resistance to authority may become justified. At the beginning of his novel Steinbeck had suggested this, describing how "the faces of the watching men lost their bemused perplexity and became hard and angry and resistant. Then the women knew that they were safe. . . . their men were whole." For this is the paradox of Protestantism: when men resist unjust and selfish authority, they themselves become "whole" in spirit.

But this American ideal of nonconformity seems negative: how can men be sure that their Protestant rebellion does not come from the devil? To this there has always been but one answer—faith: faith in the instincts of the common man, faith in ultimate social progress, and faith in the direction in which democracy is moving. So Ma Joad counsels the discouraged Tom: "Why, Tom, we're the people that live. They ain't gonna wipe us out. Why, we're the people—we go on." And so Steinbeck himself affirms a final faith in progress: "When theories change and crash, when schools, philosophies . . . grow and disintegrate, man reaches, stumbles forward. . . . Having stepped forward, he may slip back, but only half a step, never the full step back." Whether this be democratic faith, or mere transcendental optimism, it has always been the motive force of our American life and finds reaffirmation in this novel.

II

Upon the foundation of this old American idealism Steinbeck has built. But the Emersonian oversoul had seemed very vague and very ineffective—only the individual had been real, and he had been concerned more with his private soul than with other people. *The Grapes of Wrath* develops the old idea in new ways. It traces the transformation of the Protestant individual into the member of a social group—the old "I" becomes "we." And it traces the transformation of the passive individual into the active participant—the idealist becomes pragmatist. The first development continues the poetic thought of Walt Whitman; the second continues the philosophy of William James and John Dewey.

"One's-self I sing, a simple separate person," Whitman had proclaimed. "Yet utter the word Democratic, the word En-Masse." Other American writers had emphasized the individual above the group. Even Whitman celebrated his "comrades and lovers" in an essentially personal relationship. But Steinbeck now emphasizes the group above the individual and from an impersonal point of view. Where formerly American and Protestant thought has been separatist, Steinbeck now faces the problem of social integration. In his novel the "mutually repellent particles" of individualism begin to cohere.

"This is the beginning," he writes, "from 'I' to 'we.'" This is the beginning, that is, of reconstruction. When the old society has been split and the Protestant individuals wander aimlessly about, some new nucleus must be found, or chaos and nihilism will follow. "In the night one family camps in a ditch and another family pulls in and the tents come out. The two men squat on their hams and the women and children listen. Here is the node." Here is the new nucleus. "And from this first 'we,' there grows a still more dangerous thing: 'I have a little food' plus 'I have none.' If from this problem the sum is 'We have a little food,' the thing is on its way, the movement has direction." A new social group is forming, based on the word "en masse." But here is no socialism imposed from above; here is a natural grouping of simple separate persons.

By virtue of his wholehearted participation in this new group the individual may become greater than himself. Some men, of course, will remain mere individuals, but in every group there must be leaders, or "representative men." A poet gives expression to the group idea, or a preacher organizes it. After Jim Casy's death, Tom is chosen to lead. Ma explains: "They's some folks that's just theirself, an' nothin' more. There's Al [for instance] he's jus' a young fella after a girl. You wasn't never like that, Tom." Because he has been an individualist, but through the influence of Casy and of his group idea has become more than himself, Tom becomes "a leader of the people." But his strength derives from his increased sense of participation in the group.

From Jim Casy, and eventually from the thought of Americans like Whitman, Tom Joad has inherited this idea. At the end of the book he sums it up, recalling how Casy "went out in the wilderness to find his own soul, and he found he didn't have no soul that was his'n. Says he foun' he jus' got a little piece of a great big soul. Says a wilderness ain't no good 'cause his little piece of a soul wasn't no good 'less it was with the rest, an' was whole." Unlike Emerson, who had said goodbye to the proud world, these latter-day Americans must live in the midst of it. "I know now," concludes Tom, "a fella ain't no good alone."

To repeat: this group idea is American, not Russian; and stems from Walt Whitman, not Karl Marx. But it does include some elements that have usually seemed sinful to orthodox Anglo-Saxons. "Of physiology from top to toe I sing," Whitman had declared, and added a good many details that his friend Emerson thought unnecessary. Now the Joads frankly discuss anatomical details and joke about them. Like most common people, they do not abscond or conceal. Sometimes they seem to go beyond the bounds of literary decency: the unbuttoned antics of Grandpa Joad touch a new low in folk-comedy. The movies (which re-produced most of the realism of the book) could not quite stomach this. But for the most part they preserved the spirit of the book, because it was whole and healthy.

In Whitman's time almost everyone deprecated this physiological realism, and in our own many readers and critics still deprecate it. Nevertheless, it is absolutely necessary—both artistically and logically. In the first place, characters like the Joads do act and talk that way—to describe them as genteel would be to distort the picture. And, in the second place, Whitman himself had suggested the necessity of it: just as the literature of democracy must describe all sorts of people, "en masse," so it must describe all of the life of the people. To exclude the common or "low" elements of individual life would be as false as to exclude the common or low elements of society. Either would destroy the wholeness of life and nature. Therefore, along with the dust-driven Joads, we must have Grandpa's dirty drawers.

But beyond this physiological realism lies the problem of sex. And this problem is not one of realism at all. Throughout this turbulent novel an almost traditional reticence concerning the details of sex is observed. The problem here is rather one of fundamental morality, for sex had always been a symbol of sin. *The Scarlet Letter* reasserted the authority of an orthodox morality. Now Jim Casy questions that orthodoxy. On this first meeting with Tom he describes how, after sessions of preaching, he had often lain with a girl and then felt sinful afterward. This time the movies repeated his confession, because it is central to the motivation of the story. Disbelief in the sinfulness of sex converts Jim Casy from a preacher of the old morality to a practitioner of the new.

But in questioning the old morality Jim Casy does not deny morality. He doubts the strict justice of Hawthorne's code: "Maybe it ain't a sin. Maybe it's just the way folks is. Maybe we been whippin' the hell out of ourselves for nothin'." But he recognizes that love must always remain responsible and purposeful. Al Joad remains just "a boy after a girl." In place of the old, Casy preaches the new morality of Whitman, which uses sex to symbolize the love of man for his fellows. Jim Casy and Tom Joad have become more responsible and more purposeful than Pa Joad and Uncle John ever were: they love people so much that they are ready to die for them. Formerly the only unit of human love was the family, and the family remains the fundamental unit. The tragedy of *The Grapes of Wrath* consists in the breakup of the family. But the new moral of this novel is that the love of all people—if it be unselfish—may even supersede the love of family. So Casy dies for his people, and Tom is ready to, and Rose of Sharon symbolically transmutes her maternal love to a love of all people. Here is a new realization of "the word democratic, the word en-masse."

III

"An' I got to thinkin', Ma—most of the preachin' is about the poor we shall have always with us, an' if you got nothin', why, jus' fol' your hands an' to hell with it, you gonna git ice cream on gol' plates when you're dead. An' then this here Preacher says two get a better reward for their work."

Catholic Christianity had always preached humility and passive obedience. Protestantism preached spiritual nonconformity, but kept its disobedience passive. Transcendentalism sought to save the individual but not the group. ("Are they my poor?" asked Emerson.) Whitman sympathized more deeply with the common people and loved them abstractly, but trusted that God and democracy would save them. The pragmatic philosophers first sought to implement American idealism by making thought itself instrumental. And now Steinbeck quotes scripture to urge popular action for the realization of the old ideals.

In the course of the book Steinbeck develops and translates the thought of the earlier pragmatists. "Thinking," wrote John Dewey, "is a kind of activity which we perform at specific need." And Steinbeck repeats: "Need is the stimulus to concept, concept to action." The cause of the Okies' migration is their need, and their migration itself becomes a kind of thinking—an unconscious groping for the solution to a half-formulated problem. Their need becomes the stimulus to concept.

In this novel a kind of pragmatic thinking takes place before our eyes: the idea develops from the predicament of the characters, and the resulting action becomes integral with the thought. The evils of absentee ownership produce the mass migration, and the mass migration results in the idea of group action: "A half-million people moving over the country. . . . And tractors turning the multiple furrows in the vacant land."

But what good is generalized thought? And how is future action to be planned? Americans in general, and pragmatists in particular, have always disagreed in answering these questions. William James argued that thought was good only in so far as it satisfied a particular need and that plans, like actions, were "plural"—and should be conceived and executed individually. But Charles Sanders Peirce, and the transcendentalists before him, had argued that the most generalized thought was best, provided it eventually resulted in effective action. The problems of mankind should be considered as a unified whole, monistically.

Now Tom Joad is a pluralist—a pragmatist after William James. Tom said, "I'm still layin' my dogs down one at a time." Casy replied: "Yeah, but when a fence comes up at ya, ya gonna climb that fence." "I climb fences when I got fences to climb," said Tom. But Jim Casy believes in looking far ahead and seeing the thing as a whole: "But they's different kinda fences. They's folks like me that climbs fences that ain't even strang up yet." Which is to say that Casy is a kind of transcendental pragmatist. His thought seeks to generalize the problems of the Okies and to integrate them with the larger problem of industrial America. His solution is the principle of group action guided by conceptual thought and functioning within the framework of democratic society and law.

And at the end of the story Tom Joad becomes converted to Jim Casy's pragmatism. It is not important that the particular strike should be won, or that the particular need should be satisfied; but it is important that men should think in terms of action, and that they should think and act in terms of the whole rather than the particular individual. "For every little beaten strike is proof that the step is being taken." The value of an idea lies not in its immediate but in its eventual success. That idea is good which works—in the long run.

But the point of the whole novel is that action is an absolute essential of human life. If need and failure produce only fear, disintegration follows. But if they produce anger, then reconstruction may follow. The grapes of wrath must be trampled to make manifest the glory of the Lord. At the beginning of the story Steinbeck described the incipient wrath of the defeated farmers. At the end he repeats the scene. "And where a number of men gathered together, the fear went from their faces, and anger took its place. And the women sighed with relief. . . . the break would never come as long as fear could turn to wrath." Then wrath could turn to action.

IV

To sum up: the fundamental idea of *The Grapes of Wrath* is that of American transcendentalism: "Maybe all men got one big soul ever'body's a part of." From this idea it follows that every individual will trust those instincts which he shares with all men, even when these conflict with the teachings of orthodox religion and of existing society. But his self-reliance will not merely seek individual freedom, as did Emerson. It will rather seek social freedom or mass democracy, as did Whitman. If this mass democracy leads to the abandonment of genteel taboos and to the modification of some traditional ideas of morality, that is inevitable. But whatever happens, the American will act to realize his ideals. He will seek to make himself whole—i.e., to join himself to other men by means of purposeful actions for some goal beyond himself.

But at this point the crucial question arises—and it is "crucial" in every sense of the word. What if this self-reliance lead to death? What if the individual is killed before the social group is saved? Does the failure of the individual action invalidate the whole idea? "How'm I gonna know about you?" Ma asks. "They might kill ya an' I wouldn't know."

The answer has already been suggested by the terms in which the story has been told. If the individual has identified himself with the oversoul, so that his life has become one with the life of all men, his individual death and failure will not matter. From the old transcendental philosophy of identity to Tom Joad and the moving pictures may seem a long way, but even the movies faithfully reproduced Tom's final declaration of transcendental faith: "They might kill ya," Ma had objected.

"Tom laughed uneasily, 'Well, maybe like Casy says, a fella ain't got a soul of his own, but on'y a piece of a big one—an' then—'

"'Then what, Tom?'

"'Then it don' matter. Then I'll be aroun' in the dark. I'll be ever'where—wherever you look. Wherever they's a fight so hungry people can eat, I'll be there. Wherever they's a cop beating up a guy, I'll be there. If Casy knowed, why, I'll be in the way guys yell when they're mad, an'—I'll be in the way kids laugh when they're hungry an' they know supper's ready. An' when our folks eat the stuff they raise an' live in the houses they build—why, I'll be there. See?'"

For the first time in history, *The Grapes of Wrath* brings together and makes real three great skeins of American thought. It begins with the transcendental oversoul, Emerson's faith in the common man, and his Protestant self-reliance. To this it joins Whitman's religion of the love of all men and his mass democracy. And it combines these mystical and poetic ideas with the realistic philosophy of pragmatism and its emphasis on effective action. From this it develops a new kind of Christianity—not otherworldly and passive, but earthly and active. And Oklahoma Jim Casy and the Joads think and do all these philosophical things.

From *College English* 2, no. 4 (1941): 315-325. Originally published by the National Council of Teachers of English.

Christian Symbolism in *The Grapes of Wrath*_____

Martin Shockley

In their recent study (*Saturday Review*, 1954) of the Christ-symbol in modern fiction, novelist Alan Paton and theologian Liston Pope dismiss Jim Casy because their reaction to him "is essentially one of pathos rather than of awe." I hesitate to disagree with two such eminent Christians, but I do disagree. I propose an interpretation of *The Grapes of Wrath* in which Casy represents a contemporary adaptation of the Christ image, and in which the meaning of the book is revealed through a sequence of Christian symbols.

Before and after *The Grapes of Wrath* Steinbeck has used symbolism and allegory; throughout his work he has considered a wide range of Christian or neo-Christian ideas; in relation to the context of his fiction as a whole, Christian symbolism is common. His use of Biblical names, for instance, is an inviting topic yet to be investigated. *The Pearl* is an obvious allegory on the evil of worldly treasure. The Pirate in *Tortilla Flat* exemplifies a Steinbeck character type, pure in heart, simple in mind, rejected of men, clearly of the kingdom of heaven. More pertinent perhaps, the title of *The Grapes of Wrath* is itself a direct Christian allusion, suggesting the glory of the coming of the Lord, revealing that the story exists in Christian context, indicating that we should expect to find some Christian meaning.

It has, indeed, been found before. Frederic I. Carpenter has pointed out (*College English*, 1941) the relationship of the Joad philosophy to the Unitarian, transcendental pantheism of Emerson and Whitman. I would not deny that Casy preaches the gospel according to Saint Walt; but I find further, stronger, more direct relations to the Bible.

Consider first the language of the novel. Major characters speak a language that has been associated with debased Piedmont culture. It is, I suggest, easy to find in vocabulary, rhythm, imagery, and tone pronounced similarities to the language of the King James Bible. These similarities, to be seen in qualities of simplicity, purity, strength, vigor, earnestness, are easy to illustrate. The novel contains passages of moving tenderness and prophetic power, not alone in dialogue, but even in descriptive and expository passages.

Like the Israelites, the Joads are a homeless and persecuted people. They too flee from oppression, wander through a wilderness of hardships, seeking their own Promised Land. Unlike the Israelites, however, the Joads never find it.

More specifically, let us examine the Christ-Casy relationship. Jesus began his mission after a period of withdrawal into the wilderness for meditation and consecration; Preacher Casy comes into the book after a similar retreat. He tells Tom, "I went off alone, an' I sat and figured." Later when Casy and Tom meet in the strikers' tent, Casy says he has "been a-goin' into the wilderness like Jesus to try to find out sumpin." Certainly Steinbeck is conscious of the parallel.

Much has been made of Jim Conklin's name as a key to his identification in the symbolism of *The Red Badge of Courage*. Whether Steinbeck copied Crane is immaterial; Jim Casy is by the same initials identified with Jesus Christ. Like Jesus, Jim has rejected an old religion and is in process of replacing it with a new gospel. In the introductory scene with Tom Joad, Tom and Jim recall the old days when Casy preached the old religion, expounded the old concept of sin and guilt. Now, however, Casy explains his rejection of a religion through which he saw himself as wicked and depraved because of the satisfaction of natural human desires. The old Adam of the fall is about to be exorcised through the new dispensation.

It should not be necessary to point out that Jim Casy's religion is innocent of Paulism, of Catholicism, of Puritanism. He is identified simply and directly with Christ, and his words paraphrase the words of Jesus, who said, "God is love," and "A new commandment give I unto you: that ye love one another." Casy says, "What's this call, this sperit? . . . It's love. I love people so much I'm fit to bust sometimes." This is the truth Casy has found in his wilderness, the gospel he brings back to the people he loves.

Beyond this simple, central doctrine, identical and cardinal to Jesus and to Jim, there is the Emerson-Whitman-Unitarian-pantheism which Professor Carpenter notes. Jim elaborates: "There ain't no sin and there ain't no virtue. There's just stuff people do. It's all part of the same thing." I would avoid theological subtleties; I see Jim Casy as a simple and direct copy of Jesus Christ. Yet Casy's doctrine, "all that lives is holy," comes close to the doctrine of one of the most distinguished Christian theologians of our time, Albert Schweitzer, whose famous and familiar phrasing of the same concept is known to us as "reverence for life."

The third article of Casy's faith is a related one: "'Maybe,' I figgered, 'Maybe it's all men and women we love; maybe that's the Holy Sperit—the human sperit—the whole shebang. Maybe all men got one big soul ever'body's a part of.' Now I sat there thinking it, an' all of a suddent—I knew it. I knew it so deep down that it was true and I still know it." Casy's knowledge of the oversoul is derived from the same source as Emerson's and Whitman's—from within himself, or if you prefer, from God speaking within him.

Jim realizes, as did Jesus, that organized religion will reject his new teaching. Tom points this out: "You can't hold no church with idears like that," he said. "People would drive you out of the country with idears like that." In both cases, people make the rejection.

I should like to go on from this formulation of a creed to the expression of doctrine through deeds, to the unfolding of the incidents of the plot in which Jim Casy reveals himself through significant, symbolic acts.

First, he feels a compulsion to minister, to serve, to offer himself. When the Joads are preparing to leave for California, he tells them: "I got to go . . . I can't stay here no more. I got to go where the folks is goin'." Not long afterward, Casy offers himself as the sacrifice to save his people. When Tom is about to be arrested, Casy tells the police that he is the guilty one. "'It was me, all right . . . I'll go 'thout no trouble.'" So the Joads escape the consequences of their transgressions. "Between his guards Casy sat proudly, his head up and the stringy muscles of his neck prominent. On his lips there was a faint smile and on his face a curious look of conquest." Jim Casy had taken upon himself the sins of others.

Casy's death symbolically occurs in the middle of a stream to represent the "crossing over Jordan" Christian motif. Particularly significant, however, are Casy's last words directed to the man who murders him, "Listen," he said, "You fellas don' know what you're doin'." And again, just before the heavy man swings the pick handle Casy repeats, "You don' know what you're a-doin'." Jesus said, as they crucified Him, "Father forgive them; they know not what they do."

One of the major emotional climaxes of the novel is the scene in which Tom tells Ma goodbye and explains why he must leave. He has told Ma about Casy, who "Spouted out some Scripture once, an' it didn' soun' like no hellfire Scripture." He goes on to repeat what Casy told him about two being better than one. He rehearses Casy's teaching about the individual and the collective soul, recalling that Casy went into the wilderness to find his soul, then found, "His little piece of a soul wasn't no good 'less it was with the rest, an' was whole." He explains to Ma Casy's theory of Christian Socialism. "'Tom,' Ma repeated, 'What you gonna do?' 'What Casy done,' he said." At this point Tom becomes Casy's disciple. He has learned from his master, and now he takes up his master's work. Two of Jesus' disciples were named Thomas. Most of those chosen by Him to found the religion we profess were called from among people like the Joads.

Tom's answer to Ma's worry lest he lose his life is the answer he has learned from Casy.

"Then it don' matter. Then I'll be all aroun' in the dark. I'll be ever'where—wherever you look. Wherever they's a fight so hungry people can eat, I'll be there. Wherever they's a cop beatin' up a guy, I'll be there. If Casy knowed, why, I'll be in the way kids laugh when they're hungry an' they know supper's ready. An' when our folks eat the stuff they raise an' live in the houses they build—why I'll be there. See? God, I'm talkin' like Casy."

The One that Casy talked like said, "Lo, I am with you always."

These evidences of a Christ-Casy relationship mean more to me than they do to Mr. Paton and Dean Pope. I would not argue that Steinbeck's interpretation of the relationship of pathos and awe in the Christian tradition is identical with the interpretation of Paton and Pope, nor that his interpretation is more or less correct than theirs. Nevertheless, I find in the novel what seems to me to be adequate evidence to establish the author's intention of creating in Jim Casy a character who would be understood in terms of the Christ symbol.

Beyond this personal identification, I find further use of Christian symbols. The conclusion of *The Grapes of Wrath* has been said to be extreme, sensational, overwrought. The Joads have reached at last a condition of utter desolation. Rosasharn, her baby born dead, is rain-drenched, weak, her breasts heavy with milk. In the barn they come upon a boy and a starving old man, too weak to eat the bread his son had stolen for him. Ma knows what must be done, but the decision is Rosasharn's: "Ma's eyes passed Rose of Sharon's eyes, and then came back to them. And the two women looked deep into each other. The girl's breath came short and gasping.

"She said, 'Yes.'"

In this, her Gethsemane, Rosasharn says, in effect: "Not my will, but Thine be done."

The meaning of this incident, Steinbeck's final paragraph, is clear in terms of Christian symbolism. And this is the supreme symbol of the Christian religion, commemorated by Protestants in the Communion, by Catholics in the Mass. Rosasharn gives what Christ gave, what we receive in memory of Him. The ultimate mystery of the Christian religion is realized as Rosasharn "Looked up and across the barn, and her lips came together and smiled mysteriously." She smiles mysteriously because what has been mystery is now knowledge. *This is my body,* says Rosasharn, and becomes the Resurrection and the Life. Rose of Sharon, the life-giver, symbolizes the resurrective aspect of Christ, common in Christian tradition and literature, used by Mr. Eliot in his "multifoliate rose" image. In her, death and life are one, and through her, life triumphs over death.

Cited incidents occur at points of major importance in plot and action, accompany major emotional crises, and relate to the major and most familiar examples of Christian symbolism. Other less obvious examples might be brought in, such as the incident at the roadside café where the waitress lets the migrant have a loaf of bread and is immediately rewarded by large and unexpected tips from the two truck drivers: she had cast her bread upon the waters. In a recent issue of the *Colorado Quarterly* (1954) Bernard Bowron notes Noah's wandering off down the stream as possibly "a biblical association." I would not, however, try to press my point further; major examples are enough.

Certain of these symbols may be identified as pre-Christian. The motif of crossing water in death is, of course, widespread in folklore; and the Freudian, totemistic interpretation of the miracle of transubstantiation lies in the background. It is not within the scope of this paper to explore these labyrinthine shadows. Suffice it to say that we recognize in Christianity elements of older religions. Further, it is easy to identify elements of Steinbeck's ideology with other religions. For example, the principle of reverence for life, or "all that lives is holy," has been believed and practiced for centuries by Buddhists.

Such, however, I regard as incidental. In *The Grapes of Wrath* the major intended meaning is neither Buddhist nor Freudian nor Marxist; it is, I believe, essentially and thoroughly Christian. In my interpretation, Jim Casy unmistakably and significantly is equated with Jesus Christ.[1]

From *College English* 18 (1956): 87-90. Originally published by the National Council of Teachers of English.

Note

1. In the April 1954 issue of *The Annotator*, mimeographed house-organ of Purdue's English Department, "H. B." (Professor Howard Burton, I assume) lists "Biblical Analogies in *The Grapes of Wrath*" taken from term papers submitted by Barbara Hyland and John Hallett. Together they cite seven "Biblical Analogies," including "stylistic parallels," "attitude toward the rich," "Casy and Christ," "the wanderings of the children of Israel [and] . . . the migrants seeking California as a promised land," "Tom's return from McAlester [as] . . . the Prodigal Son." The most interesting analogy in relation to my purpose in this paper is the suggestion of a halo for Casy: "As Casy and Tom approach Uncle John's house, the morning sun lights Casy's brow—but not Tom's. And just before Casy is killed, an attacker says, 'That's him. It's that shiny one.'" Professor Burton's note was called to my attention after this paper was accepted for publication.

Works Cited

Bowron, Bernard. "*The Grapes of Wrath*: A 'Wagons West' Romance." *Colorado Quarterly* 3 (Summer 1954): 84-91.

Carpenter, Frederic I. "The Philosophical Joads." *College English* 2.4 (Jan. 1941): 315-25.

Paton, Alan, and Liston Pope. "The Novelist and Christ." *Saturday Review* 4 Dec. 1954: 15-16, 56-59.

Rebuttal:
Symbolism in *The Grapes of Wrath*_____

Eric W. Carlson

In his "Christian Symbolism in *The Grapes of Wrath*" (*CE*, Nov. 1956) Martin Shockley shows a commendable freedom from the usual critical stereotypes about this novel as a "propaganda tract" of the Thirties or as an example of "sociological naturalism" in fiction. In disagreeing with Paton and Pope he holds that Casy is a true Christ-symbol and that "the meaning of the book is revealed through a sequence of Christian symbols"; in agreeing with F. I. Carpenter ("The Philosophical Joads," *CE*, Jan. 1941) he nevertheless finds a "further, stronger, more direct relation to the Bible." Qualified only by the remark that Casy's religion is "innocent of Paulism, of Catholicism, of Puritanism," Shockley's interpretation of Casy identifies him "simply and directly with Christ" from the evidence of his new-found religion, his deeds, and his death, and from Tom's discipleship and Rosasharn's sacramental gift of herself in the final scene of the novel. In short, the major intended meaning, it is claimed, is "essentially and thoroughly Christian."

Now all this may seem plausible and in itself innocent enough. A closer examination of the novel as a whole, however, will lead to rather different conclusions, namely: (1) the Christian symbols and Biblical analogies function at best in a secondary capacity within a context of meaning that is so unorthodox as to be the opposite of what is generally considered "Christian"; (2) the primary symbolic structure, as well as meaning, is naturalistic and humanistic, not Christian; (3) the main theme reflects not only this foreground of natural symbolism but also the author's philosophic perspective of scientific humanism. In other words, in *The Grapes of Wrath* a few loose Biblical analogies may be identified, but these are not primary to the structure and theme of the novel, and to contend that they give it an "essentially and thoroughly Christian" meaning is to distort Steinbeck's intention and its primary framework of non-Christian symbolism.

In the first place, several of the Biblical analogies are really so tenuous as to depend entirely on other, major parallels for validity. Tom Joad as the Prodigal Son, for instance, hardly makes for a strong and direct analogy: Tom is quite unrepentant, having killed in self-defense, and Tom's homecoming is described in a most moving fashion, without benefit of analogy. Other of the cited analogies can be invoked only as the loosest sort of parallels, hardly metaphoric, much less symbolic. For example, to speak of the Joads and other migrants as wandering, like the Israelites, in a wilderness of hardships while they seek the Promised Land is but to point up by conventional metaphor the general emotional pattern of the trek westward and the long-awaited sight of California. Even when the Joads make their dramatic entrance into California, as described in Ch. 18, that fact is subordinate to the significance of Ma's stoicism (only she has known of Grandma's death), her concern for the unity of the family, Tom's idealism, etc. As for Noah's going down the river, Shockley chooses not to "press" this point, major examples being enough. But if major examples suffice, why speak of the truck drivers' generous tips (in Ch. 15) as constituting Mae's reward for "casting her bread upon the waters"? Wouldn't it be far simpler to say, without recourse to Biblical allusion, that this incident dramatizes a simple human fact: kindness breeds kindness? The strongest and most direct relationship of this incident is not to Christ but to Mae's earlier reluctance to sell the loaf of bread and, by an even more emphatic contrast, to the penny-pinching tourist couples—both suggestive of how the hard shell of economic exploitation inhibits natural sympathy and generosity. In fact, Ch. 15 is but one of a number of carefully interrelated chapters that develop the social theme of mutualism and its negative counterpart, possessive egoism, out of a pattern of human experience that is realized pragmatically, not theistically, and distilled into natural, social and epic symbols.

The title-phrase "*Grapes of Wrath*" is a good case in point. According to Shockley, it is "a direct Christian allusion, suggesting the glory of the coming of the Lord, revealing that the story exists in Christian context, indicating that we should expect to find some Christian meaning." One grants that the "Battle Hymn of the Republic" expresses the spirit of militant Christianity, the sacrificial idealism and the retribution associated with the Calvinist legacy of the South. But except for fanatics like Grandma Joad and the Jehovites, the specifically Christian association of "the grapes of wrath" has disappeared among the migrants, even as Casy had abandoned his old-style revivalism in search of something better. From the first chapter to the last, the "grapes of wrath" theme represents the indomitable spirit of man—that spirit which remains whole by resisting despair and resignation in the face of the drought of life, physical privation, exploitation, persecution, the tyranny of name-calling, and the uprooting of the very way of life itself. Out of these shared miseries there grows a spirit of resistance to the "possessive egotism" (Carpenter's term) of absentee ownership— "'a bad thing made by men, and by God that's something we can change'"; out of this nonconformity comes a sense of shared purpose and group action. Or, in the words of one of the interchapters, "From need to concept to action." In brief, then, the "grapes of wrath" theme is not specifically Christian for two reasons: it is not an expression of Christian humility and resignation; and, if one grants that the Christian spirit may on occasion be assertive and militant, here the title theme has its origin in the character and the experience of the people rather than in a body of religious concepts and beliefs. As Barker Fairley has made clear (*SR*, Apr. 1942), with special reference to the style of this novel, *The Grapes of Wrath* has behind it a long American "democratic tradition" which is embodied in its "epic form" and in its "epic tendency" of style, as well as in its folkways and philosophy.

Jim Casy belongs to this deeply rooted American liberal-democratic tradition. Like Emerson, Casy gives up the church and becomes a humble free-thinking seeker of the truth, relying on observation, shared experience, natural sympathy, and natural introspection and insight. When the revelation of his new calling comes to Casy, it comes as a result of his having lived among the migrants, sharing their hardships,

miseries, and hopes. His new faith grows out of an experiential understanding and love of his fellow man. As articulated by Casy, his new
faith has four major beliefs: (1) a belief in the brotherhood of man,
manifesting itself as "love"—i.e., good will, compassion and
mutualism; (2) a belief in the spirit-of-man as the oversoul or Holy
Spirit shared by all men in their outgoing love; (3) a belief in the unity
of man and nature; and (4) an acceptance of all life as an expression of
spirit. To Casy these beliefs are ideal spiritual values and therefore
"holy"; he seems to doubt that the word "holy" has any other valid
meaning, really, and that there is holiness enough in the ideal unity of
common purpose (spirit) when men strive together toward a worthy
goal in harmony with nature (the way of life). Here we have the social
theme again, with religious overtones associated by some readers with
Christianity—or at least that core Christianity which remains after
doctrine, dogma, sacrament, ritual, miracle, and theism itself have
been stripped away, leaving only the idealized brotherhood of man and
the unitarian Over-Soul. "'I figgered about the Holy Sperit and the Jesus road,'" Casy explained. "'I figgered, "Why do we got to hang it on
God or Jesus? Maybe," I figgered, "maybe it's all men an' all women
we love; maybe that's the Holy Sperit—the human sperit—the whole
shebang. Maybe all men got one big soul ever'body's a part of." Now I
sat there thinkin' it, an' all of a suddent—I knew it. I knew it so deep
down that it was true, and I still know it.'" Like Emerson's Brahma,
this is not the God of Christ—at least not to Casy and Steinbeck; and it
is dubious semantics to insist on labeling "Christian" so unorthodox a
creed. Christianity without Christ is hardly Christianity. And although
Carpenter concludes that "a new kind of Christianity—not otherworldly and passive, but earthly and active"—is developed from
Steinbeck's integration of "three great skeins of American thought"
(Emersonianism, Whitman's democratic religion, and pragmatism),
that integration is less a product and characteristic of Christianity than
it is of the humanist tendency and character of the American experience and the modern climate of opinion.

But if Casy's beliefs are not characteristically Christian, there is still a striking similarity to Christ in Casy's initials and his dying words. In those final words—"You don't know what you're a-doin'"—the ideas of resurrection and redemption are conspicuously absent, however. His death is not the death of a redeeming Christ, any more than the death of Jim Conklin in *The Red Badge of Courage* is such a death, even if both have names beginning with J and C. Casy does not seek death, nor is he resigned to it when it comes, though in his last words he seems to forgive his enemies. Apart from dramatizing the brutality of exploitative capitalism (not capitalism as such, necessarily), the significance of Casy's death lies in its indication of his love of man, a love that risked death even as Tom assumes Casy's mission at the same risk. This love of man, channeled by a democratic sense of social justice and a realistic sense of pragmatic action, explains Casy's compulsion to serve his fellow man, and his willingness to take the blame, after striking down the deputy, in order to save Tom from arrest. Sacrificial in appearance, this latter action is motivated by a pragmatic social idealism.

After Casy's death, Tom consciously accepts the mission of Casy's practical humanitarianism as more inspiring and realistic than Christian resignation to circumstance and the promise of heavenly reward.

The strained quality of Shockley's thesis is most apparent, however, in his interpretation of the final scene, where Rosasharn gives her breast milk to save the life of the starving old man. Here an attempt is made to cram a stark, primal symbol into the mold of orthodox Christian symbolism and doctrine. Having identified Casy's gospel as "innocent of Paulism, Catholicism and Puritanism," Shockley now identifies Rosasharn's symbolic action with Communion or Mass and with the "resurrective aspect of Christ"! How much simpler is Carpenter's remark that in this scene Rosasharn "symbolically transmutes her maternal love to a love of all people." As implied by her smile and hair-stroking gesture, Rosasharn, whose maternal instinct has been frustrated, feels a momentary satisfaction. But the beauty and the significance of this scene derive chiefly from its symbolizing the main theme of the novel: the prime function of life is to nourish life. Throughout most of the novel Rosasharn has been a weak, silly, and sentimental woman—an ironic contrast to the idealized Rose of Sharon of the "Song of Solomon." And yet in this closing scene common biology and psychology are transcended and transformed by a symbolic meaning that grows out of the natural, right, and compassionate quality of the action itself and out of the already developed structure of symbolism and meaning. In fact, I can think of no more impressive example of what William Sansom recently (*NYTBR*, 30 Dec. 1956) termed the *round* ending, one "that truly 'rounds off' the book, completing as a broad and living thing—an egg, if you like, rather than a straight thin line between arbitrary points. Round indeed as the final chords of a symphony—whose quality is not only finality but also a balanced suggestion that the music really continues . . . an ending must suggest the continuance of life, and, by definition, of that which makes life continuable and endurable, hope: the end thus must be a statement of beginning."

That this "roundness" and significance lies not in any specifically Christian symbolism can be seen in Steinbeck's careful preparation of the primary symbolic structure of the novel, a body of symbolism which, in keeping with the theme, is both naturalistic and experiential. Ch. 1, for instance, describes the way the elemental forces in nature turn into dust and death. In the last paragraph of this chapter the men attempt to think through their frustration as they face this drought of life. Here, at the outset, is implied the universal interdependence or ecological balance of man and nature. In Ch. 3, the second of a series of symbolic interchapters, the turtle is a remarkable example of creative nature symbolism, further developing the idea of interdependence and introducing the central theme, the primal drive of life. The former is implied by the description of the seeds in the opening paragraph, and of the way the head of oats caught by the turtle's leg is dropped and covered with earth by the turtle's shell. The latter theme is symbolized by the turtle's dogged movement forward, the way all life naturally seeks to go somewhere through an instinctive urge to self-realization.

In Ch. 4 Tom picks up the turtle, strokes the smooth, clean, creamy yellow underside with his finger and then rolls it up in his coat, as if identifying himself with its sensitivity, previously described by the turtle's sudden reaction when a red ant irritated the soft skin under the shell. A few pages further on in this chapter and also in Ch. 6 Tom and Casy find in the turtle's fixed sense of direction and purpose—briefly re-enforced by the sight of the shepherd dog trotting fast down the road, heedless of Tom's whistle—a point of common meaning for the idea that people too have a right to "go someplace."

This sort of nature symbolism recurs throughout the novel but, as these first chapters have illustrated, the nature symbols tend increasingly to relate to human situations and events that themselves have symbolic values. Among these we might note the tractor and its driver (5), Muley (6), the second-hand car dealer (7), Highway 66, the Joads' truck, the empty abandoned houses (11), the federal camp, the Hooverville camp, Noah's departure, the death and burial of Grampa, Casy's death, and the flood. Along with the main characters, these events are presented with such vividness and representative value as to become dramatic symbols of basic attitudes, conflicts and purposes in life—some social, others universal or epic. The social truths implied range from the tyranny of words (the handbills), the crime of monopoly (the evils of absentee ownership), economic exploitation, and the tragedy of direct action, to the positive values of folk fellowship, folk morality (the new Law of the Road) developed out of the migration (17), group action and democracy-in-process (22). But the most significant level is the epic level of the universally human: man's dependence on the primal elements (water, sun, fire, land), and the epic nature of sex, womanhood, family life, death, mutualism of spirit, and the epic idea of the race of man. The final though separate identifications with humanity of both Tom and Rosasharn underscore the epic idea that all men are brothers because all men belong to the Race of Man. This emphasis on the transcendent yet real unity of spirit is clearly more than a "biological approach to ethics" (Hyman).

The Grapes of Wrath is epic in form as well as theme, mainly through the skillful interweaving of the interchapters and the narrative chapters. It is undoubtedly this basic structure that Steinbeck had in mind when he described the structure of this novel as "very carefully worked out."

Many critics have found in Steinbeck's work an element of the mystical, the mysterious, or the religious. But as Steinbeck's search for spiritual values looks inside human experience, nature, and the life process, it is teleological only in the scientific (not the metaphysical) sense of the term. Steinbeck's naturalism goes beyond both the mechanistic determinism of Dreiser and the mystic dualism of traditional Christianity. Steinbeck lifts the biology of stimulus-response to the biology of spirit, much as Edmund W. Sinnott has done in his studies of cell and psyche. His epic mutualism is neither romantic, nor mystic, nor Christian; it is an experiential discovery of the process by which "physiological man" becomes the "whole man" (*Sea of Cortez*, p. 87). As such it is a humanistic integration of the knowledge of man made available by modern science, philosophy, and art.

From *College English* 19 (1958): 172-175. Originally published by the National Council of Teachers of English.

Works Cited

Carpenter, Frederic I. "The Philosophical Joads." *College English* 2.4 (Jan. 1941): 315-25.

Fairley, Barker. "John Steinbeck and the Coming Literature." *Sewanee Review* 50.2 (Apr.-Jun. 1942): 145-61.

Hyman, Arthur. *Philosophy in the Middle Ages: The Christian, Islamic, and Jewish Traditions*. Indianapolis: Hackett, 1952.

Sansom, William. Rev. of *The Grapes of Wrath*, by John Steinbeck. *New York Times Book Review* 30 Dec. 1956.

Shockley, Martin. "Christian Symbolism in *The Grapes of Wrath*." *College English* 18.2 (Nov. 1956): 87-90.

Sinnott, Edmund W. *Cell and Psyche: The Biology of Purpose*. Chapel Hill: U of North Carolina P, 1950.

The Grapes of Wrath as Fiction _____

Peter Lisca

When *The Grapes of Wrath* was published in April of 1939 there was little likelihood of its being accepted and evaluated as a piece of fiction. Because of its nominal subject, it was too readily confused with such high-class reporting as Ruth McKenny's *Industrial Valley*, the WPA collection of case histories called *These Are Our Lives*, and Dorothea Lange and Paul S. Taylor's *An American Exodus*. The merits of *The Grapes of Wrath* were debated as social documentation rather than fiction. In addition to incurring the disadvantages of its historical position, coming as a kind of climax to the literature of the Great Depression, Steinbeck's novel also suffered from the perennial vulnerability of all social fiction to an attack on its facts and intentions.

The passage of eighteen years has done very little to alter this initial situation. Except for scattered remarks, formal criticism of *The Grapes of Wrath* is still pretty much limited to a chapter by Joseph Warren Beach, a chapter by Harry Thornton Moore, a few paragraphs by Kenneth Burke, part of a chapter by the French critic Claude-Edmonde Magny, and an essay by B. R. McElderry, Jr.[1] In a period of such intensive analysis of the techniques of fiction as the past fifteen years, the dearth of critical material on *The Grapes of Wrath* must indicate an assumption on the part of critics that this novel cannot sustain such analysis. The present paper is an attempt to correct this assumption by exploring some of the techniques by which John Steinbeck was able to give significant form to his sprawling materials and prevent his novel of social protest from degenerating into propaganda.

The ideas and materials of *The Grapes of Wrath* presented Steinbeck with a problem of structure similar to that of Tolstoy's in writing *War and Peace*. Tolstoy's materials were, roughly, the adventures of the Bezukhov, Rostov, and Bolkonski families on the one hand, and the Napoleonic Wars on the other. And while the plot development brought these two blocks of material together, there was enough about

---

the Napoleonic Wars left over so that the author had to incorporate it in separate philosophic interchapters. Steinbeck's materials were similar. There were the adventures of the Joads, the Wilsons, and the Wainwrights; there was also the Great Depression. And like Tolstoy, he had enough material left over to write separate philosophic interchapters.

In the light of this basic analogy, Percy Lubbock's comments on the structural role of these two elements in *War and Peace* become significant for an understanding of structure in *The Grapes of Wrath*: "I can discover no angle at which the two stories will appear to unite and merge in a single impression. Neither is subordinated to the other, and there is nothing above them . . . to which they are both related. Nor are they placed together to illustrate a contrast; nothing results from their juxtaposition. Only from time to time, upon no apparent principle and without a word of warning, one of them is dropped and the other is resumed."[2] In these few phrases Lubbock has defined the aesthetic conditions not only for *War and Peace* but for any other piece of fiction whose strategies include an intercalary construction—*The Grapes of Wrath*, for example. The test is whether anything results from this kind of structure.

Counting the opening description of the drought and the penultimate chapter on the rains, pieces of straightforward description allowable even to strictly "scenic" novels (Lubbock's term for materials presented entirely from the reader's point of view), there are in *The Grapes of Wrath* sixteen interchapters, making up a total of just under a hundred pages—almost one sixth of the book. In none of these chapters do the Joads, Wilsons, or Wainwrights appear.

These interchapters have two main functions. First, by presenting the social background they serve to amplify the pattern of action created by the Joad family. Thus, for example, Chapter i presents in panoramic terms the drought which forces the Joads off their land; Chapters vii and ix depict, respectively, the buying of jalopies for the migration and the selling of household goods; Chapter xi describes at length a decaying and deserted house which is the prototype of all the houses abandoned in the Dust Bowl. In thirteen such chapters almost every aspect of the Joads' adventures is enlarged and seen as part of the social climate. The remaining interchapters have the function of providing such historical information as the development of land ownership in California, the consequent development of migrant labor, and certain economic aspects of the social lag. These three informative chapters make up only nineteen of the novel's six hundred-odd pages. Scattered through the sixteen interchapters are occasional paragraphs whose purpose is to present, with choric effect, the philosophy or social message to which the current situation gives rise. For the most part these paragraphs occur in four chapters—ix, xi, xiv, and xix.

While all of these various materials are obviously ideologically related to the longer narrative section of the novel (five hundred pages), there remains the problem of their aesthetic integration with the book as a whole. Even a cursory reading will show that there is a general correspondence between the material of each interchapter and that of the current narrative portion. The magnificent opening description of the drought sets forth the condition which gives rise to the novel's action; Highway 66 is given a chapter as the Joads begin their trek on that historic route; the chapters dealing with migrant life appear interspersed with the narrative of the Joads' actual journey; the last interchapter, xxix, describes the rain in which the action of the novel ends.

A more careful reading will make evident that this integration of the interchapters into a total structure goes far beyond this merely complementary juxtaposition. There is in addition an intricate interweaving of specific details. Like the anonymous house in the interchapter (v), one corner of the Joad house has been knocked off its foundation by a tractor (pp. 52-53, 54).[3] The man who in the interchapter threatens the tractor driver with his rifle becomes Grampa Joad, except that whereas the anonymous tenant does not fire, Grampa shoots out both headlights (pp. 53, 62). The tractor driver in the interchapter, Joe Davis, is a family acquaintance of the anonymous tenants, as Willy is an acquaintance of the Joads in the narrative chapter (pp. 50, 62). The jalopy sitting in the Joads' front yard is the same kind of jalopy described in the used-car lot of Chapter vii. Chapter viii ends with Al Joad driving off to sell a truckload of household goods. Chapter ix is an interchapter describing anonymous farmers selling such goods, including many items which the Joads themselves are selling—pumps, farming tools, furniture, a team and wagon for ten dollars. In the following chapter Al Joad returns with an empty truck, having sold everything for eighteen dollars—including ten dollars for a team and wagon. Every interchapter is tied into the book's narrative portion by this kind of specific cross-reference, which amplifies the Joads' typical actions to the level of a communal experience.

Often, this interlocking of details becomes thematic or symbolic. The dust which is mentioned twenty-seven times in three pages of Chapter i comes to stand not only for the land itself but also for the basic situation out of which the novel's action develops. Everything which moves on the ground, from insects to trucks, raises a proportionate amount of dust: "a walking man lifted a thin layer as high as his waist" (p. 4). When Tom returns home after four years in prison and gets out of the truck which had given him a ride, he steps off the highway and performs the symbolic ritual of taking off his new, prison-issue shoes and carefully working his bare feet into the dust. He then moves off across the land, "making a cloud that hung low to the ground behind him" (p. 23).

One of the novel's most important symbols, the turtle, is presented in what is actually the first interchapter (iii). And while this chapter is a masterpiece of realistic description (often included as such in Freshman English texts), it is also obvious that the turtle is symbolic and its adventures prophetic allegory. "Nobody can't keep a turtle though," says Jim Casy. "They work at it and work at it, and at last one day they get out and away they go . . ." (p. 28). The indomitable life force that drives the turtle drives the Joads, and in the same direction—southwest. As the turtle picks up seeds in its shell and drops them on the other side of the road, so the Joads pick up life in Oklahoma and carry it across the country to California. (As Grandfather in "The Leader of the People" puts it, "We carried life out here and set it down the way those ants carry eggs.") As the turtle survives the truck's attempts to smash it on the highway and as it crushes the red ant which runs into its shell, so the Joads endure the perils of their journey.

This symbolic value is retained and further defined when the turtle enters specifically into the narrative. Its incident with the red ant is echoed two hundred and seventy pages later when another red ant runs over "the folds of loose skin" on Granma's neck and she reaches up with her "little wrinkled claws"; Ma Joad picks it off and crushes it (p. 286). In Chapter iii the turtle is seen "dragging his high-domed shell across the grass." In the next chapter, Tom sees "the high-domed back of a land turtle" and picking up the turtle, carries it with him (p. 24). It is only when he is convinced that his family has left the land that he releases the turtle, which travels "southwest as it had been from the first," a direction which is repeated in the next two sentences. The first thing which Tom does after releasing the turtle is to put on his shoes, which he had taken off when he left the highway and stepped onto the land (p. 60). Thus, not only the turtle but also Tom's connection with it is symbolic, as symbolic as Lennie's appearance in *Of Mice and Men* with a dead mouse in his pocket.

In addition to this constant knitting together of the two kinds of chapters, often the interchapters are further assimilated into the narrative portion by incorporating in themselves the techniques of fiction. The general conflict between small farmers and the banks, for example, is presented as an imaginary dialogue, each speaker personifying the sentiments of his group. And although neither speaker is a "real" person, both are dramatically differentiated and their arguments embody details particular to the specific social condition. This kind of dramatization is also evident in such chapters as those concerning the buying of used cars, the selling of household goods, the police intimidation of migrants, and others.

Because Steinbeck's subject in *The Grapes of Wrath* is not the adventures of the Joad family so much as the social conditions which occasion them, these interchapters serve a vital purpose. As Percy Lubbock has pointed out, the purely "scenic" technique "is out of the question . . . whenever the story is too big, too comprehensive, too widely ranging to be treated scenically, with no opportunity for general and panoramic survey. . . . These stories, therefore, which will not naturally accommodate themselves to the reader's point of view, and the reader's alone, we regard as rather pictorial than dramatic—meaning that they call for some narrator, somebody who *knows*, to contemplate the facts and create an impression of them" (pp. 254-255).

Steinbeck's story certainly is "big," "comprehensive," and "wide ranging." But although he tried to free his materials by utilizing what Lubbock calls "pictorial" as well as "scenic" techniques, he also took pains to keep these techniques from breaking the novel in two parts. The cross-reference of detail, the interweaving symbols, and the dramatization are designed to make the necessary "pictorial" sections of the novel tend toward the "scenic." Conversely, an examination of the narrative portion of *The Grapes of Wrath* will reveal that its techniques make the "scenic" tend toward the "pictorial." Steinbeck worked from both sides to make the two kinds of chapters approach each other and fuse into a single impression.

That the narrative portion of *The Grapes of Wrath* tends toward the "pictorial" can be seen readily if the book is compared to another of Steinbeck's social novels, *In Dubious Battle*, which has a straightforward plot development and an involving action. Of course things happen in *The Grapes of Wrath*, and what happens not only grows out of what has gone before but grows into what will happen in the future. But while critics have perceived that plot is not the organizational principle of the novel, they have not attempted to relate this fact to the novel's materials as they are revealed through other techniques, assuming instead that this lack of plot constitutes one of the novel's major flaws. Actually, this lack of an informing plot is instrumental in at least two ways. It could reasonably be expected that the greatest threat to the novel's unity would come from the interchapters' constant breaking up of the narrative line of action. But the very fact that *The Grapes of Wrath* is *not* organized by a unifying plot works for absorbing these interchapters smoothly into its texture. A second way in which this tendency of the "scenic" toward the "pictorial" is germane to the novel's materials becomes evident when it is considered that Steinbeck's subject is not an action so much as a situation. Description, therefore, must often substitute for narration.

This substitution of the static for the dynamic also gives us an insight into the nature and function of the novel's characters, who often have been called "puppets," "symbolic marionettes," and "symbols," but seldom real people. While there are scant objective grounds for determining whether a novel's characters are "real," one fruitful approach is to consider fictional characters not only in relation to life but in relation to the *rest* of the fiction of which they are a part.

In his Preface to *The Forgotten Village*, which immediately followed *The Grapes of Wrath*, Steinbeck comments on just these relationships.

A great many documentary films have used the generalized method, that is, the showing of a condition or an event as it affects a group of people. The audience can then have a personalized reaction from imagining one member of that group. I have felt that this was the more difficult observation from the audience's viewpoint. It means very little to know that a million Chinese are starving unless you know one Chinese who is starving. In *The Forgotten Village* we reversed the usual process. Our story centered on one family in one small village. We wished our audience to know this family very well, and incidentally to like it, as we did. Then, from association with this little personalized group, the larger conclusion concerning the racial group could be drawn with something like participation.[4]

This is precisely the strategy in *The Grapes of Wrath*. Whatever value the Joads have as individuals is "incidental" to their primary function as a "personalized group." Kenneth Burke has pointed out that "most of the characters derive their role, which is to say their personality, purely from their relationship to the basic situation" (p. 91). But what he takes to be a serious weakness is actually one of the book's greatest accomplishments. The characters are so absorbed into the novel's "basic situation" that the reader's response goes beyond sympathy for individuals to moral indignation about their social condition. This is, of course, precisely Steinbeck's intention. And certainly the Joads are admirably suited for this purpose. This conception of character is parallel to the fusing of the "scenic" and "pictorial" techniques in the narrative and interchapters.

Although the diverse materials of *The Grapes of Wrath* made organization by a unifying plot difficult, nevertheless the novel does have structural form. The action progresses through three successive movements, and its significance is revealed by an intricate system of themes and symbols.

The Grapes of Wrath is divided into thirty consecutive chapters with no larger grouping; but even a cursory reading reveals that the novel is made up of three major parts: the drought, the journey, and California. The first section ends with Chapter x (p. 156). It is separated from the second section, the journey, by *two* interchapters. The first of these chapters presents a final picture of the deserted land—"The houses were left vacant on the land, and the land was vacant because of this." The second interchapter is devoted to Highway 66. It is followed by Chapter xiii, which begins the Joads' journey on that historic highway—"The ancient overloaded Hudson creaked and grunted to the highway at Sallisaw and turned west, and the sun was blinding" (p. 167). The journey section extends past the geographical California border, across the desert to Bakersfield (pp. 167-314). This section ends with Chapter xviii—"And the truck rolled down the mountain into the great valley"—and the next chapter begins the California section by introducing the reader to labor conditions in that state. Steinbeck had this tripartite division in mind as early as September of 1937, when he told one interviewer that he was working on "the first of three related longer novels."[5]

This structure has its roots in the Old Testament. The novel's three sections correspond to the oppression in Egypt, the exodus, and the sojourn in the land of Canaan, which in both accounts is first viewed from the mountains. The parallel is not worked out in detail, but the grand design is there: the plagues (erosion), the Egyptians (banks), the exodus (journey), and the hostile tribes of Canaan (Californians).

This Biblical structure is supported by a continuum of symbols and symbolic actions. The most pervasive symbolism is that of grapes. The novel's title, taken from "The Battle Hymn of the Republic" ("He is tramping out the vintage where the grapes of wrath are stored"), is itself a reference to Revelation: "And the angel thrust in his sickle into the earth, and gathered the vine of the earth, and cast it into the great winepress of the wrath of God" (xiv.19). Similarly in Deuteronomy: "Their grapes are grapes of gall, their clusters are bitter. Their wine is the poison of serpents" (xxxii.32); in Jeremiah: "The fathers have eaten sour grapes, and their children's teeth are set on edge" (xxxi.29). Sometimes these aspects of the symbol are stated in the novel's interchapters: "In the souls of the people the grapes of wrath are filling and growing heavy, heavy for the vintage" (pp. 447, 388).

But Steinbeck also uses grapes for symbols of plenty, as the one huge cluster of grapes which Joshua and Oshea bring back from their first excursion into the rich land of Canaan, a cluster so huge that "they bare it between two on a staff" (Num. xiii.23). It is this meaning of grapes that is frequently alluded to by Grampa Joad: "Gonna get me a whole big bunch of grapes off a bush, or whatever, an' I'm gonna squash 'em on my face an' let 'em run offen my chin" (p. 112). Although Grampa dies long before the Joads get to California, he is symbolically present through the anonymous old man in the barn (stable), who is saved from starvation by Rosasharn's breasts: "This thy stature is like to a palm tree, and thy breasts to clusters of grapes" (Cant. vii.7).[6] Rosasharn's giving of new life to the old man is another reference to the orthodox interpretation of Canticles: "I [Christ] am the rose of Sharon, and the lily of the valleys" (ii.1); and to the Gospels: "take, eat; this is my body." Still another important Biblical symbol is *Jim Casy* (Jesus Christ), who will be discussed in another connection.

Closely associated with this latter symbolic meaning of grapes and the land of Canaan is Ma Joad's frequent assertion that "We are the people." She has not been reading Carl Sandburg; she has been reading her Bible. As she tells Tom when he is looking for a suitable verse to bury with Grampa, "Turn to Psalms, over further. You kin always get somepin outa Psalms" (p. 195). And it is from Psalms that she gets her phrase: "For he is our God; and we are the people of his pasture, and the sheep of his hand" (xcv.7). They are the people who pick up life in Oklahoma (Egypt) and carry it to California (Canaan) as the turtle picks up seeds and as the ants pick up their eggs in "The Leader of the People." These parallels to the Hebrews of Exodus are all brought into focus when, near the end of the novel, Uncle John sets Rose of Sharon's stillborn child in an old apple crate (like Moses in the basket), sets the box in a stream "among the willow stems" and floats it toward the town saying, "Go down an' tell 'em" (p. 609).

As the Israelites developed a code of laws in their exodus, so do the migrants: "The families learned what rights must be observed—the right of privacy in the tent . . . the right of the hungry to be fed; the right of the pregnant and the sick to transcend all other rights" (p. 265). Chapter xvii can be seen as the "Deuteronomy" of *The Grapes of Wrath*. It is this kind of context which makes of the Joads' journey "out west" an archetype of mass migration.[7]

The novel's Biblical structure and symbolism are supported by Steinbeck's skillful use of an Old Testament prose. The extent to which he succeeded in recreating the epic dignity of this prose can be demonstrated by arranging a typical passage from the novel according to phrases, in the manner of the Bates Bible, leaving the punctuation intact except for capitals.

The tractors had lights shining,
For there is no day and night for a tractor
And the disks turn the earth in the darkness
And they glitter in the daylight.

And when a horse stops work and goes into the barn
There is a life and a vitality left,
There is a breathing and a warmth,
And the feet shift on the straw,
And the jaws champ on the hay,
And the ears and the eyes are alive.
There is a warmth of life in the barn,
And the heat and smell of life.

But when the motor of a tractor stops,
It is as dead as the ore it came from.
The heat goes out of it
Like the living heat that leaves a corpse.

(p. 157)

The parallel grammatical structure of parallel meanings, the simplicity of diction, the balance, the concrete details, the summary sentences, the reiterations—all are here. Note also the organization: four phrases for the tractor, eight for the horse, four again for the tractor. Except for the terms of machinery, this passage might be one of the psalms.

It is this echo—more, this pedal point—evident even in the most obviously "directed" passages, which supports their often simple philosophy, imbuing them with a dignity which their content alone could not sustain. The style gives them their authority:

Burn coffee for fuel in the ships. Burn corn to keep warm, it makes a hot fire. Dump potatoes in the rivers and place guards along the banks to keep the hungry people from fishing them out. Slaughter the pigs and bury them, and let the putrescence drip down into the earth.

There is a crime here that goes beyond denunciation. There is a sorrow here that weeping cannot symbolize. There is a failure here that topples all our success. The fertile earth, the straight tree rows, the sturdy trunks, and the ripe fruit. And children dying of pellagra must die because a profit cannot be taken from an orange. (p. 477)

These passages are not complex philosophy, but they may well be profound. The Biblical resonance which gives them authority is used discreetly, is never employed on the trivial and particular, and its recurrence has a cumulative effect.

There are many other distinct prose styles in the interchapters of *The Grapes of Wrath*, and each is just as functional in its place. There is, for example, the harsh, staccato prose of Chapter vii, which is devoted to the sale of used cars.

Cadillacs, La Salles, Buicks, Plymouths, Packards, Chevvies, Fords, Pontiacs. Row on row, headlights glinting in the afternoon sun. Good Used Cars.

Soften 'em up Joe. Jesus, I wisht I had a thousand jalopies! Get 'em ready to deal, an' I'll close 'em.

Goin' to California? Here's jus' what you need. Looks shot, but they's thousan's of miles in her.

Lined up side by side. Good Used Cars. Bargains. Clean runs good. (p. 89)

A good contrast to this prose style is offered by Chapter ix, which presents the loss and despair of people forced to abandon their household goods. Here the prose style itself takes on their dazed resignation.

The women sat among the doomed things, turning them over and looking past them and back. This book. My father had it. He liked a book. *Pilgrim's Progress.* Used to read it. Got his name in it. And his pipe—still smells rank. And this picture—an angel. I looked at that before the fust three come—didn't seem to do much good. Think we could get this china dog in? Aunt Sadie brought it from the St. Louis Fair. See? Wrote right on it. No, I guess not. Here's a letter my brother wrote the day before he died. Here's an old-time hat. These feathers—never got to use them. No, there isn't room. (p. 120)

At times, as in the description of a folk dance in Chapter xxiii, the prose style becomes a veritable chameleon: "Look at that Texas boy, long legs loose, taps four times for ever' damn step. Never see a boy swing aroun' like that. Look at him swing that Cherokee girl, red in cheeks and her toe points out" (p. 449). No other American novel has succeeded in forging and making instrumental so many prose styles.

This rapid shifting of prose style and technique has value as Americana and contributes to a "realism" far beyond that of literal reporting. Also, this rapid shifting is important because it tends to destroy any impression that these interchapters are, as a group, a separate entity. They are a group only in that they are not a direct part of the narrative. They have enough individuality of subject matter, prose style, and technique to keep the novel from falling into two parts, and to keep the reader from feeling that he is now reading "the other part."

In addition to the supporting Biblical structure and context, the interchapters and narrative section are held together by an interweaving of two opposing themes which make up the "plot" of *The Grapes of Wrath.* One of these, the negative one, concerns itself with the increasingly straitened circumstances of the Joads. At the beginning of their journey they have $154, their household goods, two barrels of pork, a serviceable truck, and their good health. As the novel progresses they become more and more impoverished until at the end they are destitute, without food, sick, their truck and goods abandoned in the mud, without shelter, and without hope of work. This economic decline is paralleled by a disintegration of the family's morale. The Joads start off as a cheerful group full of hope and willpower and by the end of the novel are spiritually bankrupt. As Steinbeck had noted about the migrants around Bakersfield three years earlier, they "feel that paralyzed dullness with which the mind protects itself against too much sorrow and too much pain."[8] When the Joads enter their first Hooverville they catch a glimpse of the deterioration which lies ahead of them. They see filthy tin and rug shacks littered with trash, the children dirty and diseased, the heads of families "bull-simple" from being roughed-up too often, all spirit gone and in its place a whining, passive resistance to authority. Although the novel ends before the Joads come to this point, in the last chapter they are well on their way.

And as the family group declines morally and economically, so the family unit itself breaks up. Grampa dies before they are out of Oklahoma and lies in a nameless grave; Granma is buried a pauper; Noah deserts the family; Connie deserts Rosasharn; the baby is born dead; Tom becomes a fugitive; Al is planning to leave as soon as possible; Casy is killed; and they are forced to abandon the Wilsons.

These two negative or downward movements are balanced by two positive or upward movements. Although the primitive family unit is breaking up, the fragments are going to make up a larger group. The sense of a communal unit grows steadily through the narrative—the Wilsons, the Wainwrights—and is pointed to again and again in the interchapters: "One man, one family driven from the land; this rusty car creaking along the highway to the west. I lost my land, a single tractor took my land. I am alone and I am bewildered. And in the night one family camps in a ditch and another family pulls in and the tents come out. The two men squat on their hams and the women and children listen. . . . For here 'I lost my land' is changed; a cell is split and from its splitting grows the thing you [owners] hate—'We lost *our* land'" (p. 206). Oppression and intimidation only serve to strengthen the social group; the relief offered by a federal migrant camp only gives them a vision of the democratic life they can attain by cooperation, which is why the local citizens are opposed to these camps.

Another of the techniques by which Steinbeck develops this theme of unity can be illustrated by the Joads' relationship with the Wilson family of Kansas, which they meet just before crossing the Oklahoma border. This relationship is developed not so much by explicit statement, as in the interchapters, as by symbols. Grampa Joad, for example, dies in the Wilsons' tent and is buried in one of the Wilsons' blankets. Furthermore, the epitaph which is buried with Grampa (in Oklahoma soil) is written on a page torn from the Wilsons' Bible—that page usually reserved for family births, marriages, and deaths. In burying this page with Grampa the Wilsons symbolize not only their adoption of the Joads, but their renouncing of hope for continuing their own family line. Also, note it is the more destitute Wilson family which embraces the Joads. Steinbeck makes of the two families' relationship a microcosm of the migration's total picture, its human significance.

This growing awareness on the part of the people en masse is paralleled by the education and conversion of Tom and Casy. At the beginning of the book, Tom's attitude is individualistic. He is looking out for himself. As he puts it, "I'm still laying my dogs down one at a time," and "I climb fences when I got fences to climb" (p. 237). His first real lesson comes when Casy strikes out against the trooper to save his friend and then gives himself up in his place (p. 361). The section immediately following is that of the family's stay in a federal migrant camp, and here Tom's education is advanced still further. By the time Casy is killed, Tom is ready for his conversion, which he seals by revenging his mentor. While Tom is hiding out in the cave after having struck the vigilante, he has time to think of Casy and his message, so that in his last meeting with his mother, in which he asserts his spiritual unity with all men, it is evident that he has moved from material and personal resentment to ethical indignation, from particulars to principles. It is significant that this last meeting between mother and son should take place under conditions reminiscent of the prenatal state.

The entrance to the cave is covered with black vines and the interior is damp and completely dark, so that the contact of mother and son is actually physical rather than visual; she gives him food. When Tom comes out of the cave after announcing his conversion it is as though he were reborn. When Tom says, "An' when our folks eat the stuff they raise an' live in the houses they build—why I'll be there," he is paraphrasing Isaiah: "And they shall build houses and inhabit them, they shall not build and another inhabit; they shall not plant and another eat" (lxv, 21-22).

The development of Jim Casy is similar to that of Tom. He moves from Bible-belt evangelism to social prophecy. At the beginning of the book he has already left preaching and has returned from "in the hills, thinkin', almost you might say like Jesus went into the wilderness to think His way out of a mess of troubles" (p. 109). But although Casy is already approaching his revelation of the Over-Soul, it is only through his experiences with the Joads that he is able to complete his vision. As Tom moves from material resentment to ethical indignation, so Casy moves from the purely speculative to the pragmatic. Both move from stasis to action. Casy's Christlike development is complete when he dies saying, "You don' know what you're a doin'" (p. 527). Those critics are reading superficially who, like Elizabeth N. Monroe, think that Steinbeck "expects us to admire Casy, an itinerant preacher, who, overexcited from his evangelistic revivals, is in the habit of taking one or another of the girls in his audience to lie in the grass."[9] Actually, Casy himself perceives the incongruity of this behavior, which is why he goes "into the wilderness" and renounces his Bible-belt evangelism for a species of social humanism, and his congregation for the human race. His development, like that of Tom, is symbolic of the changing social condition which is the novel's essential theme, paralleling the development of the Joad family as a whole, which is, again, but a "personalized group." Casy resembles Ralph Waldo Emerson more than he does Lewis' Elmer Gantry or Caldwell's Semon Dye. For like Emerson, Casy discovers the Over-Soul through intuition and rejects his congregation in order to preach to the world.[10]

Because these themes of education and conversion are not the central, involving action of the novel, but grow slowly out of a rich and solid context, the development of Tom and Casy achieves an authority lacking in most proletarian fiction. The novel's thematic organization also makes it possible for Steinbeck successfully to incorporate the widest variety of materials, and with the exception of romantic love, to present a full scale of human emotions.

This ability of Steinbeck's thematic structure to absorb incidents organically into its context is important for an understanding of the novel's last scene, of which there has been much criticism. The novel's materials do make a climactic ending difficult. The author faced three pitfalls: a *deus ex machina* ending; a summing up, moral essay; and simply a new level of horror. But the novel's thematic treatment of material made it possible for Steinbeck to end on a high point, to bring his novel to a symbolic climax without doing violence to credulity, structure, or theme.

This climax is prepared for by the last interchapter, which parallels in terms of rain the opening description of the drought. The last paragraphs of these chapters are strikingly similar:

The women studied the men's faces secretly. . . . After a while the faces of the watching men lost their bemused perplexity and became hard and angry and resistant. Then the women knew that they were safe and that there was no break. (p. 6)

The women watched the men, watched to see whether the break had come at last. . . . And where a number of men gathered together, the fear went from their faces, and anger took its place. And the women sighed with relief, for they knew it was all right—the break had not come. (p. 592)

With this latter paragraph, a recapitulation of the novel's two main themes as they are worked out in three movements, *The Grapes of Wrath* is brought full circle. The last chapter compactly reenacts the whole drama of the Joads' journey in one uninterrupted continuity of suspense. The rain continues to fall; the little mud levee collapses; Rosasharn's baby is born dead; the boxcar must be abandoned; they take to the highway in search of food and find instead a starving man. Then the miracle happens. As Rose of Sharon offers her breast to the old man the novel's two counter themes are brought together in a symbolic paradox. Out of her own need she gives life; out of the profoundest depth of despair comes the greatest assertion of faith.[11]

Steinbeck's great achievement in *The Grapes of Wrath* is that while minimizing what seem to be the most essential elements of fiction—plot and character—he was able to create a well-made and emotionally compelling novel out of materials which in most other hands have resulted in sentimental propaganda.

Notes

1. *American Fiction 1920-1940* (New York: Macmillan, 1941), pp. 327-347; *The Novels of John Steinbeck* (Chicago: Normandie House, 1939), pp. 54-72; *The Philosophy of Literary Form* (Louisiana State Univ. Press, 1941), p. 81; *L'Age du roman américain* (Paris: Editions du Sueil, 1948), pp. 178-195; "*The Grapes of Wrath*: In the Light of Modern Critical Theory," *College English*, v (March 1944), 308-313.

2. *The Craft of Fiction* (New York: Peter Smith, 1945), p. 33.

3. This and all subsequent references are to the 1st ed. of *The Grapes of Wrath* (Viking Press, 1939).

4. New York: Viking Press, 1941.

5. Joseph Henry Jackson, "John Steinbeck: A Portrait," *Sat. Rev. of Lit.*, xvi (25 Sept. 1937), 18.

6. One of the oddest interpretations of this scene is Harry Slochower's in *No Voice Is Wholly Lost* (New York: Creative Age Press, 1945), p. 304, n. Mr. Slochower uses this incident to explain the novel's title: "The grapes have turned to 'wrath,' indicated by the fact that the first milk of the mother is said to be bitter."

7. In a recent article Bernard Bowron fails to perceive this larger significance of the Joads' journey and attempts to make far too much out of some obvious similarities to the Covered Wagon genre. "*The Grapes of Wrath*: A 'Wagons West' Romance," *Colorado Quart.*, iii (Summer 1954), 84-91.

8. "The Harvest Gypsies," *San Francisco News*, 6 Oct. 1936, p. 3.

9. *The Novel and Society* (Univ. of North Carolina Press, 1941), p. 18.

10. Further parallels between Casy and Christ: see Martin Shockley's "Christian Symbolism in *The Grapes of Wrath*," *College English*, xviii (Nov., 1956), 87-90.

11. For parallels to this scene see Maupassant's "Idylle"; Byron's *Childe Harold*, Can. iv, St. 148-151; Rubens' painting of old Cimon taking milk from the breast of Pero; and an 18th-century play called *The Grecian's Daughter*, discussed in Maurice W. Disher's *Blood and Thunder* (London: Frederick Muller Ltd., 1949), p. 23. See also Celeste T. Wright, "Ancient Analogues of an Incident in John Steinbeck," *WF*, xiv (Jan., 1955), 50-51.

From Patriarchy to Matriarchy:
Ma Joad's Role in *The Grapes of Wrath*_____

Warren Motley

As the Joad clan disintegrates under the pressure of dispossession and migration, Ma Joad emerges as a central, cohesive force. However, critics exploring the social thinking behind *The Grapes of Wrath* have tended to give her short shrift. Many of them have looked to the articulate Jim Casy rather than to the reticent Joads to explain the family's gradual realization that their survival depends on communal cooperation.[1] I wish to correct that imbalance now. I shall argue that the Joad family shifts from a patriarchal structure to a predominantly matriarchal one. So doing, they dramatize the influence of the anthropologist Robert Briffault on John Steinbeck as he tried to understand the Depression.

Focusing too closely on the ideas of Jim Casy distorts the critical view of Ma Joad. She is too often, and mistakenly, set in opposition to the preacher, as if she shared the social values of her individualistic husband. In fact, she is receptive to Casy from the beginning and is thus marked as a cohesive rather than a fragmenting force. But the preacher does not have to convert Ma Joad. Her communal feelings emerge independently of his pronouncements. Working from Briffault's theories on the matriarchal origin of society, Steinbeck presents Ma Joad's growing power as a source of communal strength sheltering human dignity from the antisocial effects of individualism.

Steinbeck observed the Okies' migration across the Southwest at first hand and could not accept the human wreckage trailed along Route 66 as an instance of the human species sloughing off unsuccessful lower members. Seeking intellectual support, he turned to those scientists and thinkers who believed that cooperation rather than competition was the basis of both evolutionary and social progress. They strove to heal what they saw as the post-Darwinian split between scientific thinking and ethical experience. Steinbeck read Jan Smuts's *Ho-*

lism and Evolution and talked of immersing himself in the works of Jan Elif Boodin, author of *The Social Mind*.[2] In analyzing the shift from patriarchy to matriarchy in the Joad family, Steinbeck's reading in *The Mothers* is particularly important. There, Briffault unfolded a vision of social "solidarity [in the matriarchal clan] almost inconceivable and unintelligible to those who have, like ourselves, developed amid the conditions and ideas created by the strenuously competitive and suspicious individualism of modern societies."[3] As Carol Steinbeck commented to Richard Astro, Ma Joad is "pure Briffault."[4]

Briffault published a three-volume edition of *The Mothers* in 1927. No one ever wished it longer than it is, and in 1931 Macmillan printed a more accessible one-volume edition concentrating on the distinctions between matriarchal and patriarchal societies. Drawing on historical records and contemporary anthropological studies, Briffault argued that society first develops on matriarchal lines and that a matriarchal stage universally precedes the patriarchal structure of more advanced societies. Unfortunately, matriarchy is an awkward term, as Briffault himself understood; to most people it erroneously connotes a topsyturvy, Amazonian patriarchy in which "women exercise a domination over the men similar or equivalent to that exercised by the men over the women in a patriarchal social order" (p. 179). But to Briffault matriarchy describes a radically different relationship between people based on cooperation rather than power.

In defining the stages of social evolution and their economic determinants, Briffault closely parallels Friedrich Engels' *The Origin of the Family, Private Property and the State in the Light of the Researches of Lewis H. Morgan*. Briffault and Engels shared a source in Morgan's *Ancient Society* (1877), a study of matriarchal kinship groups among North American Indians. Working from Marx's abstract of *Ancient Society*, Engels declared Morgan's rediscovery of the matriarchal gens to have "the same importance for anthropology as Darwin's theory of evolution for biology and Marx's theory of surplus value for political economy." Hyperbole, no doubt, but Engels, like Briffault and Morgan, was excited to document a society that fostered "'liberty, equality and fraternity'" and that "'in a higher form'" might be revived. Although many anthropologists took up the issue of an earlier matrilineal stage, Briffault's focus on the actual roles and status of women was original. However haphazardly, he gathered copious evidence of the dominant part often played by women in the political and economic life of primitive societies.[5]

Briffault's insistence on the distinctness and precedence of the matriarchal stage reflects his theory that "all familial feeling, all group-sympathy, the essential foundation, therefore, of a social organization, is the direct product of prolonged maternal care, and does not exist apart from it" (p. 57). Gregariousness, he argues, satisfies a behaviorally conditioned need for companionship. It is not a physiological instinct, like breathing or suckling. During their nurturing period, humans develop a fear of solitude and a habit of dependence. Initially the mother appeases the fear and satisfies the need, but later on siblings are accepted as substitutes. Thus the first social groups, Briffault proposed, evolve from biologically linked maternal clans of brothers and sisters rather than from patriarchal families based on sexual bonds (p. 53).

In early societies, a woman's offspring automatically become "legitimate" members of her clan. Therefore, marriage need not regulate sexual activity. If a man forms any lasting association with a woman at all, he becomes part of her group, but his labor is dispensable: "Those functions which in the patriarchal family are discharged by the husband and father . . . are in the maternal group fulfilled by the woman's brothers" (p. 140).

Matriarchal cultures, Briffault observed, are "nothing if not equalitarian" (p. 180). The concepts of authority and domination are "entirely foreign to primitive humanity" because the economic advantages on which power rests do not exist (p. 180). Although labor is divided in matriarchies—men take charge of the hunt and women of the camp—the division is not exploitive. Both men and women work for the community; "the sexes are interdependent, and it is upon that mutual dependence that the association which constitutes society is founded" (p. 175). In fact, if there is a question of advantage, Briffault notes that all the arts and industries of primitive societies—tanning, weaving, potting, home building, and toolmaking—were invented and carried out by women. They then controlled the surplus wealth of the community. Men, on the other hand, had to devote their full energies to providing raw materials for these industries. Consequently, "the disparity in physical power, resourcefulness, enterprise, courage, capacity for endurance, observed in [more advanced, patriarchal] societies and often regarded as organic sexual differences" does not appear between men and women in matriarchies (p. 159).

According to Briffault, most civilized observers, blinded by their assumptions about femininity, misunderstood the status of women in primitive societies. They took a woman's work as a sign of "slavery and oppression" when, on the contrary, the woman in matriarchal societies "is independent because, not in spite of her labour" (p. 189). "Generally speaking," Briffault concluded, "it is in those societies where women toil most that their status is most independent and their influence greatest" (p. 189).

Patriarchy evolved when primitive economies passed from the hunting and gathering stage to the pastoral and agricultural stages and men gained predominate economic power. The domestication of animals, and the later development of advanced agriculture, gave men economic strength and freed them from hunting and the necessity of supplying raw materials for women-controlled production. As men took over home industries and agriculture, then expanding with the growth of trade, the relationship between the sexes underwent a major realignment:

Woman, instead of being the chief producer, became economically unproductive, destitute, and dependent. The contrast between the toiling primitive woman and the idle lady of civilization, which has been mistaken for an indication of the enslavement of the former and the freedom of the latter, marks the opposite relation. It is the primitive toiler who is independent and the unemployed woman who has lost her freedom and is destitute. (p. 248)

Men's monopoly of economic power allowed them to buy the privilege of taking women into their own camps instead of joining the maternal clan; the patriarchal family, based on sexual coupling, replaced the maternal clan as the controlling unit of society.

A definitive shift in values attends the transition to patriarchy. Individualism emerged, Briffault believed, only at the patriarchal stage, not before. The holding of personal and real property separated individuals both economically and psychologically from the group. Therefore, it is "not the operation of innate individualistic instincts that has given rise to the acquisition of personal property; it is, rather, the acquisition of personal property which has brought about the development of individualistic feelings" (p. 65). Briffault could not imagine that the cooperation necessary to the early evolution of man from the animals could have existed if humanity's earliest representatives had been "hordes of jealous and suspicious individualists, in which every member sought his personal advantage only," or if the incipient human social group had been ruled "by the selfishness of a despotic patriarchal male" (pp. 65, 66).

Finally, Briffault suggests that since patriarchies are based on masculine economic dominance, society could theoretically return to a matriarchal stage if our "forms of industry and wealth-production [were] to revert to the dimensions of household industry" (p. 176). The return might well be incomplete; Briffault cautions that matriarchal elements remain in societies moving into the patriarchal stage, and it follows that patriarchal elements would survive a reversion toward matriarchy. Still, in an economic catastrophe, one might expect to see "the predominance of women . . . to a large extent . . . automatically restored" (p. 177).

Supplementing his own experience with the migrants, Steinbeck's reading in Briffault offered a theoretical framework on which to measure the changes inflicted on the Joads and their fellow farmers. Steinbeck shows how the shock of dispossession suffered by the Joads undermines the frontier patriarchy and throws the family back to a more primitive economic and social stage. Briffault's belief that individualism could not have motivated the members of prepatriarchal society reinforces Steinbeck's feeling that the Oklahoma farmers could no longer rely on the values of frontier individualism. As long as they continued to think only in terms of the self-sufficient patriarchal family, their efforts to overcome oppression would be doomed.

The patriarchal structure of the Joad family, although shaken, remains intact through the early chapters of *The Grapes of Wrath*. Gathering to plan their trip to California, they arrange themselves in a hierarchical formation. Evidently habitual, it reflects the traditional authority of the pioneer as clearly as would a legislative chamber. The older men cluster around Grampa Joad, "enthroned on the running board" of the family's truck; the next generation of young men extend the semicircle around the patriarch; and the women and children stand as if in a gallery behind them.[6] Although Grampa Joad remains the "titular head" of the family as "a matter of custom," the office of greatest authority has passed to his son. Pa Joad runs the meeting according to a parliamentary procedure as well established as the positions of the participants (p. 137). He defines the meeting's agenda, calls for reports, and asks the members of the family for their opinions beginning with Grampa, who retains "the right of first comment" (p. 137). Women have a voice in the deliberations, but final responsibility for choosing a course of action lies with the older men—the "nucleus" of the family government (p. 136).

Steinbeck describes the squatting posture of the Joad men in unusual detail, as if, like Briffault, he were recording the symbolic ritual of a primitive tribe. He does so because the gesture embodies the intimate relationship between the frontiersman and his property. In times of adversity, the farmer patriarch draws his strength from his connection with the land, not from his association with society. Thus, the position of greatest authority in the Joad's ceremonial hierarchy is the position closest to the soil. The women and children stand; Grampa Joad, deprived of all but token authority by his age, sits on the truck's running board; the men who make the decisions squat. Their authority is rooted in ownership of the land where Grampa "had to kill the Indians and drive them away" and where Pa "killed weeds and snakes" (p. 45).

However, the Joads' actual, much-reduced circumstances now mock the traditional significance of the squatting posture. Banks and corporate landowners have severed the connection between family and land. The Joads gather around a converted Hudson Super-Six instead of the hearth of the patriarchal homestead. The squatting position, once a symbol of strength, has become instead a mark of their downtrodden status. Confrontation with omnipotent owners transforms the Joads and the other farmers from "squatting tenant men" into "squatters" in the traditional sense of men with no property rights and no power (p. 43).

Steinbeck signals the Joads' vulnerability by representing their patriarch as senile. Grampa Joad's incontinence and wandering mind epitomize the ineffectiveness of primitive frontier strengths without discipline and direction. His cantankerousness caricatures the inflexibility of the farmers. In defending their independence, they have clung to their fathers' ways without adjusting to the changing economics of farming. They fall prey to the banks, in part, because they do not fully comprehend that placing a mortgage on their farms deprives them of the full rights of ownership. As Grampa Joad's senility gives him the look of a "frantic child," so, following the pioneer tradition inflexibly makes the farmers childlike in their helplessness before oppression (p. 105).

Above all, the stubborn individualism embodied in the senile patriarch blinds the Joads to the necessity of collective action. When the landowner's tractor cuts across the family homestead, Grampa Joad stands up alone against his enemy with only a gun to guarantee his independence. He levels his rifle steadily at the eyes of the mechanical predator, but the tractor charges forward. The courage and pride Grampa displays mean nothing to the economic forces seizing the farm. The bank puts down the individual family as easily as the tractor caves in the house—as easily as "a dog shakes a rat" (p. 62). United the Oklahoma families might have a chance, but as self-reliant family units, they are defeated one by one.

Steinbeck emphasizes the patriarch's tragically atomistic response by placing another confrontation between tractor and solitary homesteader, similar to Grampa Joad's, in chapter five, the interchapter on the general dispossession of the Oklahoma farmers. According to this classic reading of the relationship between the Joads' saga and the interchapters, the Joad narrative develops on a more intimate level the themes of the interchapters which chronicle the plight of the migrants as a whole. But that relationship can be interpreted more fully. The power of the double narrative depends on the tension between the reader's knowledge that the Joads are representative in their suffering and the failure of the Joad men to recognize their representative status. They act as if their story were unique, when, in fact, it is typical of the tenant farmers' plight.

By establishing parallels between the oppressed and the oppressor throughout *The Grapes of Wrath*, Steinbeck also attributes the external pressures on the Joads, particularly the cruelties of the landowners, to the failure of frontier individualism as a social principle. He argues that both the powerful Californians and the shattered migrants must repudiate those aspects of individualism which deny participation in a larger community. In earlier days, the pioneers of Oklahoma and California had ignored the destructive aspect of their quest because they competed for land with Indians and Mexicans whose humanity they refused to recognize. But now that the frontier has been "closed"—that is, now that the land is owned by other white Americans—American society must confront the antisocial aspects of individualistic competition.

As the older Joad men sink into ineffectiveness and despondency, family authority shifts to Ma Joad. First she aggressively challenges patriarchal decisions that might fragment the family, and by the end of the novel she has taken the initiative. When the men cannot find work at the government camp and have forfeited their patriarchal roles "'either a-thinkin' or a-workin','" Ma Joad makes the decision to move on and rouses "her camp" for their early-morning departure (pp. 481, 491). Later she plans Tom's escape from the peach ranch after he avenges Casy's murder. During the final catastrophic chapters Ma Joad controls the family's money, handles Ruthie's betrayal of Tom's hiding place, finds the family work, leads them away from the flooded railroad car, and finally urges Rose of Sharon to suckle the starving man in the ark-like barn at the top of the hill.

On Briffault's anthropological scale this shift to matriarchal authority represents a regression to a more primitive social organization. But Steinbeck offers the step "back" to matriarchy as a promise of hope. In terms of the Joads' predicament, Ma Joad's emergence signals an essential adaptation: under the economic conditions of the migration, survival depends on the collective security of matriarchal society rather than on patriarchal self-reliance. In broader terms, Steinbeck uses Ma Joad's heightened stature to suggest that the communal values Briffault associates with matriarchy might provide an alternative basis for authority in American society as a whole.

The first extended description of Ma Joad begins in documentary detail and ends in allusions to matriarchal power. Ma Joad is an ordinary tenant farmer's wife and a "goddess" waiting to assume her new role as the representative of a dispossessed people:

> Ma was heavy, but not fat; thick with childbearing and work. She wore a loose Mother Hubbard of gray cloth in which there had once been colored flowers, but the color was washed out now, so that the small flowered pattern was only a little lighter gray than the background. The dress came down to her ankles, and her strong, broad, bare feet moved quickly and

deftly over the floor. Her thin, steel-gray hair was gathered in a sparse wispy knot at the back of her head. Strong, freckled arms were bare to the elbow, and her hands were chubby and delicate, like those of a plump little girl. She looked out into the sunshine. Her full face was not soft; it was controlled, kindly. Her hazel eyes seemed to have experienced all possible tragedy and to have mounted pain and suffering like steps into a high calm and a superhuman understanding. She seemed to know, to accept, to welcome her position, the citadel of the family, the strong place that could not be taken. . . . And from her great and humble position in the family she had taken dignity and a clean calm beauty. From her position as healer, her hands had grown sure and cool and quiet; from her position as arbiter she had become as remote and faultless in judgment as a goddess. She seemed to know that if she swayed the family shook, and if she ever really deeply wavered or despaired the family would fall, the family will to function would be gone. (pp. 99-100)

Steinbeck's portrait of Ma Joad differs in two critical aspects from classic accounts of the pioneer wife by male writers like Cooper, Mark Twain, Howe, Garland, and Rölvaag. He does not take the diurnal chores and unending childbearing as signs of Ma Joad's oppression, nor is he ill at ease with her physical strength and lack of traditional feminine beauty. Although Cooper, for example, admired at a distance the endurance and self-denial of the pioneer wife, he emphasized her sullen submission to her husband. Work and the bearing of fourteen children "amid the difficulties, privations and solitudes of stolen abodes in the wilderness" leave the once beautiful wife of a frontiersman in *The Chainbearer* "sallow, attenuated, with sunken cheeks, hollow, lack-luster eyes, and broken-mouthed." Her preoccupation with feeding and clothing her children makes her anxious and distrustful and, to Cooper's narrator, uncomfortably animalistic, like a "dam overseeing the welfare of its cubs."[7]

Steinbeck, on the other hand, follows Briffault's argument that economically productive labor is a woman's source of power. Ma Joad's work packing away the slaughtered pigs, organizing camp, buying food and cooking it over a succession of improvised stoves represents not submission but the steady shedding of her husband's control. She attains the status of arbiter "as remote and faultless in judgment as a goddess" because, not in spite, of her work. The pioneer woman's roughness threatens earlier writers, but to Steinbeck Ma Joad's thickness, her "strong, broad, bare feet," "her thin, steel-gray hair," her "strong, freckled arms" are not signs of femininity laid waste, but rather of "clean, calm beauty." His portrait places Ma Joad with Willa Cather's frontier heroines and Faulkner's black matriarchs, suggesting there may be an unheralded tradition of powerful women in early twentieth-century American literature who come forward in times of crisis and offer alternatives to the values of an individualistic and patriarchal society.

Thinking of the famous WPA photographs of the Dust Bowl, one might conclude, despite Mark Twain, that Cooper was simply more realistic about the effects of frontier conditions. But throughout *The Grapes of Wrath* Steinbeck acknowledges the reality that "'women's always tar'd'" (p. 147); in the passage on Ma Joad, with its value-loaded vocabulary, Steinbeck works on a mythical level, not to deny reality but to explain the power and endurance that survive Ma Joad's hardships. Briffault opened Steinbeck to a new interpretation of women's experience. Here and later in the novel, Steinbeck suggests that the "pain and suffering" of childbirth and the woman's role as attendant of the sick and dying leave her with an essentially tragic view of life that, in turn, generates a sustaining stoicism. Ma Joad's "high calm" and "superhuman understanding" not only endow her with the mental fortitude to be a "healer," "arbiter," and "citadel," but also spare her the kind of physically debilitating effects of depression suffered by her husband and brother-in-law. Steinbeck's view is thus quite literal. Ma Joad possesses the psychological qualities to govern her family community because she has actually given birth to it and nurtured it.

The family's dispossession deprives Pa Joad of his traditional agrarian labor, but Ma Joad's work continues and she remains strong. The tools of her husband's labor—wagons, horses, plows—are sold before the journey, but Ma Joad's kettles and pans are taken along and become, with the truck, the focus of family life. When the Joads make camp the first night, Ma Joad immediately issues an order to find firewood. Because leaving has not diminished her work, her authority is intact. Tom and Al similarly gain stature because their mechanical knowledge gives them work on the journey. But the older men have "the perplexed manner" Briffault finds common among men in primitive matriarchies (p. 177). Where Ma Joad's eyes convey "superhuman understanding," Steinbeck's initial description of Pa Joad reveals that "his bright dark eyes were failing," and Grampa's eyes move "listlessly" as soon as he leaves the farm (pp. 96, 169).

Because matriarchal strength endures as long as the household industries of camp life can be maintained, it remains available to people cast out of society. Ma Joad is a "citadel," not because she takes action, as Grampa Joad tries to do, but because she can absorb experience and "mount pain and suffering." As the image of an immovable fortress suggests, her strength gives no particular direction to the family. It simply protects the "will to function," to endure, to find some new source of strength for later action. As the family moves west, this citadel replaces the forty-acre farm that sustained the patriarch's individualism. Unlike the farm, Ma Joad's matriarchal citadel is a "strong place that cannot be taken."

Although there are moments of discouragement when Ma Joad reverts to the habits of frontier individualism, from the outset she has a broader understanding of the family's move west than does her husband. She interprets the migration according to the actual experience of the migrants rather than by the inherited and now meaningless patriarchal myth of the frontier. In the West Pa Joad thinks he will find relief from poverty through his individual labor. But his dream depends on land. When he cannot find it, he is crushed. While Ma Joad hopes one day to own a house of her own, a goal of individual fulfillment Steinbeck endorses, she gradually expands her belief that survival until that day depends on keeping the "family unbroke" to include a broader group (p. 231). Independent of Casy's philosophy, she warns her son not to stand up alone against the landowners:

> "Tommy, don't you go fightin' 'em alone. They'll hunt you down like a coyote. Tommy, I got to thinkin' an' dreamin' an' wonderin'. They say there's a hun'erd thousand of us shoved out. If we was all mad the same way, Tommy—they wouldn't hunt nobody down—" She stopped. (p. 104)

When she first asserts her authority over her husband with the jack handle, she places her family first, but even then she is willing to include Casy and the Wilsons, and earlier she speaks up for Tom and Al's idea of traveling with the Wilsons as a "unit" (pp. 202, 222).

Steinbeck suggests that Ma Joad's experience as a woman has made her see the individual as part of a larger whole; when Rose of Sharon grows frightened at her grandmother's illness, Ma Joad soothes her explaining that "dyin' is a piece of all dyin', and bearin' is a piece of all bearin'" (p. 286). As Ma Joad experiences the scorn and savagery of the California deputies, this matriarchal intuition is tempered into political faith. Ma counsels patience: "Why, Tom—us people will go on livin' when all them people is gone. Why, Tom, we're the people that live. They ain't gonna wipe us out. Why, we're the people—we go on" (p. 383).[8]

Ma Joad's matriarchal understanding of unity opens her to the possibility of a new frontier myth founded on the westward migration as a process which brings a dispossessed people together:

> In the evening a strange thing happened: the twenty families became one family, the children were the children of all. The loss of home became one loss, and the golden time in the West was one dream. And it might be that a sick child threw despair into the hearts of twenty families, of a hundred people; that a birth there in a tent kept a hundred people quiet and awestruck through the night and filled a hundred people with the birth-joy in the morning. (p. 264)

To Pa Joad (Job-road), life on the road seems meaningless. Route 66 is a trial by brutality, inhumanity, and contempt. Stretching to an unknown destination from an irretrievable starting point, the road confronts Pa with an image of time slipping by without the reassuring cyclical pattern of farm life to give him a sense of progress or permanence. Without a farm of his own, Pa Joad feels that "life's over an' done," but Ma Joad contradicts him:

> "No, it ain't," Ma smiled. "It ain't, Pa. An' that's one more thing a woman knows. I noticed that. Man, he lives in jerks—baby born an' a man dies, an' that's a jerk—get a farm an' loses his farm, an' that's a jerk. Woman, it's all one flow, like a stream, little eddies, little waterfalls, but the river, it goes right on. Woman looks at it like that. We ain't gonna die out. People is goin' on." (p. 577)

By the time she offers her husband this reassurance late in the novel, she has extended her belief in the importance of collective strength from the family to the migrants as a people: "Use' to be the fambly was fust. It ain't so now. It's anybody" (p. 606). Her statement on the end of the family's primacy has been taken to mark her conversion to Jim Casy's transcendental collectivism, but Ma Joad's sense of belonging to the stream of her race has its deepest origins in her own matriarchal nature.[9]

In his account of the government camp at Weedpatch, where the Joads temporarily find sanctuary from the brutalities of the road, Steinbeck offers an image of a society founded on the communal spirit of the matriarchy. Raising themselves from the more primitive life of roadside bivouacs and Hoovervilles, the migrants return to a life as well ordered as they knew on their farms.

In keeping with Briffault's stages of social development, the more complex government of the camp has shifted back toward patriarchal form. But it has done so without sacrificing the matriarchal impulse to keep the "family unbroke." The migrant men are no longer seen as dull and stupid as they were on the road because organizing the camp and its defenses again gives them a sphere of action. But the division of labor in the camp is consistent with the communal economy of the matriarchy in which the people's needs, instead of being supplied by the accumulation of private property, are provided for by communal division of labor between the sexes. Similarly, while the camp is managed by a male government agent, Steinbeck makes clear that his authority is entirely compatible with the egalitarian character of matriarchal society. He is not a chief, but a representative.

Steinbeck uses the meeting between Ma Joad and the camp manager as his principal metaphor for the matriarchal basis of governmental authority. Unlike the sheriffs and deputies Ma Joad confronts along the way, this man greets Ma Joad without condescension or hostility. With a gesture that Steinbeck has carefully prepared, the government agent squats down beside Ma Joad in the traditional posture of the tenant farmer: "He came to the fire and squatted on his hams, and the last of Ma's resistance went down" (p. 416). The emotional impact of this simple act of kindness and decency after so much insult and brutality drives home the symbolic significance of the gesture: the representative of the government meets the representative of the people's collective strength to "go on" at her own level. As the Oklahoma farmer drew strength from his independent plot of soil, this government will draw strength from the people.

Steinbeck proposes the paradox that a stronger communal government would be necessary to protect individual freedom and dignity and anticipates his readers' suspicions. Taking symbols of the red scare, political committees and barbed-wire fences, he transforms them into symbols of a democracy that protects the propertyless and allows them to participate in government. It is not the imposed patriarchal power of a totalitarian regime that protects the camp from the farmers' associations; it is not "that little guy in the office is a-stoppin' 'em," but the community's own collective strength—"'cause we're all a-workin' together" (p. 488).

However, Steinbeck doubts that his America will adopt Ma Joad's matriarchal sense of community as a governing principle. He knew where power lay, and his experience forbad optimism. The camp presents only a utopian vision; it cannot provide jobs to the migrants, and the Joads are forced back to the road.[10] As in other accounts of westward migration in our literature, Steinbeck correlates the redemption of American values with the rescue of the distressed patriarchal family. For the Joads the outlook is bleak. Ma Joad retards the family's disintegration but cannot prevent it.

At the end of the novel, Steinbeck preserves some hope, however, by insisting that Ma Joad's legacy passes on to Rose of Sharon, to Tom, and, by extension, to a future generation of Americans that might incorporate her values into democratic society. The significance of Ma Joad's bequest differs according to the sex of the two children; traditional male and female roles persist in Steinbeck's working out of matriarchal values. Rose of Sharon inherits her mother's sense of community through her womb; Tom through his mind. When Rose of Sharon offers her breast to a starving man, her smile announces her initiation into a matriarchal mystery: the capacity to nurture life. The scene confirms Ma Joad's belief that family unity can be extended to the wider community, and its shock, springing from the denial of sexuality in the meeting of man and woman, asserts Briffault's thesis that society originates not in sexual union but in maternal nurturing.[11] As Steinbeck wrote to his editor, Rose of Sharon's offering is "a survival symbol": as a woman, she represents not the alleviation of oppression but the ability to endure it.[12]

Tom Joad carries communal values into a more active mode. From the beginning of the novel, Tom is Ma Joad's chosen child; the core of the Joad family, as of the matriarchal clan, becomes mother and offspring rather than husband and wife. After his years in jail, Tom shares his mother's ability to live day by day on the road. Hunting down Uncle John or calming Al, Tom executes his mother's belief that the family must stay "unbroke." His eventual conversion to the labor cause is convincing in part because his new faith is firmly rooted in his mother's values. When he explains his plans to join the union—"maybe like Casy says, a fella ain't got a soul of his own, but on'y a piece of a big one," his language is not only Casy's. He follows as well his mother's more humble expression of faith—"people is goin' on" (pp. 572, 577). In the last days before Tom begins his mission as a labor organizer, Ma Joad claims the task of carrying food to his hiding place among the rushes. When he leaves, he receives the family's meager savings, not from his father but from Ma Joad—not when he takes over as patriarch of the family, but when he leaves the family to work for the people. Tom will tap strength that has come to the migrants by the shared experience of dispossession rather than by the individualism of his frontier heritage.

Tom's chances of staying alive, much less of relieving his people's oppression, are slim. The uncertainty of his future reflects Steinbeck's pessimism not only about the labor movement's prospects, but also about curbing the antisocial effects of individualism. However, the final image of Tom disappearing into the rushes at night has a power independent of his realistic chances of success. In the symbolic drama of the novel, his decision to follow Jim Casy and to act on the matriarchal sense of community represents the potential of the oppressed to take action—of passive endurance to become active resistance.

From *American Literature* 54, no. 3 (1982): 397-412. Copyright © 1982 by Duke University Press. All rights reserved. Used by permission of the publisher.

Notes

1. Frederic I. Carpenter, "The Philosophical Joads," *College English*, 2 (1941), 315-25; rpt. in *Steinbeck and His Critics: A Record of Twenty-Five Years*, ed. E. W. Tedlock, Jr., and C. V. Wicker (Albuquerque: Univ. of New Mexico Press, 1957), pp. 241-49; Chester E. Eisinger, "Jeffersonian Agrarianism in *The Grapes of Wrath*," *University of Kansas City Review*, 14 (1947), 149-54; in Viking Critical Library edition of *The Grapes of Wrath*, ed. Peter Lisca (New York: Viking, 1972), pp. 720-28; Wood-

burn O. Ross, "John Steinbeck: Naturalism's Priest," *College English*, 10 (1949), 432-38; rpt. in Tedlock, pp. 206-15; Peter Lisca, "The Dynamics of Community in *The Grapes of Wrath*," in *From Irving to Steinbeck: Studies of American Literature in Honor of Harry R. Warfel*, ed. Motley Deakin and Peter Lisca (Gainesville: Univ. of Florida Press, 1972), pp. 125-40; Richard Astro, *John Steinbeck and Edward F. Ricketts: The Shaping of a Novelist* (Minneapolis: Univ. of Minnesota Press, 1973); Jackson J. Benson, "John Steinbeck: Novelist as Scientist," *Novel*, 10 (1977), 248-64.

2. Astro, pp. 47-52; I am indebted throughout to Astro's uncovering of Steinbeck's reading.

3. *The Mothers: The Matriarchal Theory of Social Origins* (New York: Macmillan, 1931), p. 59; subsequent quotations will be taken from this edition and noted in the text.

4. Astro, p. 133.

5. *The Origin of the Family, Private Property and the State*, introd. Eleanor Burke Leacock (New York: International Publishers, 1972), pp. 83, 237 (Engels quotes Morgan), 30, 37; to trace Briffault's debt to Engels see particularly three chapters of *The Origin of the Family*, "The Stages of Prehistoric Culture," "The Family," and "Barbarism and Civilization"; for a review of the anthropological research on matriarchy see Leacock's helpful Introduction.

6. *The Grapes of Wrath* (New York: Viking, 1939), p. 140; subsequent quotations will be taken from this edition and noted in the text.

7. *The Chainbearer* (New York: Stringer & Townsend, 1857), p. 228.

8. Lisca refers to this passage as evidence of Ma Joad's sense of participation in a historical community, p. 133.

9. Warren French, *John Steinbeck* (New York: Twayne, 1961), pp. 103-07.

10. French, p. 110.

11. Astro, p. 133; Joseph Fontenrose, *John Steinbeck: An Introduction and Interpretation* (New York: Barnes & Noble, 1963), pp. 73-74.

12. "To Pascal Covici," 16 January 1939, *Steinbeck: A Life in Letters*, ed. Elaine Steinbeck and Robert Wallsten (New York: Viking, 1975), p. 178; Steinbeck explains his refusal to change the ending as Covici had requested.

The Fully Matured Art:
*The Grapes of Wrath*_____

Howard Levant

The enormous contemporary social impact of *The Grapes of Wrath*[1]
can encourage the slippery reasoning that condemns a period novel to
die with its period.[2] But continuing sales and critical discussions suggest that *The Grapes of Wrath* has outlived its directly reportorial ties
to the historical past; that it can be considered as an aesthetic object, a
good or a bad novel *per se*. In that light, the important consideration is
the relative harmony of its structure and materials.

The Grapes of Wrath is an attempted prose epic, a summation of national experience at a given time. Evaluation proceeds from that identification of genre. A negative critical trend asserts that *The Grapes of
Wrath* is too flawed to command serious attention: the materials are local and temporary, not universal and permanent; the conception of life
is overly simple; the characters are superficial types (except, perhaps,
Ma Joad); the language is folksy or strained by turns; and, in particular,
the incoherent structure is the weakest point—the story breaks in half,
the nonorganic, editorializing interchapters force unearned general
conclusions, and the ending is inconclusive as well as overwrought and
sentimental.[3] The positive trend asserts that *The Grapes of Wrath* is a
great novel. Its materials are properly universalized in specific detail;
the conception is philosophical, the characters are warmly felt and
deeply created; the language is functional, varied, and superb on the
whole; and the structure is an almost perfect combination of the dramatic and the panoramic in sufficient harmony with the materials. This
criticism admits that overwrought idealistic passages as well as propagandistic simplifications turn up on occasion, but these are minor flaws
in an achievement on an extraordinary scale.[4] Relatively detached
studies of Steinbeck's ideas comprise a third trend. These studies are
not directly useful in analytical criticism; they do establish that
Steinbeck's social ideas are ordered and legitimate extensions of bio-

logical fact, hence scientific and true rather than mistaken or senti-mental.[5]

The two evaluative positions are remarkable in their opposition. They are perhaps overly simple in asserting that *The Grapes of Wrath* is either a classic of our literature or a formless pandering to sentimen-tal popular taste. Certainly these extremes are mistaken in implying (when they do) that somehow, *The Grapes of Wrath* is *sui generis* in re-lation to Steinbeck's work.

Trends so awkwardly triple need to be brought into a sharper focus. By way of a recapitulation in focus, consider a few words of outright praise:

> For all of its sprawling asides and extravagances, *The Grapes of Wrath* is a big book, a great book, and one of maybe two or three American novels in a class with *Huckleberry Finn*.[6]

Freeman Champney's praise is conventional enough to pass unques-tioned if one admires *The Grapes of Wrath*, or, if one does not, it can seem an invidious borrowing of prestige, shrilly emotive at that. After-thought emphasizes the serious qualification of the very high praise. Just how much damage is wrought by those "sprawling asides and ex-travagances," and does *The Grapes of Wrath* survive its structural faults as *Huckleberry Finn* does, by virtue of its mythology, its charac-terization, its language? If the answers remain obscure, illumination may increase (permitting, as well, a clearer definition of the aesthetic efficacy of Steinbeck's ideas) when the context of critical discussion is the relationship of the novel's structure to materials.

Steinbeck's serious intentions and his artistic honesty are not in question. He had studied and experienced the materials intensely over a period of time. After a false start that he rejected (*L'Affaire Lettuce-berg*), his conscious intention was to create an important literary work rather than a propagandistic shocker or a journalistic statement of the topical problem of how certain people faced one aspect of the Great

Depression.[7] Therefore, it is an insult to Steinbeck's aims to suggest that somehow *The Grapes of Wrath* is imperfect art but a "big" or "great" novel nevertheless. In all critical justice, *The Grapes of Wrath* must stand or fall as a serious and important work of art.

The consciously functional aspect of Steinbeck's intentions—his working of the materials—is clarified by a comparison of *The Grapes of Wrath* with *In Dubious Battle*. Both novels deal with labor problems peculiar to California, but that similarity cannot be pushed too far. The Joads are fruit pickers in California, but not of apples, the fruit mentioned in *In Dubious Battle*. The Joads pick cotton, and in the strike novel the people expect to move on to cotton. The Joads become involved in a strike but as strikebreakers rather than as strikers. Attitudes are less easy to camouflage. The strikers in *In Dubious Battle* and the Okies in *The Grapes of Wrath* are presented with sympathy whereas the owning class and much of the middle class have no saving virtue. The sharpest similarity is that both the strikers and the Okies derive a consciousness of the need for group action from their experiences; but even here there is a difference in emphasis. The conflict of interest is more pointed and the lessons of experience are less ambiguous in *The Grapes of Wrath* than in *In Dubious Battle*. The fact is that the two novels are not similar beyond a common basis in California labor problems, and Steinbeck differentiates that basis carefully in most specific details. The really significant factor is that different structures are appropriate to each novel. The restricted scope of *In Dubious Battle* demands a dramatic structure with some panoramic elements as they are needed. The broad scope of *The Grapes of Wrath* demands a panoramic structure; the dramatic elements appear as they are needed. Therefore, in each case, the primary critical concern must be the adequacy of the use of the materials, not the materials in themselves.

Steinbeck's profound respect for the materials of *The Grapes of Wrath* is recorded in a remarkable letter in which he explained to his literary agents and to his publisher the main reason for his withdrawing

L'Affaire Lettuceberg, the hurried, propagandistic, thirty-thousand-word manuscript novel that preceded *The Grapes of Wrath*:

> I know I promised this book to you, and that I am breaking a promise in withholding it. But I had got smart and cagey you see. I had forgotten that I hadn't learned to write books, that I will never learn to write them. A book must be a life that lives all of itself and this one doesn't do that. You can't write a book. It isn't that simple. The process is more painful than that. And this book is fairly clever, has skillful passages, but tricks and jokes. Sometimes I, the writer, seem a hell of a smart guy—just twisting this people out of shape. But the hell with it. I beat poverty for a good many years and I'll be damned if I'll go down at the first little whiff of success. I hope you, Pat, don't think I've double-crossed you. In the long run to let this book out would be to double-cross you. But to let the bars down is like a first theft. It's hard to do, but the second time it isn't so hard and pretty soon it is easy. If I should write three books like this and let them out, I would forget there were any other kinds.[8]

This is Steinbeck's declaration of artistic purpose—and his effort to exorcise a dangerous (and permanent) aspect of his craft. Much of the motivation for Steinbeck's career is stated in this letter. After all, he did write *L'Affaire Lettuceberg*; and "tricks and jokes," detached episodes, and detached ironic hits, as well as a twisting of characters, are evident enough in much of Steinbeck's earlier work. But the depression materials were too serious to treat lightly or abstractly, or to subject to an imposed structure (mistaken idealism, nature worship, a metaphysical curse, a literary parallel). Such materials need to be in harmony with an appropriate structure.

From that intentional perspective, the central artistic problem is to present the universal and epical in terms of the individual and particular. Steinbeck chooses to deal with this by creating an individual, particular image of the epical experience of the dispossessed Okies by focusing a sustained attention on the experience of the Joads. The result is an organic combination of structures. Dramatic structure suits the family's particular history; panoramic structure proves out the representative nature of their history. To avoid a forced and artificial "typing," to assure that extensions of particular detail are genuinely organic, Steinbeck postulates a conceptual theme that orders structure and materials: the transformation of the Joad family from a self-contained, self-sustaining unit to a conscious part of a group, a whole larger than its parts. This thematic ordering is not merely implicit or ironic, as it is in *The Pastures of Heaven*, or withheld to create mystery as in *Cup of Gold* or *To a God Unknown*. Steinbeck chances the strength of the materials and the organic quality of their structure. And he defines differences: the group is not group-man. The earlier concept is a "beast," created by raw emotion ("blood"), short-lived, unwieldy, unpredictable, mindless; a monster that produces indiscriminate good or evil. The group is quite different—rational, stable, relatively calm—because it is an assemblage of like-minded people who retain their individual and traditional sense of right and wrong as a natural fact. Group-man lacks a moral dimension; the group is a morally pure instrument of power. The difference is acute at the level of leadership. The leaders have ambiguous aims in *In Dubious Battle*, but they are Christ-like (Jim Casy) or attain moral insight (Tom Joad) in *The Grapes of Wrath*.

The Grapes of Wrath is optimistic; *In Dubious Battle* is not. That the living part of the Joad family survives, though on the edge of survival, is less than glowingly optimistic, but that survival produces a mood that differs considerably from the unrelenting misery of *In Dubious Battle*. Optimism stems from the theme, most openly in the alternation of narrative chapter and editorial interchapter. While the Joads move slowly and painfully toward acceptance of the group, many of the interchapters define the broad necessity of that acceptance. Arbitrary plotting does not produce this change. Its development is localized in Ma Joad's intense focus on the family's desire to remain a unit; her recognition of the group is the dramatic resolution.[9] Optimism is demonstrated also in experience that toughens, educates, and enlarges the stronger Joads in a natural process. On the simplest, crudest level, the family's journey and ordeal is a circumstantial narrative of an effort to reach for the good material life. Yet that is not the sole motive, and those members who have only that motive leave the family. On a deeper level, the family is attempting to rediscover the identity it lost when it was dispossessed; so the Joads travel from order (their old, traditional life) through disorder (the road, California) to some hope of a better, rediscovered order, which they reach in Ma's recognition and Tom's dedication. Their journey toward order is the ultimate optimistic, ennobling process, the earned, thematic resolution of the novel.

I do not intend to imply that Steinbeck pretties his materials. He does not stint the details of the family's various privations, its continual losses of dignity, and the death or disappearance of many of its members. On the larger scale, there is considerable objective documentation of the general economic causes of such misery—a circumstantial process that lifts *The Grapes of Wrath* out of the merely historic genre of the proletarian novel. Optimism survives as the ultimate value because of the will of the people to understand and to control the conditions of their lives despite constant discouragement.

This value is essentially abstract, political. Steinbeck deepens and universalizes it by developing the relationship between the family unit and "the people." The family is made up of unique individuals. "The people" embraces a timeless entity, a continuing past, present, and future of collective memory—but free of any social or political function.[10] Time lag confounds the usefulness of "the people" as a guide for the present. The Joads and others like them know they may keep the land or get new land if they can kill or control "the Bank," as the old people killed Indians to take the land and controlled nature to keep it.[11] But "the Bank" is more complicated an enemy than Indians or nature because it is an abstraction.[12] So the Okies submit to dispossession in Oklahoma (forced by mechanized cheaper production of cotton) and to the huge migration into California (encouraged by landowners to get cheap field labor), motivated by the time lag that confuses them, for none of them comprehends the monstrous logic of modern economics. Despite their ignorance, in a process that is unifying in itself and is second only to survival, the families work at some way of prevailing against "the Bank." The older, agrarian concept of "the people" is succeeded in time by the new concept of the group, an instrument of technology and political power—an analogue that works. Steinbeck makes this succession appear necessary and legitimate by a representation that excludes alternate solutions.[13] The permitted solution seems a natural evolution, from people to group, because it is a tactic, not a fundamental change in folkways. Its process is long and painful because the emotive entity, "the people," needs to feel its way toward redefinition as the group—the abstract, political entity which emerges as an organic, particularized whole. This is brilliant literary strategy, in its grasp of operative metaphor and its avoidance of an overly obvious, loaded opposition. Steinbeck is scrupulously careful to keep to precise and exact circumstantial detail in this developed metaphor. Concretely, the panicky violence of "the Bank" is the reverse of the fact that (seemingly by habit) the Joads are kind to those who need their help and neighborly to people who are like them. The metaphor is persuasive.

Steinbeck is quite as scrupulous in the use of allegory as a way of universalizing an abstract particular. In his earlier work this method can produce a tangibly artificial, forced result, but allegory is a credible and functional device in *The Grapes of Wrath*. The turtle episode in chapter 3 is justly famous. Objectively, we have a fully realized description of a land turtle's patient, difficult journey over dust fields, across a road and walled embankment, and on through the dust. The facts are the starting point; nature is not distorted or manipulated to yield allegorical meaning. The turtle seems awkward but it is able to survive, like the Joads, and like them it is moving southwest, out of the dry area.[14] It can protect itself against a natural danger like the red ant it kills, as the Joads protect themselves by their unity. The turtle's eyes are "fierce, humorous," suggesting force that takes itself easily; the stronger Joads are a fierce, humorous people.[15] When mismanaged human power attacks, as when a truck swerves to hit the turtle, luck is on the animal's side—it survives by luck. The Joads survive the mismanagement that produced the Dust Bowl and the brutalizing man-made conditions in California as much by luck as by design. The relation to the Joads of the life-bearing function of the turtle is more obscure, or perhaps overly ambitious. The factual starting point is that, unknowingly, the turtle carries an oat seed in its shell and unknowingly drops and plants the seed in the dust, where it will rest until water returns. The most obvious link in the Joad family is the pregnant Rose of Sharon, but her baby is born dead. Perhaps compassion is "born," as in Uncle John's thoughts as he floats the dead baby down the flooding river in its apple box coffin:

> Go down an' tell 'em. Go down in the street an' rot an' tell 'em that way. That's the way you can talk. . . . Maybe they'll know then.[16]

But this appeal is strained, too greatly distanced from the factual starting point. The link works in the restricted sense that Ruthie and Winfield are "planted," and will perhaps take root, in the new environment of California. At this point the careful allegory collapses under its own weight, yet care is taken to join the device to the central narrative. In chapter 4, Tom Joad picks up a turtle, and later Casy remarks on the tenacity of the breed:

> "Nobody can't keep a turtle though. They work at it and work at it, and at last one day they get out and away they go—off somewheres."[17]

This recognition of the turtle's purposeful tenacity interprets and places the preceding interchapter in the central narrative. Tom calls the turtle "an old bulldozer," a figure that works in opposition to the threatening insect life the tractors suggest as self-defeating, destructive tools of "the Bank."[18] Again, a purposeful turtle is opposed to homeless domestic animals, like the "thick-furred yellow shepherd dog" that passes Tom and Casy, to suggest precisely the ruined land and the destruction of the old ways of life on the most basic, animal level, where the wild (or free) animal survives best.[19] These and other supporting details extend the exemplum into the narrative; they continue and deepen Steinbeck's foreshadowing, moralizing insight naturally, within the range of biological imagery. It is true, allowing for the one collapse of the allegory, that none of Steinbeck's earlier work exhibits as profound a comprehension of what can be done to "place" an allegorical narrative device.

The turtle interchapter is masterful enough. Steinbeck does even more with an extended instance of allegorizing—the introduction of the lapsed preacher, Jim Casy, into the Joad family. Casy has a role that is difficult to present within the limits of credibility. Casy may look too much like his function, the Christ-like force that impels the family toward its transformation into the group. If the novel is to have more significance than a reportorial narrative of travel and hardship, Casy's spiritual insights are a necessary means of stating a convincing philosophical optimism. The technical difficulty is that Casy does not have a forthright narrative function. He drops out of the narrative for almost one hundred and fifty pages, although his presence continues through the Joads' wondering at times what had happened to him. When he reenters the novel, he is killed off within fifteen pages—sacrificed for the group in accord with his Christ-like function, with a phrase that recalls Christ's last words.[20] In spite of the obvious technical difficulty in handling such materials, Steinbeck realizes Casy as fully as any of the major Joads. Casy's struggle with himself to define "sin" to include the necessary facts of the natural world lends him a completely human aspect. He earns the right to make moral statements because he bases all judgments on his own experience. This earned right to "witness" serves to keep Casy human, yet it permits him to function as if he were an allegorical figure. This is a brilliant solution, and Casy is Steinbeck's most successful use of a functional allegorical figure in a major role. His narrative sharpness contrasts amazingly with the dim realization of Sir Henry Morgan or Joseph Wayne.

Even Casy's necessary distance is functional rather than arbitrary. He exists outside the narrative in the sense that he travels with the Joads but he is not a member of the family, and there is no danger of confusing his adventures with theirs. Further, by right of his nature and experience, he has the function of being the living moral conscience of "the people." He travels with the Joads to witness the ordeal of the Okies, to understand its causes, and to do what he can to help. Steinbeck's convincing final touch is that, at the end, Tom Joad aspires to Casy's role. In this shift, Steinbeck manipulates allegory, he does not submit to its rigid quality, for Tom is not like Casy. Tom is far more violent, more capable of anger; having been shown the way, however, he may be more successful as a practical missionary than Casy. One might say that if Casy is to be identified with Christ, the almost human god, Tom is to be identified with Saint Paul, the realistic, tough organizer. The allegorical link by which Tom is "converted" and assumes Casy's role is deeply realized and rich with significance, not simply because it is a technical necessity, but because it is a confirmation of Casy's reality as a man and a teacher. The parallels to Christ and Saint Paul would be only and technical facts if they were not realized so profoundly. The trivial fact that Casy has Christ's initials dims beside this more profound and sustained realization.

Function, not mere design, is as evident in the use of characterization to support and develop a conflict of opposed ideas—mainly a struggle between law and anarchy. The one idea postulates justice in a moral world of love and work, identified in the past with "the people" and in the present with the government camp and finally with the union movement, since these are the modern, institutional forms the group may take. The opposed idea postulates injustice in an immoral world of hatred and starvation. It is associated with buccaneering capitalism, which, in violent form, includes strikebreaking and related practices that cheapen human labor.

The Joads present special difficulties in characterization. They must be individualized to be credible and universalized to carry out their representative functions. Steinbeck meets these problems by making each of the Joads a specific individual and by specifying that what happens to the Joads is typical of the times. The means he uses to maintain these identities can be shown in some detail. The least important Joads are given highly specific tags—Grandma's religion, Grandpa's vigor, Uncle John's melancholy, and Al's love of cars and girls. The tags are involved in events; they are not inert labels. Grandma's burial violates her religion; Grandpa's vigor ends when he leaves the land; Uncle John's melancholy balances the family's experience; Al helps to drive the family to California and, by marrying, continues the family. Ma, Pa, Rose of Sharon, and Tom carry the narrative, so their individuality is defined by events rather than through events. Ma is the psychological and moral center of the family; Pa carries its burdens; Rose of Sharon means to ensure its physical continuity; and Tom becomes its moral conscience. On the larger scale, there is much evidence that what happens to the family is typical of the times. The interchapters pile up suggestions that "the whole country is moving" or about to move.[21] The Joads meet many of their counterparts or outsiders who are in sympathy with their ordeal; these meetings reenforce the common bond of "the people."[22] Both in the interchapters and the narrative, the universal, immediate issue is survival—a concrete universal.

On the other hand, the individualized credibility of the Joads is itself the source of two difficulties: the Joads are too different, as sharecroppers, to suggest a universal or even a national woe, and they speak an argot that might limit their universal quality.[23] Steinbeck handles these limitations with artistic license. The narrative background contains the Joads' past; their experience as a landless proletariat is highlighted in the narrative foreground. The argot is made to seem a typical language within the novel in three ways: it is the major language; people who are not Okies speak variations of their argot; and that argot is not specialized in its relevance, but is used to communicate the new experiences "the people" have in common as a landless proletariat. However, because these solutions depend on artistic license, any tonal falseness undermines severely the massive artistic truthfulness the language is intended to present. So the overly editorial tone in several of the interchapters has a profoundly false linguistic ring, although the tonal lapse is limited and fairly trivial in itself.

The Joads are characterized further in comparison with four Okie types who refuse to know or are unable to gain the knowledge the family derives from its collective experience. They are the stubborn, the dead, the weak, and the backtrackers; they appear in the novel in that order.

Muley Graves is the stubborn man, as his punning name suggests. He reveals himself to Tom and Casy near the beginning of the novel. His refusal to leave Oklahoma is mere stubbornness; his isolation drives him somewhat mad. He is aware of a loss of reality, of "jus' wanderin' aroun' like a damn ol' graveyard ghos'," and his blind violence is rejected from the beginning by the strongest, who oppose his pessimism with an essential optimism.[24]

Deaths of the aged and the unborn frame the novel. Grandpa and Grandma are torn up by the roots and die, incapable of absorbing a new, terrible experience. Rose of Sharon's baby, born dead at the end of the novel, is an index of the family's ordeal and a somewhat contrived symbol of the necessity to form the group.

The weak include two extremes within the Joad family. Noah Joad gives up the struggle to survive; he finds a private peace. His character is shadowy, and his choice is directed more clearly by Steinbeck than by any substance within him.[25] Connie has plenty of substance. He is married to Rose of Sharon and deserts her because he had no faith in the family's struggle to reach California. His faith is absorbed in the values of "the Bank," in getting on, in money, in any abstract goal. He wishes to learn about technology in order to rise in the world. He does not admire technique for itself, as Al does. He is a sexual performer, but he loves no one. Finally, he wishes that he had stayed behind in Oklahoma and taken a job driving a tractor. In short, with Connie, Steinbeck chooses brilliantly to place a "Bank" viewpoint within the family. By doing so, he precludes a simplification of character and situation, and he endorses the complexity of real people in the real world. (*In Dubious Battle* is similarly free of schematic characterization.) In addition, the family's tough, humanistic values gain in credibility by their contrast with Connie's shallow, destructive modernity. The confused gas station owner and the pathetic one-eyed junkyard helper are embodied variations on Connie's kind of weakness.[26] Al provides an important counterpoint. He wants to leave the family at last, like Connie, but duty and love force him to stay. His hard choice points the moral survival of the family and measures its human expense.

The Joads meet several backtrackers. The Wilsons go back because Mrs. Wilson is dying; the Joads do not stop, in spite of death. The ragged man's experience foreshadows what the Joads find in California; but they keep on. Some members of the Joad family think of leaving but do not, or they leave for specific reasons—a subtle variation on backtracking. Al and Uncle John wish deeply at times to leave, but they stay; Tom leaves (as Casy does) but to serve the larger, universal family of the group. Backtracking is a metaphor, then, a denial of life, but always a fact as well. The factual metaphor is deepened into complexity because the Joads sympathize with the backtrackers' failure to endure the hardships of the road and of California, in balance with where they started from—the wasteland—while knowing they cannot accept that life-denying solution. All of these choices are the fruit of the family's experience.

A fifth group of owners and middle-class people are accorded no sympathetic comprehension, as contrasted with the Joads, and, as in *In Dubious Battle*, their simply and purely monstrous characterization is too abstract to be fully credible. The few exceptions occur in highly individualized scenes or episodes (chapter 15 is an example) in which middle-class "shitheels" are caricatures of the bad guys, limited to a broad contrast with the good guys (the truck drivers, the cook), who are in sympathy with a family of Okies.[27] This limitation has the narrative advantage of highlighting the importance and vitality of the Okies to the extent that they seem by right to belong in the context of epic materials, but the disadvantage of shallow characterization is severe. Steinbeck can provide a convincing detailed background of the conditions of the time; he cannot similarly give a rounded, convincing characterization to an owner or a disagreeable middle-class person.

On the whole, then, fictive strength and conviction are inherent in the materials of *The Grapes of Wrath*. The noticeable flaws are probably irreducible aspects of the time context and of narrative shorthand, counterpointed by a complex recognition of human variety in language and behavior.

The ordering of the structure supports this conclusion. *The Grapes of Wrath* has three parts: Tom's return and his witnessing of events; the family's departure and experiences on the road; its arrival and experiences in California. The interchapters "locate" and generalize the narrative chapters, somewhat like stage directions. They supply, in a suitably dramatic or rhetorical style, information the Joads cannot possess, and they are involved more often than not in the narrative.[28] This device provides for both precise detail and epic scope. The imagery fulfills the structural purpose of pitting life against death.

The first part contains ten chapters. The opening is a "location" interchapter. The dead land of the Dust Bowl in Oklahoma provides the imagery of a universal death, but at the close the women watch their men to see if they will break in the stress of that natural disaster. The men do not break; the scene is repeated in California at the close of the novel in a rising rhetoric.[29] The objective imagistic frame sets life against death, and life endures in the will of the people to endure. The following nine chapters center on Tom's return from a kind of death— prison. With Casy, Tom is an external observer, witnessing with fresh eyes the dead land and the universal dispossession. Death seems to prevail. The turtle interchapter is recapitulated ironically in the narrative. Pa carries handbills that promise jobs in California, an analogue to the turtle carrying a head of oats; but the handbills falsely promise renewal; their intention is to cheapen the labor market. Later events prove the group concept is the genuine renewal, the true goal. Immediately, death is associated with "the Bank," an abstraction presented concretely in symbolic form as the tractor—the perfect tool of the abstract "Bank," which dehumanizes its driver and kills the fertility of the land.

When he sees the abandoned Joad home, Tom says, "Maybe they're all dead," but Muley Graves tells Tom the family is alive, with Uncle John, and about to leave without him for California.[30] Tom is reborn or returned to life within the family, but its vital center has shifted (as represented in charged, frankly mystical terms) to a life-giving machine:

> The family met at the most important place, near the truck. The house was dead, and the fields were dead; but this truck was the active thing, the living principle.[31]

The family's certainties develop from an ironically hopeful innocence, a failure to realize that a new basis for life has overtaken them, replacing family with group. The trek is an instinctive flight from death, but the economic system is more deadly than the drought. The Joads accept the promise of the handbills, they are cheated when they sell their farm equipment, but they do not doubt that they will transplant themselves in California. The real certainty is the death of the past, as in the burning of relics by an unnamed woman in an interchapter, and by Ma herself, just before the trek begins.

All that is not dead is altered. Pa's loss of authority to Ma and Al's new authority (he knows automobiles) represent the shifts in value within the family. They retain a living coherence as farmers. They work as a unit when they kill and salt down the hogs in preparation for the trek. They are innocent of the disgusting techniques of close dealing in business, but Tom explains to Casy how the Joads can deal closely enough in their accustomed agrarian context. Their innocence, therefore, is touching, not comic, and their literal preparations support a symbolic preparation, a blindly hopeful striving to find life. Their journey is an expression, despite all shocks and changes, of the will to survive; hence, it has an epic dignity, echoing their retained, personal dignity.

In all the imagery of life and death, Steinbeck is consistent in that his symbols grow out of objective, literal facts. He thus achieves imagery in a more fully realized texture in this novel than in earlier work. This organically realized symbolism is maintained and developed in the seven chapters of the second section.

With the dead land behind them, the family carries the death of the past on its journey. Grandpa dies on the first night. Probably his stroke is caused, at least in part, by the "medicine" that Ma and Tom dope him with to take him away from the land—for the good of the family as a whole. An incipient group concept emerges in this overriding concern for the whole. Grandpa's death is offset by the meeting of the Joads and the Wilsons. At the beginning, Grandpa's illness and death join the two families in bonds of sympathy. There are other unifying forces; the language bar becomes senseless, and the two families help each other. Casy sees the emergence of the group, the whole absorbing the individual, in his sermon for Grandpa:

> Casy said solemnly, "This here ol' man jus' lived a life an' jus' died out of it. I don't know whether he was good or bad, but that don't matter much. He was alive, an' that's what matters. An' now he's dead, an' that don't matter. Heard a fella tell a poem one time, an' he says, 'All that lives is holy. . . .'"[32]

A modest dignity embodies the vitalistic dogma. As a further push from individual to group, the family decides to break the law by burying Grandpa secretly beside the road; a conventional funeral would eat up the money they need to reach California. Grandma's grisly, circumstantial death is delayed until the end of the section; it outweighs the achievement of reaching their destination and foreshadows the reality of California. True, the family can absorb death, even new kinds of death, into its experience. Ruthie and Winfield react most violently to the dog's death at the first stop on the road; they are less affected by Grandpa's death, still less by Grandma's. Late on the night of Grandpa's death after the Joads and Wilsons have agreed to join forces, Ma remarks: "Grandpa—it's like he's dead a year."[33] Experience breeds a calm in the face of loss that fills in the past. Tom points this harshly realistic network of difference after Grandma's death:

> "They was too old," he said. "They wouldn't of saw nothin' that's here. Grampa would a been a-seein' the Injuns an' the prairie country when he was a young fella. An' Granma would a remembered an' seen the first home she lived in. They was too ol'. Who's really seein' it is Ruthie and Winfiel'."[34]

Life matters. The narrative context supports this fruit of the family's private experience. Between the deaths of Grandpa and Grandma, the Joads meet several symbolically dead people on the road. The gas station owner is incapable of learning the meaning of his own experience even when it is explained to him. The one-eyed junkyard helper lives in a prison of self, inside his ugly face and unclean body. Tom (who was in an actual prison) tries unsuccessfully to force him from his death into life. The several returning sharecroppers have come to accept a living death as the only reality. They have cut themselves off from the inchoate struggle to form a group, admittedly against severe odds, so they have no choice but to return to the dead, empty land.

But to outsiders, seeing only the surface, the Joads are not heroic life-bearers but stupidly ignorant, as in a dialogue between two service station boys when the family leaves on the final lap of the trek, the night trip across the Mojave Desert:

"Jesus, I'd hate to start out in a jalopy like that." "Well, you and me got sense. Them goddamn Okies got no sense and no feeling. They ain't human. A human being wouldn't live like they do. A human being couldn't stand to be so dirty and miserable. They ain't a hell of a lot better than gorillas." "Just the same, I'm glad I ain't crossing the desert in no Hudson Super-Six. . . ." "You know, they don't have much trouble. They're so goddamn dumb they don't know it's dangerous. And, Christ Almighty, they don't know any better than what they got. Why worry?"[35]

The dialogue is exactly true, but the truth is ironic. The Joads do have the appearance of death, and ignorant, dirty, dispossessed yokels seem to be unlikely carriers of an affirmation of life. The ironic truth defines the heroism of the Joads. The family is aware of the dangers of the desert crossing, and Grandma dies during it, "for the fambly," as Ma says.[36] In general the family is more aware than the boys at the service station are allowed to know. After meeting a second returning sharecropper, the Joads are even aware of the actual conditions in California; Uncle John, the family's weakest moral agent, voices the family's rejection of despair when he says, "We're a-goin' there, ain't we? None of this here talk gonna keep us from goin' there."[37] The service station boys express, so we can dismiss, a superficially sentimental view of the Joads. The ironic truth is that the family goes ahead, knowing the dangers and aware that California may not be Eden. Their genuine heroism and nobility are all the more valid for being tested by irony.

Yet there is no suggestion that the Joads are merely deterministic formulae. They are pawns of circumstance up to a point. They react to events they do not understand fully, and no doubt partial ignorance and pure necessity keep them on the road and get them to California. But Ma and Tom undergo certain developments of character that exclude determinism. Ma's constantly increasing moral authority is her response to the forces that are tearing the family apart, but she acts out of love that is restricted to the family, that is not universalized until very near the end of the novel. Tom's role is more extensive and more complex. He begins by regarding himself as a creature of necessity— "I ruther jus'—lay one foot down in front a the other"—but his quietism relates to a prison experience he does not want to live "over an' over."[38] His natural understanding of why and how people behave forces him into a moral concern that is larger but as intense as Ma's. His knowledge of people is established at the beginning of the novel, in his shrewd, unflattering understanding of the truck driver who gives him a lift, and it widens subsequently with experience on the road. His disdain for the gas station owner precedes his tough moral lecture to the one-eyed junkyard helper and an equally tough lecture to Al. That is to say, Tom is involved. His moral development follows Casy's, with the significant difference that his is the more difficult to achieve. Casy is a relatively simple character; he can express moral concern easily. Tom's emotional numbness following his time in prison does not permit meditation or cancel personality, so the awakening of his moral consciousness on the road is a more rigorous, more painful experience than Casy's time in the desert. Consequently, because of its special quality, Tom's growing awareness of good and evil is a highly credible mirror of the general experience that drives the family toward the group. The logic is paradoxical, but the artistic insight is realized deeply in Tom's circumstantial journey from moral quietism to moral concern for the group.

Enduring all the harsh experiences of their journey, the family gains moral stature and finds that it can function as a unit in the new environment of the road. Its survival in California is a result in part of its redefinition gained on the road.

The interchapters underscore and generalize these particulars. Chapter 14 states the growth of the group concept as a shift in the thinking of the migrants from *I* to *we*. The narrative context is Grandpa's death and the unity of the Joads and Wilsons. Chapter 15 suggests that the Joads' ordeal is a moral experience that affects society at large. Chapter 17 continues the theme that the road furthers the growth of the group concept:

Every night relationships that make a world, established; every morning the world torn down like a circus. At first the families were timid in the building and tumbling worlds, but gradually the technique of building worlds became their technique. Then leaders emerged, then laws were made, then codes came into being. And as the worlds moved westward they were more complete and better furnished, for their builders were more experienced in building them.[39]

The formation of a group is a "technique" with its basis in the older agrarian order. As with the Joads, the experience of building produces a new moral stature and a redefinition of the family.

In the relation of these events and changes, the narrative chapters and interchapters cohere in an organic unity. Their common theme is movement from and through death to a new life inherent in the group concept. The symbolic level extends the narrative level of movement on the road through time and space. The texture is fully realized. No generalization violates narrative particulars or exists apart from them. Steinbeck's work is careful, convincing, flawless.

The third part—the family's arrival and experience in California—marks an artistic decline. The materials alter and at times the structure is defective.

The chief difference in the materials is an absolute focus on man-made misery. In Oklahoma and on the road, survival can seem to be mainly a struggle against natural conditions. Drought is the cause of the migration. "The Bank" dispossesses the Okies, but it is not the effective cause of the drought. In California the struggle is almost entirely against men, and there is no possibility of an escape by further migration. The chief difference in structure stems from Steinbeck's need to begin to think of how to conclude the novel, which presents structural choices and manipulations not present in the first two parts of the novel. For a time the narrative thrust remains coherent, an organic unity disguising these changes.

Grandma's undignified burial establishes the pattern of the family's experience in California. Her pauper's funeral by the state contrasts with the full dignity and free will the family expressed in burying Grandpa. Landless poverty is a moral insult to family pride, and it affects their will to survive. For the moment, as their moral spokesman, Ma expresses a will to recover as quickly as possible for the sake of the future:

> "We got to git," she said. "We got to find a place to stay. We got to get to work an' settle down. No use a-lettin' the little fellas go hungry. That wasn't never Granma's way. She always et a good meal at a funeral."[40]

The conserving lesson of the past is negated by the present economic reality. Ma's brave gesture fails as the family learns that California is a false goal. The imagery associated with California indicates these negations. Peter Lisca and Joseph Fontenrose have pointed to the major biblical parallels in *The Grapes of Wrath*, including those associating California and the Promised Land.[41] The parallels are intensive, even more so than Lisca and Fontenrose suggest, and their function is ironic rather than associative. To begin with, California evokes images of plenty to eat and drink. The ironic fact is that California is the literal reverse of Canaan; there is little to eat and drink, at least for Okies; but California is the Promised Land so far as the family's experience there forces the full emergence of the group concept. Appropriately, the family enters California with a foreboding that runs counter to their expectations:

> Pa called, "We're here—we're in California!" They looked dully at the broken rock glaring under the sun, and across the river the terrible ramparts of Arizona.[42]

They have crossed over, but the physical imagery foreshadows their actual human environment. The land is green across the river, but the biblical lists of landscape features are framed by the fact that they have been carrying Grandma's corpse. The human reality of California life is a living death, as the first camp, the Hooverville, suggests: "About the camp there hung a slovenly despair," everything is "grey" and "dirty," there is no work, no food, and no evident means of overcoming "despair."[43] The deadly economic reality is explained by a young man in the Hooverville, when Tom asks why the police "shove along" the migrants:

> "Some says they don' want us to vote; keep us movin' so we can't vote. An' some says so we can't get on relief. An' some says if we set in one place we'd get organized."[44]

That reply announces the political solution, the humanly possible way of countervailing power through organization. But the words are programmatic, not a revelation of character.

The difference in materials and in structure begins to appear at this point. The root of the matter is that Steinbeck is so compelled by the documentary facts that he permits their narration to take precedence over the central theme of the family's transformation into the group. And in moving the novel toward an affirmation of life in response to the facts, Steinbeck allows the Joads' experience in California to become a series of allegorical details within a panoramic structure. The narrowed scope of the materials and the schematic handling of the structure are visible in nearly every event in this part of the novel.

Casy's alternative to "despair," sacrificing himself for "the people," is almost wholly an allegorical solution. It is so abstractly schematic that at first none of the family understands its meaningful allegorical force—that loss of self leads to the group concept and thus to power to enforce the will of the group. Instead, the narrative is largely an account of the family's efforts to avoid starvation. The phrase "We got to eat" echoes through these concluding chapters.[45] Ma's changing attitude toward hungry unknown children is ambiguous: "I dunno what to do. I can't rob the fambly. I got to feed the fambly."[46] Ma grows more positive, later, when she is nagged by a storekeeper in the struck orchard:

> "Any reason you got to make fun? That help you any?" . . . "A fella got to eat," he began; and then, belligerently, "A fella got a right to eat." "What fella?" Ma asked.[47]

Ma asserts finally that only "the poor" constitute a group that practices charity:

> "I'm learnin' one thing good," she said. "Learnin' it all a time, ever' day. If you're in trouble or hurt or need—go to poor people. They're the only ones that'll help—the only ones."[48]

"The poor" are identified with "the people," who, in turn are the emerging group. Their purity is allegorical, and, in its limitation, incredible. Steinbeck's handling of "the poor" in *In Dubious Battle* is much less schematic, and therefore far more credible. In general, romanticizing "the poor" is more successful in an outright fantasy like *Tortilla Flat* but Steinbeck commits himself to a measure of realism in *The Grapes of Wrath* that does not sort well with the allegorical division of "good" from "evil."

Romanticizing "the poor" extends beyond Ma's insight to an idealization of the "folk law" that Tom envisions as the fruit of his own experience in California—at a great distance from the "building" experience on the road:

> "I been thinkin' how it was in that gov'ment camp, how our folks took care a theirselves, an' if they was a fight they fixed it theirself; an' they wasn't no cops wagglin' their guns, but they was better order than them cops ever give. I been a-wonderin' why we can't do that all over. Throw out the cops that ain't our people. All work together for our own thing—all farm our own lan'."[49]

Presenting the reverse of Tom's beatific vision in an interchapter, Steinbeck draws on the imagery of the novel's title:

> This vineyard will belong to the bank. Only the great owners can survive. . . . Men who can graft the trees and make the seed fertile and big can find no way to let the hungry people eat their produce. . . . In the souls of the people the grapes of wrath are filling and growing heavy, growing heavy for the vintage.[50]

It is not vitally important that Steinbeck's prediction of some kind of agrarian revolt has turned out to be wrong. The important artistic fact is that "good," divided sharply, abstractly, from "evil," argues that Steinbeck is not interested in rendering the materials in any great depth. Consider the contrast between the people in the government camp and in the struck orchard. Point by point, the camp people are described as clean, friendly, joyful, and organized, while in the struck orchard they are dirty, suspicious, anxious, and disorganized by the police.[51] Credibility gives way to neat opposites, which are less than convincing because Steinbeck's government camp is presented openly as a benevolent tyranny that averages out the will of "the people" to live in dignity and excludes people unable or unwilling to accept that average.

Neat opposites can gather fictive conviction if they are realized through individuals and in specific detail. There is something of that conviction in specific action against specific men, as when the camp leaders exclude troublemakers hired by business interests to break up the camp organization. There is more awkwardness in the exclusion of a small group of religious fanatics obsessed with sin. An important factor is that these people are genuinely Okies, not tools of the interests; another is that the exclusion is necessary, not realistic, if the secular values of the group concept are to prevail. Allowing for his selection and schematic treatment of these materials, Steinbeck does engineer his manipulated point with artistic skill. Fanaticism is considered a bad thing throughout the novel, both as a religious stance and as a social phenomenon. Tom's first meeting with Casy identifies "spirit" with emotional release, not a consciousness of sin, and Casy announces his own discovery, made during his time in the desert, of a social rather than an ethical connection between "spirit" and sexual excitement.[52] Further, fanaticism is identified repeatedly with a coercive denial of life. Rose of Sharon is frightened, in the government camp, by a fanatic woman's argument that dancing is sinful, that it means Rose will lose her baby. The woman's ignorance is placed against the secular knowledge of the camp manager:

> "I think the manager, he took [another girl who danced] away to drop her baby. He don' believe in sin. . . . Says the sin is bein' hungry. Says the sin is bein' cold."[53]

She compounds ignorance by telling Ma that true religion demands fixed economic classes:

> "[A preacher] says 'They's wicketness in that camp.' He says, 'The poor is tryin' to be rich.' He says, 'They's dancin' an' huggin' when they should be wailin' an' moanin' in sin.'"[54]

These social and economic denials of life are rooted in ignorance, not in spiritual enlightenment, and they are countered by the materialistic humanism of the camp manager. So fanaticism is stripped of value and associated with business in its denial of life. The case is loaded further by the benevolent tyranny of the group. Fanatics are not punished for their opinions, or even for wrongdoing. They are merely excluded, or they exclude themselves.

A similar process is apparent in the group's control of social behavior, as when Ruthie behaves as a rugged individual in the course of a children's game:

The children laid their mallets on the ground and trooped silently off the court. . . . Defiantly she hit the ball again. . . . She pretended to have a good time. And the children stood and watched. . . . For a moment she stared at them, and then she flung down the mallet and ran crying for home. The children walked back on the court. Pig-tails said to Winfield, "You can git in the nex' game." The watching lady warned them, "When she comes back an' wants to be decent, you let her. You was mean yourself, Amy."[55]

The punishment is directive. The children are being trained to accept the group and to become willing parts of the group. The process is an expression of "folk law" on a primary level. There is no doubt that Ruthie learned her correct place in the social body by invoking a suitably social punishment.

Perhaps the ugliness implicit in the tyranny of the group has become more visible lately. Certainly recent students of the phenomenon of modern conformity could supply Steinbeck with very little essential insight. The real trouble is precisely there. The tyranny of the group is visible in all of Steinbeck's instances (its ambiguity is most evident in Ruthie's case), which argues for Steinbeck's artistic honesty in rendering the materials. But he fails to see deeply enough, to see ugliness and ambiguity, because he has predetermined the absolute "good" of group behavior—an abstraction that precludes subtle technique and profound insight, on the order of Doc Burton's reservations concerning group-man. The result is a felt manipulation of values and a thinning of credibility.

Given this tendency, Steinbeck does not surprise us by dealing abstractly with the problem of leadership in the government camp. Since there is minimal narrative time in which to establish the moral purity of Jim Rawley, the camp manager, or of Ezra Huston, the chairman of the Central Committee, Steinbeck presents both men as allegorical figures. Particularly Jim Rawley. His introduction suggests his allegorical role. He is named only once, and thereafter he is called simply "the camp manager." His name is absorbed in his role as God. He is dressed "all in white," but he is not a remote God. "The frayed seams on his white coat" suggest his human availability, and his "warm" voice matches his social qualities.[56] Nevertheless, there is no doubt that he is God visiting his charges:

> He put the cup on the box with the others, waved his hand, and walked down the line of tents. And Ma heard him speaking to the people as he went.[57]

His identification with God is bulwarked when the fanatic woman calls him the devil:

> "She says you was the devil," [says Rose of Sharon]. "I know she does. That's because I won't let her make people miserable. . . . Don't you worry. She doesn't know."[58]

What "she doesn't know" is everything the camp manager does know; and if he is not the devil, he must be God. But his very human, secular divinity—he can wish for an easier lot, and he is always tired from overwork—suggests the self-sacrifice that is Casy's function. The two men are outwardly similar. Both are clean and "lean as a picket," and the camp manager has "merry eyes" like Casy's when Tom meets Casy again.[59] These resemblances would be trivial, except for a phrase that pulls them together and lends them considerable weight. Ezra Huston has no character to speak of, beyond his narrative function, except that when he has finished asking the men who try to begin a riot in the camp why they betrayed "their own people," he adds: "They don't know what they're doin'."[60] This phrase foreshadows Casy's words to his murderer just before he is killed in an effort to break the strike: "You don't know what you're a-doin'."[61] Just as these words associate Casy with Christ, so they associate the leaders in the government camp with Casy. Steinbeck's foreshortening indicates that, because Casy is established firmly as a "good" character, the leaders in the government camp must resemble Casy in that "good" identity.

The overall process is allegorical, permitting Steinbeck to assert that the camp manager and Ezra Huston are good men by definition and precluding the notion that leadership may be a corrupting role, as in *In Dubious Battle*. It follows that violence in the name of the group is "good," whereas it is "evil" in the name of business interests. The contrast is too neat, too sharp, to permit much final credibility in narrative or in characterization.

A still more extreme instance of Steinbeck's use of allegory is the process by which Tom Joad assumes the role of a leader. Tom's pastoral concept of the group is fully developed, and as the novel ends, Tom identifies himself through mystic insight with the group. Appropriately, Tom explains his insight to Ma because Tom's function is to act while Ma's function is to endure—in the name of the group. More closely, Ma's earlier phrase, "We're the people—we go on," is echoed directly in Tom's assurance when Ma fears for his life:

"Well, maybe like Casy says, a fella ain't got a soul of his own, but on'y a piece of a big one—an' then—" "Then what, Tom?" "Then it don't matter. Then I'll be all aroun' in the dark. I'll be ever'where—wherever you look. . . . See? God, I'm talkin' like Casy. Comes of thinkin' about him so much. Seems like I can see him sometimes."[62]

This anthropomorphic insight, borrowed from *To a God Unknown* and remotely from Emerson, is a serious idea, put seriously within the allegorical framework of the novel's close. Two structural difficulties result. First, Tom has learned more than Casy could have taught him—that identification *with* the group, rather than self-sacrifice *for* the group, is the truly effective way to kill the dehumanized "Bank." Here, it seems, the Christ/Casy, Saint Paul/Tom identifications were too interesting in themselves, for they limit Steinbeck's development of Tom's insight to a mechanical parallel, such as the suggestion that Tom's visions of Casy equate with Saint Paul's visions of Christ. Second, the connection between the good material life and Tom's mystical insight is missing. There is Steinbeck's close attention to Tom's political education and to his revival of belief in a moral world. But, in the specific instance, the only bridge is Tom's sudden feeling that mystical insight connects somehow with the good material life. More precisely, the bridge is Steinbeck's own assertion, since Tom's mystical vision of pastoral bliss enters the narrative only as an abstract announcement on Steinbeck's part.

Characterization is, as might be assumed, affected by this abstracting tendency. Earlier, major characters such as Tom and Ma are "given" through actions in which they are involved, not through detached, abstract essays; increasingly, at the close, the method of presentation is the detached essay or the extended, abstract speech. Steinbeck's earlier, more realized presentation of Tom as a natural man measures the difference. Even a late event, Tom's instinctive killing of Casy's murderer, connects organically with Tom's previous "social" crimes—the murder in self-defense, for which Tom has finished serving a prison term when the novel begins, and the parole that Tom jumps to go with the family to California. In all of these crimes, Tom's lack of guilt or shame links with the idea that "the people" have a "natural" right to unused land—not to add life, liberty, and the pursuit of happiness—and that "the Bank" has nothing but an abstract, merely legal right to such land. Tom's mystical vision is something else; it is a narrative shock, not due to Tom's "natural" responses, but to the oversimplified type of the "good" man that Tom is made to represent in order to close the novel on a high and optimistic note. Tom is a rather complex man earlier on, and the thinning out of his character, in its absolute identification with the "good," is an inevitable result of allegorizing.

Style suffers also from these pressures. Tom's speech has been condemned, as Emerson's writing never is, for mawkishness, for maudlin lushness, for the soft, rotten blur of intellectual evasion.[63] Style is a concomitant of structure; its decline is an effect, not a cause. Tom's thinking is embarrassing, not as thought, but as the stylistic measure of a process of manipulation that is necessary to close the novel on Steinbeck's terms.

The final scene, in which Rose of Sharon breastfeeds a sick man, has been regarded universally as the nadir of bad Steinbeck, yet the scene is no more or no less allegorical than earlier scenes in this final part. Purely in a formal sense, it parallels Tom's mystical union or identification with the group: it affirms that "life" has become more important than "family" in a specific action, and, as such, it denotes the emergence of the group concept. In that light, the scene is a technical accomplishment. Yet it is a disaster from the outset, not simply because it is sentimental; its execution, through the leading assumption, is incredible. Rose of Sharon is supposed to become Ma's alter ego by taking on her burden of moral insight, which, in turn, is similar to the insight that Tom reaches. There is no preparation for Rose of Sharon's transformation and no literary justification except a merely formal symmetry that makes it desirable, in spite of credibility, to devise a repetition. Tom, like Ma, undergoes a long process of education; Rose of Sharon is characterized in detail throughout the novel as a protected, rather thoughtless, whining girl.[64] Possibly her miscarriage produces an unmentioned, certainly mystical change in character. More likely the reader will notice the hand of the author, forcing Rose of Sharon into an unprepared and purely formalistic role.

Once given this degree of manipulation, direct sentimentality is no surprise. Worse, the imagistic shift from anger to sweetness, from the grapes of wrath to the milk of human kindness, allows the metaphor to be uplifted, but at the cost of its structural integrity. The novel is made to close with a forced image of optimism and brotherhood, with an audacious upbeat that cries out in the wilderness. I have no wish to deny the value or the real power of good men, optimism, or brotherhood. The point is that Steinbeck imposes an unsupported conclusion upon materials which themselves are thinned out and manipulated. The increasingly grotesque episodes (and their leading metaphors) prove that even thin and manipulated materials resist the conclusion that is drawn from them, for art visits that revenge on its mistaken practitioners.

To argue that no better conclusion was available at the time, granting the country's social and political immaturity and its economic innocence, simply switches the issue from art to politics. No artist is obliged to provide solutions to the problems of the socio-politico-economic order, however "engaged" his work may be. Flaubert did not present a socio-educational program to help other young women to avoid Emma Bovary's fate. The business of the artist is to present a situation. If he manipulates the materials or forces them to conclusions that violate credibility—especially if he has a visible design upon us—his work will thin, the full range of human possibility will not be available to him, and to that extent he will have failed as an artist.

We must not exclude the likelihood, not that Steinbeck had no other conclusion at hand, but that his predisposition was to see a resolution in the various allegorical and panoramic arrangements that close out *The Grapes of Wrath*; Steinbeck's earlier work argues for that likelihood.

Yet that is not all there is to John Steinbeck. If he becomes the willing victim of abstract, horrendously schematic manipulations as *The Grapes of Wrath* nears its close still he is capable of better things. He demonstrates these potentialities particularly in minor scenes dealing with minor characters, so the negative force of the imposed conclusion is lessened.

Consider the scene in which Ruthie and Winfield make their way (along with the family) from the flooded boxcar to the barn where Rose of Sharon will feed the sick man. The intention of the scene is programmatic: the children's identification with the group concept. The overt content is the essentially undamaged survival of their sense of fun and of beauty. Significantly, the action makes no directly allegorical claim on the reader, unlike the rest of the concluding scenes.

Ruthie finds a flower along the road, "a scraggly geranium gone wild, and there was one rain-beaten blossom on it."[65] The common flower, visualized, does not insist on the identity of the beaten but surviving beauty in pure nature with the uprooted, starved children of all the migrants. The scene is developed implicitly, in dramatic, imagistic terms. Ruthie and Winfield struggle to possess the petals for playthings, and Ma forces Ruthie to be kind:

> Winfield held his nose near to her. She wet a petal with her tongue and jabbed it cruelly on his nose. "You little son-of-a-bitch," she said softly. Winfield felt for the petal with his fingers, and pressed it down on his nose. They walked quickly after the others. Ruthie felt how the fun was gone. "Here," she said. "Here's some more. Stick some on your forehead."[66]

The scene recapitulates the earlier scene on the playground of the government camp. Here, as there, Winfield is the innocent, and Ruthie's cruelty is changed by external pressure (the other children, Ma's threat) to an official kindness that transcends itself to become a genuine kindness when "the fun was gone." The observed basis of the present scene is the strained relationship, that usually exists between an older sister and a younger brother. There is no visible effort to make the scene "fit" a predetermined allegorical scheme. Ruthie's kind gesture leads into Rose of Sharon's, as child to adult, and both scenes project the affirmative values—the survival of optimism, brotherhood, kindliness, goodness—that are the substance of the group concept at the conclusion. The children's quarrel and reconciliation is a relatively unloaded action, an event in itself. Tom's affirmation is nondramatic, a long, deeply mystical speech to Ma. Rose of Sharon's affirmation is out of character and frankly incredible. Uncle John's symbolic action derives from his own guilt but expresses a universal anger.

As the scene between the children is exceptional, Steinbeck's development of the flood scene is typical. Allegorical intentions override narrative power: the family's struggle against the flood is intended to equate with its surviving will to struggle against hopelessness; Pa, Uncle John, and Al are exhausted but not beaten. Tom's insight precedes the flood; Rose of Sharon's agreement to breastfeed the sick man follows it. In the larger frame, neither extreme of drought or flood can exhaust the will and the vitality of the people. The dense texture of these panoramic materials is impressive. They lie side by side, at different levels of the "willing suspension of disbelief," depending on whether they are convincing narrative actions or palpable links in an arranged allegory. Hence, there is no great sense of a concluding "knot," an organic fusion of parts; there is no more than a formulated ending, a pseudoclose that does not convince because its design is an a priori assertion of structure, not the supportive and necessary skeleton of a realized context. Here structure and materials fail to achieve a harmonious relationship.

These final scenes are not hackwork. We cannot apply to Steinbeck, even here, the slurring remark that F. Scott Fitzgerald aimed at Thomas Wolfe: "The stuff about the GREAT VITAL HEART OF AMERICA is just simply corny."[67] Steinbeck's carefully interwoven strands of character, metaphor, and narrative argue a conscious, skillful intention, not a sudden lapse of material or of novelistic ability. Even in failure, Steinbeck is a formidable technician. His corn, here, if it exists, is not a signal of failed ability.

Steinbeck's feeling that *The Grapes of Wrath* must close on an intense level of sweetness, of optimism and affirmation, is not seriously in doubt. His ability to use the techniques of structure to this end is evident. The earlier novels demonstrate his able willingness to skillfully apply an external structure, to mold, or at least to mystify, somewhat recalcitrant materials. The letter withdrawing *L'Affaire Lettuceberg* suggests that Steinbeck is aware of having that willing skill—"just twisting this people out of shape"—and of having to resist its lures in this most serious work. So for the critic there is a certain horrid fascination in Steinbeck's consistent, enormously talented demonstration of aesthetic failure in the last quarter of *The Grapes of Wrath*.

The failure is not a matter of "sprawling asides and extravagances," or the more extreme motivational simplicities of naturalism, or a lapse in the remarkably sustained folk idiom and the representative epic scope. The failure lies in the means Steinbeck utilizes to achieve the end.

The first three quarters of the novel are masterful. Characters are presented through action; symbolism intensifies character and action; the central theme of transformation from self to group develops persuasively in a solid, realized documentary context. The final quarter of the novel presents a difference in every respect. Characters are fitted or forced into allegorical roles, heightened beyond the limits of credibility, to the point that they thin out or become frankly unbelievable. Scenes are developed almost solely as links in an allegorical pattern. Texture is reduced to documentation, and allegorical signs replace symbolism. The result is a hollowed rhetoric, a manipulated affirmation, a soft twist of insistent sentiment. These qualities deny the conceptual theme by simplifying it, by reducing the facts of human and social complexity to simple opposites.

The reduction is not inherent in the materials, which are rendered magnificently in earlier parts of the novel. The reduction is the consequence of a structural choice—to apply allegory to character, metaphor, and theme. In short, *The Grapes of Wrath* could conceivably have a sweetly positive conclusion without an absolute, unrestrained dependence on allegory. Yet the least subtle variety of that highly visible structural technique, with its objectionably simplified, manipulative ordering of materials, is precisely the element that prevails in the final part of *The Grapes of Wrath*.

Why? Steinbeck is aware of various technical options, and he is able to make use of them earlier in the novel. As we have seen in the previous novels, with the exception of *In Dubious Battle*, Steinbeck draws on allegory to stiffen or to heighten fictions that are too loose—too panoramic—to achieve the semblance of a dramatic structure purely by means of technique. Apparently Steinbeck was not offended aesthetically by the overwhelming artificiality that results from an extreme dependence on allegory. That the contemporary naturalistic or symbolic novel requires a less simple or rigid structure clearly escapes Steinbeck's attention.

On the contrary, Steinbeck is greatly attracted to some extreme kind of external control in much of the immediately preceding work and in much of the succeeding work. During the rest of his career, Steinbeck does not attempt seriously, on the massive scale of *The Grapes of Wrath*, to achieve a harmonious relationship between structure and materials. He prefers some version of the control that flaws the last quarter of *The Grapes of Wrath*.

This judgment offers a certain reasonableness in the otherwise wild shift from *The Grapes of Wrath* to the play-novelettes.

Notes

1. John Steinbeck, *The Grapes of Wrath* (New York: The Viking Press, Inc., 1939). Hereafter cited as *GW*.

2. Louis Kronenberger, *The Nation*, 148 (April 15, 1939), 440. "It is, I think, one of those books—there are not very many—which really do some good."

3. I list a typical range of such criticism by date of publication.

   a. James T. Farrell, "The End of a Literary Decade," *The American Mercury*, 48 (December 1939), 408-14.

   b. Edmund Wilson, "The Californians: Storm and Steinbeck," *The New Republic*, 103 (December 9, 1940), 784-87.

   c. Stanley Edgar Hyman, "Some Notes on John Steinbeck," *Antioch Review*, 2 (Summer 1942), 185-200.

   d. Maxwell Geismar, *Writers in Crisis* (Boston: Houghton Mifflin Company, 1942), pp. 237-70.

   e. Alfred Kazin, *On Native Grounds* (New York: Harcourt, Brace & Co., 1942), pp. 393-94.

   f. W. M. Frohock, "John Steinbeck's Men of Wrath," *Southwest Review*, 31 (Spring 1946), 144-52.

   g. John S. Kennedy, "John Steinbeck: *Life Affirmed and Dissolved*," in *Fifty Years of the American Novel*, ed. H. C. Gardiner, S.J. (New York: Charles Scribner's Sons, 1951), pp. 217-36.

   h. Frederick J. Hoffman, *The Modern Novel in America: 1900-1959* (Chicago: Henry Regnery Company, 1951), pp. 146-53.

   i. Edmund Fuller, "The New Compassion in the American Novel," *The American Scholar*, 26 (Spring 1957), 155-63.

j. Walter Fuller Taylor, "*The Grapes of Wrath* Reconsidered," *Mississippi Quarterly*, 12 (Summer 1959), 136-44.

4. I list a typical range of such criticism by date of publication.

a. Harry Thornton Moore, *The Novels of John Steinbeck* (Chicago: Normandie House, 1939), pp. 53-72

b. Frederic I. Carpenter, "The Philosophical Joads," *College English*, 2 (January 1941), 315-25.

c. Joseph Warren Beach, *American Fiction: 1920-1940* (New York: The Macmillan Company, 1941), pp. 327-47.

d. Chester E. Eisinger, "Jeffersonian Agrarianism in *The Grapes of Wrath*," *University of Kansas City Review*, 14 (Winter 1947), 149-54.

e. Peter Lisca, "*The Grapes of Wrath* as Fiction," *PMLA*, 72 (March 1957), 296-309.

f. Eric C. Carlson, "Symbolism in *The Grapes of Wrath*," *College English*, 19 (January 1958), 172-75.

g. Theodore Pollock, "On the Ending of *The Grapes of Wrath*," *Modern Fiction Studies*, 4 (Summer 1958), 177-78.

5. I list a typical range of such criticism by date of publication.

a. Woodburn Ross, "John Steinbeck: Earth and Stars," in *University of Missouri Studies in Honor of A. H. R. Fairchild* (XXI), ed. Charles T. Prouty (Columbia: University of Missouri Press, 1946), pp. 177-91.

b. Frederick Bracher, "Steinbeck and the Biological View of Man," *The Pacific Spectator*, 2 (Winter 1948), 14-29.

c. Woodburn Ross, "John Steinbeck: Naturalism's Priest," *College English*, 10 (May 1949), 432-37.

6. Freeman Champney, "John Steinbeck, Californian," *The Antioch Review*, 7:3 (Fall 1947), 355. Reprinted by permission of *The Antioch Review.*

7. The main sources are:

a. John Steinbeck, "Dubious Battle in California," The *Nation*, 143 (September 12, 1936), 302-4.

b. John Steinbeck, "The Harvest Gypsies," *San Francisco News*, October 5-12, 1936. Reprinted with a 1938 epilogue and retitled *Their Blood Is Strong*, under the auspices of the Simon J. Lubin Society of California, Inc., April 1938. Reprinted in *A Companion to "The Grapes of Wrath,"* ed. Warren French (New York: The Viking Press, Inc., 1963), pp. 53-92.

c. Lewis Gannett, "Introduction: John Steinbeck's Way of Writing," *The Viking Portable Steinbeck* (New York: The Viking Press, Inc., 1946), pp. xx-xxiv.

d. Moore, pp. 53-54, 85, 88, 90.

e. Peter Lisca, *The Wide World of John Steinbeck* (New Brunswick: Rutgers University Press, 1958), pp. 144-48.

8. Gannett, pp. xxii-xxiii.

9. *GW*, p. 606. "Use' ta be the fambly was fust. It ain't so now. It's anybody. Worse off we get, the more we got to do."

10. *GW*, pp. 37, 45-46, 73, 312, 535-36, 597-98.

11. *GW*, pp. 45-46, 406-7, 432.

12. *GW*, pp. 45-46, 50-53, 63-65. That buccaneering capitalism is an abstract or allegorical monster of evil is left to implication in *In Dubious Battle*. Steinbeck is far more directly allegorical in characterizing "the Bank" as an evil, nonhuman monster. Consequently there is, I think, a gain in horror but a relative loss of credibility.

13. It would be too severe to blame Steinbeck for failing to foresee a quite different solution, a war that produced jobs for the Okies. But a cropper does plead to keep his land because with so many wars in sight cotton will go up (p. 44). That logic is rejected, possibly to motivate the emergence of the group—an insight that has turned out to be too shallow or too simple. *The Grapes of Wrath* has lost readers most often in our time because of its serious loss of historic relevance.

14. I am indebted to Harry Thornton Moore for the directional suggestion. See Moore, p. 55.

15. *GW*, p. 20.

16. *GW*, p. 609. The reversal of values is evident in the reversed symbolism; the river bears death—not life, the coffin—not water to seeds in the earth.

17. *GW*, p. 28.

18. *GW*, p. 28.

19. *GW*, p. 29.

20. *GW*, pp. 364, 520, 527.

21. *GW*, pp. 6-7, 43-47, 65, 104, 196-97, 206, 236, 259, 264-70, 273, 279, 317-18, 324-25.

22. *GW*, pp. 165, 171,174-75, 215-20, 245-46.

23. It is a curious fact that Steinbeck attempts to create a so-called "universal language" in *Burning Bright*, a far more theory-ridden novel than *The Grapes of Wrath*. In any event, the attempt produces a fantastic, wholly incredible language.

24. *GW*, pp. 67-71, 151.

25. Noah does not suggest earlier "idiot" characters—the two Burgundians in *Cup of Gold*, Willie in *To a God Unknown*, and Tularecito in *The Pastures of Heaven*. Instead, Noah's shadowy, directed character recalls one aspect of Lennie in *Of Mice and Men*.

26. *GW*, pp. 170-74, 242, 343-44, 372.

27. Fifteen years later, Steinbeck detailed this technique in a witty article, "How to Tell Good Guys from Bad Guys," *The Reporter*, 12 (March 10, 1955), 42-44. In that quite different, political context, Steinbeck demonstrates that he knows the technique is too bluntly black and white to permit any but the broadest cartoon characterization. There is every reason to think he knew as much in 1935 or 1939.

28. Because of that involvement, it is incorrect to think of the interchapters as choral. We see the difference in comparing the four detached interchapters in *Cup of Gold* with any interchapters in *The Grapes of Wrath*, and we see as well Steinbeck's artistic growth in the organic integration of chapter and interchapter in the later novel. For an excellent analysis of style in the interchapters, see Lisca, pp. 160-65. The stylistic variety always suited to its content is further evidence of a conscious, intentional artistry.

29. *GW*, pp. 6, 592-94.

30. *GW*, p. 55.

31. *GW*, p. 135.

32. *GW*, p. 196.

33. *GW*, p. 203.

34. *GW*, p. 313.

35. *GW*, pp. 301-2.

36. *GW*, pp. 311-12.

37. *GW*, p. 283.

38. *GW*, p. 241.

39. *GW*, p. 265.

40. *GW*, p. 328.

41. Lisca, pp. 169-70; Joseph Fontenrose, *John Steinbeck: An Introduction and Interpretation* (New York: Barnes & Noble, Inc., 1963), pp. 74-83.

42. *GW*, p. 275.

43. *GW*, pp. 327-29.

44. *GW*, pp. 332-33.

45. *GW*, pp. 479, 483, 487, 497, 512-13.

46. *GW*, p. 351.

47. *GW*, p. 512.

48. *GW*, pp. 513-14.

49. *GW*, p. 571.

50. *GW*, p. 476

51. *GW*, pp. 389-491, 558.

52. *GW*, pp. 27, 29, 30, 31-32.

53. *GW*, p. 423.

54. *GW*, p. 437.

55. *GW*, pp. 433-34.

56. *GW*, pp. 415-16.

57. *GW*, p. 416.

58. *GW*, p. 424.

59. *GW*, pp. 25-26, 415, 521.

60. *GW*, p. 470.

61. *GW*, p. 527.

62. *GW*, p. 572.

63. See references in endnote 3.

64. *GW*, pp. 129-30, 134-35, 175-77, 285-86, 343-44, 366, 371-72, 378-79, 413-14, 420-425, 440, 460-61, 482-85, 504, 508, 537, 539, 548, 580-81, 586-88.

65. *GW*, p. 615.

66. *GW*, pp. 615-16.

67. F. Scott Fitzgerald, *The Letters of F. Scott Fitzgerald*, edited, with an introduction by Andrew Turnbull (New York: Charles Scribner's Sons, 1963), p. 97. Reprinted by permission of Charles Scribner's Sons. Copyright © 1963 Frances Scott Fitzgerald Lanahan.

John Steinbeck:
*The Grapes of Wrath*_____

Donald Pizer

Steinbeck's most famous novel is enshrouded in a number of myths about its origin and nature. Here is a work which appears to be the epitome of the 1930s proletarian novel in that all its good people speak bad English, which sweetens its animal view of human nature with an anomalous mixture of Christian symbolism and scientific philosophy, and which appeals principally on the level of sentimentality and folk humor. *The Grapes of Wrath*, in short, is naturalism suffering the inevitable consequences of its soft thinking and its blatant catering to popular interests.[1]

The Grapes of Wrath is indeed closely linked to the 1930s. Unlike either *Studs Lonigan* or *U.S.A.*, *The Grapes of Wrath* is set entirely within the 1930s and is concerned with a distinctive condition of the depression. The novel is also a work of the 1930s in the sense that it is a product of Steinbeck's artistic maturation during that decade. His first three novels, all of the late 1920s, are marked by excessive fantasy and turgid allegory. In 1930 Steinbeck married Carol Henning, met the marine biologist Ed Ricketts, and began to interest himself in economic and social problems.[2] His wife's deep commitment to his career, Ricketts' philosophical naturalism, and the impingement of contemporary social events on his writing seemed to push Steinbeck not into a denial of his earlier "romantic" strain but toward a hybrid form in which symbol making and ideas have a solid base in contemporary life. In the mid-1930s Steinbeck became absorbed in the plight of the migrant farm workers of the central California valleys. He reported their conditions, talked at great length about their ways in the prairie West and California with the sympathetic manager of a government camp,[3] and thus gained an awareness of the substantive detail which crowds *The Grapes of Wrath*.

The Grapes of Wrath is also a depression novel in its often doctrinaire 1930s economic, social, and political ideas. As late as 1960, in a reminiscence of the 1930s, Steinbeck still held a melodramatic view of the decade, one in which Hoover epitomized the forces of social evil and Roosevelt of good.[4] *The Grapes of Wrath* has something of the same character. Evil is epitomized by the great banks and corporations which oppress the common worker and manipulate, by fear, the lower middle class. The California portion of the novel even enacts an American version of European fascism, in which the deputies and vigilantes are proto-fascists and the migrants are hounded Jews. To this 1930s mix, Steinbeck adds an appropriately Marxist interpretation of history and of economic processes. The migrants can be exploited because labor is abundant, the "lesson of history" is that the increasing chasm between the haves and the have-nots will result in revolution, and organization of the masses—from camp sanitation committees to labor unions—is the solution to all social problems.

There is also an element of truth in the view that *The Grapes of Wrath* contains an uneasy amalgam of what Edmund Wilson called "biological realism"[5] and an overapparent Christian symbolism. Few readers today would accept Wilson's remark of 1940 that Steinbeck's characters are "so rudimentary that they are almost on the animal level" or the obsessive concern in the 1950s and early 1960s with Biblical parallels in the novel.[6] Nevertheless, the Joads are primitive folk who live close to the natural processes of life, Steinbeck does occasionally indulge in a blatant animism (the turtle crossing the road is a famous example), and the Joads' exodus and Casy's life and death are immediately evocative of Christian myth.

Perhaps the most troublesome matter involving the background of *The Grapes of Wrath* in recent decades has been the relationship between the themes of the novel and the philosophical ideas expressed by Steinbeck in his *Sea of Cortez*. Ostensibly a record of a voyage in 1940 by Steinbeck and Ricketts to study marine life in Lower California, *Sea of Cortez* also contains a number of philosophical meditations. The most significant of these is an "Easter Sermon" on the advantages of

---

"non-teleological" or "is" thinking.[7] The non-teleological thinker accepts the fatuousness of man's belief that his will can control events and thus concentrates on understanding experience rather than on judging men. Steinbeck also expresses in *Sea of Cortez* a belief in group identity,[8] an identity which he elsewhere calls the "phalanx." As individuals, all creatures, including man, are usually weak and unknowing; as members of a group they can "key in" to the strength and knowledge of the group. A group can thus have a distinctive identity. As Steinbeck wrote in a letter of 1933, when he first became interested in this idea, "the fascinating thing to me is the way the group has a soul, a drive, an intent, an end, a method, a reaction and a set of tropisms which in no way resembles the same things possessed by the men who make up the group. These groups have always been considered as individuals multiplied. And they are not so. They are beings in themselves, entities."[9]

The two ideas, non-teleological thinking and the phalanx, have long been thought to be the product of Steinbeck's association with Ed Ricketts, but they have also been viewed as irreconcilable ideas both in *Sea of Cortez* and in Steinbeck's fiction. The amoral passivity of "is" thinking and the possibility for beneficial and self-directed group action by the phalanx appear to be incompatible, and "is" thinking in particular seems to be foreign to the moral indignation present in much of Steinbeck's fiction of the decade. But with the recent publication of Richard Astro's *John Steinbeck and Edward F. Ricketts: The Shaping of a Novelist* and Elaine Steinbeck and Robert Wallsten's *Steinbeck: A Life in Letters* it can be seen that the problem in fact does not exist. Although both Steinbeck's and Ricketts' names appear on the title page of *Sea of Cortez*, it was always believed that Steinbeck himself wrote the narrative portion of the book and that he therefore assumed full responsibility for all of the ideas in that portion. We now know, however, that Steinbeck incorporated verbatim sections from Ricketts' unpublished philosophical writing, including the passage on non-teleological thinking.[10] Although Steinbeck occasionally used or referred to Ricketts' non-teleological beliefs, he was absorbed most of all during the 1930s, as his letters reveal, by the phalanx idea. He could thus either ignore or contradict "is" thinking when other, more compelling beliefs attracted him. In *Sea of Cortez*, for example, the narrator of the voyage (here presumably Steinbeck) records his anger at the Japanese factory fishing boats which were depleting the waters off Lower California and thus causing hardship among the Mexicans.[11] And so in *The Grapes of Wrath* itself Casy's early defense of non-teleological thinking—"There ain't no sin and there ain't no virtue. There's just stuff people do"[12]—is clearly in the context of an attack on a puritan sexual morality. The issue of the anomaly of Steinbeck's non-teleological philosophy is really a non-issue. The concept was largely Ricketts', and though Steinbeck does occasionally endorse it in special contexts, his own deepest involvement was in the emotionally and morally compelling social activism implied by the phalanx idea.

Thus, there indeed are primitivist, Marxist, Christian, and scientific elements in *The Grapes of Wrath*. But no one of them is the single most dominant element and none is present in a single and obvious way. Rather, they exist in a fabric of complex interrelationship which constitutes both the power and permanence of *The Grapes of Wrath* as a naturalistic tragedy.

* * *

The first two portions of *The Grapes of Wrath*—the Joads in Oklahoma and on the road to California—enforce upon us the realization that the more we come to know and admire the humanity of the Joads the more inhumanely they are treated. Steinbeck's success in involving us in this irony derives in part from his ability to place the Joads within two interrelated mythic sources of value: they are primitives and they are folk. Their "natural" ways and feelings touch upon a core belief which in various forms runs through American life from the Enlightenment to the primitivistic faith of such moderns as Faulkner and Hemingway.

The Joads are close to the natural processes and rhythms of life. They are farmers who have always farmed and hunted. They have little education and little association with town or city. Their unit of social life is the family with its "natural" crests of birth, puberty, and marriage at one end of life and aging and death at the other. Indeed, the Joads seem to live in a pre-tribal stage of social evolution, since their principal contacts are with other families rather than with school, church, or state. Spoken and written expression to them is always a barrier; they communicate largely by action and by an instinctive sensitivity to unspoken feelings. We first encounter them not in person but rather in the long series of anecdotes about them which Tom and Casy share at the opening of the novel, anecdotes which establish their shrewdness, openness, and understanding in a context of crudity and occasional bestiality. But even this texture of animality in their lives helps establish their naturalness.

As primitives, the Joads have an "honest" relationship to their land. They farm to live, not for profit, and out of the intrinsic relationship between their work and their existence there emerges the life-sustaining values of industry and pride as well as an instinctive generosity and compassion. They seem at first lawless because of their opposition to those who wish to remove them from their land, but their experiences on the road reveal that regulation and order in their lives arise organically out of their needs and conditions. The different families meeting each night in makeshift camps along Route 66 quickly establish unwritten codes of behavior which maintain order and equity in the camps.

The care with which Steinbeck molds our sense of the primitive strength of the Joads early in the novel is especially revealed in two areas of their experience. The Joads are attuned to solving the problems of their lives without outside aid. They raise and prepare their own food, they make their own clothes, and they create and maintain their own special form of transportation. We thus come to accept that the Joads are latter-day pioneers, that the myth of the self-sustaining pioneer family still lives in them. But the Joads not only solve problems by the exercise of individual skills but also by the maintenance of a group strength and efficiency. Here Steinbeck is at pains to dramatize his phalanx notion of the distinctive identity of the group. So, for example, in the family councils just before departure or soon after Grandpa's death, the family when it meets to solve its problems becomes a powerful and cohesive single body, "an organization of the unconscious. They obeyed impulses which registered only faintly in their thinking minds" (135).

The Joads are folk as well as primitives; that is, we also experience the comic and the ritualized in their naturalness. For example, the three generations of the Joads constitute a gallery of family folk types: earthy and querulous grandparents, eccentric and even occasionally demented uncles and brothers, cocky and sexually vibrant late adolescents, and over-curious and problem-creating children. Above all, the Joads contain the archetypal center of the folk family, the mother as source of love, wisdom, and strength. The Joads as folk salt the novel with the sexuality and excrementality of folk humor and with the ritualized forms of folk life, particularly of courtship and death. Some of the folk attributes and experiences of the Joads have both a Dickensian predictability of repetitive motif and a freakish humor characteristic of Erskine Caldwell's portrayal of poor whites. (The Joads' discovery of the flush toilet is pure Caldwell.) But the folk element in the lives of the Joads, when combined with the central strain of their primitivism, contributes to rather than diminishes our sense of their basic humanity. The earthiness and humor of the Joads as folk permit Steinbeck to avoid the heavy-breathing and lush primitivism of his early fiction—notably of *To a God Unknown*—and encourage us to respond to them not only as symbols but as "real" people.

The Joads as primitive folk appear to be opposed by the life-denying forces of the mechanical, institutional, and intellectual. In Oklahoma these forces are allegorized by the banks and corporations which have the law and wealth on their side but which lack the human attributes of understanding and compassion. The forces are symbolized above all by the impersonal and mechanical tractor which destroys the farmers' homes and by the anonymous car which attempts to run over the turtle as it goes about its "business" of spreading the seed of life. Yet the mechanical and the commercial are not inherently evil. The Joads' jerry-built truck soon becomes a symbol of family unity as well as a means of fulfilling their striving for a better life. And the small businessmen along the road and the small California ranchers are themselves threatened with destruction. If the tractor were owned and used by the Joads, Steinbeck tells us, it would be a beneficial mechanical force. The real evils in the Joads' life are thus not the abstractions of the mechanical or the institutional but the human failings of fear, anger, and selfishness. Those who cheat or beleaguer or harass the Joads in Oklahoma and on the road and in California may symbolize the opposition of the structured in life to the natural but they are above all greedy or frightened men who wish to preserve or add to what they own. Steinbeck's depiction of this essentially human conflict suggests that his attempt in *The Grapes of Wrath* was not to dramatize a labored and conventional primitivistic ethic. It was rather to engage us, within the context of primitivistic values, in one of the permanent centers of human experience, that of the difficulty of transcending our own selves and thereby recognizing the nature and needs of others.

Although the Joads as a family are the matrix of this growth, the process of transcendence occurs most pointedly and fully in the lives of Tom, Ma, and Casy. The experiences of these characters illustrate Steinbeck's faith in the ability of man to move from what he calls an "I" to a "We" consciousness.[13] The "conversion" of Tom, Ma, and Casy to a "We" state of mind is both the theme and the form of *The Grapes of Wrath*; it is also Steinbeck's contribution both to the naturalistic theme of the humanity of all sorts and conditions of men and to the naturalistic tragic novel of the 1930s.

Tom is initially the symbol of "natural man." He is big and raw-boned, is uncomfortable in store-bought clothes, and he can roll a cigarette or skin a rabbit expertly. He has humor, understanding, and a commonsense shrewdness and he is proud and independent. He judges men and events with generosity of spirit, but his faith in his judgment and in a natural order in life has been tempered by his imprisonment for killing a man in self-defense during a drunken brawl. He cannot understand his punishment and emerges from prison with the belief that it is better to live from moment to moment than to seek to understand and thus to plan.

If Tom is natural man, Ma is natural woman in the roles of wife and mother. Steinbeck's initial description of her renders with a blatantly exultant religiosity her character and function as preserver of the family:

> Her full face was not soft; it was controlled, kindly. Her hazel eyes seemed to have experienced all possible tragedy and to have mounted pain and suffering like steps into a high calm and a superhuman understanding. She seemed to know, to accept, to welcome her position, the citadel of the family, the strong place that could not be taken. . . . And from her great and humble position in the family, she had taken dignity and a clean calm beauty. . . . She seemed to know that if she swayed the family shook, and if she ever really deeply wavered or despaired the family would fall, the family will to function would be gone. (100)

Tom's power lies in his pride and shrewdness, Ma's in her capacity to love and in her sense of continuity. To her, life is not a series of beginnings and endings but rather "all one flow, like a stream, little eddies, little waterfalls. . . . Woman looks at it like that. We ain't gonna die out. People is goin' on—changin' a little, maybe, but goin' right on" (577). If Tom represents natural strength, Ma represents natural religion. She is appalled by the religion of fear and sin which she encounters in the woman in black at Grandma's death and in the "Jesus-lover" at Weedpatch. Her religion is of love, and love to her means constant rededication to preserving the family, just as Tom's strength means solving the problems which this pledge demands.

Whereas Tom and Ma are fully realized both as characters and as symbols, Casy functions principally as a symbol. Dissatisfied with conventional religious truth because it runs counter to his own impulses, he seeks to find God in his own spirit rather than in Bible or church. On the morning of the Joads' departure, he is asked to say grace before breakfast. He seizes the opportunity to tell them of his attempt to commune with God in the hills. He felt a oneness with all things, he explains,

> "An' I got thinkin', on'y it wasn't thinkin', it was deeper down than thinkin'. I got thinkin' how we was holy when we was one thing, an' mankin' was holy when it was one thing. An' it on'y got unholy when one mis'able little fella got the bit in his teeth an' run off his own way, kickin' and draggin' an' fightin'. Fella like that bust the holiness. But when they're all workin' together, not one fella for another fella, but one fella kind of harnessed to the whole shebang—that's right, that's holy." (110)

The Joads, however, scarcely listen; they are absorbed in the expectation of breakfast. And Casy does not really understand the implications of his insight into the nature of "holiness" as a kind of phalanx of group oneness. The journey of the Joads, and particularly of Tom, Ma, and Casy, is thus not so much to California as toward a full understanding and acceptance of this vision of human sanctity and strength.

* * *

The "I" quality of life, man's selfishness in its various forms, is the dominant force in the Oklahoma portion of *The Grapes of Wrath*. It exists not only in the corporate "I" of the banks and land companies which are displacing the Joads but in the Joads themselves. Their intense and instinctive commitment to family unity and preservation is a superficially attractive but nevertheless narrow and limited form of self-absorption. It has already been revealed as ineffective in that it has not prevented their eviction. And the local young man who is driving the tractor which is bulldozing their home displays its vital flaw when he says, in defense of his turning against his own people, "'You got no call to worry about anybody's kids but your own'" (51). Not to worry about someone else's children, however, as the novel makes clear in incident after incident involving a child, is to aid not only in the destruction of the children of others but of one's own.

The Oklahoma section of the novel also contains several strains of "We" thinking, strains which emerge more clearly and fully as the novel proceeds. The famous description of the turtle crossing the road is a parable not only of persistence within nature—of the turtle continuing his journey with ingenuity and strength despite hazards and setbacks—but of the relatedness and unity of all life. The turtle unconsciously carries in a crevice of his shell a seed from a plant he has brushed against; he thus has both a specific goal and the general function of contributing to the perpetuation of other forms of life. Tom and Ma at this point are somewhat like the turtle in that while pursuing a specific narrow goal they also reveal in several ways an unconscious acceptance of a "We" ethic. Ma, when she reflects on the number of tenant farmers being evicted, moves instinctively toward a Marxist idea of unity: "'They say there's a hun'erd thousand of us shoved out. If we was all mad the same way . . . —they wouldn't hunt nobody down'" (104). And Tom accepts without question Muley's observation that "'If a fella's got somepin to eat an' another fella's hungry—why, the first fella ain't got no choice'" (66). But these "We" qualities, like those of the turtle and other animals, are both instinctive and ungeneralized. They have not taken on the human qualities of consciousness and abstraction, the qualities which Steinbeck later in the novel associates with "Manself"—the distinctive ability of man to give up something material, even life itself, for a concept. The "We" in man, though an attribute of the universal potential for a phalanx identity, is distinguished by conscious awareness and direction.

The tension between the primitive folk "I-ness" of the Joads' commitment to family and their tentative reaching out toward a "We-ness" continues on the road. Now, however, new conditions and experiences

---

impress on the Joads a greater sense of the meaning and validity of "We." "I-ness" is of course still paramount in their minds, particularly after Grandpa's death raises the specter of eventual dispersal of the family. Their response to the crisis of his death—the decision to bury him by the side of the road—renews a pioneer custom and thus affirms the primacy of the family in the westering experience. But on the road the Joads encounter families like them in intent and need, such as the Wilsons, and so begin to move out of their isolation.[14] And in the wayside camps the Joads begin to realize the benefits of group cooperation. Perhaps most of all they begin to sense the potential strength in the fact that so many share the same condition; they are beginning to shape in their minds the vital difference, as Steinbeck expresses it in an interchapter, between "I lost my land" and "We lost *our* land" (206).

The California experiences of the Joads—and particularly of Ma and Tom—make explicit to them the difference between "I" and "We." This portion of the novel is divided into four segments. The first two (the Hooverville and Weedpatch) demonstrate concretely to the Joads the opposition between the "I" and "We" ways of life; the second two (the peach ranch and the boxcar) demand of them a conscious allegiance either to "I" or "We." The Hooverville and the government camp at Weedpatch represent, as many readers have complained, a loaded contrast in human values. The Hooverville is an allegorical representation of anarchistic animality, of the anger, cruelty, and desperation of men seeking to survive in a world in which they are pitted against each other. Put in Marxist terms, the Hooverville is a free market economy when the supply of labor exceeds demand and when labor is unorganized. The government camp, though it is an island in a hostile sea, is maintained on the principle of the surrender of some individual rights for the greater good of the whole. Its method is organization to achieve group aims, and its operative unit is the committee. Put in Marxist terms, it is the proletarian state.

The Joads are almost immediately involved in the destructive violence of the Hooverville; at Weedpatch they flourish and contribute to the suppression of violence. As throughout the novel, the ethical distinction between the "I" of the Hooverville and the "We" of Weedpatch is revealed by the treatment of children at the two camps. When the Joads arrive at the Hooverville Ma prepares supper and soon finds herself surrounded by starving children. She is torn between her commitment to her own family and her responsiveness to the silently begging children, and can only cry out, "'I dunno what to do. I got to feed the fambly. What'm I gonna do with these here?'" (350). In Weedpatch the problem of hungry children is resolved not by depriving one's own—not by the "I" principle of the conflict between mine and yours—but by maintaining a camp fund which dispenses loans to those in need.

The peach ranch to which the Joads are forced to move in order to get work unites the Hooverville and Weedpatch principles in one volatile setting. Inside the ranch, in a kind of prison, are the families driven to the "I" of scabbing because of their desperate need; outside are striking migrants who have organized to help all migrants. Casy had been separated from the Joads at the Hooverville when he had been arrested for coming to the aid of a man being framed by the deputies. He now reappears as a strike leader and union organizer, and explains his conversion to Tom. "'Here's me, been a-goin' into the wilderness like Jesus to try to find out somepin. Almost got her sometimes, too. But it's in the jailhouse I really got her'" (521). What he had learned in prison, in the incident of the men acting in unison to gain better food, was the principle of group action to achieve just ends. Life had a holy unity both in the wilderness and in jail, but he has discovered in jail that his function was not passively to accept this holiness but to seek actively to render it concrete in social life. Tom, however, doesn't fully understand Casy's explanation, and Casy says, "'Maybe I can't tell you. . . . Maybe you got to find out'" (522).

The vigilantes attack the strikers, and as Casy is about to be clubbed down, he says, "'You fellas don' know what you're doin'. You're helpin' to starve kids'" (527). The first sentence of this speech (and its repetition by Casy just before his death) is often cited as a specific parallel between Casy and Christ. In fact, Casy is a Christ-figure only in the social-activist sense of the Christian life in *The Grapes of Wrath*. The vigilantes are not killing the son of God but children who have been denied their humanity, and Casy is not sacrificed to vouchsafe a heaven for man but to aid man to achieve a better life on earth. Holiness is not a condition between God (or his son) and man but between man and man, between all the members of the "whole shebang," as Casy put it earlier. Helping to starve children is thus unholy or parallel to killing Christ; helping to create a society in which children will be fed is man's true Christlike role on earth.

Even though Tom fails to grasp Casy's meaning at this point, he has been growing in understanding. True, his two acts of involvement so far—his coming to the aid of the Hooverville migrant earlier and of Casy now—were instinctive responses to blatant acts of bullying. But he has also been absorbing a sense of the social injustice and of the fundamental inhumanity in the condition of the migrants which is now reaching the level of consciousness. He realizes that the landowners wish not only to employ the migrants but to turn them into a kind of obedient domestic animal. "'They're a-workin' away at our spirits,'" he tells the family. "'They're a-tryin' to make us cringe an' crawl like a whipped bitch. They tryin' to break us'" (381).

In defending Casy, Tom has killed a man and therefore has to live in the fields when the family moves on to pick cotton and live in an abandoned boxcar. Musing over Casy's ideas and experiences, he now accepts what he had earlier neither understood nor had even consciously heard. Casy, he recalls,

> "went out in the wilderness to find his own soul, an' he foun' he didn' have no soul that was his'n. Says he foun' he jus' got a little piece of a great big soul. Says a wilderness ain't no good, 'cause his little piece of a soul wasn't no good 'less it was with the rest, an' was whole. Funny how I remember. Didn' think I was even listenin'. But I know now a fella ain't no good alone." (570)

Tom here expresses both Casy's wilderness vision and his later social expansion and application of that vision. The wilderness (contemplation and passivity) is not a true joining of one's soul to that of all men; only in social unity and action can this be achieved. So Tom decides to pursue a true "We-ness"; like Casy, he will now attempt to organize the migrants.

The Joads, and particularly Ma, move in an analogous direction. In the crisis of Rose's delivery during the flood, the Wainwrights, who are as beleaguered as the Joads, come to their aid. When Ma tries to thank Mrs. Wainwright, she replies,

> "No need to thank. Ever'body's in the same wagon. S'pose we was down. You'd a give us a han'."
>
> "Yes," Ma said, "we would."
>
> "Or anybody."
>
> "Or anybody. Use' ta be the fambly was fust. It ain't so now. It's anybody. Worse off we get, the more we got to do." (606)

So Ma, the staunchest defender of the "I" of the family, has come to accept consciously the principle of "We" embodied in the "anybody" of those in need.

The conclusion of the novel, when Rose of Sharon gives her breast to the starving man in the barn, unites in one symbolic act various themes which have been fully dramatized in the conversions of Tom and Ma. Throughout the novel Rose's pregnancy has represented one of the major strands in the primitive character of the Joads as a family. Her child-bearing is honored because it is a contribution to family continuity, and it constitutes, because of her intense self-preoccupation, the inward-turning nature of the family. But with the birth of her still-born child—a child who is the last "starving kid" of the novel—she is freed from these "I" roles. Encouraged by Ma, she can now—in a climactic gesture of conversion—move outward to the "We" of the starving man. She is saying, in effect, that all those who hunger are her children, just as Tom has given himself to the anonymous migrants who require leadership and Ma to the "anybody" who needs.

By the close of the novel the Joads have been stripped clean in several senses. They have lost most of their possessions, including the truck which had served since their departure from Oklahoma as a symbol of family unity. In the family itself, the weak (Grandpa and Grandma) and the irredeemably self-preoccupied (Noah, Connie, and finally Al) have fallen away. Left is a core of Ma and Pa, Uncle John and Rose, and the two children, Ruth and Winfield. With the exception of the children but including Tom, this is a group in which each figure has conformed to the Biblical promise that to lose all is often to gain one's salvation; that is, each has struggled through to a form of "We" consciousness. Tom in his decision to trade a day-to-day existence for militant organizing, Ma in her acceptance at last of commitments beyond that of saving the family, Rose in the translation of her biological self-absorption into an almost blissful giving, Pa in his neglect of his anger at his loss of status in the family as he marshals the boxcar migrants into a group effort to save their dwellings, and even John, in that for once his lifelong preoccupation with his guilt is replaced by an outward-directed anger (it is he who sets Rose's dead baby afloat in a box to remind the nearby townspeople that they are starving children)—each has made the journey from "I" to "We."

In one of the major ironic motifs of *The Grapes of Wrath*, this reduction of the Joads to an almost animal struggle for survival also bares fully their essential humanity, their Manself. Throughout the novel the migrants' poverty has been viewed by others as an index of their inhumanity. The gas station attendant at Needles cries, "'Them goddamn Okies got no sense and no feeling. They ain't human. A human being wouldn't live like they do. A human being couldn't stand it to be so dirty and miserable'" (301). But it is the very absence of that which defines humanity to the limited understanding which at last helps shape the penetrating clarity of spiritual insight of the Joads and thus enables them to discover a transcending sense of oneness with all men.

* * *

Our understanding of and response to the Joads' journey to aware-ness are aided by a number of fictional devices. Of these, the natural and Biblical symbolism requires little detailed discussion. The one serves to establish certain similarities between the Joads and natural life, the other between them and man's spiritual character. Together they contribute to Steinbeck's theme of the enriching unity of all life, in which the natural is also the spiritual and the spiritual is also the natu-ral. Less obvious in their function are the interchapters and the cyclic structure of the novel. Both serve as forms of editorial commentary through which the Joads' experience is translated into a statement on the human condition. The interchapters have a number of forms, from generalized narrative and prose poem to dramatic exchange and authorial philosophizing. They also vary in content from social realism to expressionistic exaggeration and in tone from humor and satire to bombast and supplication. But they are bound together, whatever their form, content, or tone, by the underlying authorial emotion of anger. Steinbeck uses the narrative of the Joads to involve us in the tragic pa-thos of the life of a migrant family, and the interchapters to involve us in the anger we must feel when we understand the inhumanity to man which their lives illustrate. The interchapters not only allegorize the Joads into universal figures of the poor and downtrodden but also en-gage us, through Steinbeck's devices in these sections, in an intensity of emotion usually foreign to allegory and other forms of abstraction. The interchapters are not extraneous to the novel but rather are central to its ability to move us.

Anger, yet an anger which contains an element of hope, is also an important characteristic of the cyclic form of *The Grapes of Wrath*. The novel begins with the Joads poor and landless in a drought-stricken Oklahoma; it ends with them even poorer and still landless in a flooded California. In Oklahoma, the men are at first silent and puzzled but then become "hard and angry and resistant" as they sit "thinking—

figuring" (6-7). In California, the men, in a parallel moment, are at first fearful and then angry (592). Anger is thus a source of both strength and continuity. In California, moreover, anger has found a focus and therefore a potential resolution. Nature, whether drought or flood, is not to blame for the condition of the migrants, nor is the Oklahoma tractor driver or the California deputy or ranch foreman. To blame is the greed exemplified by the economic system, and against this force, the Joads, who have thought and figured, have begun to find an answer in their willingness (as symbolized by Tom) to mold themselves into a group force equal in strength. So the last two chapters of the novel end with images of renewal in the midst of the carnage. After the starvation of the winter, "Tiny points of grass came through the earth, and in a few days the hills were pale green with the beginning year" (592); and after the Joads are driven from the boxcar by the flood, Rose nurses the starving man in the barn.

* * *

Much that is central in *The Grapes of Wrath* as a naturalistic novel of the 1930s can be understood by noting the remarkable number of similarities, as well as some significant differences, between it and an earlier naturalistic novel of social conflict in California, Frank Norris' *The Octopus*. In both works a struggle for land occurs within a cycle of natural growth, and in both the weaker figures in the conflict—the wheat ranchers and the migrants—suffer a tragic defeat. But in both instances, the most insightful and feeling of those crushed—Annixter, Vanamee, and Presley, and Tom, Ma, and Casy—struggle through to an understanding both of the underlying nature of the conflict and the essential nature of life. The three young men in *The Octopus* learn that the machinations of men cannot affect the omnipotence and benevolence of the natural process of growth, and the Joads learn to accept the oneness of all existence. Both works are fundamentally naturalistic despite these religious overtones. As is also true of *The Octopus*, the naturalism of *The Grapes of Wrath* resides in the theme that man can find in verifiable natural and social life the basic truths he should live by. In *The Octopus* the continuity of life is discovered not in the Pauline symbol of the seed—that man shall be reborn in heaven—but in the real seed, that man and nature reproduce themselves. And in *The Grapes of Wrath*, Casy's discovery that all things are united in holiness is only a vaguely felt concept until its meaning is completed by his finding that oneness is union organization and that holiness is the power to correct injustice. Men may come to know these truths initially by an instinctive or intuitive reaching out, but the truth itself must be not only felt but also observed and validated in experience. Both novels are thus conversion allegories, but the "religion" to which the characters are converted is that of the sanctity of life itself rather than of some aspect of man, God, or nature which is different from or superior to the life we lead and know.

The Grapes of Wrath also has its own distinctive character as a naturalistic novel of the 1930s. *The Octopus* proclaims that "all things, surely, inevitably, resistlessly work together for good,"[15] since the natural process of growth is both omnipotent and beneficent. Although the railroad monopoly is a bad thing which affects individuals adversely, it does not adversely affect mankind in general, since society and its conflicts are subsumed under the cosmic beneficence of the natural order. Men have died in the struggle for a crop of wheat, but the wheat itself will feed the starving millions of India. Steinbeck's perspective is quite different. Much of the fruit grown by the San Joaquin ranchers doesn't reach anyone because it is destroyed to maintain high prices, an act which aids the wealthy but harms the poor, including the migrant children who hunger for the oranges they see all around them. Steinbeck views the American economic system not as part of a natural process but as a baneful social illustration of the "I" principle. Men can and must struggle through to a "We" activism of camp committees and unions rather than accept that good will eventually accrue to the greatest number through cosmic beneficence. Although Steinbeck in *The*

Grapes of Wrath occasionally appears to be endorsing a Marxist theory of historical necessity by his references to the inevitability of class conflict if class divisions continue to grow, he is really endorsing a naturalistic version of a traditional social gospel activism in which one's beliefs must be realized in social life as well as be expressed in the temple.

Some of the obvious and often noted defects of *The Grapes of Wrath* stem from its character as a 1930s naturalistic novel, though a good many of these are less disturbing if the allegorical mode of the novel is at once accepted. Parables such as the turtle crossing the road, characters who exist principally as symbols, the hell-paradise contrast of the Hooverville and Weedpatch—these are major weaknesses only if one adopts the notion that naturalism is limited to the probabilities of social realism. Much more significant as a flaw in *The Grapes of Wrath* is the conflict between its tragic and social impulses. Steinbeck asks us to respond to the fate of the Joads with the compassion we bring to other accounts of men who must be stripped naked and suffer before they can understand the needs of the poor naked wretches around them. But he also generates intense anger toward those causing the misery of the Joads and points out ways in which their condition can be improved. The two intents seem to be related. It is the economic system as a whole which is the equivalent of the Joads' initial "I" values. Thus, compassion for their suffering as they move toward a "We" consciousness, and anger at the economic system for failing to undergo this change appear to be coordinate sentiments. But in fact the presence of these two emotions both diffuses and confuses the tragic theme and form of the novel. Steinbeck has succeeded so well in engaging us in the nature and quality of the Joads as primitive folk that the family assumes a validity at odds with his ultimate goal for them. We wish the Joads to find a better life in California, but we are not really persuaded that the committees and unions and other activities which represent the "We" principle in their lives are really better than the folk inwardness and the clearly definable entity that is their family. Here we are perhaps victims of a change in perspective since the 1930s in that we are no longer convinced that committees are inherently superior to other forms of awareness and action. We are also reacting in a way unforeseen by Steinbeck to his conviction that the humblest man can rise to the wisest thoughts. Steinbeck believed that it would be primarily the "thoughts"—the acceptance by the Joads of "We-ness"—which would hold us. But instead it is the Joads themselves who are the source of the enduring power of the novel.

Notes

1. Two collections of Steinbeck criticism contain most of the pertinent commentary on *The Grapes of Wrath*: *A Casebook on "The Grapes of Wrath,"* ed. Agnes McNeill Donohue (New York: Crowell, 1968), and *Steinbeck: A Collection of Critical Essays*, ed. Robert M. Davis (Englewood Cliffs, N.J.: Prentice-Hall, 1972). The two most important views of Steinbeck as a naturalist are Woodburn O. Ross, "John Steinbeck: Naturalism's Priest," *College English* 10 (May 1949): 432-38 and Warren French, "John Steinbeck: A Usable Concept of Naturalism," in *American Literary Naturalism: A Reassessment*, ed. Yoshinobu Hakutani and Lewis Fried (Heidelberg: Carl Winter, 1975), pp. 122-35 (also in French's second edition of his *John Steinbeck* [New York: Twayne, 1975]). Ross stresses the mysticism at the center of Steinbeck's naturalism, and French views *The Grapes of Wrath* as a move by Steinbeck from naturalism to a "drama of consciousness." My "John Steinbeck and American Naturalism," *Steinbeck Quarterly* 9 (Winter 1976): 12-15, concentrates on *Of Mice and Men*.

2. In the absence of a full-scale biography, Peter Lisca's *The Wide World of John Steinbeck* (New Brunswick, N.J.: Rutgers Univ. Pr., 1958) and Elaine Steinbeck and Robert Wallsten's *Steinbeck: A Life in Letters* (New York: Viking, 1975) are the best sources for information about Steinbeck's life.

3. See Jackson J. Benson, "'To Tom, Who Lived It': John Steinbeck and the Man from Weedpatch," *Journal of Modern Literature* 5 (Apr. 1976), 151-94.

4. "A Primer on the 30's," *Esquire* 53 (June 1960): 85-93.

5. "John Steinbeck: The Boys in the Back Room," *Classics and Commercials* (New York: Farrar, Straus, 1950), p. 44.

6. Wilson, *Classics*, p. 36, and J. Paul Hunter, "Steinbeck's Wine of Affirmation in *The Grapes of Wrath*," in *Essays in Modern American Literature*, ed. Richard E. Langford (DeLand, Fla.: Stetson Univ. Pr., 1963), pp. 76-89.

7. *Sea of Cortez* was initially published in 1941. A useful later edition is Steinbeck's *The Log from the Sea of Cortez: The Narrative Portion of the Book "Sea of Cortez" with a Profile "About Ed Ricketts"* (London: Heinemann, 1958 [1951]). The "Easter Sunday" chapter in the *Log* is pp. 131-51.

8. *The Log from the Sea of Cortez*, p. 165.

9. *Steinbeck: A Life in Letters*, p. 76. See also pp. 81 and 87.

10. As early as 1948 Frederick Bracher, in his "Steinbeck and the Biological View of Man," *Pacific Spectator* 2 (Winter 1948): 14-29, announced that Steinbeck had derived the non-teleological thinking passage in *Sea of Cortez* from Ricketts' journals. Not until the appearance of Astro's study in 1973, however, was Ricketts' responsibility for the passage fully substantiated. Nevertheless, some critics—for example, Jackson J. Benson, in his "John Steinbeck: Novelist as Scientist," *Novel* 10 (Spring 1977): 248-64—continue to attempt to reconcile the ideas of the passage with Steinbeck's ideas in his fiction.

11. *The Log from the Sea of Cortez*, pp. 247-50.

12. *The Grapes of Wrath* (New York: Viking, 1939), p. 32. Citations will hereafter appear in the text.

13. Steinbeck first uses the "I" to "We" formulation on pp. 206-7, soon after the Joads begin their journey to California.

14. In perhaps a conscious effort to make a connection between the Wilsons and other such families later in the novel—the Wallaces at Weedpatch and the Wainwrights in the boxcar—Steinbeck begins all three surnames with the same letter.

15. *The Octopus*, in *Collected Writings of Frank Norris* (Garden City, N.Y.: Doubleday, Doran, 1928), vol. 2, p. 361.

The Wine of God's Wrath:
The Grapes of Wrath

The Grapes of Wrath may well be the most thoroughly discussed novel—in criticism, reviews, and college classrooms—of twentieth-century American literature. It is a treasure trove, ceaselessly yielding up new jewels under the probing hands of historians, theologians, and critics of every caste, method, and meaning. A thorough bibliography of articles and book chapters on the novel would cover pages, and anyone reading all these discussions comes away amazed at the ingenuity of those who wrote them. Doing so also deepens one's admiration for the original, which rewards readers time after time with new insights. That it marks Steinbeck's permanence in American literature no one questions; that it was the basis for the Nobel Award given twenty-three years later few people doubt.

In his concluding Chronicle of Narnia, *The Last Battle*, C. S. Lewis described heaven as an onion with the inside bigger than the outside, so that with each ring you peel off you seem to go further in but also further out into new visions and new understanding. The analogy may apply as well to all great works of literature. The challenge becomes, finally, to excise one ring whole and clean rather than attempting to lift a great many tangled chunks of the onion that is the work. In this chapter I focus on just two of those "inner rings" of the novel, and they form an essential part of the whole. Further, they are allied with the themes Steinbeck was exploring during the entire decade of the 1930s. First, in the portrait of Ma Joad and her dream of "the fambly of man," Steinbeck provides a clear response to the ongoing tension between the individual and the Group Man, freedom and restraint. Like Cathy Ames in *East of Eden*, Ma Joad is the pivot of *The Grapes of Wrath*. Second, in his realistic characterization and particularly in the use of profanity, Steinbeck developed an important aesthetic approach to the issue of censorship, an issue that has attended the novel from its publication until the present.

The Wine of God's Wrath

Background to the Novel: Structural Technique

In early 1936, Steinbeck began writing what he called his "flock of experimentation," which was to develop into *Of Mice and Men*. Although interrupted by the growing critical interest in *Tortilla Flat* and by the move from the Pacific Grove cottage (which was being too frequently visited by the critics and the merely curious) to the cabin at Los Gatos, the work began in earnest in March. Steinbeck completed the second writing in August. About that time, George West, of the *San Francisco News*, approached him with the idea of writing a series of articles on disturbing conditions in the agricultural belt of the San Joaquin Valley. The focus was to be on the plight of the migrants and the government's efforts to supply sanitary camps for them.

The idea appealed to Steinbeck immediately. Outfitting an old bakery truck in a manner foreshadowing the 1960 trip in *Rocinante*, he set out for the squatters' camps in the company of the director in charge of management of migrant-camp programs, Eric H. Thomsen. Such camps were hardly a new experience for Steinbeck. Hobos and migrants were familiar people to him. Even Salinas had a so-called Little Oklahoma on its outskirts. But somehow this trip imprinted the human misery and need on him as never before. His response can be sensed from the articles he wrote for the *News*. The sentences are terse, clipped, unornamented. Portrait after heartrending portrait emerged on those pages. And it was clear from the outset that the journalist was also the novelist with a larger story to tell, the story behind that misery and need.

The Dust Bowl migration, which had begun around 1930, had reached an apex at the time Steinbeck undertook his trip down the San Joaquin Valley. Over 80,000 new migrants had wandered into California that year alone. Throughout the decade between three and four hundred thousand migrants—fiercely independent people who were also terribly dependent on new jobs that did not exist—entered the agricultural fields. The portraits submitted to the *News* brought individual stories to light, but Steinbeck's literary instinct was for the large story, the whole life environment of the people. As he traveled farther with Thomsen, Steinbeck arrived at the Arvin Sanitary Camp, or "Weed-patch," run by Tom Collins. Collins supplied Steinbeck with innumerable firsthand experiences, with his own journals and camp reports, and also with his unique idealism centered in the common man. The reports in particular provided a valuable resource for *The Grapes of Wrath*. Beyond the mandatory statistics they were filled with anecdotes and details that brought to reality the large story sought by Steinbeck.

It was nearly two years before Steinbeck could fully assimilate and objectify his material and experiences. In a sense he had grown too close to the reality. In time he found the necessary artistic distance to write a story rather than a diatribe. During those two years, however, he was never far from the story, writing occasionally, mulling it over, revising. By March, 1938, the work had reached a crisis. He confessed to Elizabeth Otis that "I want to put a tag of shame on the greedy bastards who are responsible for this" (*LL*, p. 162). By April he had finished a draft of the satirical work that he called "L'Affaire Lettuceberg," a draft that profoundly disappointed him. Within weeks he had decided to burn the manuscript and begin anew.

The new work started in early June and proceeded rapidly through its completion in December, 1938. The fact that Steinbeck wrote a 200,000-word novel in this half-year period is daunting enough, but the hard work was exacerbated by all kinds of demands on his time and energy, including Carol's serious illness with a strep infection in August and the bankruptcy of Pascal Covici's publishing company. That he wrote so many words is a feat in itself, that he told a powerful story is incredible. But surely the most fascinating aspect lies in the stylistic skill with which the novel is written. The artistic complexity that provides the novel its hard, focused energy may, indeed, be a partial result of the feverish conditions under which it was written.

Several items of that stylistic technique may seem the result of fortunate coincidence. For example, as was observed in chapter 1, titles were often a matter of large significance—and no small difficulty—for

Steinbeck. He wanted titles that somehow suggested at once the narrative accounting, the tone of the accounting, and its symbolic significance.

Steinbeck credited Carol with the selection of "The Grapes of Wrath," and he was ecstatic over the choice, even insisting to Elizabeth Otis that the entire "Battle Hymn of the Republic," "one of the great songs of the world," be published—music and words—on a page at the beginning. He further suggested to Otis that "as you read the book you will realize that the words have a special meaning in this book" (*LL*, p. 173). Indeed they do, at several symbolic levels. The first level, of course, derives from the song itself. "He is trampling out the vintage where the grapes of wrath are stored" encapsulates the rage of the oppressed, prophesies the overthrow of suppression, and envisions a strong freedom.

The most familiar biblical analogue, at a second level of symbolism, occurs in Revelation 14:19-20: "And the angel thrust in his sickle into the earth, and cast it into the great winepress of the wrath of God. And the winepress was trodden without the city, and blood came out of the winepress, even unto the horse bridles, by the space of a thousand and six hundred furlongs."[1] Someone who has read the Bible as carefully as Steinbeck would observe that the actions of the avenging angel, sent here by the Lamb, follow the oppression of the Beast detailed in previous chapters. The familiar New Testament passage, however, is rooted solidly in the Old Testament. In passages such as Deuteronomy 32:32, "For their vine is of the vine of Sodom, and of the fields of Gomorrah: their grapes are grapes of gall, their clusters are bitter," and Jeremiah 31:29, "In those days they shall say no more, The fathers have eaten a sour grape, and the children's teeth are set on edge," grapes are used symbolically as prefiguration of divine retribution upon the oppressor.

Ironically, however, in the Bible the grapes of wrath are juxtaposed and contrasted to the equally strong theme of the grapes of plenty. Such instances are found, for example, in Numbers 13:23-27, where the spies come to the Brook of Eshcol in Canaan and return with a huge branch of grapes as a sign of "the land of milk and honey." This parallels the prophecy of Deuteronomy 23:24 that the Israelites would eat their fill of grapes. Steinbeck perceived the contrast, of course, for the dream of grapes of plenty recurs in *The Grapes of Wrath*. Grampa dreams of it: "'Jus' let me get out to California where I can pick me an orange when I want it. Or grapes. There's a thing I ain't never had enough of. Gonna get me a whole big bunch of grapes off a bush, or whatever, an' I'm gonna squash 'em on my face an' let 'em run offen my chin'" (p. 112). Again, Grampa proclaims: "'They's grapes out there, just a-hangin' over inta the road. Know what I'm a-gonna do? I'm gonna pick me a wash tub full a grapes, an' I'm gonna set in 'em, an' scrooge aroun', an' let the juice run down my pants'" (p. 126). And yet a third time: "'I'm gettin' hungry. Come time we get to California I'll have a big bunch a grapes in my han' all the time, a-nibblin' off it all the time, by God!'" (p. 141). For Grampa, grapes represent the possible dream of the promised land, imaged in an almost sexual and animal indulgence. But the promised land is a fallen land, riddled by greed, and as the prophecy of the sweet grapes is replaced by the reality of thin stew, the grapes of wrath take root in their place.

Other techniques of structural unity and symbolic suggestiveness focus the novel. Perhaps the most conspicuous (and intriguing) such technique is the artistic use of the intercalary chapters, which can be observed to function in several ways.

The intercalary chapters, first of all, provide aesthetic richness by symbolic analogies that frame or support the narrative plot. Perhaps the most notable example occurs in chapter 3, where the turtle functions as a symbol of the migrants. The turtle carries its house on its back as the migrants carry their households on the backs of ancient vehicles. The turtle's "horny beak" and his "fierce, humorous eyes" resemble both the grim determination and the quick capacity for joy in the migrants but especially resemble the description of Grampa Joad with "his shrewd, mean, merry eyes" and also Jim Casy with his "nose, beaked and hard." The turtle's instinctive sense of direction toward the southwest, even after being upset by Tom's boot, resembles the Okies' dogged determination to arrive in California despite the obstacles in their way. The turtle's awkward gait, as it "jerked itself along," resembles the lurching, overloaded migrant trucks. And, finally, the turtle is one of the oldest of reptiles, resembling this oldest of urges in man to move on to a new place, what Grandfather in *The Red Pony* calls the "Westering" urge. Further use of animal imagery in the novel, and particularly in the intercalary chapters, could be explored at some length. In chapter 16, as the Wilsons' car breaks down, the shadow of a buzzard flits over the earth. In intercalary chapter 17, Steinbeck uses insect imagery, a recurring pattern discussed by Robert J. Griffin and William E. Freeman in their essay on the topic, "Machines and Animals: Pervasive Motifs in *The Grapes of Wrath*."[2]

The intercalary chapters also provide historical background that throws the narrative event into relief. Chapter 5, for example, evokes the historical environment through the Bank-as-Monster image that frames the immediate plight of the Okies. Such passages also serve to universalize the story for the reader; by being placed in historical context, the Joads become part of our own story. Chapter 9 functions the same way, as a vast farmering consciousness allows the author to compress history and retain focus on the narrative. Chapter 21 serves as another example of how the intercalary chapters fill in historical detail to frame the narrative. In such chapters the narrator speaks in the same omniscient "overvoice" that we find in such works as *Cup of Gold*, *East of Eden*, and *Sweet Thursday*.

Furthermore, the intercalary chapters provide aesthetic pace or rhythm to frame the events of the narrative plot. Chapter 7, the intercalary chapter on car sales, follows immediately on the sense of loss and movement in the preceding chapter. It is an important chapter because the car will become a character in its own right in the novel, and here we get to know the "character" well. More important, however, the caroming pace of chapter 7 plays off against the hollowness that ends chapter 6. The forty-two-word final sentence of that chapter spirals downward with a particular emphasis on heavy *o* and *u* sounds: "They were silent, and gradually the skittering life of the ground, of holes and burrows, of the brush, began again; the gophers moved, and the rabbits crept to green things, the mice scampered over clods, and the winged hunters moved soundlessly overhead" (p. 82). The syntactical pace of chapter 7 opens like the crack of a whip as short prepositional phrases careen across the page. Steinbeck uses elliptical syntactical structures with the main verbs eliminated for the impressionistic quickness and crispness of roaring engines. The pace quickens until it roars through staccato sentences that average about five words each. Similarly, chapter 23, which recounts the dance at Weedpatch, breaks into the ring-shout pattern of the square dance:

> Look at that Texas boy, long legs loose, taps four times for ever' damn step. Never seen a boy swing aroun' like that. Look at him swing that Cherokee girl, red in her cheeks an' her toe points out. Look at her pant, look at her heave. Think she's tired? Think she's winded? Well, she ain't. Texas boy got his hair in his eyes, mouth's wide open, can't get air, but he pats four times for ever' darn step, and he'll keep a-goin' with the Cherokee girl. [P. 449]

These are the caller's lines, used here to provide the festive beat of Weedpatch.

Mary Ellen Caldwell has pointed out, in one of the more consistent studies of the intercalary chapters, that these chapters as a whole fold in on the central chapter 15 of the book by chapter count and by theme. Caldwell says of chapter 15 that "neither [is it] a purely intercalary chapter as the others are nor is it a part of the Joad narrative. It is an epitome of the whole book, having its own narrative paragraphs and intercalary paragraphs."[3] In this chapter Steinbeck juxtaposes the rush of the highway with the one small act of kindness to a migrant family. Significantly, this chapter is preceded by one detailing the first coalescence of the people from "I" to "we":

Here is the anlage of the thing you fear. This is the zygote. For here "I lost my land" is changed; a cell is split and from its splitting grows the thing you hate—"We lost our land." The danger is here, for two men are not as lonely and perplexed as one. And from this first "we" there grows a still more dangerous thing: "I have a little food" plus "I have none." If from this problem the sum is "We have a little food," the thing is on its way, the movement has direction. . . . This is the beginning—from "I" to "we." [P. 206]

Chapter 15 provides the "how" of the equation. The chapter begins with the same pounding rhythm of the highway notable in other intercalary chapters. Billboards march by in a blur; legends slap at weary eyes. But here we find a change from the car and junk dealers of chapter 9 who deal in "junked lives" to little kindnesses that grow and balance the cruelty. In Caldwell's estimation, "Chapter 15 is not only a microcosm of *The Grapes of Wrath* but also a microcosm of the United States."[4]

Taking Steinbeck at his word that "its structure is very carefully worked out,"[5] that structure is evident in the careful interweaving of the intercalary chapters and the way in which they fold in, both stylistically and thematically, on chapter 15. In precisely the same way that chapter 15 becomes a structural pivot in the novel, Ma Joad becomes a thematic pivot between the "I" and the "we" forces with her concept of the "fambly of man." She is the spiritual pivot with her enduring faith and loving-kindness.

Ma Joad's thematically pivotal role can best be considered in the general context of Steinbeck's female characters.[6] Female characters play a significant role in Steinbeck's fiction, and their roles, as well as the author's comments on them, merit close attention. If one of his ongoing concerns is freedom and constraint and individual dreams of fulfillment, female characters play an important part as examples of that theme.

Not surprisingly, the vast majority of female characters in Steinbeck's work are there without particular sanction or censure; they are there simply as human characters in the ceaseless drama of life that he witnessed. One such grouping is the whorehouse women, who are generally characterized in the fiction as spirited and wholesome. Several of these rise to major roles in the fiction; for example, Fauna, the indomitable matron of the Bear Flag, who "could easily have been chairman of the board of a large corporation," who tutors her girls in fine etiquette, and who keeps her "star board" of those girls who marry well. Another might be Suzy of *Sweet Thursday*, who possesses such native grace that she can make a cottage of a cast-off boiler. Suzy also struggles mightily to clean up her language to fit the ladylike portrait Fauna provides for her. In another grouping we find the rambunctious paisano women of *Tortilla Flat*, whose volcanic emotions sometimes threaten to blow up Monterey Bay. And in yet another grouping we find the stirring human portraits from the short fiction: Helen Van Deventer of "The White Quail," who struggles with her psychotic daughter; Mary Teller, a fascinating literary counterpart to Elisa Allen; and the ladies of the Long Valley, who contend with themselves, their husbands, and their families, and who sometimes find peace. Women are the focal point of many of these stories, and perhaps one of the most notable is Molly Morgan of *The Pastures of Heaven*, whose interview with John Whiteside forms a kind of intricate psychoanalytic journey into her past.

Several women gain preeminent roles. Curley's wife in *Of Mice and Men* is a significant character despite her namelessness. She is selfish, but not evil in the way that Cathy Ames is. She is lonely, comparable perhaps to Crooks and Candy in the novel, and thereby a part of George's general lament, "We're the loneliest guys in the world." She is a victim of accident, it seems, the worst accident being her marriage to Curley. To Claire Booth Luce, who played Curley's wife in the stage play, Steinbeck elaborated on her character with surprising specificity:

Now, she was trained by threat not only at home but by other kids. And any show of fear or weakness brought an instant persecution. And she learned she had to be hard to cover her fright. And automatically she became hardest when she was most frightened. She is a nice, kind girl and not a floozy. No man has ever considered her as anything except a girl to try to make. She has never talked to a man except in the sexual fencing conversation. She is not highly sexed particularly but knows instinctively that if she is to be noticed at all, it will be because some one finds her sexually desirable. [*LL*, p. 154-55]

Steinbeck goes on to describe her loneliness, and how it is allied with her sexuality:

If anyone—a man or a woman—ever gave her a break—treated her like a person—she would be a slave to that person. Her craving for contact is immense but she, with her background, is incapable of conceiving any contact without some sexual context. With all this—if you knew her, if you could ever break down the thousand little defenses she has built up, you would find a nice person, an honest person, and you would end up by loving her. [*LL*, p. 155]

But, more important, Steinbeck points out that "I've known this girl and I'm just trying to tell you what she is like" (*LL*, p. 155). That is the key; she also emerges from Steinbeck's perception of and experience in the living drama.

One of the strongest female characters is Juana, who is discussed in chapter 7 of this book, as is Cathy Ames in chapter 8. Cathy, like Ma Joad, is the pivotal character of a novel but is Ma Joad's diametrical opposite—a thoroughly evil center in contrast to Ma Joad's thoroughly good center.

While he frequently uses female protagonists, Steinbeck's personal comments on women should be separated from his characters since the comments usually reflect his psychological state in relation to his marriages. Thus after his divorce from Gwyn, when he announces to Bo Beskow that "I do not think now I will remarry," Steinbeck engages in a long reflection comparing American women to their European counterparts (*LL*, pp. 342-43). The comments—such as "American married life is the doormat to the whore house"—should be understood in their personal context and no other. At times these personal reflections lap over into the fiction in generalized statements. Describing Elizabeth in *Cup of Gold*, Morgan reflects: "She was a thing of mystery. All girls and women hoarded something they never spoke of. His mother had terrific secrets about biscuits, and cried, sometimes, for no known reason. Another life went on inside women—some women—ran parallel to their outward lives and yet never crossed them" (*COG*, p. 21). In *East of Eden*, Lee reflects on his mother in general terms: "My father said she was a strong woman, and I believe a strong woman may be stronger than a man, particularly if she happens to have love in her heart. I guess a loving woman is almost indestructible" (*EOE*, p. 357).

In short, with the exception of Cathy Ames, Steinbeck observes with appreciation the following character traits in his major female characters: endurance through adversity, a patient ability to ride with changing circumstances and yet retain an individual point of view, and a loving-kindness that, while not immune to adversity, nonetheless finds a straight and sure path through that adversity. Each of these traits is exemplified particularly well in Ma Joad as, despite the pull of a solipsistic individualism on the one hand and a subsuming into a great, amorphous Group Man force on the other, she strikes a path she calls the "fambly of man." Consider first her thematic counterparts in the novel, and then the way in which these counterparts, as the intercalary chapters fold in on the pivotal 15th chapter, gather around Ma Joad for thematic resolution.

Thematic Conflict

The background conflict of the novel, rich versus poor, is established at the outset when Tom Joad, newly released from McAlester Penitentiary, tries to hitch a ride with the truck driver. When the driver points to the "No Riders" sticker, Tom responds: "Sure—I seen it. But sometimes a guy'll be a good guy even if some rich bastard makes him carry a sticker" (p. 11). The brief exchange foreshadows the tragedy of the devastated farms, amalgamated by the "Machine" of the nameless rich into one vast possession. The first person Tom meets on that blasted farmland is the former "Burning Busher," the Reverend Jim Casy, who has forsaken his call from the Holy Spirit in search of the spirit of man.

Casy is one of the most significant characters in the novel, and through him Steinbeck establishes the broad view typified in earlier works by a character like Doc Burton. Richard Astro has argued that Doc Burton and Jim Casy are figures of Ed Ricketts, and to a certain extent both Burton and Casy represent the non-teleological view of Ricketts. Astro sees Casy as a more successful spokesman than Burton for that view in that "unlike Burton, whose vision of the whole is never converted into meaningful action, Casy knows that 'we got a job to do' and applies the principles of his perceptions to help 'the folks that don' know which way to turn.'"[7] Casy becomes a spokesman for the movement from "I" to "we" and assumes a degree of leadership in it before he is cut down by the landowners' goons. But it is precisely that futility of leadership of a mob that stands apart from Ma Joad's enduring loving-kindness toward the family. In a sense Ma Joad is closer to Doc Burton's character than Jim Casy's; not a "party" person, she merely battles in her quiet way for human dignity. It is these quiet, almost forgotten people, like George and Lennie, that Steinbeck brings to public recognition and in whom he finds a resilient nobility.

Casy plays a significant role in the dramatic action of *The Grapes of Wrath*, however, and one can better understand Ma Joad's character by a closer examination of Casy. He has, as he says, forsaken the Holy

Spirit (which he sees as being apart from man) for the human spirit. In his initial conversation with Tom, Casy provides rather unclear reasons for his conversion. He says, first, that "'the Sperit ain't in the people no more'"; they seem forsaken, lost, and lonely. Second, "'The Sperit ain't in me no more,'" a statement that he qualifies immediately by saying that the spirit is still strong in him but has changed from an abstract divinity to concrete action. He does not fully understand this new spirit that calls him to be a part of the people rather than apart from the people, but he recognizes that "'I got the call to lead the people, an' no place to lead 'em.'" His effort now is to come to grips with what he calls the "human sperit." While Casy has been popularly interpreted as a Christ figure and dozens of convincing analogies are provided in the text (analogies that I would suggest Steinbeck uses to provide backdrop or "coloring" for Casy's actions), it is necessary that Casy be seen first in aesthetic terms, as a profound and moving psychological study of a man grappling with sin and human nature.

From the early portraits of Tom Joad and Jim Casy one can trace two primary themes developing in the novel. The first, which we may call theme A, observable immediately in the scene of Tom and the truck driver, suggests that, when threatened by the huge force of the "machine" or "monster," each person must care for himself. Every man for himself will be answered in the novel by Ma Joad's idea of the family of man—although Tom also finds his own response in the family of strikers. Theme B is represented by Jim Casy and may be considered as parallel to A, the movement from some ideal outside and imposed on humanity to the spirit in humanity. Ma Joad finally ties these two together, perhaps as theme C. We consider first Steinbeck's careful development of the two themes, A and B, to appreciate fully Ma's response.

As Tom and Jim trek over the land, gouged by the iron claws of the tractor, theme A, each man for himself, is exemplified by Joe Davis's boy and his migrant counterpart, the sad and irascible Muley Graves. Joe Davis's boy puts his own needs ahead of others. When reminded by a tenant farmer that "'nearly a hundred people have to go out and wander on the roads for your three dollars a day,'" Joe Davis's boy responds: "'Can't think of that. Got to think of my own kids. Three dollars a day, and it comes every day. Times are changing, mister, don't you know?'" (p. 50). Muley Graves, whose character is exemplified by both his names, stubbornly refuses to leave the land of ruined lives and dreams. His life is a portrait of desolation, his whiskered face a study in bereavement, as he tries to understand how others can think only of themselves. Casy is right when he says to Muley, "'You're lonely—but you ain't touched.'" But touched by the malignant hand of the monster, Muley too is reduced to the man living only for himself, unable to leave, as he says, wandering "'aroun' like a ol' graveyard ghos'.'"

In the novel the movement of the migrants is from the "I" of each man for himself to the "we" where people, partly out of desperation, are driven to a unit. The first mention of this occurs when Grampa dies. When the family sets out, they are anything but a unit. In fact, although cast together by the necessity of the journey, each harbors his or her own individual motivations and dreams, from Grampa, who wants to frolic in a tub of grapes, to Connie, who builds a little dream world that leaves no room for either his wife or their unborn child. In this novel the familiar dream motif can actually threaten the family. But around the rude grave of Grampa's burial, in a sodden little ditch shared with the Wilsons, "the family became a unit" (p. 189). And that unity is echoed in the following intercalary chapter with its refrainlike measures:

One man, one family driven from the land; this rusty car creaking along the highway to the west. I lost my land, a single tractor took my land. I am alone and I am bewildered. And in the night one family camps in a ditch and another family pulls in and the tents come out. The two men squat on their hams and the women and children listen. Here is the node, you who hate change and fear revolution. Keep these two squatting men apart. [P. 206]

That unity is not easily maintained, however, and will be strained throughout the novel. The threat is made clear by the returning migrant who, in chapter 16, explains the handbill ruse and the landowners' theory of bring together, divide, and conquer. Significantly, this occurs in a camp where the owner exemplifies the theme of each man for himself by overcharging the Okies for their night's lodging. That theme prevails to the end of the novel. After Tom decides to take up Casy's banner, he says to Ma Joad, "'I know now a fella ain't no good alone,'" and he quotes Ecclesiastes 4:9-12 to verify it. While Tom does not quote the first verse of that chapter, it provides the significant context for the later verses as well as for Tom's decision:

> So I returned, and considered all the oppressions that are done under the sun: and behold the tears of such as were oppressed, and they had no comforter; and on the side of their oppressors there was power; but they had no comforter. [Eccles. 4:1]

At the close of the novel the two sides of theme A, the "I" and the "we," clash dramatically—not just landowners versus migrants, but the migrants among themselves, so that the unity is threatened from within. This time the causes emanate from nature itself in the relentless rain and the rising flood. As children sicken, the migrants pound desperately on doors for help and are turned away, collecting in a hard, hopeless unit at the railroad yards. Quietly at first the whispers of desperation run through the unit: "Wainwright said, 'We was jes' talkin'. Seems like we oughta be gettin' outa here'" (p. 595). The strain deepens. As Rose of Sharon's birth pangs start, the floods continue their inexorable tide, and Pa Joad tries to unify the men to build a dam:

> Pa sloshed through the mud to the stream. His marking stick was four inches down. Twenty men stood in the rain. Pa cried, "We got to build her. My girl got her pains." The men gathered around him.
> "Baby?"

"Yeah. We can't go now."

A tall man said, "It ain't our baby. We kin go."

"Sure," Pa said. "You can go. Go on. Nobody's stoppin' you. They's only eight shovels." He hurried to the lowest part of the bank and drove his shovel into the mud. The shovelful lifted with a sucking sound. He drove it again, and threw the mud into the low place on the stream bank. And beside him the other men ranged themselves. [P. 599]

For a time the men coalesce in a frenetic battle against the flood, but finally the families are forced to separate, and the Joads wander to the old barn, where once again the unit, the family of man, is reestablished by Rose of Sharon offering her breast to the starved man.

Theme B, the movement from a transcendent spirit to a spirit immanent in man, parallels the "I" to "we" theme, and is focused in the developing character of Jim Casy. Casy has to find this spirit in himself before he can find it in others, and the development of his character parallels this discovery. Before his "conversion" Jim Casy struggled desperately against his human drives and could find no sanctification for them. After preaching, he would roll with a girl in the bushes. He seemed set apart by the word he preached, but actually he had set himself apart by his failure to account for human fallibility. That recognition dawns on him slowly. After Tom tells the slightly risqué story of Willy Feeley's heifer, Jim Casy laughs softly and reflects: "'You know . . . it's a nice thing not bein' a preacher no more. Nobody use' to tell stories when I was there, or if they did I couldn' laugh. An' I couldn' cuss. Now I cuss all I want, any time I want, an' it does a fella good to cuss if he wants to'" (p. 94). His self-recognition deepens when he is driven into reciting a breakfast "prayer." What can he say that will articulate his belief? With whom will he commune in the human spirit? The prayer edges him another step forward in his thinking:

"An' I got to thinkin', on'y it wasn't thinkin', it was deeper down than thinkin'. I got thinkin' how we was holy when we was one thing, an' mankin' was holy when it was one thing. An' it on'y got unholy when one mis'able little fella got the bit in his teeth an' run off his own way, kickin' an' draggin' an' fightin'. Fella like that bust the holiness. But when they're all workin' together, not one fella for another fella, but one fella kind of harnessed to the whole shebang—that's right, that's holy." [P. 10]

Again, Casy is driven to prayer at Grampa's rude committal service, and here he finds inspiration in Emerson: "All that lives is holy." The third time Casy is driven to prayer, when Sairy Wilson is dying, he can find no words at all but merely bows his head in silence, to which Sairy responds: "'That's good. . . . That's what I needed. Somebody close enough—to pray'" (p. 298). What she needed was simply someone *close enough*, and Casy's silent presence seals his transformation.

It is not surprising, then, that at the California migrant camp Casy gives himself up in place of another. If, as so many critics have argued, Jim Casy is a Christ figure, he is a thoroughly humanized one, acting as man for man: "Far down the line Floyd came in sight, sprinting for the willows. The deputy, sitting on the ground, raised his gun again and then, suddenly, from the group of men, the Reverend Casy stepped. He kicked the deputy in the neck and then stood back as the heavy man crumpled into unconsciousness" (p. 361). Casy gives himself up, but is not to be held long, not with the jail cells jammed with migrants, and upon his release he takes up the cause of man that leads to his death. He dies with the echo of Christ on his lips: "'You fellas don' know what you're doin'. You're helpin' to starve kids'" (p. 527). His transformation is complete and extends beyond his death. He has changed his loyalty to the spirit of man and that spirit will endure, as is exemplified by Tom's picking up the bloody banner of the cause.

Ma Joad as Thematic Pivot

Between the poles of Tom Joad and Jim Casy, Ma Joad is the lodestar that evinces calm and grants direction. Her concept of the family of man, which she holds intuitively from the start, is the final point at which the others arrive like grim pilgrims, knowing the place for the first time. The enigmatic ending of the novel in this instance is indeed a thematic fulfillment, and it is no wonder that Steinbeck fought his editors to retain it. Strip away that ending and one destroys the thematic structure of the novel. The ending represents the direction Ma Joad has been traveling since the start of the novel, and it is no accident that Rose of Sharon's action occurs at Ma Joad's behest. But to arrive properly at that ending, we consider first the character development of Ma Joad in relation to the thematic development—this woman who says, "'I ain't got faith,'" but whose faith finally proves sufficient to undergird the whole family.

Ma Joad is typified from the outset by a generosity that, along with patient loving-kindness, will guide her actions in relations to the family of man throughout. She is, in a sense, the female counterpart to Doc Burton in her steadfast performance of altruistic deeds. When Pa Joad plays his little trick of introducing Tom and Casy as strangers, "'Ma, there's a couple fellas jus' come along the road, an' they wonder if we could spare a bite,'" Ma's reaction is immediate: "'Let 'em come. . . . We got a'plenty'" (p. 99). That they do not have a'plenty is undeniable, but not as undeniable as the need of others that Ma will always try to meet. This idea of the woman as matriarchal "Feeder" is important in twentieth-century southern fiction and characteristic of real migrant families on their long pilgrimage to California. The father is the worker-provider, the mother the nourisher-feeder—source of spiritual as well as physical nourishment.

Among the migrants Steinbeck would, no doubt, have witnessed the "feeder" ritual dozens of times. One such scene may have had direct impact on *The Grapes of Wrath*. Migrant-camp director Tom Collins had asked Steinbeck to write a foreword to his manuscript "Bringing in the

Sheaves," written under the pseudonym Windsor Drake. In the foreword Steinbeck recollects an experience in the migrant camps with Collins:

> I dropped to sleep in my chair. A baby's crying near at hand awakened me. Windsor was gone. He came back in a few moments and stood turning the burnt bacon.
>
> "What happened?" I asked.
>
> "Baby lost the breast. Mother was too tired to wake up."
>
> "What did you do?"
>
> "Found the breast and gave it back to the baby."
>
> "Didn't the mother wake up then?"
>
> "No,—too tired. Been working all day in the rain."
>
> Later in the year Windsor and I traveled together, sat in the ditches with the migrant workers, lived and ate with them. We heard a thousand miseries and a thousand jokes. We ate fried dough and sow belly, worked with the sick and the hungry, listened to complaints and little triumphs.
>
> But when I think of Windsor Drake, I remembered first, the tired eyes, and I think of the baby that lost the breast in the night, and the mother too tired to wake up.[8]

With the starvation rampaging among the migrants, the "Feeder" attained a role of huge significance. Her very food became symbolic of hope and unity and spiritual nourishment. In Collins's manuscript another stirring scene is related:

> We frightened the little children we found in the tent, the two little children. . . . And the bulging eyes of those two children, the sunken cheeks,— the huge lump on the old bed,—they frightened John [Steinbeck] and me. Inside the tent was dry because it was on high land, but it was an island in a sea of mud and water all around it. Everything under that bit of canvas was dry—Everything—the make-shift stove was without heat; all shapes of cans were empty; pans, pots and kettles—all were dry. Everything, for there was not a morsel of food—not a crumb of bread.

"Mommy has been like that a long time. She won't get up. Mommy won't listen to us. She won't get up." Such was the greeting cried to us by the two little children.

Mommy couldn't get up. She was the lump on the old bed. Mommy was ill and she hadn't eaten for some time. She had skimped and skimped so that the children would have a bite. A bite is a banquet when there is nothing but a bite.[9]

Steinbeck himself records one such scene in *The Grapes of Wrath* at the first California migrant camp. The scene is preceded by intercalary chapter 19, which raises the cry of hunger as a backdrop: "How can you frighten a man whose hunger is not only in his own cramped stomach but in the wretched bellies of his children? You can't scare him— he has known a fear beyond every other" (p. 323). In chapter 20 the Joads find the reality of the intercalary chapter at the Hooverville camp. Over and over the refrain rises: "'S'pose they's a hundred men wants that job. S'pose them men got kids, an' them kids is hungry. S'pose a lousy dime'll buy a box a mush for them kids. S'pose a nickel'll buy at leas' somepin for them kids'" (p. 334). And in the center of that raging hunger Ma Joad fixes the family meal, while the camp children watch with wolfish eyes: "The children, fifteen of them, stood silently and watched. And when the smell of the cooking stew came to their noses, their noses crinkled slightly" (p. 344). Finally Ma, the Feeder and Nourisher, ladles out her stew for the others, saying as she does so, "'I can't send 'em away . . . I don't know what to do'" (p. 351). This same Feeder motif operates at the end of the novel, where Ma asks Rose of Sharon to give her breast to the starved man, an ending structurally and thematically anticipated from the first meeting with Ma Joad.

Gradually, in the development of the novel, as the men are torn between the "I" and the "we", Ma Joad also takes over the dominant male role of the family so that her generosity and loving-kindness will prevail. She is no one's apathetic servant. As Feeder, she must be indomitably strong, for if the Feeder weakens, the family falls apart. Her fight is for the family—and indeed for the family of man—rather than for herself.

Ma Joad is not immune to the sense of catastrophe and of hope mixed with fear, that accompanies the migrant exodus. In fact, she finds some solace in the sheer numbers of people leaving, and at one point she anticipates the war cry of the California migrant camps:

> She came near to him then, and stood close; and she said passionately, "Tommy, don't you go fightin' 'em alone. They'll hunt you down like a coyote. Tommy, I got to thinkin' an' dreamin' an' wonderin'. They say there's a hundred thousand of us shoved out. If we was all made the same way, Tommy—they wouldn't hunt nobody down—." [P. 104]

There is steel in this woman's hope. And when hopelessness first begins to descend upon the others, in chapter 16, Ma Joad begins to exert control, threatening Pa with a jack-handle until she gets her way. While Pa gives in with some obligatory curses, Tom questions her: "'What's the matter'th you anyways? You gone johnrabbit on us?'" To which Ma responds: "'You done this 'thout thinkin' much. . . . What we got lef' in the worl'? Nothin' but us. Nothin' but the folks'" (p. 230). To protect the family she will stand up to anyone, even her own.

Ma's steel-like courage and control are strengthened on the desert crossing. While Connie and Rose of Sharon try in their desperate little privacy to make love, Ma Joad cradles the dying Granma's head in her lap, and even after Granma dies, Ma retains the courage to bluff her way past the border inspection. Spiritually and psychologically she assumes control over the family.

The Weedpatch camp poses a crisis for both the psychological well-being of the family and the spiritual control of Ma Joad. Having sojourned in tribulation, having been demeaned by the common epithet "Okies" on the lips of calloused and angry men, the family has its dignity reaffirmed at Weedpatch. Ma sighs, "'Why, I feel like people again.'" The camp is marked by small items that seem to validate human worth: from flush toilets to dances to the dignity of labor as a commodity for barter. And while the dubious battle rages outside the walls of Weedpatch, one feels that one could harbor in its port forever. But ironically Weedpatch has its own psychological nettles. For example, it robs the people of their will. At ease with their heaven-sent manna, the migrants do not want to risk the struggle into Canaan. In the camp the migrants find themselves becoming more and more dependent, depleted in will and direction. The Joad resources prove insufficient to sustain the family. Ma rises to goad them on, and the argument that rises to meet her is precisely the desirability of being at ease. "'This here hot water an' toilets—'" Pa argues, to which Ma responds, "'Well, we can't eat no toilets.'" Again Ma exerts her authority and issues the command:

> Ma plunged the dish into the bucket. "We'll go in the mornin'," she said.
>
> Pa sniffled. "Seems like times is changed," he said sarcastically. "Time was when a man said what we'd do. Seems like women is tellin' now. Seems like it's purty near time to get out a stick."
>
> Ma put the clean dripping tin dish out on a box. She smiled down at her work. "You get your stick, Pa," she said. "Times when they's food an' a place to set, then maybe you can use your stick an' keep your skin whole."
> [Pp. 480-81]

And again, it is Tom who presses her for her reasons, to which Ma responds:

> "Take a man, he can get worried an' worried, an' it eats out his liver, an' purty soon he'll jus' lay down and die with his heart et out. But if you can take an' make 'im mad, why, he'll be awright. Pa, he didn't say nothin', but he's mad now. He'll show me now. He's awright." [P. 481]

Yet a third time the issue of control rises, notable here because Ma uses the occasion to reflect on the nature of women. Suffused with a vast loneliness for his old homestead and feeling lost in the new land, Pa Joad exclaims: "'Funny! Woman takin' over the fambly. Woman sayin' we'll do this here, an' we'll go there. An' I don' even care.'" Ma soothes him by responding: "'Woman can change better'n a man. . . . Woman got all her life in her arms. Man got it all in his head. Don' you mind.'" After a short pause Ma adds: "'Man, he lives in jerks—baby born an' a man dies, an' that's a jerk—gets a farm, an' loses his farm, an' that's a jerk. Woman, it's all one flow, like a stream, little eddies, little waterfalls, but the river, it goes right on. Woman looks at it like that. We ain't gonna die out. People is goin' on—changin' a little, maybe, but goin' right on'" (p. 577).

Like Faulkner's Dilsey in *The Sound and the Fury*, Ma Joad endures; somehow she sees past the fiery emotions of the moment to one sure light that guides her path. In so doing she keeps the dream alive, nurtures and feeds it, of a "fambly" of man united in the same love and generosity she exhibits. The spirit is infectious, in a sense replacing—or perhaps the alternative to—the Group Man infection of the Mob that Doc Burton analyzes in *In Dubious Battle*. In Ma's hour of need, Mrs. Wainwright reciprocates:

> Ma fanned the air slowly with her cardboard. "You been frien'ly," she said. "We thank you."
>
> The stout woman smiled. "No need to thank. Ever'body's in the same wagon. S'pose we was down. You'd give us a han'."
>
> "Yes," Ma said, "we would."
>
> "Or anybody."
>
> "Or anybody. Use' to be the fambly was fust. It ain't so now. It's anybody. Worse off we get, the more we got to do." [P. 606]

A new movement has started, and its beginning—not its ending—is exemplified at the close of the novel as Ma's eyes and Rose of Sharon's meet in acknowledgment:

"Hush," said Ma. She looked at Pa and Uncle John standing helplessly gazing at the sick man. She looked at Rose of Sharon huddled in the comfort. Ma's eyes passed Rose of Sharon's eyes, and then came back to them. And the two women looked deep into each other. The girl's breath came short and gasping.

She said "Yes."

Ma smiled. "I knowed you would. I knowed!" [P. 618]

From the dust-filled skies of Oklahoma to the rain-laden skies and scudding clouds of California, Ma Joad points a straight path for her family. Similarly she is the thematic center of the novel.

Ma Joad represents a quality of the novel too often overlooked, that is, the warm, sympathetic, and often humorous portrayal of character. Too often readers focus on the fiery scenes in California and miss the quiet little nights that provide enduring illumination. If the turtle symbolizes the Okies, it is easy to focus only on its hard shell and hard, horny beak and to miss its fierce, humorous eyes. That humor attends the migrants also. We see it in the comedy of Grampa Joad fumbling with his pants buttons, casting lecherous glances at Granma, or dreaming of a tub bath in grape juice. It is there too when Granma Joad falls asleep in the privy:

"Where is Granma?" Rose of Sharon asked.

"I dunno. She's aroun' here somewheres. Maybe in the out-house."

The girl went toward the toilet, and in a moment she came out, helping Granma along. "She went to sleep in there," said Rose of Sharon.

Granma grinned. "It's nice in there," she said. "They got a patent toilet in there an' the water comes down. I like it in there," she said contentedly. "Would of took a good nap if I wasn't woke up." [P. 178]

Humor is there also in the frolicking dance at Weedpatch. These thoroughly human touches continually mitigate the anger of the book and make it finally a book about people rather than a political tract.

As a book about people, captured in all their ornery and humorous and noble and despicable reality, *The Grapes of Wrath* also raises the issue of profanity and censorship. The issue warrants attention for two reasons: first, it has fueled many censorship campaigns against *The Grapes of Wrath*, and, second, it is revealing of Steinbeck as a literary artist. The literary history of *The Grapes of Wrath* is, in part, a history of literary censorship in America.

Profanity, the Artist, and Censorship

Although Steinbeck advised his agent, Elizabeth Otis, against a large print run of *The Grapes of Wrath* under the opinion that "this will not be a popular book," the novel quickly seized the attention of the nation. Despite Steinbeck's prediction, "It will be a loss to do anything except to print a small edition and watch and print more if there are more orders" (*LL*, p. 173), Covici could hardly keep ahead of sales. By April, 1939, advance sales were past 90,000 copies. By November the book was selling 11,000 copies a week, and Steinbeck had just sold the movie rights for $75,000. The novel remained on the best-seller lists for much of 1940.

From the start the novel was accompanied by censorship, and for two major reasons. The first was clearly political, as Martin Shockley has ably demonstrated in "The Reception of *The Grapes of Wrath* in Oklahoma."[10] But political censorship diminished with the passage of time. With the onset of World War II, the migrants found new jobs. Regional suspicions waned. Political and ideological charges eventually died down. But also from the start there was a second torrent of censorship that remains very much alive today, that is, censorship owing to the book's profane language. As Jackson Benson points out, in the early period the charges of profanity may have been in fact politically motivated:

Charges of filth against the novel were widespread and led to bannings and burnings in several localities, including Buffalo, New York; East Saint Louis, Illinois; and Kern County, California. (Since these early responses, the book has remained among the most frequently banned, as reported by school and library associations.) But this aspect of the controversy didn't bother Steinbeck nearly as much as the one that was essentially political (although, as [Joseph Henry] Jackson noted, some of the charges of obscenity were no doubt politically inspired).[11]

But the issue had predated that; it had, in fact, occurred in the editorial offices of Viking Press before publication:

> The manuscript had gone on to Viking, where there was much concern over the novel's language. It was felt that if some passages were not changed and some words altered, bookstores would simply refuse to handle the book and it would be banned throughout much of the country. The problem was a delicate one. Viking would not censor the offensive language, yet the editors were quite aware that Steinbeck would not willingly alter anything, especially for reasons of placating an audience or insuring sales.[12]

It is clear, however, that Steinbeck both recognized the issue and dealt with it from the start and that he had an artistic theory of language that included profanity and guided him throughout his career.

For Steinbeck the heart of the issue lay in his effort to capture the whole life environment of a character and in his recognition that in certain groups of people and certain environments profanity is a customary form in which characters express emotions or convictions. The words chosen for this expression do not necessarily carry the same meaning or weight of meaning that they do for other people in other environments. The novelist's task, however, is to capture accurately the people and environment of his story and not to appease readers from a wholly other environment. An early indication of this belief occurs in

Cup of Gold. When Henry Morgan ventures forth on ship for the first time, "To his lips came the peculiar, clean swearing of sailors; phrases of filth and blasphemy and horror, washed white by their utter lack of meaning in his mouth" (pp. 46-47). In this environment, from the lips of these people, profanity is a natural thing, "washed white" by the lack of profane intention.

Steinbeck wrote at some length about this relativity of language to people and environment in *The Log from the Sea of Cortez*. The passage is important in relation to the novelist's task, which is, like the marine biologist's, fidelity to the truth of the people and environment he perceives:

> We have wondered about the bawdiness this book must have if it is to be true. Bawdiness, vulgarity—call it what you will—is such a relative matter, so much a matter of attitude. A man we knew once long ago worked for a wealthy family in a country place. One morning one of the cows had a calf. The children of the house went down with him to watch her. It was a good normal birth, a perfect presentation, and the cow needed no help. The children asked questions and he answered them. And when the emerged head cleared through the sac, the little black muzzle appeared, and the first breath was drawn, the children were fascinated and awed. And this was the time for their mother to come screaming down on the vulgarity of letting the children see the birth. This "vulgarity" had given them a sense of wonder at the structure of life, while the mother's propriety and gentility supplanted that feeling with dirtiness. If the reader of this book is "genteel," then this is a very vulgar book. [P. 70]

While he was at work on *Tortilla Flat*, Steinbeck observed the problem, emphasizing the novelist's prerogative to see things his own way: "Dad doesn't like characters to swear. But if I had taken all the writing instructions I've been given, I would be insane. I try to write what seems to me true. If it isn't true for other people, then it isn't good art. But I've only my own eyes to see with. I won't use the eyes of other people" (*LL*, p. 90). This attitude crystallized while Steinbeck was at work on *In Dubious Battle*. His acute consciousness that he must keep his fictional characters faithful to real-life prototypes affected his language: "The talk, and the book is about eighty percent dialogue, is what is usually called vulgar. I have worked along with working stiffs, and I have rarely heard a sentence that had not some bit of profanity in it. And in books I am sick of the noble working man talking very like a junior college professor" (*LL*, p. 99).

Throughout this period, with a growing sense of sureness and purpose in his own artistry, Steinbeck was adamant in what he called "the sound of authenticity." Any tampering with that would lessen and cheapen a work. A revealing episode occurred in November, 1937, when Jack Kirkland was given the task of providing the dramatic adaptation of *Tortilla Flat*. Seeing the script for the first time, Steinbeck alternated between outrage and "howls of laughter" at the linguistic mangling. A week and a half after firing off an angry salvo at Kirkland, Steinbeck reflected a bit more temperately:

> These are little things but I have a feeling that unless they are taken care of, the play is not going to have any sound of authenticity. You can argue that it doesn't matter because no one in the east ever heard of these people, anyway. Just remember some of the phony dialect in pictures and you will see that it does matter. No one believes that, in fact scorns it. [*LL*, p. 150]

This "sound of authenticity" became a creed for Steinbeck as novelist.

It is clear that Steinbeck had sharply formed attitudes toward language and authentic characterization by the time of *The Grapes of Wrath*. He anticipated problems with the profanity and did not avoid them. When the editors questioned the language, he remained firm in his conviction.

Elizabeth and I went over the mss and made some changes. I made what I could. There are some I cannot make. When the tone or overtone of normal speech requires a word, it is going in no matter what the audience thinks. The book wasn't written for delicate ladies. If they read it at all they're messing in something not their business. I've never changed a word to fit the prejudices of a group and I never will. The words I changed were those which Carol and Elizabeth said stopped the reader's mind. I've never wanted to be a popular writer—you know that. And those readers who are insulted by normal events or language mean nothing to me. [*LL*, p. 175]

Steinbeck never varied in this attitude. Seldom did he use profanity gratuitously—perhaps only in *The Winter of Our Discontent*, in which the profanity seems somewhat at odds with character and environment. With the publication of *Travels with Charley* and its notorious "cheerleaders" scene, he faced a conflict similar to that of *The Grapes of Wrath*. Steinbeck's letter to Elizabeth Otis of February 1, 1962, bears an interesting statement. Because of the danger of sensationalism there was a concomitant danger of losing the truth. Therefore Steinbeck worked out the cheerleader passage by suggestion and implication rather than quotation:

What started out as a simple piece of truth now wears all the clothing of sensationalism and has lost every vestige of its purity. It doesn't feel clean to me any more. The only value of the passage lay in its shock value. Now it has become that book with the dirty words and by a magical turnabout the dirty words are no longer the cheer leaders' but mine. When I get the galleys I shall see what I want to do. I know that by simple suggestion I can make them much uglier without saying them. [*LL*, pp. 733-34]

In its final form the simple suggestiveness goes like this:

No newspaper had printed the words these women shouted. It was indicated that they were indelicate, some even said obscene. On television the sound track was made to blur or had crowd noises cut in to cover. But now I heard the words, bestial and filthy and degenerate. In a long and unprotected life I have seen and heard the vomitings of demoniac humans before. Why then did these screams fill me with a shocked and sickened sorrow?

The words written down are dirty, carefully and selectedly filthy. But there was something far worse here than dirt, a kind of frightening witches' Sabbath. Here was no spontaneous cry of anger, of insane rage.

Perhaps that is what made me sick with weary nausea. Here was no principle good or bad, no direction. [*TWC*, pp. 227-28]

Clearly, this is more than "suggestiveness." It is also condemnation for the feral gratuitousness of the language of the cheerleaders whose sole purpose was to express hatred, to vilify and to demean, being therefore absolutely opposed to Steinbeck's whole point of view. The language was sordid, ugly, and obscene by virtue of willfulness. In *The Grapes of Wrath* Jim Casy quotes Emerson, "All that lives is holy"; Casy says this with awe and reverence for the mystery that is life. Although John Steinbeck expressed no particular fondness for D. H. Lawrence, he might have agreed with Lawrence that obscenity constitutes anything that degrades the holiness of life. As a matter of fact, Lawrence's derision for pornography roughly parallels Steinbeck's derision for obscenity such as the cheerleaders'. In his essay "Pornography and Obscenity," Lawrence wrote:

Pornography is the attempt to insult sex, to do dirt on it. This is unpardonable. Take the very lowest instance, the picture postcard sold underhand, by the underworld, in most cities. What I have seen of them have been of an ugliness to make you cry. The insult to the human body, the insult to a vital human relationship! Ugly and cheap they make the human nudity, ugly and degraded they make the sexual act, trivial and cheap and nasty.[13]

The same can be said about Steinbeck's view of language as used by the cheerleaders. When language threatens the family of man, it is, like the brute power of the landowners in *In Dubious Battle* and in *The Grapes of Wrath*, an obscene and malevolent thing.

* * *

Critics have sometimes spoken of a series of apexes in Steinbeck's work, with *The Grapes of Wrath* representing the highest and a series of lesser heights represented in *East of Eden* and finally *The Winter of Our Discontent*. While one might find fault with such a scheme because of the great variety of Steinbeck's work—that is, *The Pearl* may be an apex as parable, *Tortilla Flat* as comedy, *Of Mice and Men* as novella—it is true that Steinbeck achieved a work of rare complexity and merit in *The Grapes of Wrath*. When he spoke of five layers of meaning he put into the novel, he probably did not guess that readers would easily double the number of layers. In terms of thematic complexity and artistic skill, however, the work stands also as one of the masterpieces of American literature.

Notes

1. A dozen or more critical articles have explored, with varying degrees of success, biblical symbolism in *The Grapes of Wrath*. Among the better studies are Chris Browning, "Grape Symbolism in *The Grapes of Wrath*," *Discourse* 11 (Winter, 1968): 129-40; Gerard Cannon, "The Pauline Apostleship of Tom Joad," *College English* 24 (December, 1962): 222-24; Eric W. Carlson, "Symbolism in *The Grapes of Wrath*," *College English* 19 (January, 1958): 172-75; Charles T. Dougherty, "The Christ-Figure in *The Grapes of Wrath*," *College English* 24 (December, 1962): 224-26; Joseph Fontenrose, *John Steinbeck: An Introduction and Interpretation*, chap. 6; J. P. Hunter, "Steinbeck's Wine of Affirmation in *The Grapes of Wrath*," in Richard E. Langford,

Guy Owen, and William E. Taylor, eds., *Essays in Modern American Literature*; Alan Paton and Liston Pope, "The Novelist and Christ," *Saturday Review* 37 (December 4, 1954): 15-16, 56-59; Martin S. Shockley, "Christian Symbolism in *The Grapes of Wrath*," *College English* 18 (November, 1956): 87-90. Peter Lisca has provided a fine analysis of the history of criticism on *The Grapes of Wrath* and a bibliography of such criticism in the Viking Critical Library edition of the novel.

2. Robert J. Griffin and William E. Freeman, "Machines and Animals: Pervasive Motifs in *The Grapes of Wrath*," *Journal of English and Germanic Philology* 62 (April, 1963): 569-80.

3. Mary Ellen Caldwell, "A New Consideration of the Intercalary Chapters in *The Grapes of Wrath*," *Markham Review* 3 (May, 1973): 117-18.

4. Ibid., p. 119.

5. John Steinbeck, "A Letter on Criticism," *Colorado Quarterly* 4 (1955): 218-19. Steinbeck added that "it is no more intended to be inspected than the skeletal structure of a pretty girl. Just read it, don't count it." Nevertheless, the structure does "count" and is crafted in many subtle ways. For example, in chapter 9 the Okies' old homeland ends in a fire (p. 121), and in the final chapter their new home ends in a flood. The flood, however, can bring renewal, as is symbolized in Rose of Sharon. The spiritual pilgrimage is structured geographically, the descent into hell being represented by Toprock and Needles, and the ascent into the blighted paradise by a movement in the itinerary that occurs approximately midway in the novel. Premonitory devices weld the novel's structural parts, the handbills, for example, which are first revealed as a ruse on p. 124, and proved to be a ruse during the strikes in California (see also pp. 201, 259, and 333 for development of the handbills as a plot motif). Further, the biblical symbolism that structures the novel throughout has been so carefully and thoroughly scrutinized as to need no additional comment here.

6. For discussion of Steinbeck's female characters consider also *Steinbeck's Women: Essays in Criticism*, Monograph 9, Steinbeck Monograph Series (Muncie, Ind., Ball State University, Steinbeck Society of America, 1979).

7. Richard Astro, *John Steinbeck and Edward F. Ricketts: The Shaping of a Novelist*, p. 130.

8. John Steinbeck, Foreword to "Bringing in the Sheaves," Windsor Drake [Tom Collins], *Journal of Modern Literature* special issue, (*Background of* The Grapes of Wrath) 5 (April, 1976): 213.

9. Drake, "Bringing in the Sheaves," p. 222. In his "Background of *The Grapes of Wrath*" in the same issue (see n. 8 above), Jackson J. Benson discusses at length the relation between Collins and Steinbeck and the manuscript "Bringing in the Sheaves."

10. Martin Shockley, "The Reception of *The Grapes of Wrath* in Oklahoma," *American Literature* 15 (May, 1944): 351-61; reprinted in E. W. Tedlock, Jr., and C. V. Wicker, eds., *Steinbeck and His Critics*; and in Warren French, ed., *A Companion to* The Grapes of Wrath.

11. Jackson J. Benson, *The True Adventures of John Steinbeck, Writer*, p. 418.

12. Ibid., p. 389.

13. D. H. Lawrence, "Pornography and Obscenity," in Harry T. Moore, ed., *Sex, Literature, and Censorship*, p. 69.

"A Truly American Book":
Pressing *The Grapes of Wrath*_____

Robert DeMott

> The idea of an art detached from its creator is not only outmoded; it is false.
>
> —Albert Camus

I

There is nothing detached or slickly objective about John Steinbeck's masterpiece. For its creator, *The Grapes of Wrath* was a thoroughly engaging, utterly consuming novel; it arose from the sympathetic psychic wound brought on by his witnessing the cataclysmic migrant-farm-worker situation in California in the mid-1930s. *The Grapes of Wrath* is a harrowing cry from the heart, and Steinbeck's passionate investment took on a kind of sacramental air: "What some people find in religion a writer may find in his craft . . . a kind of breaking through to glory," he said in 1965.[1] The pressure of living through the research, creation, publication, reception, and aftermath of this novel—over a span of nearly four years—changed Steinbeck so profoundly that he became a different kind of artist after *The Grapes of Wrath*. But the breakthrough and transformation, the notoriety and glory, and the critical backlash were still in the future when, on June 18, 1938, three weeks or so after starting the final version of *Grapes*, thirty-six-year-old Steinbeck—head full of lament—sang a doleful tune: "If I could do this book properly it would be one of the really fine books and a truly American book. But I am assailed with my own ignorance and inability. I'll just have to work from a background of these. Honesty. If I can keep an honesty it is all I can expect of my poor brain. . . . If I can do that it will be all my lack of genius can produce. For no one else knows my lack of ability the way I do. I am pushing against it all the time."[2]

Pushing against limits was Steinbeck's forte. His first novel, *Cup of*

Gold (1929), a swashbuckling historical romance based on the life of the seventeenth-century Welsh buccaneer Henry Morgan, gave no indication that Steinbeck would eventually be capable of producing a graphic novel with the startling originality, magnitude, and compassion of *The Grapes of Wrath*. What transpired in the ten years between the two books is as arresting an example of self-willed artistic growth as we have in American letters, for in the nine volumes of prose (mostly fiction) that Steinbeck produced in that decade, he simply became better and better as a writer. His achievement is especially moving because he did not think of himself as naturally gifted and rarely believed he had ever "arrived" as a writer: "I was not made for success. I find myself with a growing reputation. In many ways it is a terrible thing. . . . Among other things I feel that I have put something over. That this little success of mine is cheating" (*WD*, [1]).

Steinbeck's self-accusations were constant during *Grapes*'s composition, and yet ironically it not only turned out to be a "fine" book, but it also is generally considered to be the greatest of his seventeen novels. Like other rough-hewn products of American genius—Stowe's *Uncle Tom's Cabin*, Twain's *Adventures of Huckleberry Finn*, Kesey's *One Flew over the Cuckoo's Nest*, and Walker's *The Color Purple* (four "flawed" novels that also humanize America's downtrodden by exposing social ills)—*The Grapes of Wrath* has a home-grown quality: part naturalistic epic, part jeremiad, part captivity narrative, part road novel, part transcendental gospel. Steinbeck's aggressive mixture of native philosophy, New Deal politics, blue-collar radicalism, working-class characters, folk wisdom, and homespun literary form—all set to a jazzy, rhythmic style, bold, improvisational form, and nervy, raw dialogue—gave the novel its "American" qualities, its fusion of experience and discourse. Even the novel's title, taken from Julia Ward Howe's "Battle Hymn of the Republic," was clearly in the American grain: "[I]t is a march and this book is a kind of march . . . in our own revolutionary tradition," Steinbeck announced on September 10, 1938, to Elizabeth Otis, his literary agent and confidante.[3]

After its composition from late May through late October, 1938, *The Grapes of Wrath* passed from the 751-page typescript prepared by his wife, Carol, to published novel in record time—four months. In March 1939, when Steinbeck received copies from one of three advance printings, he told Pascal Covici, his editor at Viking Press, that he was "immensely pleased with them" (*SLL*, 182). The novel's impressive physical and aesthetic appearance was the result of its imposing size (619 pages) and Elmer Hader's striking dust-jacket illustration of the Joads looking out on a lush California valley. And partly true to Steinbeck's insistence that *The Grapes of Wrath* be "keyed into the American scene," Covici had Viking print the first page of the words and music from the "Battle Hymn" inside the book's front and rear covers in an attempt (unsuccessfully, it turned out) to deflect accusations of Communism against the book and its author. In gratitude for their assistance, Steinbeck had dedicated the novel to Carol and to Thomas Edwards Collins, a government-relief-camp specialist (their roles will be examined below).

Given his emotional commitment to the California migrant laborers' situation, Steinbeck refused to write a book cynically calculated to court commercial success. "Funny how mean and little books become in the face of such tragedies," he confessed to Otis (*SLL*, 159). It was doubly ironic, then, that shortly after its official publication date, April 14, 1939, spurred by the nearly ninety reviews (mostly positive) that appeared in newspapers, magazines, and literary journals between April and June, *The Grapes of Wrath* went to the top of best-seller lists and stayed there for most of the year, selling 428,900 copies in hardcover at $2.75 each. *The Grapes of Wrath* won the 1940 Pulitzer Prize (Steinbeck gave the $1,000 prize to a Monterey friend and fellow writer Ritch Lovejoy). By 1941, when the Sun Dial Press issued a cloth reprint for a dollar, the publisher announced that over 543,000 copies of *Grapes* had already been sold. It eventually became the cornerstone of Steinbeck's 1962 Nobel Prize award and proved itself to be among the most enduring works of fiction by any American author. In spite of

the flaws its critics perceive—frequent sentimentality, flat character-
izations, heavy-handed symbolism, and unconvincing dialogue—or
perhaps because of them (general readers tend to embrace the book's
mystic soul and are less troubled by its imperfect body), *The Grapes of
Wrath*, during the past half century, has sold more than fourteen million
copies.[4] It has, in short, emphatically entered both the American consciousness and the American conscience.

Grapes has also had a charmed life on screen and stage. Steinbeck
sold the novel's film rights for $75,000 to producer Darryl F. Zanuck.
Then Nunnally Johnson scripted a film version, directed by John Ford
and released in 1940, which, though truncated, was nonetheless memorably paced, photographed, and acted, especially by Henry Fonda as
Tom Joad, Jane Darwell as Ma, and John Carradine as Jim Casy. (A
"hard, straight picture . . . that looks and feels like a documentary film
and . . . has a hard, truthful ring," Steinbeck reported after seeing its
Hollywood preview [*SLL*, 195].) A few years ago, Frank Galati faithfully adapted the novel for his Chicago-based Steppenwolf Company,
whose Broadway production won a Tony Award as Best Play in 1990.
Ike Sallas, the hero of Ken Kesey's latest novel, *Sailor Song* (1992),
prizes the novel and places it among his collection of classic American
books—"the essential heavies," he calls them—a status the book
clearly holds worldwide, for *The Grapes of Wrath* has also been translated into over thirty languages. It seems that Steinbeck's words continue, in Warren French's apt phrase, "the education of the heart."[5]

All this public fanfare and hoopla has overshadowed the private history of the novel's background and creation. The story of the novel's
making is an intriguing and dramatic one in itself, full of some of the
same twists and turns, travails, triumphs, and ironies that characterize
the Joad family's journey to the Promised Land. While Steinbeck's pu-
ritanical doubts about his ability to carry out the plan of his ambitious
novel surface repeatedly in his daily journal, he rarely questioned the
risks involved in bringing his whole sensibility—the leverage of his
entire heart—to bear upon its writing. Like another populist manifesto

of the American spirit, Whitman's *Leaves of Grass*, Steinbeck's novel had a complicated, tumultuous growth. *The Grapes of Wrath* was the product of Steinbeck's increasing immersion in the "matter of the migrants," which required a zigzag walk before he discovered the proper means of doing the topic justice. In one way or another, from August 1935, when Steinbeck told Louis Paul he had discovered a subject "like nothing in the world" (*SLL*, 129), through October 1939, when he resolved privately to put behind him "that part of my life that made the *Grapes*" (*WD*, 105), the migrant issue, which had wounded him deeply, was the central obsession of this obsessive writer.

First, he produced a seven-part series of newspaper articles, "The Harvest Gypsies"; then he worked on an unfinished novel, "The Oklahomans," and on a completed, but destroyed, satire, "L'Affaire Lettuceberg"; and finally—in a five-month stretch in 1938—he wrote *The Grapes of Wrath*. Each version of the story shared a fixed core of elements: on one side, the entrenched power, wealth, authority, and consequent tyranny of California's industrialized agricultural system (symbolized by Associated Farmers, Inc.), which produced flagrant violations of the migrants' civil and human rights and ensured their continuing peonage through threats, reprisals, and violence; on the other side, the powerlessness, poverty, victimization, and fear of the nomadic American migrants whose willingness to work, desire to retain their dignity, and wish to settle land of their own were kept alive by their innate resilience and resourcefulness and by the democratic benefits of the government sanitary camps. From the moment he entered the fray, Steinbeck had no doubt that the presence of the migrants would change the fabric of California life, though he had little foresight about what his own role in that change would be (or, for that matter, what changes would be wrought in him). His purpose was avowedly humanitarian and partisan; he wanted to be an effective advocate, but he did not want to appear presumptuous: "Every effort I can bring to bear is and has been at the call of the common working people to the end that they may eat what they raise, use what they produce, and in every way and in completeness share in the works of their hands and their heads," he declared unequivocally to *San Francisco News* columnist John Barry (*WD*, 152).

II

The Grapes of Wrath's communal vision began in the fire of Steinbeck's own labor, but the flames were fanned by numerous people. Few major American novels are more indebted to the generosity of others than *Grapes* is. Before continuing this narrative of the novel's genesis and growth, it will be necessary to sketch the chief benefactors, especially Carol Steinbeck and Tom Collins, both of whom had significant impact on Steinbeck's work. Carol Henning Steinbeck, his outgoing first wife (they married in 1930), was far more politically radical than John, and she actively supported members of northern California's local fugitive agricultural labor movement before he did.[6] Carol was an energetic, talented person in her own right, and she agreed to relinquish a career of her own in favor of helping to manage her husband's. Their partnership and marriage were smoother and more egalitarian in the struggling years of Steinbeck's career; with the enormous success—and pressures—brought first by the runaway best-seller *Of Mice and Men* (1937), and then by *The Grapes of Wrath*, their situation became more tenuous and volatile. Carol Steinbeck was an extremely strong-willed, demonstrative person, and she was often frustrated and resentful and sometimes jealous; her husband, inordinately shy, was frequently beleaguered, confused, and demanding. In the late 1930s, whenever he was writing daily, which was much of the time, Carol handled—but didn't always like—most of the routine domestic duties. She also shielded her husband as much as possible from unwarranted disruptions and intrusions, and oversaw some of the financial arrangements between Steinbeck and his literary agents, an increasingly large job. "Carol does so much," Steinbeck admitted on August 2, 1938 (*WD*, 50).

Carol also served as John's cultural envoy and stand-in. In January 1938, on a trip to New York City to attend a performance of George S. Kaufman's long-running Broadway production of *Of Mice and Men*, she met with documentary filmmaker Pare Lorentz and arranged his first visit to the Steinbecks' home in Los Gatos, California, to discuss a joint Steinbeck/Lorentz movie version of *In Dubious Battle* (which was never made) and a private showing of *The Plow That Broke the Plains* (1936) and *The River* (1937). These pioneering documentary films, made by Lorentz for President Franklin D. Roosevelt's New Deal-inspired Resettlement Administration (forerunner of the Farm Security Administration [FSA]), dealt with human displacement and natural erosion caused by storms in the Dust Bowl and floods in the Mississippi Valley—themes that were, of course, close to Steinbeck's heart. After their initial meeting, Lorentz became an extremely important figure in the novelist's life, providing everything from practical advice on politics to spirited artistic cheerleading.

Carol left her stamp on *The Grapes of Wrath* in many ways. As Steinbeck told Otis, Carol's time was "too valuable to do purely stenographic work" (*SLL*, 171), but she did type the manuscript, which was a formidable task in itself because her husband could cram fifty-five or more lines of his spidery hand on a single page of his outsized ledger book. She began typing from the early part of the holograph manuscript while her husband was still writing its latter sections, and she sometimes smoothed and edited the text as she went along, serving in the early stages as a rigorous critical commentator (after typing 300 pages, she confessed to Otis that she had lost "all sense of proportion" and felt unfit "to judge it at all"). In a brilliant and justly celebrated stroke, on September 2, Carol chose the novel's title from Howe's "Battle Hymn of the Republic," perhaps inspired by her hearing of Lorentz's radio drama, *Ecce Homo!*, which ends with a martial version of Howe's song.[7] Steinbeck was impressed with the "looks of it— marvelous title. The book has being at last"; he considered it "Carol's best title so far" (*SLL*, 171). ("Tell Carol she is a whiz at picking titles and she has done it again with the new one," his drama agent, Annie Laurie Williams, exulted.) Her role as facilitator is recorded permanently in one half of the novel's dedication: "To CAROL who willed it." On February 23, 1939, Steinbeck told Pascal Covici at Viking that he had given Carol the holograph manuscript of *The Grapes of Wrath*: "You see I feel that this is Carol's book" (*SLL*, 180).[8]

Eventually, Carol's brittle efficiency, brusque managerial style, and violent mood swings seemed to cause more problems than they solved. She, too, was exhausted by the novel's completion and at her wit's end over its histrionic reception. Steinbeck told Otis on June 22, 1939, "The telephone never stops ringing, telegrams all the time, fifty to seventy-five letters a day all wanting something. People who won't take no for an answer sending books to be signed. . . . Something has to be worked out or I am finished writing. I went south to work and I came back to find Carol just about hysterical. She had been pushed beyond endurance" (*SLL*, 185). His willful involvement with a much younger woman, a Hollywood singer named Gwyndolyn Conger, whom he met in mid-1939 and who quickly came to represent everything Steinbeck felt romantically lacking in Carol, signaled the beginning of the end of their marriage. They separated rancorously in 1941 and divorced two years later.

The second part of the novel's dedication—"To TOM who lived it"—refers to Tom Collins, the novelist's chief source of accurate migrant information. Collins not only put Steinbeck in touch with people like the Joads and Jim Casy, but he also served as Steinbeck's real-life prototype for the character Jim Rawley, the manager of the Weedpatch government camp, which became an oasis of relief for the harried Joads and is featured in chapters 22 through 26 of *The Grapes of Wrath*. The Weedpatch camp is an accurate rendering of Collins's Arvin camp. Steinbeck portrayed Collins with photographic accuracy in chapter 22: "A little man dressed all in white stood behind [Ma Joad]—a man with a thin, brown, lined face and merry eyes. He was as lean as a picket. His white clean clothes were frayed at the seams."[9] Steinbeck also caught Collins's effective interpersonal technique in Jim Rawley's wearing frayed clothes and in his winning over Ma Joad by the simple request of a cup of her coffee (*GW*, 416).

An intrepid, idealistic, and exceptionally compassionate man, Collins was the manager of a model Region IX FSA camp, located in Kern County, at the southern end of California's Central Valley. The twenty-acre Arvin Sanitary Camp was one of several proposed demonstration tent camps intended to provide humane, clean, and democratic—but temporary—living conditions for ninety-six families at a time from the growing army of migrant workers entering California from the lower Midwest's Dust Bowl region. (More than two dozen camps were planned in 1935 by the Resettlement Administration; by 1940, with New Deal budgets slashed by conservatives in Congress, only fifteen were actually completed or under construction.) Collins possessed a genius for camp administration and was widely respected throughout California. Labor historian Anne Loftis calls Collins a "hands on" administrator.[10] Collins had the right mix of fanaticism, vision, and tactfulness. He and Steinbeck, both New Deal Democrats, hit it off immediately. One of the many legends that grew up around *The Grapes of Wrath* purported that Steinbeck traveled with a migrant family all the way from Oklahoma to California; that never happened, though he and Carol did follow Route 66 on a car trip from Chicago to Los Gatos in 1937. Actually, Tom Collins was the novelist's companion on several grueling research trips made from 1936 to 1938 to investigate field conditions in the Central Valley.

Fortunately, Collins was a punctual and voluminous report writer (a plan to publish his reports eventually fell through [*WD*, lii-liii]). His colorful weekly accounts of the workers' activities, diets, entertainments, beliefs, music, and observations provided Steinbeck with a ready documentary supplement to his own researches. Collins guided Steinbeck through the intricacies of the agricultural labor scene, put him in direct contact with migrant families, and permitted him to incorporate "great gobs" of information into his own writing. "Letter from Tom. . . . He is so good, I need this stuff. It is exact and just the thing that will be used against me if I am wrong," Steinbeck noted on June 24, 1938 (*WD*, 33).

In 1939, at Steinbeck's recommendation, Collins worked as a well-paid technical advisor to John Ford's Twentieth Century-Fox production of *The Grapes of Wrath* ("Tom will howl his head off if they get out of hand," Steinbeck told Elizabeth Otis). And later—probably spurred by the success of both novel and film—Collins himself (under the pseudonym Windsor Drake) wrote an autobiographical/fictional memoir, to which Steinbeck, who appears as a character, added a foreword: "Windsor and I traveled together, sat in the ditches with the migrant workers, lived and ate with them. We heard a thousand miseries and a thousand jokes. We ate fried dough and sow belly, worked with the sick and the hungry, listened to complaints and little triumphs."[11] The book was accepted but never reached print because the publisher reneged on the deal. After that, Collins resigned from the FSA, and he and Steinbeck passed out of each other's lives.

Clearly, Steinbeck had a knack for associating himself with gifted, far-sighted, generous people, many of whom helped provide the context of *The Grapes of Wrath*. George West, chief editorial writer for the progressive Scripps-Howard newspaper the *San Francisco News*, instigated Steinbeck's initial investigations of the migrant-labor situation. Frederick R. Soule, the enlightened regional information advisor at the San Francisco office of the FSA, and his assistant Helen Horn (who later, as Helen Hosmer, directed the Simon Lubin Society) provided statistics and documents for Steinbeck's seven-part series on migrants in the *News* and otherwise opened official doors for Steinbeck that might have stayed closed. Soule's colleague Eric Thomsen, regional director of the FSA office in San Francisco, personally escorted Steinbeck to the Central Valley and introduced him to Tom Collins at the Arvin camp for the first time. Indeed, as Jackson Benson was quick to recognize, in an unintentional and ultimately ironic way the federal government underwrote part of Steinbeck's research and smoothed the path of this first major written account of the deplorable California agricultural situation.[12]

III

Not counting the scotched plan to edit and publish Tom Collins's reports, an abandoned play laid in "a squatter's camp in Kern County," and a warm-up essay published in *The Nation* called "Dubious Battle in California" and intended to "give a mild idea" of the civil war brewing under his "nose," Steinbeck's first lengthy excursion into the migrants' problems was published in the liberal, pro-labor *San Francisco News*. His series "The Harvest Gypsies," produced at West's invitation, formed the foundation of Steinbeck's concern for a long time to come, raised issues and initiated forces, gave him a working vocabulary with which to understand current events, and furthered his position as a reliable interpreter. This stage resulted from the notoriety caused by his recently published strike novel, *In Dubious Battle* (1936), after which Steinbeck found—often against his will—that he was fast becoming considered a spokesman for the contemporary agricultural labor situation in a state that was primarily pro-management. This was ironic because while *In Dubious Battle* exposed the capitalist dynamics of corporate farming, it took no side for or against labor, preferring instead to see the fruit strike as a symbol of "man's eternal, bitter warfare with himself" (*SLL*, 98).

The articles in "The Harvest Gypsies," peppered with Dorothea Lange's graphic photographs of migrants, appeared from October 5 to 12, 1936. Steinbeck's gritty reports detailed the plan of California's feudal agricultural industry. The pieces introduced the antagonists, underscored the anachronistic rift between the Okie agrarian past and the mechanized California present, explained the economic background and insidious effects of the labor issue, examined the deplorable migrant living conditions, and exposed the unconscionable practices of the interlocking conglomerate of corporation farms. (These elements remained central to the core and texture of *The Grapes of Wrath*.) Primarily, though, Steinbeck's eye was on the "nomadic, poverty-stricken harvesters," the "150,000 homeless migrants" who were "gypsies by force of circumstance," as he announced in his opening piece: "And so they move, frantically, with starvation close behind them. And in this series of articles we shall try to see how they live and what kind of people they are, what their living standard is, what is done for them, and what their problems and needs are. For while California has been successful in its use of migrant labor, it is gradually building a human structure which will certainly change the state, and may, if handled with the inhumanity and stupidity that have characterized the past, destroy the present system of agricultural economics."[13]

Although Steinbeck later admitted that he was taken "over completely, heart and soul" by the "fine, brave people," he still maintained a measured style to promote understanding and intelligent solutions. Steinbeck's articles are full of case studies, chilling factual statistics, and an unsettling catalogue of human woes (illness, incapacitation, persecution, death) observed from close contact with field workers he had met. In the spirit of advocacy journalism, Steinbeck concluded with prophetic recommendations for alleviating the problem with federal aid and local support; this in turn would create subsistence farms, establish a migratory labor board, encourage unionization, and punish terrorism. When they were published in 1936 and again when they were reprinted in 1938 as a twenty-five-cent pamphlet called *Their Blood Is Strong* by the nonprofit Simon J. Lubin Society (which sold 10,000 copies in four printings), Steinbeck's articles solidified his credibility—both in and out of the migrant camps—as a serious commentator in a league with sociologist Carey McWilliams and Paul Taylor, Dorothea Lange's husband, two other influential, respected investigators.[14]

Steinbeck understood that the migrants wouldn't disappear, even though California officials hoped they would. He also knew that the subject he had dipped into reached further than he had imagined and was beginning to present itself as a possible novel. Consequently, Steinbeck built on his *News* pieces and on at least one more month-long field trip with Tom Collins in October and November of 1937. In Steinbeck's old panel truck (a pie delivery wagon in its former life), they started from Gridley, where Collins was managing a new camp, but then roamed California from Stockton to Needles, wherever migrants were gathered to work.[15] His purpose was to gather more research for his next version, the "big" book of fiction which had apparently been on his mind for most of that year, and which Steinbeck and Collins had obviously discussed. [In an undated letter probably written in the spring of 1937, he said to Collins, "You know of course my plans for the long novel dealing with the migrant" [*WD*, lii].) A letter to Elizabeth Otis, written on January 27, 1937, indicates he had been wrestling with this version since the previous winter: "The new book has struck a bad snag. . . . The subject is so huge it scares me to death." Several months later, in an interview in the *Los Gatos Mail-News*, Steinbeck publicly claimed for the first time that he had started a book whose topic was the Dust Bowl refugees, the "Oklahomans." Though he was "reluctant to discuss the characters and plot," he said it was "one third complete and will be about 1000 pages in length."[16] Given his comment to Otis in January and the fact that he traveled a good deal that year (including a trip with Carol to the Soviet Union), three hundred pages of completed manuscript at this point may have been wishful thinking on his part, or it may have represented the total number of pages of Collins's reports and his own research notes (which have never been found) he had accumulated during the year. If nothing else, the interview announced his proprietary attention to the material, about which he was known to have been protective and, as Horace Bristol later learned, even secretive.

In a second interview, with journalist Louis Walther, published January 8, 1938, in the *San Jose Mercury Herald*, he apparently had not progressed much, if at all. After hitting several "snags," he was working on a "rather long novel" allegedly called "The Oklahomans," which was "still a long way from finished." Steinbeck, generally guarded with interviewers, revealed enough to Walther to indicate his novel's focus was the salutary, irrepressible character of the "southern dust bowl immigrants" who, he believed, would profoundly alter the tenor of life in California. "Their coming here now is going to change things almost as much as did the coming of the first American settlers." Furthermore, "The Californian doesn't know what he does want. The Oklahoman knows just exactly what he wants. He wants a piece of land. And he goes after it and gets it" (*CJS*, 11-12). In *The Grapes of Wrath*, Steinbeck did not relinquish his land-hunger theme, or his belief that the migrants formed a specific phalanx group within the large national mass movement of the 1930s, but he certainly dropped his somewhat condescending, imperious, and naive tone in favor of a more inevitably tragic one.

As nearly as can be determined, between January and March 1938 Steinbeck quietly stopped work on this manuscript Walther had named "The Oklahomans." Steinbeck never mentioned it again by name, the manuscript has never been found, and his boasts of three hundred completed pages aside, it is doubtful that he had actually written a substantial amount of it at all. In the first entry of *Working Days*, on February 7[?], 1938, he mentioned having written "ten pages" of an otherwise unidentified book: "You pages . . . are the dribble cup—you are the cloth to wipe up the vomit. Maybe I can get these fears and disgusts on you and then burn you up. Then maybe I won't be so haunted" (6). And six weeks later, on March 23, 1938, he again told Elizabeth Otis: "I've been writing on the novel but I've had to destroy it several times. I don't seem to know any more about writing a novel than I did ten years ago. You'd think I would learn. I suppose I could dash it off but I want this one to be a pretty good one. There's another difficulty too. I'm trying to write history while it is happening and I don't want to be wrong" (*SLL*, 162). These troubled comments in early 1938 have long been thought to refer to the beginnings of "L'Affaire Lettuceberg" (discussed below), but it is far more likely that they refer to his difficulties in writing one or more avatars of the Oklahomans book, the Ur-*Grapes of Wrath*, which had, after more than a year and a couple of starts and stops, not yet found its proper impetus or creative urgency and in fact may have blown up in his face following his interview in the *San Jose Mercury Herald*. But in mulling over, rehearsing, and living with the subject of this "long novel dealing with the migrant" for so long ("I've been three years on the material," he told critic Harry T. Moore in July), Steinbeck was staking his claim to that imaginative territory, repeatedly experimenting with a way to fictionalize material that was until then the stuff of contemporary reportage. The general chapters in *Grapes* would be especially influenced by his long rehearsal.

Actually, the migrant situation had worsened, and along with it Steinbeck's capacity for anger and his need for direct involvement had grown. The workers' misery was increasing in the winter of 1938, especially in Visalia and Nipomo, where thousands of families were marooned by floods. From Los Gatos, Steinbeck wrote Otis in February:

> I must go over into the interior valleys. There are about five thousand families starving to death over there, not just hungry but actually starving. The government is trying to feed them and get medical attention to them with the fascist group of utilities and banks and huge growers sabotaging the thing all along the line. . . . in one tent there are twenty people quarantined for smallpox and two of the women are to have babies in that tent this week. I've tied into the thing from the first and I must get down there and see it and see if I can't do something to help knock these murderers on the heads. . . . They think that if these people are allowed to live in camps with proper sanitary facilities, they will organize and that is the bugbear of the large landowner and the corporation farmer. The states and counties will give them nothing because they are outsiders. But the crops of any part of this state could not be harvested without these outsiders. I'm pretty mad about it. (*SLL*, 158)

In late February and early March 1938 Steinbeck witnessed these deplorable conditions firsthand at Visalia, where, after three weeks of steady rain, "the water is a foot deep in the tents and the children are up on the beds and there is no food and no fire, and the county has taken off all the nurses because 'the problem is so great that we can't do anything about it.' So they do nothing," he informed Otis on March 7, 1938 (*SLL*, 161). In the company of *Life* magazine photographer Horace Bristol, Tom Collins, and other FSA personnel, Steinbeck worked day and night for nearly two weeks, sometimes dropping in the mud from exhaustion, to help relieve the people's misery, though of course no aid seemed adequate. Steinbeck was supposed to be writing an article with Bristol for *Life* magazine, but what he encountered was so devastating, he told Otis, that he was utterly transfixed by the "staggering" conditions; the "suffering" was so great that objective reporting would only falsify the moment.[17] Suddenly, Steinbeck realized that the issue was not as simple as portraying the "naive directness" of the migrants' desire for land. Indeed, the cauldron of his own soul was beginning to boil with anger, frustration, and impotence. Apparently neither the "Oklahomans" version nor the proposed article could adequately redress the injustices he had recently witnessed. "When I wrote *The Grapes of Wrath*," he declared in a 1952 Voice of America radio interview, "I was filled . . . with certain angers . . . at people who were doing injustices to other people" (quoted in *WD*, xxxiii).

In his work as a novelist, Steinbeck often experienced a delayed reaction to piercing events. Perhaps as early as February—but certainly no later than early April ("New book goes very fast but I am afraid it is pretty lousy. I don't care much," he told Otis on April 26, 1938)—through approximately mid-May 1938, Steinbeck worked at the third stage of his effort, and produced "L'Affaire Lettuceberg." With this abortive—but necessary—sidetrack venture, Steinbeck's migrant subject matter took its most drastic turn, inspired by an ugly event in Salinas, California, his hometown, two years earlier. In September 1936 Steinbeck had encountered the vicious clash between workers and growers in a lettuce strike—"there are riots in Salinas and killings in the streets of that dear little town where I was born," he told novelist George Albee (*SLL*, 132). The strike was smashed with "fascist" terrorism, including gas bombings, shootings, and strict lockouts, and recollections of the workers' defeat and the systematic violation of their civil rights festered in Steinbeck for more than a year. "I am treasonable enough not to believe in the liberty of a man or a group to exploit, torment, or slaughter other men or groups. I believe in the despotism of human life and happiness against the liberty of money and possessions," he said in a 1937 statement for the League of American Writers.[18]

Perhaps as early as the first week of February 1938, and no later than the first week of April, galvanized by reports of the worsening conditions in Visalia and Nipomo, Steinbeck felt the urgent need to do something direct in retaliation. He never became what committed activists would consider fully radicalized (his writings stemmed more from his own feelings and humane sensibility than from the persuasiveness of the Left's economic and social ideas), but by putting his pen to the service of this cause, he was stepping as close to being a firebrand as he ever would. He launched into "L'Affaire Lettuceberg," a vituperative satire aimed at attacking the leading citizens of Salinas, a cabal of organizers called "the committee of seven," who foment the army of armed vigilantes (a thousand strong) recruited from the common populace of Salinas—clerks, service-station operators, shopkeepers. "L'Affaire" was a detour from his main concern for the migrant workers, already recorded in "The Harvest Gypsies" and adumbrated in the "Oklahoman" rehearsals. In fact, "L'Affaire" wasn't "literary" at all, rather, it was a "vulgar" tract concocted to do a specific job. Sometime in early May 1938 Steinbeck, who had already written approximately 50,000 words (and was aiming for 10,000 more), confessed to Annie Laurie Williams: "I'll have the first draft of this book done in about two weeks. . . . And it is a vicious book, a mean book. I don't know whether it will be any good at all. It might well be very lousy but it has a lot of poison in it that I had to get out of my system and this is a good way to do it" (quoted in *WD*, xxxix).

Shortly after that prediction, however, Steinbeck wrote again to Otis and to his publisher, Pascal Covici (who had already announced the publication of "L'Affaire"), to inform them that he would not be delivering the manuscript they expected:

> This is going to be a hard letter to write. . . . this book is finished and it is a bad book and I must get rid of it. It can't be printed. It is bad because it isn't honest. Oh! these incidents all happened but—I'm not telling as much of the truth about them as I know. In satire you have to restrict the picture and I just can't do satire. . . . I know, you could sell possibly 30,000 copies. I know that a great many people would think they liked the book. I myself have built up a hole-proof argument on how and why I liked it. I can't beat the argument but I don't like the book. And I would be doing Pat [Covici] a greater injury in letting him print it than I would by destroying it. Not once in the writing of it have I felt the curious warm pleasure that comes when work is going well. My whole work drive has been aimed at making people understand each other and then I deliberately write this book the aim of which is to cause hatred through partial understanding. My father would have called it a smart-alec book. It was full of tricks to make people ridiculous. If I can't do better I have slipped badly. And that I won't admit, yet. (quoted in *WD*, xl-xli)

Urged on by Carol, who hated "L'Affaire," Steinbeck made the right move. On May 24, 1938, Annie Laurie Williams, speaking for the staff at McIntosh and Otis literary agents, replied: "I admire you for having the courage of your convictions and know you would feel better if you could have heard what Elizabeth and Pat both said when they read your letter. . . . [W]e all admire you more than ever for sticking by your instincts about your work" (quoted in *WD*, lv).

IV

Steinbeck rebounded immediately and hit the ground running. Traditionally, he did not work weekends or holidays, so he probably took off Memorial Day weekend, which means that—judging from the fact that he wrote the "turtle episode," or the third chapter (*WD*, 20), on Tuesday, May 31, and calculating backwards from there at 2,000 words per day—he began *The Grapes of Wrath* on Wednesday, May 25, and certainly no later than Thursday, May 26. His conscience squared, his integrity restored, Steinbeck quickly embarked on the longest sustained writing job of his career. Ridding himself of poison by passing through a "bad" book proved beneficial, he told Otis on June 1, 1938: ". . . it is a nice thing to be working and believing in my work again. I hope I can keep the drive. . . . I only feel whole and well when it is this way" (*SLL*, 167). Naturally, his partisanship for the workers and his sense of indignation at California's labor situation carried over, but they were given a more articulate and believable shape.

From the moment Steinbeck struck the first lines of the new novel to paper—"To the red country and part of the gray country of Oklahoma, the last rains came gently, and they did not cut the scarred earth. The plows crossed and recrossed the rivulet marks"[19]—through the winter of 1939, when the last of the corrections and editorial details were negotiated—"I meant, Pat, to print *all all all* the verses of the Battle Hymn. They're all pertinent and they're all exciting. And the music if you can," he chastised (*SLL*, 175)—*The Grapes of Wrath* was a task which fully commanded Steinbeck's artistic energy and attention. Everything he had written earlier—from his 1936 *Nation* article, through "Starvation under the Orange Trees," an impassioned April 1938 essay that functioned as the epilogue to *Their Blood Is Strong*, and even through "Breakfast," a poignant short story/sketch included in his short story collection *The Long Valley* (1938)—became grist for his final attempt. "For the first time I am working on a book that is not limited and that will take every bit of experience and thought and feeling that I have," he claimed on June 11, 1938 (*WD*, 26).

From his numerous field travels with Collins, and from countless hours of talking to migrant people, working beside them, listening to them, and sharing their problems, Steinbeck summoned all the concrete details of human form, language, and landscape that ensure artistic verisimilitude, as well as the subtler, imaginative nuances of dialect, idiosyncratic tics, habits, and gestures that animate fictional characterization and would make his "people . . . intensely alive the whole time" (*WD*, 40).[20] From the outset in creating the Joad family to occupy the narrative chapters of *The Grapes of Wrath*, Steinbeck endowed his novel with a specific human context, a felt emotional quality, and a capacious dramatic dimension his earlier versions lacked: "Begin the detailed description of the family I am to live with. Must take time in the description, detail, detail, looks, clothes, gestures. . . . We have to know these people. Know their looks and their nature," he reminded himself on June 17 (*WD*, 29). Most importantly, by deliberately conceiving the Joads as "an over-essence of people," Steinbeck elevated the entire history of the migrant struggle into the realm of art and joined the mythic westering journey with latently heroic characters, according to this key notation on June 30: "Yesterday . . . I went over the whole of the book in my head—fixed on the last scene, huge and symbolic, toward which the whole story moves. And that was a good thing, for it was a reunderstanding of the dignity of the effort and the mightyness of the theme. I feel very small and inadequate and incapable but I grew again to love the story which is so much greater than I am. To love and admire the people who are so much stronger and purer and braver than I am" (*WD*, 36). His transformation of Rose of Sharon from "silly pregnant" teenager to mysterious madonna figure in the novel's final scene was not only long prepared for in his imagination but became, in a sense, the novel's alpha and omega, at once its point of departure and its finale.

It is a critical commonplace that many American authors, often with little in the way of a shared novelistic tradition to emulate, or finding that established fictional models don't suit their sensibilities, forge their own way by synthesizing their personal vision and experience with a variety of cultural forms and literary styles. Steinbeck was no exception. To execute *The Grapes of Wrath* he drew on the jump-cut technique of John Dos Passos's *U.S.A.* trilogy (1937), the narrative tempo of Pare Lorentz's radio drama *Ecce Homo!*, the sequential quality of Lorentz's films *The Plow That Broke the Plains* (1936) and *The River* (1937), the stark visual effects of Dorothea Lange's photographs of Dust Bowl Oklahoma and California migrant life, the timbre of the Greek epics, the rhythms of the King James Bible, the refrains of American folk music, and the biological impetus of his and Edward F. Ricketts's ecological phalanx, or group-man, theory, in which an aggregate group of individuals acts according to a single purpose, and in so doing, their identity as a group organism transcends individual personalities. Steinbeck's imagination transformed these resources, especially Old and New Testament themes, parallels, and inversions, into his own holistic structure, his own individual signature. Malcolm Cowley's claim that a "whole literature is summarized in this book and much of it is carried to a new level of excellence" is especially pertinent and underscores the capacious dimension of the novel.[21]

If Steinbeck's artistic influences were disparate, his conception of the novel's structure was uniform in its growth. The epic scale and technical plan of *Grapes* apparently crystallized between May 15 and May 25, 1938. During that fertile transitional moment the organizational design of the novel clearly established itself in Steinbeck's mind. Unlike William Faulkner, say, Steinbeck was not an elite literary practitioner or formal innovator, but he still achieved in *Grapes* a compelling combination of individual style, visual realism, and rambunctious, symphonic form that was at once accessible and experimental, documentarian and fictive, expository and lyrical. He anticipated almost precisely the novel's length and the amount of time it would take to complete it. He apparently did not work from a formal outline (at least no written one has ever turned up); rather, he sketched out the novel in his head in aggregate first (he appears to have assembled a nearly complete list of potential topics for his intercalary, or general, chapters by the time he started writing), followed by a brief planning session each day, or every few days if he happened to be working on a long chapter, such as chapter 20.[22] On August 18, he noted: "Now away from the daily life and into the book. I read a couple of chapters to company last night and could see the whole thing clearly. Also it doesn't sound bad. Today is going to take a long time, I have to get on the line of my family again. The outline of today will carry over some days. Must get it straight, must get it clear and straight" (*WD*, 58). Sticking to his outline became increasingly important, because this chapter, continually disrupted by intrusions, took him from August 18 to September 3 to complete. When it was finished, Steinbeck scrawled at the bottom of manuscript page 109, "long son of a bitch too."

In early July 1938 Steinbeck confided to Harry T. Moore that he was employing what was for him a "new method" of fictional technique which purposefully combined a suitably elastic form and elevated style to express the far-reaching tragedy of the migrant drama.[23] Influenced by Tolstoy's construction in *War and Peace*—which Steinbeck told Merle Danford a few months later was his favorite "literary creation" (*CJS*, 23)—he devised for *The Grapes of Wrath* a contrapuntal structure, alternating in the thirty chapters between short lyrical ones of exposition and background pertinent to the migrants as a group (Chapters 1, 3, 5, 7, 9, 11, 12, 14, 15, 17, 19, 21, 23, 25, 27, 29) and the long narrative chapters of the Joad family's dramatic exodus to California (all the other chapters), Steinbeck structured his novel by juxtaposition. His "particular" chapters are the slow-paced and lengthy narrative chapters that embody traditional characterization and advance the dramatic plot, while his jazzy, rapid-fire "interchapters" work at another level of recognition by expressing an atemporal, universal, synoptic view of the migrant condition. As he composed chapters 5 and 6, for instance, Steinbeck reminded himself that, for maximum effect, "I want the reader to be able to keep [the general and particular chapters] separate in his mind" (*WD*, 23-24). In fact, his "general" or intercalary chapters ("pace changers," Steinbeck called them), were expressly designed to "hit the reader below the belt. With the rhythms and symbols of poetry one can get into a reader—open him up and while he is open introduce things on an intellectual level which he would not or could not receive unless he were opened up," as Steinbeck revealed to Columbia undergraduate Herbert Sturz in 1953.[24]

The Grapes of Wrath is an engaged novel with a partisan posture and many complex voices and passionate prose styles: "No other American novel has succeeded in forging and making instrumental so many prose styles," Peter Lisca believes.[25] Except for *Grapes*'s unflinching treatment of the Great Depression's climatic, social, and economic conditions, and those non-teleologically inspired interchapters which serve to halt the slide of his characters' emotions toward sentimentality, there is nothing cynically distanced about it, nothing coolly modernist, in the way we have come to understand the elite literary implications of that term in the past seventy-five years. (*The Grapes of Wrath* is in some ways an old-fashioned novel, even down to its curious avoidance of human sexuality.) It is not narrated from the first-person point of view, yet the language has a consistently catchy eyewitness quality about it; and the vivid biblical, empirical, poetical, cinematic, and folk styles Steinbeck employed demonstrate the remarkable tonal and visual acuity of his ear and eye. Passages like this one, written on September 22, come from a place far deeper than the intellect, come from the visceral center of the writer's being:

> There is a crime here that goes beyond denunciation. There is a sorrow here that weeping cannot symbolize. There is a failure here that topples all our success. The fertile earth, the straight tree arrows, the sturdy trunks, and the ripe fruit. And children dying of pellagra must die because a profit cannot be taken from an orange . . . and in the eyes of the people there is the failure; and in the eyes of the hungry there is a growing wrath. In the souls of the people the grapes of wrath are filling and growing heavy, growing heavy for the vintage. (*GW*, 477)

The tempo of this passage—one of the most striking in *Grapes*—indicates the importance of musical and harmonic analogies to the novel. Steinbeck told Merle Armitage on February 17, 1939, that in "composition, in movement, in tone and in scope," *The Grapes of Wrath* is "symphonic."[26] Steinbeck's covenant was with his own radical sense of the fiction-making process, not with a well-made linear formula. Indeed, his fusion of intimate narrative and panoramic editorial chapters enforces a dialogic concert. Chapters, styles, voices all speak to each other, set up resonances, send echoes back and forth—point and counterpoint, strophe and antistrophe—as in a huge symphony whose total tonal and spatial impression far surpasses the sum of its discrete and sometimes dissonant parts. It should come as no surprise that Steinbeck listened almost religiously to classical music either before or during his writing sessions. Tchaikovsky's ballet *The Swan Lake*, Stravinsky's "very fine" *Symphony of Psalms*, and Beethoven's symphonies and sonatas created a mood conducive to writing and established a rhythm for the day's work. For instance, on June 21, in preparation for writing chapter 9, the short interchapter about the migrants deciding which, if any, of their belongings they can take west, Steinbeck played *The Swan*, "because there too is the loss of a loved thing of the past" (*WD*, 31). And when he didn't have the record player going, he contented himself with the chug and whir of the washing machine.

Steinbeck's novel belongs to that vital class of fictions whose shape issues not from an ideal blueprint of aesthetic propriety, but from the generative urgency of their authors' experience ("It had to be written," Stanley Kunitz said in *Wilson Library Bulletin* in October 1939). Steinbeck's direct involvement with the plight of hundreds of thousands of Dust Bowl migrants in the latter half of the 1930s created his obsessive urge to tell their story honestly but also movingly. "This must be a good book," he wrote on June 10, 1938. "It simply must. I haven't any choice. It must be far and away the best thing I have ever attempted—slow but sure, piling detail on detail until a picture and an experience emerge. Until the whole throbbing thing emerges" (*WD*,

25). Making his audience see and feel that living picture was paramount. "I am not writing a satisfying story," he claimed to Pascal Covici on January 16, 1939: "I've done my damndest to rip a reader's nerves to rags, I don't want him satisfied. . . . I tried to write this book the way lives are being lived not the way books are written. . . . Throughout I've tried to make the reader participate in the actuality, what he takes from it will be scaled entirely on his own depth or hollowness. There are five layers in this book, a reader will find as many as he can and he won't find more than he has in himself" (*SLL*, 178-79). Steinbeck's participatory aesthetic was based on a circle of complicity which linked "the trinity" of writer, text, and reader to ensure maximum affective impact. On June 7, 1938, as he completed chapter 5, for instance, he kept his eye steadily on target: "Today's work is the overtone of the tractors, the men who run them, the men they displace, the sound of them, the smell of them. I've got to get this over. Got to because this one's tone is very important—this is the eviction sound and the tonal reason for movement. Must do it well" (*WD*, 23).

As he said, Steinbeck conceived his novel on five simultaneous levels of existence, ranging from socioeconomic determinism to transcendent spirituality. Louis Owens explains how biblical parallels illuminate four of Steinbeck's layers: "On one level it is the story of a family's struggle for survival in the Promised Land. . . . On another level it is the story of a people's struggle, the migrants'. On a third level it is the story of a nation, America. On still another level, through . . . the allusions to Christ and those to the Israelites and Exodus, it becomes the story of mankind's quest for profound comprehension of his commitment to his fellow man and to the earth he inhabits."[27] Thus Steinbeck pushed back the normative boundaries of traditional mimetic fiction and redefined the proletarian form. Like most significant American novels, *The Grapes of Wrath* does not offer codified social solutions. Even though it privileges a particular section of the white American migrant labor scene (Steinbeck ignores the problems of the nonwhite migrant workers—Filipino, Chinese, Japanese, and Mexican—who made up a large percentage of California's agricultural labor force, according to Carey McWilliams's 1939 sociological study, *Factories in the Field*), his book—if the testimony of the late César Chávez is any indication—still speaks to the universal experience of human disenfranchisement, still looks toward an authentic human ecology. In this sense it is both a hermeneutical and a heuristic text. At every level *The Grapes of Wrath* enacts the process of its author's belief and embodies the shape of his faith, as in this ringing synthesis from chapter 14: "The last clear definite function of man—muscles aching to work, minds aching to create beyond the single need—this is man. To build a wall, to build a house, a dam, and in the wall and house and dam to put something of Manself, and to Manself take back something of the wall, the house, the dam; to take hard muscles from the lifting, to take the clear lines and form from conceiving. For man, unlike any other thing organic or inorganic in the universe, grows beyond his work, walks up the stairs of his concepts, emerges ahead of his accomplishments" (*GW*, 204).

V

John Steinbeck lived to write. He believed it was redemptive, transformative work. Each day, as early as possible, but generally no later than 11:15 A.M., he brewed a pot of "ranch" coffee (clarified with a raw egg) and sequestered himself in the eight-by-eight-foot work room of "Arroyo del Ajo" ("Garlic Gulch"), the house he and Carol built in 1936 on Greenwood Lane in Los Gatos: "Just big enough for a bed and a desk and a gun rack and a little book case. I like to sleep in the room I work in," he confided to George Albee (*SLL*, 133). In his study, or some days out on their porch deck or in their guest cottage, he warmed up religiously with letters to Otis or Covici and an all-important entry in his working journal to give him "the opening use of words every day" (*WD*, 38). Thus, Steinbeck created a disciplined working rhythm and what he called a "unity feeling"—a sense of continuity and cohabitation with his material that made "it easy and fun to work" (*WD*, 27). "Let the damn book go three hundred thousand words if it wants to. This is my life. Why should I want to finish my own life? The confidence is on me again. I can feel it. It's stopping work that does the damage," he wrote on July 7, 1938 (*WD*, 39). Ideally, for a few hours each day, the world Steinbeck created took precedence over the one in which he lived. Because, for an artist, both worlds can be considered "real," at times during 1938 Steinbeck didn't know where one began and the other left off, walking back into the domestic world from the world of imagination was not always a smooth shift for him (or for Carol). His work demanded his attention so completely that he finally refused to dissipate his energy in extraliterary pursuits: "I won't do any of these public things. Can't. It isn't my nature and I won't be stampeded. And so the stand must be made and I must keep out of politics," he promised himself, though he continually worried about the migrant situation in California and news of Nazi/Fascist advances in Eastern Europe, which contributed to the book's edginess, its sense of doom.

But as the summer wore on, emerging ahead of his accomplishments seemed an insurmountable task for Steinbeck because, besides losing the "threads" that tied him to his characters, he was low on patience and had lost his sense of humor. "Was ever a book written under greater difficulty?" (*WD*, 63), he moaned. Nearly every day brought unsolicited requests for his name, his money, and his time, including unscheduled visitors, unanticipated disruptions and reversals. Domestic and conjugal relations with Carol were often strained (Steinbeck apparently remained mostly celibate when he was deeply immersed in his writing [*WD*, 34]). Houseguests trooped to Los Gatos all summer, including his sisters, Beth Ainsworth and Mary Dekker, and longtime friends Carlton Sheffield, George and Gail Mors, Ed Ricketts, Ritch and Tal Lovejoy, plus new celebrity acquaintances Wallace Ford and Broderick Crawford (stars of the recently closed New York Drama Critics' Circle Award-winning play, *Of Mice and Men*), Charlie Chaplin, and Pare Lorentz. As if that weren't enough to erode the novelist's composure, the Steinbecks' tiny house on Greenwood Lane was besieged with the noise of neighborhood building and boisterous activity, which nearly drove them to distraction. By midsummer, hoping for permanent sanctuary, they decided to buy the secluded Biddle Ranch, a forty-seven-acre spread on Brush Road in the Santa Cruz Mountains above Los Gatos. Even though it was the most "beautiful" location they had seen (*WD*, 42), its original homestead was in disrepair, so besides buying the land they would also have to build a new house, and that too became a source of added distractions. The Steinbecks didn't move there until November 1938, a month after the novel was finished (final typing of the manuscript and corrections of the typescript and galley proofs took place at the Biddle Ranch from November 1938 to early February 1939), but preparations for the purchase ate a great deal of Steinbeck's time and energy from mid-July onward.

August proved the most embattled period. Early in the month—on the third—Steinbeck noted in his journal, "There are now four things or five rather to write through—throat, bankruptcy, Pare, ranch, and the book. If I get this book done it will be remarkable" (*WD*, 51). His litany of woes included Carol's tonsillectomy, which incapacitated her; the bankruptcy of Steinbeck's publisher, Covici-Friede, which threatened the end of their current income and posed an uncertain publishing future for the novel he was writing; Pare Lorentz's arrangements for making a film version of *In Dubious Battle*; the purchase of the Biddle Ranch, which they both wanted badly; and the book itself, still untitled (and therefore without "being"), which seemed more recalcitrant than ever. By mid-August, roughly halfway through the novel, Steinbeck took stock of his situation; the Viking Press had bought his contract, hired Pat Covici as a senior editor as part of the deal, and planned a first printing of 15,000 copies for Steinbeck's collection of short stories, *The Long Valley*; a string of famous houseguests had either just departed or were about to arrive; and he and Carol had closed on the Biddle property for $10,500. On August 16, in the middle of what he called a "Bad Lazy Time," he lamented, "Demoralization complete and seemingly unbeatable. So many things happening that I can't not be interested. . . . All this is more excitement than our whole lives put together. All crowded into a month. My many weaknesses are beginning to show their heads. I simply must get this thing out of my system. I'm not a writer. I've been fooling myself and other people. . . . This success will ruin me as sure as hell. It probably won't last and that will be all right" (*WD*, 56). Four days later, on August 20, Lorentz, the newly appointed director of the United States Film Service, arrived for the weekend. His visit broke Steinbeck's depression and logjam. They discussed further a full-length movie of *In Dubious Battle*, then rushed off to visit Chaplin at Pebble Beach, where they stayed up all night drinking and talking about the state of America.[28] Though their film project would ultimately fall through, Steinbeck was encouraged by Lorentz's optimism about the country at large and his prediction that Steinbeck's "monumental" book would be one of "the greatest novels of the age." Steinbeck doggedly kept up his daily stint (he aimed for 2,000 words at each sitting, some days managing as few as 800, some days, when the juices were flowing, as many as 2,200) through what Carol called the "interminable details and minor crises" of August and September (*WD*, 17-18).

That Steinbeck lost only four or five working days during that entire stretch points up just how deeply he augmented his talent with discipline and hard work. Where his characters use tools to elevate work to a dignified level, Steinbeck turned to his "comfortable and comforting" pen, an instrument that became an "extension" of the best part of himself: "Work is the only good thing," he claimed on July 6, 1938 (*WD*, 39). For Steinbeck, writing was a means of textual habitation, a way of living in the world he created. He wrote books methodically the way other people built houses, word by word, sentence by sentence. His act of composing was also self-creation, a way of fulfilling his emotional and psychological dream of belonging by being at home, by living in the architectural spaces created by his imagination. In fact, this creative, interior, or "architextual" level of engagement is the elusive, unacknowledged fifth layer of Steinbeck's novel.

Although Steinbeck insisted on effacing his own presence in *The Grapes of Wrath* (*SLL*, 180-81), the fact remains that it is a very personal book, rooted in his own compulsion. Aspects of Steinbeck's life bore directly on manuscript decisions. During his planning session on July 13, admittedly confused by the increasing lure of owning the Biddle Ranch—"I want that ranch" (*WD*, 42)—he decided to write chapter 14, the general chapter on Manself, which became one of the most important theoretical chapters and perhaps the most significant summation of organismal philosophy Steinbeck had yet written. The first half includes the paean to the universal human capacity for creation. The second half expresses the core of Steinbeck's mature phalanx theory, his belief in the possibility of the creation of an aggregate, dynamic "We" from distinct, myriad selves (*GW*, 206). The summary quality of this chapter suggests that Steinbeck intended to use it later as a kind of climactic crescendo (he ended up using chapter 25). Instead he inserted the Manself chapter at the midpoint of the novel for several reasons: its dithyrambic tone and heightened language reawakened his flagging interest; its optimistic, theoretical bias restored focus and clarity to the narrative line; its extolment of creativity, based on humanity's willingness to "suffer and die for a concept" (*GW*, 205), provided an immediate reminder that his own compositional process could be endured for the sake of the cause he espoused; and its concern for families who had lost their land and homes may have partly assuaged his guilt, if not his sense of irony, as he was about to make the biggest property purchase of his life. Furthermore, the "plodding" pace of Steinbeck's writing schedule informed the slow, "crawling" movement of the Joads' journey, while the harried beat of his own life gave the proper "feel" and tone to his beleaguered characters. Their unsavory weaknesses and vanities, their struggle for survival, their unsuspecting heroism are Steinbeck's as well. If *The Grapes of Wrath* praises the honorableness of labor and ratifies the obsessive quest for a home it is because the author himself felt that these twin acts called into being the most committed, the most empathetic, the most resourceful qualities of the human psyche.

By early October, Steinbeck, rebuked often by his wife, roused himself from another bout of "self indulgence" and "foolishness" to mount the final drive (*WD*, 81). Like a gift, the last five chapters of the novel came to him so abundantly that he had more material than he could use (Rose of Sharon was to contract measles, which in turn would cause the death of her infant). On Wednesday, October 5, and again on Friday, October 7, he planned chapter 26:

> And my story is coming better. I see it better. Ma's crossing with the clerk, and then Tom's going out—meeting Casy, trying to move the men in the camp. Arrest and beating. Return in secret. Move. Cotton—flood. And the end—Tom comes back. Stolen things. Must go. Be Around. Birth. And the rising waters. And the starving man. And the end. What more? (*WD*, 82-83)

> This leisurelyness must go on although the tempo gets faster the details must be as slow. Today the hiding of Tom and the scene with his mother. The cut in wages. Tom has to go. Getting together. The drop to starvation level of the wages. The trapped duality. Must get it in—Difficulty of getting clean. No soap. No money to buy soap. Then peaches. The rush of workers and the fight for the peaches. Fight to get them. Must get this all in. There's so damned much in this book already. I must keep it coming. . . . (*WD*, 84)

Here the full force of Steinbeck's experience at Visalia eight months earlier came into play, prompting his metamorphosis from right-minded competency to inspired vision. What Steinbeck had witnessed in that "heart-breaking" sea of mud and debris called forth every ounce of his moral indignation, social anger, and empathy, which in turn profoundly affected his novel's climax. His internal wounding opened the floodgates of his affection, created *The Grapes of Wrath*'s compelling justification, provided its haunting spiritual urgency, and rooted it in the deepest wellsprings of democratic fellow-feeling. In the same way that rain floods the novel's concluding chapters, so the memory of Steinbeck's cataclysmic experience, his compensation for the futility and impotency of Visalia, pervades the ending of the book; its ominous emotional climate is charged by a terrible beauty symbolized by Rose of Sharon's gratuitous act of sharing her breast with a starving stranger. "It must be an accident, it must be a stranger, and it must be quick," Steinbeck instructed Covici. "To build this stranger into the structure of the book would be to warp the whole meaning of the book. The fact that the Joads don't know him, don't care about him, have no ties to him—that is the emphasis. The giving of the breast has no more sentiment than the giving of a piece of bread" (*SLL*, 178). This prophetic final tableau scene—often decried and misunderstood, but for that no less subversively erotic, mysteriously indeterminate—refuses to fade from view; before the apocalypse occurs, before everything is lost in otherness, Steinbeck suggests, all gestures must pass from self to world, from flesh to word, from communication to communion. It was the perfect ending for his book.[29]

Steinbeck's participation at Visalia also empowered his transformation of Tom Joad, the slowly awakening disciple of Jim Casy. Tom's acceptance of the crucified preacher's gospel of social presence occurs just as the deluge is about to begin: "Wherever they's a fight so hungry people can eat, I'll be there. Wherever they's a cop beatin' up a guy, I'll be there. If Casy knowed, why, I'll be in the way guys yell when they're mad an'—I'll be in the way kids laugh when they're hungry an' they know supper's ready. An' when our folks eat the stuff they raise an' live in the houses they build—why, I'll be there. See? God, I'm talkin' like Casy. Comes of thinkin' about him so much. Seems like I can see him sometimes" (*GW*, 572).

In one of those uncanny transferences artists can make in moments of extreme exhaustion or receptivity, Steinbeck not only believed that his fictive alter ego, Tom Joad, floated above *The Grapes of Wrath*'s "last pages . . . like a spirit," but also imagined that Joad actually entered the novelist's work space, the private chamber of his room: "'Tom! Tom! Tom!' I know. It wasn't him. Yes, I think I can go on now. In fact, I feel stronger. Much stronger. Funny where the energy comes from. Now to work, only now it isn't work any more," he recorded in his journal on October 20 (*WD*, 91). With that breakthrough—at once a visitation and a benediction—Steinbeck arrived at the intersection of novel and journal, that luminous point, that fifth layer of involvement, where the life of the writer merges with his created world. He entered the architecture of his own novel, and, however briefly, lived in its fictive space, where, like Tom Joad, Steinbeck discovered it was no longer necessary to lead people toward a distant new Eden or illusory Promised Land; rather, the most heroic action was simply to learn to be present, to inhabit the "wherever" fully and at once.

The terms of his complex investment fulfilled, Steinbeck needed only a few more days to finish his novel. Around noon on Wednesday, October 26, 1938, feeling "so dizzy" he could "hardly see the page" (*WD*, 93), he completed the last 775 words of the novel; at the bottom of the concluding manuscript page, Steinbeck, whose writing was normally tiny, scrawled in letters an inch and a half high "END#."[30] It should have been cause for wild celebrating, but between bouts of bone-weary tiredness and nervous exhaustion, Steinbeck felt only numbness and perhaps some of the mysterious satisfaction that comes from having transformed the weight of his whole life into the new book. In *The Grapes of Wrath* the multiple streams of subjective experience, amelioration, graphic realism, biblical themes, and symbolic forms gather to create the "truly American book" Steinbeck had planned. "Finished this day," his final journal entry concluded simply, "and I hope to God it's good" (*WD*, 93).

VI

In 1963 Steinbeck told Caskie Stinnett: "I wrote *The Grapes of Wrath* in one hundred days, but many years of preparation preceded it. I take a hell of a long time to get started. The actual writing is the last process" (*CJS*, 87-88). Though Steinbeck made 99 entries in his daily journal, and actually wrote the novel in 93 sittings, it was his way of saying that *The Grapes of Wrath* was an intuited whole which embodied the form of his devotion. The entire 200,000-word manuscript took up 165 handwritten pages (plus one smaller sheet) of a 12″ × 18″ lined ledger book. When he was hot, Steinbeck wrote fast, paying little or no attention to proper spelling, punctuation, or paragraphing. On top of that his script was so small he was capable of cramming over 1,300 words on a single oversized ledger sheet (page 156 of the manuscript is the equivalent of four pages of the Viking text). In short, the novel was written with remarkably preordained motion and directed passion; the relative cleanness and clarity of the holograph manuscript is awesome. To British scholar Roy S. Simmonds it displays a "phenomenal" unity of purpose, an example of "spontaneous prose" created long before Kerouac's *On the Road*.[31]

In one instance Steinbeck inserted an unnumbered sheet between pages 87 and 88 of the manuscript. This contained three short bridge passages (totaling approximately 500 words) to explain Noah Joad's abandonment at the Colorado River. There is also a very ungainly passage of 159 words, originally intended to be part of chapter 21, which one of the Steinbecks wisely canceled when proofreading the typescript:

> Once the Germans in their hordes came to the rich margin of Rome; and they came timidly, saying 'we have been driven, give us land.' And the Romans armed the frontier and built forts against the hordes of need/ . ~~And the Romans armed the frontier~~ And the legions patrolled the borders, cased in metal, armed with the best steel. And the barbarians came, naked, across the border, humbly, humbly. They received the swords in their

breasts and marched on; and their dead bore down the swords and the bar-barians marched on and took the land. And they were driven by their need, and they conquered with their need. In battle the women fought in the line, and the yellow-haired children lay in the grass with knives to ham-string the legionaries, to snick through the hamstrings of the horses. But the le-gions had no needs, no wills, no force. And the best trained. best armed troops in the world went down before the hordes of need.[32]

Not in the manuscript or in the typescript, but in the galleys of the Vi-king text, a passage of 82 words was later added to chapter 26 and one of 228 words designed for effective pacing was added to chapter 30. Otherwise, the emendations are neither major nor substantive—often just changes in syntax, punctuation, paragraphing, spelling, and names (the family that shares the flooding boxcar with the Joads at novel's end were called the Hamills in manuscript, but Steinbeck changed that to the Wainwrights in Carol's typescript). Page after page went essen-tially unmodified from autograph manuscript to typescript to pub-lished novel. Though Steinbeck severely doubted his own artistic abil-ity, and in fact wavered sometimes in regard to such niceties as chapter divisions (he originally conceived the novel in three parts), in writing this novel he was creating with the full potency of his imaginative powers. His ability to execute a work of its magnitude places him among the premier creative talents of his time. From the vantage point of history, the venture stands as one of those happy occasions when a writer simply wrote better than he thought he could.

Steinbeck had completely lost sight of the novel's effectiveness and had little grasp on its potential popularity, so he warned Covici and the Viking Press against a large first printing. Viking ignored him and spent $10,000 on publicity and printed an initial run of 50,000 copies. After recuperating in San Francisco from the stress of writing the book, the Steinbecks moved to their new Brush Road mountain home. It was still under construction, so they camped awhile in the old homestead, where Carol finished the huge typescript, and together they made "routine" final corrections. After Covici had read 400 pages of the typescript on a visit to Los Gatos in late October (*WD*, 91), he badgered Steinbeck for his own copy of the manuscript; Steinbeck gave in and sent the first two chapters to him on November 29. The whole of Carol's cleanly typed copy, which was actually only the second draft of the book (*SLL*, 171), was sent to his New York agents on December 7, 1938, roughly six months after Steinbeck had started the novel. Elizabeth Otis visited Los Gatos in late December to smooth out some of Steinbeck's rough language, like the dozen or so appearances of the words *fuck*, *shit*, *screw*, and *fat ass*, which were the chief offenders. They reached a workable compromise: Steinbeck agreed to change only those words "which Carol and Elizabeth said stopped the reader's mind"; beyond that, "those readers who are insulted by normal events or language mean nothing to me," he told Covici on January 3, 1939 (*SLL*, 175). The novel's enthusiastic reception at Viking was spoiled by the wrangling that ensued over the controversial Rose of Sharon ending, which the firm wanted Steinbeck to change, not only to make it more "integral" to the plot, but also because it seemed larcenously close to de Maupassant's tale "Iddyle" (1884). On January 16, 1939, Steinbeck fired back:

> I am sorry but I cannot change that ending. . . . The giving of the breast has no more sentiment than the giving of a piece of bread. I'm sorry if that doesn't get over. It will maybe. I've been on this design and balance for a long time and I think I know how I want it. And if I'm wrong, I'm alone in my wrongness. As for the Maupassant story, I've never read it but I can't see that it makes much difference. There are no new stories and I wouldn't like them if there were. The incident of the earth mother feeding by the breast is older than literature. You know that I have never been touchy about changes, but I have too many thousands of hours on this book, every incident has been too carefully chosen and its weight judged and fitted. The balance is there. (*SLL*, 178)

The entire postwriting flurry, including answering the persistent marginal queries on the typescript posed by a copy editor (whose initials were DZ), proofreading the galleys, and fending off Viking's requests for public appearances, struck the novelist, by then suffering from sciatica and tonsillitis, as anticlimactic; "[D]o you really think we've lost a single reader by refusing to do the usual things? By not speaking at luncheons do you think I've lost sales? I don't. And if it were true I'd rather lose that kind of readers" (*SLL*, 181).

Steinbeck may not have been interested in the promotional activities surrounding his book, but plenty of other people were. *The Grapes of Wrath* was widely and favorably reviewed, and its fidelity to fact, its degree of social realism were discussed and debated in the popular press when it was first published. It has been praised by the Left as a triumph of proletarian writing, nominated by critics and reviewers alike as "The Great American Novel," given historical significance by Senator Robert M. La Follette's inquiries into California's tyrannical farm labor conditions, and validated by Carey McWilliams, whose own great work, *Factories in the Field*, is the classic sociological counterpart to Steinbeck's novel. But *The Grapes of Wrath* has also been attacked by elitist scholars as sentimental, unconvincing, and inartistic; banned repeatedly by school boards and libraries for its rebellious theme and frank language; and denounced by right-wing ministers, corporate farmers, and politicians as communistic, immoral, degrading, warped, and untruthful. The Associated Farmers mounted a smear campaign to discredit the book and its author, who often felt his life was in danger. Rebuttals intended to whitewash the Okie situation, such as *Of Human Kindness*, written by Steinbeck's Los Gatos neighbor Ruth Comfort Mitchell, had no impact whatsoever.

Since it was published, *The Grapes of Wrath* has been steadily studied and analyzed by literary critics, scholars, historians, and creative writers. It is no exaggeration to say that, during the past half century, few American novels have attracted such passionate attacks and equally passionate defenses. It seems hard to believe that critics are all reading the same novel. Philip Rahv's complaint in the *Partisan Review* (Spring 1939) that "the novel is far too didactic and long-winded" and "fails on the test of craftsmanship" should be weighed against Charles Angoff's assessment in the *North American Review* (Summer 1939) that it is "momentous, monumental, and memorable," and an example of "the highest art." This dialectic still characterizes the novel's critical reception. In a 1989 speech, critic Leslie Fiedler attacked the novel as "maudlin, sentimental, and overblown"; a month later, in a review, novelist William Kennedy praised it for standing "tall . . . a mighty, mighty book."[33]

If the past fifty years have seen little consensus about the exact nature of the novel's achievement, at least contemporary analysts treat the book as a legitimate work of fiction rather than as a propagandistic tract. No matter which lens *Grapes* is viewed through, its textual richness, its many layers of action, language, and characterization continue to pay enormous dividends. As John Ditsky discovered, "the Joads are still in motion, and their vehicle with them."[34] Academic theories to the contrary, reading remains a subjective act, and perhaps the only sure thing about *The Grapes of Wrath* is its capacity to elicit powerful audience responses, This of course was Steinbeck's intention from the first. "I don't think *The Grapes of Wrath* is obscure in what it tries to say, " he claimed in 1955. "Its structure is very carefully worked out. . . . Just read it, don't count it!"[35]

As a result of shifting political emphases, the enlightened recommendations of the La Follette Committee (that the National Labor Relations Act include farm workers), the effects of loosening or abolishing some labor laws (such as California's discriminatory "anti-migrant" law, established in 1901, which was struck down by the Supreme Court in 1941 in a decision *The Grapes of Wrath* helped bring about), the creation of compulsory military service, and the inevitable recruitment of migrant families into defense-plant and shipyard jobs caused by the booming economy of World War II that signaled the beginning of their successful assimilation (California growers soon complained of an acute shortage of seasonal labor), the particular set of epochal conditions that crystallized Steinbeck's awareness in the first place passed from his view.[36] Like other momentous American novels that embody the bitter, often tragic, transition from one way of life to another, *The Grapes of Wrath* possessed, among its other attributes, perfect timing. Its appearance permanently changed the literary geography of the United States.

It also changed Steinbeck permanently. Many "have speculated," Jackson Benson writes, "about what happened to change Steinbeck after *The Grapes of Wrath*. One answer is that what happened was the writing of the novel itself."[37] Writing 260,000 words in a single year "finished" him, he told Lawrence Clark Powell on January 24, 1939. After his long siege with the "matter of the migrants" ("I don't know whether there is anything left of me," he confided in October 1939), his "will to death" was so "strengthened" that by the end of the thirties he was sick of writing proletarian fiction, so he decided to quit it. This was a decision many critics and reviewers held against him for the rest of his life; they wanted him to write *The Grapes of Wrath* over and over again, which he refused to do. "The process of writing a book is the process of outgrowing it," he told Herbert Sturz. "Disciplinary criticism comes too late. You aren't going to write that one again anyway. When you start another—the horizons have receded and you are just as cold and frightened as you were with the first one."[38]

The unabated sales, the frenzied public clamor, and the vicious personal attacks over *The Grapes of Wrath* confirmed Steinbeck's worst fears about the fruits of success and pushed the tension between the Steinbecks to the breaking point, a situation exacerbated by his romance with Gwyn Conger (they were married from 1943 to 1948) and his repeated absence on trips to Hollywood and Mexico. By the early 1940s, "finishing off a complete revolution" and having "worked the novel" as far as he could "take it" (*SLL*, 193-94), Steinbeck was no longer content to be the man—or the artist—he had once been. Steinbeck's change from social realist to metafictionist was not caused by a bankruptcy of talent, a change of venue, or a failure of honesty. Rather, it was the backlash from an unprecedented and unanticipated success, a repugnant "posterity." "I have always wondered why no author has survived a best-seller," he told John Rice in a June 1939 interview. "Now I know. The publicity and fan-fare are just as bad as they would be for a boxer. One gets self-conscious and that's the end of one's writing" (*CJS*, 15). His new writing lacked the aggressive bite of his late 1930s fiction, but it had the virtue of being different and varied. After 1940 much of his important work centered on explorations of a new topic—the implications of individual choice and imaginative consciousness. A prophetic postmodernist, Steinbeck's subject in *Sea of Cortez* (1941), *Cannery Row* (1945), *East of Eden* (1952), *Sweet Thursday* (1954), *The Winter of Our Discontent* (1961), and *Journal of a Novel* (1969) was the creative process itself, the epistemological dance of the law of thought and the law of things.

The Grapes of Wrath remains among the most wrenching fictional indictments of the myth of California as a promised land. Ironically, as John Steinbeck composed this novel that tested a social group's capacity for survival in a hostile world, he was himself unraveled. As a consequence, the particular angle of vision, the vital signature, the moral indignation, that made his art exemplary in the first place could never be repeated with the same integrated force. Once his name became inseparably linked with the title of his most famous novel, Steinbeck could never escape the influence of his earlier life, but thankfully, it is tempting to say, neither can we. Wherever human beings dream of a dignified and free society in which they can harvest the fruits of their own labor, *The Grapes of Wrath*'s voice can still be heard. Every strong novel redefines our conception of the genre's dimensions and reorders our awareness of its possibilities. As a tale of dashed illusions, inhuman suffering, and betrayed promises—all strung on a gossamer thread of hope—*The Grapes of Wrath* not only sums up the depression era's socially conscious art, but, beyond that, with its emotional urgency, evocative power, and sustained drama, has few peers in American fiction in general.

Notes

This essay, substantially expanded for the present collection, builds upon three earlier versions: the introduction and bridging commentaries to my edition of *Working Days* (1989), the essay "'Working Days and Hours': Steinbeck's Writing of *The Grapes of Wrath*" (1990), and my introduction to the Penguin Twentieth-Century Classics Series edition of *The Grapes of Wrath* (1992). I thank Elaine Steinbeck, McIntosh and Otis Inc., Viking Penguin, Inc., and *Studies in American Fiction* for permission to quote. I also thank Roy Simmonds and Susan Shillinglaw for generous readings of earlier versions; this version is dedicated to John Ditsky and Pare Lorentz.

1. John Steinbeck, interview by Herbert Kretzmer, in *Conversations with John Steinbeck*, ed. Thomas Fensch (Jackson: University Press of Mississippi, 1988), 95. Hereafter cited parenthetically in the text as *CJS*. Joseph Henry Jackson, "Why Steinbeck Wrote *The Grapes of Wrath*," *Booklets for Bookmen*, no. 1 (New York: Limited Editions Club, 1944), 3, was among the first to suggest that the book issued from Steinbeck's profound shock and "hurt."

2. John Steinbeck, *Working Days: The Journals of "The Grapes of Wrath," 1938-1941*, ed. Robert DeMott (New York: Viking, 1989), 29-30. Hereafter cited parenthetically in the text as *WD*. Steinbeck was a fairly scrupulous observer of his own writerly processes and intentions. This private journal records his day-to-day struggles with the composition of the novel and includes additional entries which cover its conflicted aftermath. Entries 2 through 100 complement the public novel; read together, journal and novel provide a twin-voiced, parallel discourse and perhaps one of our most intriguing blow-by-blow accounts of the making of any major twentieth-century American novel.

3. Steinbeck to Otis, *Steinbeck: A Life in Letters*, ed. Elaine Steinbeck and Robert Wallsten (New York: Viking, 1975), 171. Hereafter cited parenthetically in the text as *SLL*.

4. William Strachan, a former senior editor at Viking Penguin, provided sales information to me in a March 1985 letter. According to the novelist's widow, Elaine Steinbeck, *Grapes* still sells 100,000 paperback copies each year.

5. Warren French, *John Steinbeck's Fiction Revisited* (New York: Twayne Publishers, 1999), 75. See Robert B. Harmon, *"The Grapes of Wrath": A Fifty Year Bibliographic Survey* (San Jose; Steinbeck Research Center/San Jose State University, 1989), 15-32, for a handy list of translations of *Grapes*.

6. Contrary to popular belief, Steinbeck was never a Marxist or a member of the Communist party. According to his biographer, Steinbeck was not interested in doctrinaire political theories at this point of his career. See Jackson J. Benson, "The Back-

ground to the Composition of *The Grapes of Wrath,*" in *Critical Essays on Steinbeck's "The Grapes of Wrath,"* ed. John Ditsky (Boston: G. K. Hall, 1984), 52-53.

7. See also Pare Lorentz, *FDR's Moviemaker: Memoirs and Scripts* (Reno: University of Nevada Press, 1992), 121. Jackson, "Why Steinbeck Wrote *The Grapes of Wrath,*" 10-11, was first to note the impact of Lorentz's work on Steinbeck's novel.

8. In 1954, Carol sold the manuscript to Clifton Waller Barrett through book dealer John Howell of San Francisco. The typescript was presented to the Library of Congress in 1941 by Frank J. Hogan, a lawyer and book collector.

9. John Steinbeck, *The Grapes of Wrath* (New York: Viking, 1939; reprint, New York: Penguin Books, Twentieth Century Classics Series, 1992), 415 (page references are the same for both editions). Hereafter cited parenthetically in the text as *GW*. Unlike the portrait of Collins in Rawley, the equation between other historical human beings and fictional characters is blurred and conjectural. Most of the major characters that eventually came to populate *Grapes* were probably composite creations of historical antecedents. See Benson, "Background to the Composition," 52-53.

10. Anne Loftis, "Steinbeck and the Federal Migrant Camps," *San Jose Studies* 16 (Winter 1994): 80.

11. John Steinbeck, foreword to *Bringing in the Sheaves,* by Windsor Drake [Thomas Collins], in Jackson J. Benson, "'To Tom Who Lived It': John Steinbeck and the Man from Weedpatch," *Journal of Modern Literature* 5 (April 1976): 213.

12. Benson, "'To Tom Who Lived It,'" 184.

13. *The Harvest Gypsies: On the Road to "The Grapes of Wrath,"* ed. Charles Wollenberg (Berkeley: Heyday Books, 1988), 19.

14. The text of *Their Blood Is Strong,* which includes an additional entry, "Epilogue: Spring 1938," is reprinted in Warren French, ed., *A Companion to "The Grapes of Wrath"* (New York: Viking, 1963), 53-92.

15. The probable destinations and routes of Steinbeck's and Collins's 1937 travels inside California are provided in Benson, "'To Tom Who Lived It,'" 183-85, and in his "Background to the Composition," 64-65.

16. Dorothy Steel, "'Oklahomans' Topic of Steinbeck," *Las Gatos Mail-News,* November 4, 1937, p. 1. Susan Shillinglaw, "Local Newspapers Report on 'The Oklahomans,'" *Steinbeck Newsletter* 2 (Fall 1988): 4, rightly notes the "unconvincing" tone and sanitized political view (emphasizing the migrants' upward social mobility) that emerges in this conservative interview and in the next one, with Louis Walther. She wonders whether Steinbeck wasn't making a "bid for hometown favor at a time when he feared reprisal from the Associated Farmers and law enforcement officers?" To make things more confusing—or more interesting—Joseph Henry Jackson, "John Steinbeck, A Portrait," *Saturday Review of Literature* 16 (September 25, 1937): 18, claimed Steinbeck was working on "three related longer novels" during 1937.

17. After Visalia, Steinbeck pulled back from his work with Bristol, preferring instead to throw his efforts into his own factional version, which he was beginning to conceive in tragic terms and which he knew would require his undivided attention. This led to hard feelings on the photographer's part (*WD*, lv-lvi). Bristol's Visalia photographs, with some captions from *The Grapes of Wrath,* turned up in *Life* on June 5, 1939, pp. 66-67, and again on February 19, 1940, pp. 10-11, where they were used to

show the authenticity of John Ford's cinematic version of the novel. For a different, more suspicious, view of Steinbeck's motives concerning Bristol and the meaning of the Visalia experience, and for a discussion of his allegiances and affinities with journalism, see William Howarth, "The Mother of Literature: Journalism and *The Grapes of Wrath,*" in *New Essays on "The Grapes of Wrath,"* ed. David Wyatt (New York: Cambridge University Press, 1990), 71-99.

18. John Steinbeck, letter in *Writers Take Sides: Letters about the War in Spain from 418 American Authors* (New York: League of American Writers, 1938), 57. The Salinas lettuce strike extended from September 4 to November 3, 1935, and was especially violent. (It is still considered the Salinas Valley's worst agricultural strike.) Less certain is whether Steinbeck actually went to Salinas to investigate events for himself or viewed the battle from a distance, either from Los Gatos or from the site(s) of his field research. The strike was a nationally covered event, so plenty of information was available in newspapers, especially the *San Francisco Chronicle.* In any case, the labor situation was so "tense" throughout California that Steinbeck felt the *News* might not print "The Harvest Gypsies" after all (*SLL*, 132),

19. "The Grapes of Wrath," autograph manuscript, 1938, page 1, Item 6239, John Steinbeck Collection, Clifton Waller Barrett Library, Manuscripts Division, Special Collections Department, University of Virginia Library, Charlottesville, Virginia. Pagination given here refers to Steinbeck's handwritten numerals at the top right- or top left-hand side of each page, not to the numbers printed on each ledger page. To be precise, Steinbeck's first words on the paper were "New Start," superposed over "Big Writing." This referred to his new start after "L'Affaire" and the fact that Carol made him promise to write in larger and more legible script to make her typing job easier.

20. Part of Steinbeck's expertise was knowing how to employ his generative sources. He returned frequently for inspiration and material to Tom Collins's reports. For instance, in a section called "Bits of Migrant Wisdom," noted in the "Kern Migratory Labor Camp Report for week ending May 2, 1936," Collins records a heated discussion with two women about how best to cut down on the extravagant use of toilet paper. Steinbeck saw the humor in the account of "the great toilet paper scandal" (*WD*, 71) and utilized some of the original material on September 13 for chapter 22 of *Grapes*: "Hardly put a roll out 'fore it's gone. . . . One lady says we oughta have a little bell that rings ever' time the roll turns oncet. Then we could count how many ever'body takes" (430). See Benson, "'To Tom Who Lived It,'" 174-79, for more examples of the kind of detailed material and observations Collins incorporated in his reports, and Martha Heasley Cox, "Fact into Fiction in *The Grapes of Wrath*: The Weedpatch and Arvin Camps," in *John Steinbeck: East and West,* ed. Tetsumaro Hayashi, Yasuo Hashiguchi, and Richard F. Peterson, Steinbeck Monograph Series, no. 8 (Muncie, Ind.: Ball State University/Steinbeck Society of America, 1978), 18-19, for other parallels not developed in Benson.

21. Malcolm Cowley, *Think Back on Us . . . A Contemporary Chronicle of the 1930s,* ed. Henry Dan Piper (Carbondale: Southern Illinois University Press, 1967), 350.

22. Steinbeck's autograph manuscript and his published novel both have thirty chapters in exactly the same sequence, though the former begins with an alternating system of roman and arabic numerals (to indicate general and narrative chapters, re-

spectively), then shifts to arabic numbers at manuscript page 29. Uniform numbering of chapters 1-30 first took place on the typescript and may have been Carol's suggestion. Chapter 20 in the typescript and in the published novel was originally chapter 8 of Book II of the autograph manuscript. Roy S. Simmonds, "The Original Manuscript," *San Jose Studies* 16 (Winter 1990): 131-32, brings some order to Steinbeck's "chaotic" numbering by providing a handy appendix that compares the text of the manuscript with Viking's first edition.

23. John Steinbeck to Harry T. Moore, July 6, 1938. Moore, working on *The Novels of John Steinbeck: A First Critical Study* (Chicago: Normandie House, 1939), had written Steinbeck for "information for a critique of some kind" (*WD*, 38).

24. John Steinbeck to Herbert Sturz, February 10, 1953. Mr. Sturz kindly provided me with a photocopy of Steinbeck's autograph original before donating it to the Rare Book Room of the B. Davis Schwartz Library of Long Island University at Greenvale, New York. The letter was published in the *New York Times* on August 6, 1990, and again in Phyllis T. Dircks, "Steinbeck's Statement on the Inner Chapters of *The Grapes of Wrath*," *Steinbeck Quarterly* 24 (Summer-Fall 1991): 91-92.

25. Peter Lisca, *The Wide World of John Steinbeck* (New Brunswick, N.J.: Rutgers University Press, 1958), 164. In their Bakhtinian study, Louis Owens and Hector Torres, "Dialogic Structure and Levels of Discourse in Steinbeck's *The Grapes of Wrath*," *Arizona Quarterly* 45 (Winter 1989): 77, put it another way: "Steinbeck shows no interest in substituting one 'monologic' voice for another. Instead . . . he creates a text in which no single voice speaks with final authority: the endings of neither the Joad chapters, nor the interchapters, nor the novel as a whole can be taken as final narrative closures. Rather, these endings foreground Steinbeck's complex view of the subject and subjects of his novel and the complex levels of discourse contained within it."

26. Quoted in Robert DeMott, "'Working Days and Hours': Steinbeck's Writing of *The Grapes of Wrath*," *Studies in American Fiction* 18 (Spring 1990): 14. In a letter to Otis (*Letters to Elizabeth: A Selection of Letters from John Steinbeck to Elizabeth Otis*, ed. Florian J. Shasky and Susan F. Riggs [San Francisco: Book Club of California, 1978], 11), Steinbeck claimed that he employed "the mathematics of musical composition in writing" *Grapes*.

27. Louis Owens, *The Grapes of Wrath: Trouble in the Promised Land* (Boston: Twayne Publishers, 1989), 45.

28. Part of Steinbeck's cryptic entry for August 23, 1938, reads: "Pare came over the weekend. Big time. Carol sprained her ankle q.t. Went down to the peninsula with Pare and spent the night at Chaplin's place. Talked all night" (*WD*, 59). Lorentz, *FDR's Moviemaker*, 117-19, recalls the excursion to Chaplin's house in more vivid style and provides details that indicate that pressure from writing the novel made relations between the Steinbecks not just tense but nearly callous.

29. Martha Heasley Cox, "The Conclusion of *The Grapes of Wrath*: Steinbeck's Conception and Execution," *San Jose Studies* 1 (November 1975): 73-81, was the first to see the novel's ending positively in light of Steinbeck's stated intentions in the as-yet-unpublished "Diary of a Book" (later titled *Working Days*).

30. "The Grapes of Wrath," autograph manuscript, 165.

31. Simmonds, "The Original Manuscript," 129,

32. This passage appears on p. 110 of the autograph manuscript and, in its canceled form, on p. 462 of the typescript of *The Grapes of Wrath*, Item MMC-1713, Box 1, Manuscripts Division, Library of Congress.

33. Leslie Fiedler, "Looking Back after 50 Years," *San Jose Studies* 16 (Winter 1990): 55; William Kennedy, "'My Work Is No Good,'" *New York Times Book Review*, April 9, 1989, 44-45. Contemporary reviews by Philip Rahv and Charles Angoff are available in John Ditsky, ed., *Critical Essays on Steinbeck's "The Grapes of Wrath"* (Boston: G. K. Hall, 1989), 30-31, 33-35. See Ray Lewis White, "*The Grapes of Wrath* and the Critics of 1939," *Resources for American Literary Study* 13 (Autumn 1983): 134-63, for a compilation of 108 annotated contemporary reviews. Harmon, *Fifty Year Bibliographic Survey*, 37-152, lists 844 reviews and scholarly articles on *Grapes*.

34. Ditsky, introduction to *Critical Essays*, 15. Ditsky's introduction is the most exhaustive overview of *Grapes* criticism since Lisca undertook a survey for the Viking Critical Library edition, *The Grapes of Wrath: Text and Criticism* (New York: Viking, 1972), 695-707 (Lisca is currently revising the book). Ditsky updated his overview in "*The Grapes of Wrath* at Fifty: The Critical Perspective," in *The Grapes of Wrath: A Special Issue*, ed. Susan Shillinglaw, *San Jose Studies* 16 (Winter 1990): 46-53.

35. John Steinbeck, "A Letter on Criticism," *Colorado Quarterly* 4 (Autumn 1955): 53; reprinted in *Steinbeck and His Critics: A Record of Twenty-five Years*, ed. E. W. Tedlock and C. V. Wicker (Albuquerque: University of New Mexico Press, 1957), 53.

36. Information in this paragraph is gleaned from Philip Brooks, "Notes on Rare Books," *New York Times Book Review*, February 1, 1942, 22; Walter J. Stein, *California and the Dust Bowl Migrants* (Westport, Conn.: Greenwood Press, 1973), 279-81; James N. Gregory, *American Exodus: The Dust Bowl Migration and the Okie Culture in California* (New York: Oxford University Press, 1989), 172-73; and Dick Meister and Anne Loftis, *A Long Time Coming: The Struggle to Unionize America's Farm Workers* (New York: Macmillan, 1977).

37. Jackson J. Benson, *The True Adventures of John Steinbeck, Writer* (New York: Viking, 1984), 392.

38. John Steinbeck to Herbert Sturz, February 10, 1953; also Dircks, "Steinbeck's Statement on the Inner Chapters," 92.

Steinbeck's Myth of the Okies_____

Keith Windschuttle

John Steinbeck performed a rare feat for a writer of fiction. He created a literary portrait that defined an era. His account of the "Okie Exodus" in *The Grapes of Wrath* became the principal story through which America defined the experience of the Great Depression. Even today, one of the enduring images for anyone with even a passing familiarity with the 1930s is that of Steinbeck's fictional characters the Joads, an American farming family uprooted from its home by the twin disasters of dust storms and financial crisis to become refugees in a hostile world. Not since Dickens's portrayal of the slums of Victorian England has a novelist produced such an enduring definition of his age.

According to Penguin Books, which produced a very handsome series of paperbacks to mark the centenary of his birth this February, Steinbeck's novels still generate a combined sale of around two million books a year. Originally published in 1939, *The Grapes of Wrath* remains a widely studied text in both high schools and universities, and the 1940 John Ford film of the book still enjoys healthy sales on videotape and frequent reruns on classic movie shows on cable television. The story that these various audiences hear goes like this:

Dust storms and bank foreclosures during the Great Depression forced a mass migration of hundreds of thousands of small landowners and sharecroppers from the American southwest, especially Oklahoma, Arkansas, and east Texas. Enticed by false advertising, impoverished farming families loaded their possessions onto ramshackle automobiles and pickup trucks to brave the thousand-mile journey westward to California where they hoped to revive their fortunes and regain their livelihood on the land. This American version of Exodus faced its own Sinai crossing in the Arizona desert, where many vehicles broke down or ran out of gas. Those who survived the hazardous passage to the promised land, however, found the large corporations that controlled California agriculture used the rapidly growing number of migrants to continually beat down harvest wages. Police and vigilantes set upon those who complained or resisted, especially if they were suspected of being "reds" or Communist agitators. The Okies ended up landless, homeless, and impoverished, forced to watch their children starve in a land of plenty. Folk singers like Woody Guthrie, in his Dust Bowl Ballads, expressed their bitterness and anger: "I'm goin' down the road feelin' bad. Lawd. Lawd. And I ain't gonna be treated this-a-way."

Although it is about the experiences of the fictional Joad family, *The Grapes of Wrath* was always meant to be taken literally. Borrowing from John Dos Passos's *U.S.A.* trilogy and other works in the realist or documentary genre of the time, Steinbeck interspersed his fictional chapters with passages that gave a running account of the prevailing social, climatic, economic, and political conditions. Steinbeck himself had researched the living conditions of the Okies for a series of newspaper articles he wrote for a San Francisco newspaper, and, soon after his novel appeared, its tale was confirmed by the publication of America's most famous work of photographic essays, Dorothea Lange and Paul S. Taylor's *American Exodus*, which traced every step of the Okies' tragic journey across the country. In other words, Steinbeck's book was presented at the time as a work of history as well as fiction, and it has been accepted as such ever since. Unfortunately for the reputation of the author, however, there is now an accumulation of sufficient historical, demographic, and climatic data about the 1930s to show that almost everything about the elaborate picture created in the novel is either outright false or exaggerated beyond belief.

* * *

For a start, dust storms in the Thirties affected very little of the farming land of Oklahoma. Between 1933 and 1935, severe wind erosion did create a dust bowl in the western half of Kansas, eastern Colorado, and the west Texas/New Mexico border country. While many Oklahoma farms suffered from drought in the mid-1930s, the only dust-affected region in that state was the narrow panhandle in the far west. Steinbeck wrote of the dust storms:

> In the morning the dust hung like fog, and the sun was as red as ripe new blood. All day the dust sifted down, and the next day it sifted down. An even blanket covered the earth. It settled on the corn, piled up on the tops of the fence posts, piled up on the wires; it settled on roofs, blanketed the weeds and trees.

But nothing like this happened anywhere near where Steinbeck placed the Joad family farm, just outside Sallisaw, Oklahoma, part of the cotton belt in the east of the state, almost on the Arkansas border. In the real dust bowl, it is true that many families packed up and left, but the historian James N. Gregory has pointed out that less than 16,000 people from the dust-affected areas went to California, barely six percent of the total from the southwestern states. Gregory blames contemporary journalists for the misunderstanding:

> Confusing drought with dust, and assuming that the dramatic dust storms must have had something to do with the large number of cars from Oklahoma and Texas seen crossing the California border in the mid-1930s, the press created the dramatic but misleading association between the Dust Bowl and the Southwestern migration.

It is true that many people left Oklahoma for California in the 1930s. This was anything but a novel phenomenon, however. People had been doing the same since before World War I, as the southwestern states' economy failed to prosper and as better opportunities were available in other regions. Between 1910 and 1930, 1.3 million people migrated from the southwest to other parts of the United States. In the 1920s, census data show that about 250,000 of them went to California, while in the 1930s this total was about 315,000. The real mass migration of

Okies to California actually took place in the 1940s to take advantage of the boom in manufacturing jobs during World War II and its aftermath. In this period, about 630,000 of them went to the west coast. It was not the Depression of the 30s but the economic boom of the 40s that caused an abnormal increase in Okie migration.

Moreover, most of the migrants who did leave Oklahoma in the Depression were not farmers. Most came from cities and towns. The 1940 Census showed that in the period of the supposed great Okie Exodus between 1935 and 1940, only thirty-six percent of southwesterners who migrated to California were from farms. Some fifty percent of these migrants came from urban areas and fitted occupational categories such as professionals, proprietors, clerical/sales, skilled laborers, and semi-skilled/service workers. Predictably, they had a similar distribution when they joined the Californian workforce. Their favorite destination was Los Angeles, which attracted almost 100,000 Okies between 1935 and 1940, with about a quarter as many going to the cities of San Francisco and San Diego. Of the two major destinations for agricultural workers, the San Joaquin Valley attracted 70,000 and the San Bernardino/Imperial Valley region 20,000 migrants. This fell considerably short of their demographic portrait in *The Grapes of Wrath*:

> And the dispossessed, the migrants, flowed into California, two hundred and fifty thousand, and three hundred thousand. Behind them new tractors were going on the land and the tenants were being forced off. And new waves were on the way, new waves of the dispossessed and the homeless, hardened, intent and dangerous.

Steinbeck blamed the banks for their plight. Rather than allowing small farms and tenant farmers the right to exist, the banks fostered competition, mechanization, land consolidation, and continual expansion. "The bank—the monster has to have profits all the time. It can't wait. When the monster stops growing, it dies. It can't stay one size."

He compared this inhuman imperative to the rights of those who worked the land:

> We were born on it, and we got killed on it, died on it. Even if it's no good, it's still ours. That's what makes it ours—being born on it, working on it, dying on it. That makes ownership, not a paper with numbers on it.
>
> We're sorry [say the owner men]. It's not us. It's the monster. The bank isn't like a man.

* * *

Ironically, for someone whose politics have been described by his several biographers as a "typical New Deal Democrat," Steinbeck identified the wrong culprit. In two separate studies of the plight of southern tenant farmers in the 1930s, the historians David Eugene Conrad and Donald H. Grubbs have blamed not the banks but the agricultural policies of the New Deal itself. In the early 1930s, some sixty percent of farms in Oklahoma, Arkansas, and Texas were operated by tenants. However, during the Depression they found themselves victims of Franklin Roosevelt's 1933 Agricultural Adjustment Act, which required landlords to reduce their cotton acreage. Fortified by AAA subsidies, the landlords evicted their tenants and consolidated their holdings. It was government handouts, not bank demands, that led these landlords to buy tractors and decrease their reliance on tenant families. By 1940, tenant farmer numbers had declined in the southwest by twenty-four percent.

In *The Grapes of Wrath*, thirteen members of the Joads' extended family set out in the one vehicle, including grandparents and grandchildren. In two moving scenes, both Grampa and Granma die en route. Along the way, in-laws and uncles also abandon them, leaving Ma Joad, who is in her fifties, to try to keep the rest of the family together. This entourage would have been demographically unusual. Rather than large families extending over several generations, the most common trekkers from the southwest to California were composed of husband, wife, and children, an average of 4.4 members. Only twenty percent of households included other relations. Most were young. Of the adults, sixty percent were less than thirty-five years old. They were also better educated than those of the same age group who stayed behind. In other words, they were typical of those who have undertaken migration in every era, whether over the Rockies or across the Atlantic: upwardly rather than downwardly mobile young people seeking better opportunities for themselves and their children.

The most comprehensive historical study of the background of the Okie migrants was written by James N. Gregory in 1989. Its title, *American Exodus: The Dust Bowl Migration and Okie Culture in California*, indicates that the author did not set out to demolish any of the myths generated by Steinbeck, Guthrie, and Lange. This, however, is what he actually does accomplish, especially in his account of the motivations of those who went to California. The Joads packed up and left for no better reason than a yellow handbill Pa Joad found saying there were good wages and plenty of work in California. According to later chapters of the novel, this was simply an advertising ploy by the "great owners" of California to entice more men than they needed to their harvest so they could reduce wages. Hence the Joads set out for a region about which they knew nothing. To find work, they could only wander helplessly from one location to the next.

Gregory argues that the real migrants were much better informed than this. Most had direct information about working conditions from relatives already there. Two-thirds of Okies interviewed in the Salinas Valley had relatives living in California before they came west. In two other surveys in Sacramento Valley and Kern County, the majority of migrants said relatives or friends had been instrumental in their decision to relocate. "All of this suggests," Gregory writes, "that the Dust Bowl migration was not an atomistic dispersion of solitary families but a guided chain migration of the sort very typical for both trans-Atlantic immigrants and rural-to-urban immigrants." Some families generated their own migration chains, sending out a teenage son or young male relative to explore California before deciding whether to follow him. Gregory provides examples of some young men who made several such exploratory trips west during the 1930s.

In the film of *The Grapes of Wrath*, Steinbeck's statement that people owned their land not because they had a piece of paper but because they had been born on it, worked on it, and died on it is given to the half-crazy character Muley Graves. His sentiments, and the injustice of the dispossession behind them, resonate throughout the drama. Again, however, these remarks bear very little relationship to the real farmers of Oklahoma. American rural communities have rarely been populated by the permanent, hidebound settlers that urban journalists and novelists have so condescendingly assumed. Southwestern farmers in the early twentieth century were highly mobile people who felt free to move about in search of better land or even to leave the land for opportunities in town. At the 1930 Census, forty-four percent of Oklahoma farmers and forty-seven percent of those in Arkansas said they had been on their current farms for less than two years. They were actually more mobile than the national farm average, where only twenty-eight percent answered the same. A 1937 study by a sociologist found that the average Oklahoma farmer moved four times in his working life, five times if he was a tenant. The Joads, who had all grown up in the same place where Grampa had fought off snakes and Indians in the nineteenth century, would have been most unusual Oklahomans.

* * *

A large part of Steinbeck's success with his reading public lay in his ability to merge deep, mythical concerns with the American experience. One of the reasons why his Okie story defined the era, while other Depression tales of poverty and hardship did not, was its theme from Exodus. But, once more, this part of the tale had very little historical authenticity. The road the migrants took was not a Biblical camel track but the comparatively new national highway Route 66, which since the 1920s had provided a direct route from the southwest to the California coast. Steinbeck treats the road more like a covered wagon trail than the fast, modern highway it actually was. In reality, if their car was in good shape, an Oklahoma family in the 1930s could make it to California in three days. Rather than taking weeks while yarning about their hardship with other travellers and singing folk songs around campfires, the real migrants slept en route in auto courts (motels) for two or three nights. While some used the highway several times in the 1930s to test job prospects, others did the same simply to pay short visits to relatives. Gregory writes:

> Ease of transportation was the key both to the volume of migration and to the special frame of mind with which the newcomers began their California stay. The automobile gave these and other twentieth-century migrants a flexibility that cross-country or trans-Atlantic migrants of earlier eras did not share. By reducing the costs and inconveniences of long distance travel, it made it easy for those who were tentative or doubtful, who under other circumstances would have stayed behind, to go anyway. They went knowing that for the price of a few tanks of gasoline they could always return.

Even if all they had was an old jalopy of the kind that broke down, this by no means necessitated the tragedy implied by Dorothea Lange's photographs. Gregory points out that farming families had a number of options to make money en route. Some of them planned their journey to coincide with the Arizona cotton-picking season. Others who were less well organized nonetheless found plenty of agricultural employment along the way in the newly developed irrigation fields of the desert state. In the 1930s, Arizona acquired thousands of new citizens in this way.

* * *

This version of the story, in which agricultural migrants had many more active choices than the powerless victims of Steinbeck's novel, was also true of California. Although the state was hit particularly hard by the Depression, with the unemployment rate reaching twenty-nine percent in early 1933, its economy bounced back comparatively quickly between 1934 and 1937. In this period, Californian agriculture suffered not unemployment but labor shortages. At the time, Californian growers needed thousands of harvesters for their crops. In the San Joaquin Valley, cotton acreages quadrupled between 1932 and 1936. As a result, demand for cotton pickers soared and wages more than doubled. From forty-five cents for one hundred pounds in 1932, the rate for cotton picking rose to ninety cents in 1934 and one dollar in 1936. A new bout of recession in 1937-38 reduced wages to seventy-five cents per one hundred pounds, but this still paid twenty to fifty percent more than the going rate in the southwest. In almost every other industry where low-skilled Okie agricultural laborers sought work, such as meat packing, oil, cement, clay, machinery, railroad, and ice manufacturing, Californian wages were twenty to fifty percent higher than back home.

California also had a much more generous unemployment relief system: $40 a month for a family of four, compared to $10 to $12 a month in the southwest. Although paying relief to migrants generated resentment among Californian taxpayers, it was an important consideration for agricultural workers. It obviated the need to follow the harvests up and down the state all year and allowed them to drop their nomad status and settle with their children in one place, working part of the year on the harvests, part in construction and similar laboring occupations, and part on relief. The combined income from these varied sources lifted them out of poverty, giving them a modest but decent standard of living.

The social policy Steinbeck favored for them was quite different. He was part of a group of west-coast writers and intellectuals who urged Washington to expand the Farm Security Administration Camps funded under the New Deal. *The Grapes of Wrath* described a model camp of this kind in the form of Weedpatch where the Joads stay for a while. The author dedicated his novel to Tom Collins, a social worker who administered one of these camps and who was one of his principal informants about Okie customs and language. The FDA camps comprised orderly rows of tents with clean water and sanitation. They encouraged the migrants to form self-management committees to handle chores like garbage disposal and ablution block cleaning.

Most Okies who went to the agricultural valleys, however, preferred other options. "Little Oklahoma" or "Okieville" settlements sprung up on subdivisions on the outskirts of larger inland cities like Bakersfield. For as little as $5 to $10 down and the same each month, migrant families could own land on which to build their own houses. They constructed them of cheap building materials and they initially had poor water supply and sewage disposal and no electricity. However downmarket they might have seemed to other neighborhoods, who often resented their presence, these typical Okie settlements were still a long way from either the canvas lean-tos and abandoned railway carriages Steinbeck made his characters inhabit in the novel, or the prim government camps he urged the New Deal to provide for them. The great majority of real Okies voted with their feet and went to the private market to buy their own land and build their own houses.

* * *

Rather than a tragedy, the Okie migration was a success story by almost any measure. By 1940, well before the World War II manufacturing boom transformed the Californian economy, a substantial majority of Okies had attained the goals that had brought them west. Eighty-three percent of adult males were fully employed, a quarter in white-collar jobs and the rest evenly divided between skilled, semi-skilled, and unskilled occupations. About twenty percent earned $2,000 or more a year, a sum that elevated them to middle-class status after less than five years in their new state. While their average incomes were beneath those of longer established Californian families, their earnings were significantly higher and their unemployment rate significantly lower than that of their compatriots who remained in the southwest. In short, despite the Depression, California delivered on its promise.

It should be emphasized, however, that the received story of the great Okie Exodus was not entirely an invention. Instead of Steinbeck's 300,000, there were actually about 90,000 agricultural workers fitting the Okie category who migrated to and settled in Californian farming valleys in the 1930s. While the great majority of them prospered, a small minority did not. In 1937, when the problem of migrant homelessness was at its worst, a Californian government health survey estimated there were 3,800 of these families living in squatter villages of the kind portrayed in *The Grapes of Wrath*. This would appear to be the most accurate estimate of the number of people who experienced what the Joads went through. This is not an insignificant number, but neither is it a quantity that warrants being the received image of the Great Depression. This number amounted to about five percent of the dimension claimed by Steinbeck and gives a fair idea of the scale of exaggeration his book has perpetrated. If this is so, it raises the question: how did such a grossly false picture become so entrenched in the popular imagination?

The Okie myth owes its existence not only to the Old Testament but also to *Das Kapital*. Today, Steinbeck is known as an admirer of Franklin Roosevelt, a friend of Lyndon Johnson, and a patriotic supporter of the Vietnam War of the 1960s. In the 1930s, however, he inhabited a west coast literary milieu that was much more Marxist than New Deal. One of his friends in the early 1930s was Francis Whitaker, then a leading figure in the Communist Party's John Reed Club for writers. Through Whitaker he met the organizers of the wave of strikes conducted by the Communist-controlled Cannery and Agricultural Workers' Industrial Union from 1933 to 1936. In these years, several young members of the John Reed Club and the Young Communist League were regular visitors to the author at his cottage in Pacific Grove.

At the time, his west coast mentors also included the aging radical author Lincoln Steffens and his wife Ella Winter. At the height of the Depression, Steffens was one of a group of celebrated writers who produced the manifesto *Culture and the Crisis* in which they announced their support for Communist Party political candidates. Steinbeck had begun visiting the Steffens' household at Carmel in 1933 where he was introduced to George West, an editor at the *San Francisco News*, who later commissioned him to write the series of newspaper articles that became the genesis of *The Grapes of Wrath*. After the Communist Party proclaimed the Popular Front in 1935 to forge alliances with non-party identities and movements, Steinbeck joined the League of American Writers, the organization formed by the Communists to succeed its more militant John Reed Club. Steinbeck's first wife, Carol Henning, was a Marxist who took him to radical political meetings in San Francisco throughout the time he wrote the novel. In 1937, the pair made what at the time was, for those intellectuals who could afford it, an almost obligatory pilgrimage to the Soviet Union to inspect the "new civilization" created by the Bolshevik regime.

These kind of political connections were not especially unusual for a hopeful young novelist in the 1930s. This was the "Red Decade" in artistic and intellectual circles when many took Marxism and Communism seriously. The Great Depression had, for some, shaken their faith in the market-based economic system; for others, it had confirmed their belief in Marxist theory, which they equated with modernism. Among aspirant writers, Marxism inspired a great deal of experimentation in literary forms, including realist prose, newsreel formats, proletarian novels, and books combining history, fiction, and documentary. Many writers on the left regarded themselves as a "proletarian avant-garde," waging a "literary class war" against the establishment. They wrote novels, plays, poems, and songs about the strikes and the political conflicts of coal miners, steel workers, laundry hands, textile workers, and sharecroppers. One 1929 textile strike in North Carolina alone produced four novels in the subsequent decade. While much of this material was crude ideological cheerleading, some of the better proletarian novels included Upton Sinclair's *Little Steel* and Harriette Arnow's *Dollmaker.* The movement especially affected the publishing industry in New York. Many publishers, editors, agents, reviewers, and book sellers sought to transform what they regarded as the spirit of the age into a literary form.

Steinbeck's first commercially successful novel, *In Dubious Battle,* was conceived and written within this atmosphere. This book tells how a group of Communist union leaders organize a protracted strike among agricultural workers in the Californian apple industry. The experience of getting it published, however, soured the author's attitude towards party members. The manuscript was assessed and rejected by Harry Black, a Marxist editor at Steinbeck's publisher, Covici-Friede, on the grounds that it was inaccurate and that its less than heroic portrayal of the strike leaders would offend readers on the left. Steinbeck was reportedly furious because "some cocktail circuit communist back in New York" had accused him of being inaccurate. Later, the critic Mary McCarthy repeated Black's sentiments that the text was not sufficiently orthodox for a proletarian novel, a response that generated a lifelong enmity between her and Steinbeck.

* * *

Today, these quibbles over Marxist orthodoxy might seem like splitting hairs. *In Dubious Battle* is a grim and inelegant work, but it does toe the Marxist ideological line fairly well, especially by preserving that theory's central inconsistency: a worker's revolution is inevitable but needs a vanguard of activists to bring it off. There was, however, a real disagreement between Steinbeck's temperament and the demands of the party. He had more faith in the ability of the workers, rather than the party leadership, to manage their affairs. That is why, in *The*

Grapes of Wrath, he endorsed the idea of the migrant workers running self-management committees at the Weedpatch FDA camp. To apply a label that the author himself would not have appreciated, in the great debate over Marxism within the American left during the period of the Popular Front, Steinbeck was more Trotskyite than Stalinist. He was a non-conformist Marxist who eventually became an anti-Communist in the Cold War of the 1950s, a not unfamiliar American intellectual trajectory of the era.

Even though the author's more enthusiastic biographers would dispute calling him a Marxist, the text of *The Grapes of Wrath* makes it plain that he was both predicting and justifying nothing less than a proletarian revolution in America. In one of his nonfiction interludes he provides the rationale for the coming conflagration:

And the great owners, who must lose their land in an upheaval, the great owners with access to history, with eyes to read history and to know the great fact: when property accumulates in too few hands it is taken away. And that companion fact: when a majority of the people are hungry and cold they will take by force what they need. And the little screaming fact that sounds throughout all history: repression works only to strengthen and knit the repressed. The great owners ignored the three cries of history. The land fell into fewer hands, the number of the dispossessed increased, and every effort of the great owners was directed at repression.

The development of the capitalist system, he tells the reader, makes revolution almost inevitable:

The tractors which throw men out of work, the belt lines which carry loads, the machines which produce, all were increased; and more and more families scampered on the highways, looking for crumbs from the great holdings, lusting after the land beside the roads. The great owners formed associations for protection, and they met to discuss ways to intimidate, to kill, to gas. And always they were in fear of a principal—three hundred thousand—if they ever move under a leader—the end. Three hundred thousand, hungry and miserable; if they ever know themselves, the land will be theirs, and all the gas, all the rifles in the world won't stop them.

On their great trek, this is a lesson that Steinbeck's fictional characters learn as well. The preacher Casy, who plays the novel's prophet, muses over the meaning of the exodus:

> "They's stuff goin' on that the folks doin' it don't know nothing about— yet. They's gonna come somepin outa all these folks goin' wes'—outa all their farms lef' lonely. They's gonna come a thing that's gonna change the whole country."

By the end of the book, Ma Joad, who was initially concerned to keep the family together and to preserve their food and supplies for their own use, now identifies herself as one with all the other poor and oppressed.

> The stout woman smiled. "No need to thank. Everybody's in the same wagon. S'pose we was down. You'd a give us a han'."
> "Yes," Ma said, "we would."
> "Or anybody."
> "Or anybody. Use' ta be the fambly was fust. It ain't so now. It's anybody. Worse off we get, the more we got to do."

In other words, the Depression had taken the individualistic American farming family and turned it into a proletariat with a new set of collectivist values. Many of Steinbeck's admirers claim that he is an observer of the human condition rather than the proselytizer of a political position, but passages like the above are little more than Marxist wishful thinking.

* * *

This was, in fact, widely recognized when the book was published. Many Californians were outraged at a story they believed was a grotesque misrepresentation that defamed their state. There were a number of anti-Steinbeck public meetings organized and several angry pamphlets produced. Steinbeck's neighbor and fellow author Ruth Comfort Mitchell, wife of the Republican State Senator, called one of these meetings in San Francisco where she promised to write a reply to the libel and set the record straight. The sentimental novel she eventually produced, *Of Human Kindness*, however, was hardly a match for her rival's ability to generate powerful literary mythology.

At the time, Whittaker Chambers showed the most insight into why such a piece of propaganda had become so popular. He contrasted the book with the film, arguing that the latter brought out the essence of what was actually a great story. Reviewing the film in *Time* in February 1940, Chambers wrote:

It will be a red rag to bull-mad Californians who may or may not boycott it. Others, who were merely annoyed at the exaggerations, propaganda and phony pathos of John Steinbeck's best selling novel, may just stay away. Pinkos who did not bat an eye when the Soviet Government exterminated 3,000,000 peasants by famine, will go for a good cry over the hardship of the Okies. But people who go to pictures for the sake of seeing pictures will see a great one. For *The Grapes of Wrath* is possibly the best picture ever made from a so-so book. . . . Camera craft purged the picture of the editorial rash that blotched the Steinbeck book. Cleared of excrescences, the residue is a great human story which made thousands of people, who damned the novel's phony conclusions, read it. It is the saga of an authentic U.S. farming family who lose their land. They wander, they suffer, but they endure. They are never quite defeated, and their survival is itself a triumph.

I think Chambers is right. *The Grapes of Wrath* is the only example of the proletarian novel to survive. Why *it* became the story that defined the Great Depression for America is a question that still calls for an answer. Why weren't other novels from this genre and this period—stories of battles at Carolina textile mills, Pennsylvania steel towns, or Appalachian coal mines—the ones that did the job? The ultimate answer does not lie in the proletarian novel or any other version of Marxist literary endeavor. The enduring appeal of Steinbeck's story—though not his book—is its application of a great Biblical theme to the experience of an ordinary American farming family.

None of this, however, has much connection to the history of the Great Depression or the experience of the great majority of the Okies. Rather than a proletariat who learned collectivist values during a downward spiral towards immiseration, all the historical evidence points the other way. The many sociological studies made over the last forty years confirm the same picture. In the 1940s and beyond, the migrants retained their essentially individualist cultural ethos, preserved their evangelical religion, and prospered in their new environment. In popular music, Woody Guthrie's Dust Bowl Ballads proved a bigger hit with New York bohemians than with California Okies, who much preferred Gene Autry and Merle Haggard. By the 1960s, the Okies and their offspring constituted an important part of the conservative coalition that twice elected Ronald Reagan governor of California.

From *The New Criterion* (20 June 2002): 24-32. Copyright © 2002 by Keith Windschuttle. Reprinted by permission of Keith Windschuttle.

Rethinking the Politics of
The Grapes of Wrath_____

Charles Cunningham

Paradoxically, *The Grapes of Wrath* is both an exemplary radical analysis of the exploitation of agricultural workers and the culmination in the thirties of an implicitly racist focus on whites as victims. The novel scarcely mentions the Mexican and Filipino migrant workers who dominated the California fields and orchards into the late thirties, instead implying that Anglo-Saxon whites were the only subjects worthy of treatment. This focus also seems to join contemporary journalistic representations in mythologizing the Okies as quintessential American pioneers—an ideological convention that resonated with the implicit white supremacism of Jeffersonian agrarianism and of manifest destiny.[1] Yet, the novel also attacks the very assumptions about private property and class difference on which the social order rests ideologically. Far from being merely racist, it presents one of the most radical critiques of the social order in all of popular—and canonical—literature. Thus, its political intervention was—and is—contradictory. In fact, *The Grapes of Wrath* (along with the Okie mythology in general) arguably became a site of confrontation between the thirties anti-capitalist consciousness and the American racist tradition—between manifest destiny and manifest exploitation and dispossession.

Ironically, we can see vestiges of this confrontation in comparing recent criticism of the novel with its reception in 1939. Michael Denning has lately remarked the implicit racism of *The Grapes of Wrath* in his encyclopedic account of thirties left cultural production, *The Cultural Front: The Laboring of American Culture in the Twentieth Century*—a work that has been reshaping the field. For Denning, the novel is not typical of the Popular Front cultural production he celebrates, because it is imbued with "racial populism"—in contrast with what he sees as the PF's nascent multiculturalism. Yet, this is a view that was apparently unavailable to critics during the thirties, when racial essentialism was only recently coming to be understood as racist.[2] They instead emphasized the novel's critique of capitalism. On the left, Granville Hicks's 1939 review in *The New Masses* declared *The Grapes of Wrath* an exemplary proletarian novel, noting that Steinbeck's "insight into capitalism illuminates every chapter of the book." He went on to remark that "No writer of our time has a more acute sense of economic forces, and of the way they operate against the interests of the masses of the people." In contrast, Denning never mentions the implicit Marxism in the novel.[3] He is more than sympathetic with leftists, but from his point of view, the triumph of the thirties and of the Popular Front was to have working-class people become cultural workers and enter the culture industries. For him, the "laboring" of American culture means that the working class came to be included as both subjects and producers of culture. Questions about what it means to be compelled to sell one's labor power or to be co-opted against one's class interests— hardly an unlikely scenario in big business cultural production—drop out of his analysis.

My contrast of Hicks and Denning is intended to prompt questions about what a current left analysis of the thirties should look like. Hicks, the thirties leftist, well-recognized *The Grapes of Wrath*'s condemnation of the capitalist mode of production (as did many mainstream reviewers[4]), but, like most of his contemporaries, was blind to the novel's racism. Denning, our contemporary leftist, sees the racism, but not the anti-capitalism. I would argue that neither perspective is adequate as left analysis: missing the racism means failing to realize that a working class divided by race cannot change the world; on the other hand, to ignore the impact of capital accumulation on workers is to misunderstand why workers need to band together in the first place— across race and other lines. Denning's analysis is in many ways more troubling because it fails to draw on the knowledge of thirties leftists; rather than offering supplemental and corrective critiques that would invigorate our current knowledge of the relationship between class and race, his book seems to forget the Depression's radical challenge. Instead, I believe that *The Grapes of Wrath* in effect wrestles with the contradiction between a radical class politics and American racial nationalism. Understanding how the novel deals with that contradiction may help us to better understand the class/race relationship today.

Here, I will begin by trying to place the novel's cultural intervention in historical context, first by assessing its relationship to other popular accounts of the "Okie" migration, then by giving an account of the labor struggles in California agriculture up to that point. Finally, I will look at Steinbeck's 1936 reportage of the migrant problem and contrast its politics with the novel's. According to Denning, the novel reproduces the racial nationalism of the reporting, a charge I will argue is reductive given a careful reading of both.

Most people remember the cause of the Okie migration as the Dust Bowl disaster, which took place in the Great Plains states. According to this narrative, the soil literally blew away during the great drought of the mid-thirties because the plains should never have been cultivated in the first place. The resulting dust storms of topsoil left some areas buried and others denuded, generally rendering farming impossible and causing the agrarian inhabitants to have to migrate. This version was attractive to the press because the Dust Bowl and drought were spectacular and, as represented, were often uncomplicated by reference to power relations. Margaret Bourke-White photographed dust storms for *Fortune* in October of 1934, wrote about them for *The Nation* (22 May 1935), and many other magazines reported the story, often with accompanying photographs. *Life* ran gruesome photographs of desiccated animals and cracked earth (4 Jan. 1937), followed a few months later by Alexandre Hogue's forlorn drought and dust paintings (21 June 1937).[5] The early reports of the Dust Bowl did not connect it strongly with the California migration, but most did by the late thirties.

A paradigmatic example of the "dust" explanation was offered in Pare Lorentz's documentary film *The Plow That Broke the Plains*, made for the Resettlement Administration in 1936. As titles announce from the start, the film's focus is not so much the migrants; instead, it is "a story of land, soil—rather than people." The narrator notes that the westward march across the continent brought cattle-grazing to the Great Plains and later the plow. Then, millions of acres of grassland were planted with crops in order to make as much profit as possible. At this point, and throughout the rest of the film, the narrator ominously declares that this cultivation took place in a land of "high winds and sun." The film then remarks the coincidence between the replacement of the horse drawn plow with the tractor and World War I's extraordinarily high demand for wheat. A counterposing montage of military tanks marching across the battlefields and tractors marching across the plains suggests that both technologies are destructive. Indeed, after the war boom, drought follows and the soil begins to blow away, unchecked by its native grass cover. Towards the end of the film, migrants in their old cars are seen fleeing the dust storms and arriving "blown out, baked out, and broke" in California. The narrator tells us that 30,000 people a day are moving west and that sun and wind are responsible.

The film identifies technology and a drive for profits as complicit in breaking the plains. Yet both forces are disembodied; technology is without human agents, as is the profit drive. As a critique, this aspect of the film resembles what might be called the "man's folly" genre, attributing problems to humanity in general, erasing class interests and complex histories. In this genre, there is no distinction between the tenant farmer and the conglomerate based in Chicago that he or she might ultimately work for. But overall the film primarily relies on the "wind and sun" analysis, leaving the migrants as helpless victims of natural forces.[6] A drawing over which the closing credits roll depicts covered wagons and pioneers marching up a long hill, not in Sisyphean misery, but in steadfast progress. The explanation offered little insight into the migration, and by focusing on the past, offered little in the way of solution to the present problem.

It is important to note that the mythology of the Okie migration actually involved two distinct, but related problems. The outmigration of people from the Southwest, South, and upper Midwest to California was an ongoing twentieth century phenomenon that received the most public notoriety in the thirties. On the other hand, the migrant labor problem in California dated back to the mid-nineteenth century but also became famous in the thirties. As for the westward migration, James Gregory notes that it came in three major phases: the teens and twenties, the Depression years, and during and after World War II (3-35). Of these three, the thirties period was perhaps the largest, and the one that concerns us here. Challenging previous assumptions, Gregory convincingly argues that refugees from the dust bowl accounted for only six percent of the southwestern migrants to California, and he reminds us that only the panhandle of Oklahoma was in the dust area (which encompassed mainly eastern Colorado, western Kansas, eastern New Mexico, and the Texas panhandle) (11).

The reasons for the outmigration from the principal feeder states, Oklahoma, Texas, Arkansas, and Missouri are complex, but a few main ones can be discerned. The first is directly related to the collapse of the tenant system, which pushed people off the land and into cities and towns while impoverishing those who stayed on farms. The Depression exacerbated the collapse because the non-agricultural industries of the urban areas slowed down considerably, greatly hindering the absorption of displaced agricultural workers. The land retirement policies of the Agricultural Adjustment Act (AAA) furthered that displacement, as did the mechanization of farming, which was more pronounced in the Southwest than in the old South. The drought of the mid-thirties—the worst in a century—only worsened conditions for the working people of the region, an area where unemployment was higher than the already soaring national average (Gregory 14).

Contrary to the Okie mythology, not all the migrants were farmers, who actually composed slightly less than half the total. The next largest segments were workers from cities and towns, although many of these may have been recently displaced rural people (17). Gregory also argues that the migration was not the result only of the push of economic crisis, but the pull of California. The image of the state as a paradise had been well-marketed for years and its economy had mushroomed since the turn of the century. California growers also advertised for agricultural labor in the outmigrating states, if perhaps to a lesser degree than the myth usually suggests. Thus, Gregory surmises that choice was a critical element of the migration.

While Gregory rejects a narrow determinism—be it economic or meteorological—it is important to note the extent to which choices are determined—have their limits set—by structural conditions.[7] As the older structures such as tenancy collapsed because of internal contradictions, or because they failed to generate enough capital, they were pushed aside or abandoned, leaving displaced and dispossessed workers to try to attach themselves to the other sites of accumulation—in this case, California industry and agribusiness.

Once in California, the story of the migration westward becomes distinct from that of the migrant farmworkers who were Okies. In general, the southwesterners tended to migrate towards the kinds of locales they had come from; city and town dwellers predominantly settled in the Los Angeles area and most of the farm people headed into the agricultural San Joaquin Valley (Gregory 36-77). The latter area became the principal locus of the mythical Dust Bowl Okie and of *The Grapes of Wrath*. If the migrants began with dreams of sharing the wealth of the great agricultural valleys by eventually becoming small landowning farmers, what they found was an entrenched corporate agribusiness that mocked agrarian myths. As Cletus Daniel documents, California agriculture since the latter half of the nineteenth century had been controlled by large growers who banded together in corporate cooperatives to dominate the industry. Ownership of the grower corporations often rested with banks, utilities, and other investment companies, and thus the farms themselves were often absentee-owned and managed by corporate employees. Even smaller farmers were under the sway of the large growers, because the latters' connection with the banking industry meant that they controlled credit—a necessity for farming. The corporate growers also effectively set wages and determined the character of working conditions throughout the industry. Dissenting farmers could be bullied by banks, or sometimes squeezed out of business by large growers with vertical operations that included processing, canning, distribution, and shipping.[8] Thus, it becomes clear that the title of Carey McWilliams's history of California agriculture, *Factories in the Field*, was not merely a simile but an apt description.[9]

The conditions for agricultural laborers were as bad as or worse than those for southern tenant farmers and sharecroppers. While there were small permanent workforces on California farms, the vast majority of the labor was needed at harvest time, and was performed by migrant laborers who followed the crops as they matured over a six-month harvest season. By the 1930s, the pay and working conditions had both been terrible for at least sixty years. Migrant workers had few possessions, lived in substandard company housing or in makeshift camps, and had to provide their own transportation—usually ancient "jalopies." Their children had limited or no access to schools, and they had little healthcare, making malnutrition and preventable diseases common.

The ethnic makeup of the migrant workforce changed over the years, but the groups involved usually had in common that they were minorities not considered citizens of the United States—or at least *proper* citizens. As "aliens," they were thus particularly vulnerable to exploitation. Before the Civil War, Native Americans were the first group to dominate the workforce, because the black slavery advocated by some growers was politically untenable in California. Native Americans were followed by Chinese immigrants, who were followed by the Japanese. By the 1920s, Mexicans and Mexican-Americans were the majority, with a significant Filipino minority. As Daniel recounts, growers initially felt that Mexican workers were attractive because their vulnerability would make them docile.[10] Natives of Mexico could be readily deported at government expense and Americans of Mexican descent could be fraudulently deported. Nevertheless, this hoped-for docility quickly disappeared under the "nearly intolerable" conditions in the industry (Daniel 26). Work stoppages and spontaneous strikes were not uncommon and intensified with the onset of the Great Depression. Growers anxious about reduced profits decided to extract the difference from workers, who responded with "angry militancy" (68). Into this contentious situation stepped the Communist Party-sponsored Cannery and Agricultural Workers Industrial Union (CAWIU), which after faltering first steps garnered an excellent record of organizing between 1929 and 1934. The American Federation of Labor (AFL) had traditionally thought migrant labor too difficult to organize, but the majority Mexican and Filipino workers proved committed unionists.

In response both to this militancy and to the general surplus of workers produced by Depression conditions, a sentiment rose in the state to deport Mexican and Filipino workers. Anti-immigrant racism was mobilized as a false palliative for unemployment, and as a result, about one third of the Mexican and Filipino populations of the U.S. were deported or repatriated between 1931 and 1934 (Ruiz 8, 51). While the threat of deportation made life precarious for migrant farmworkers, other factors also undermined the union movement of the early thirties. California had an anti-syndicalism statute that made labor organizing very difficult; under its auspices, several of the best CAWIU leaders were prosecuted and served years in prison before finally winning appeals and being released (see Daniel, especially 252-55). The unconstitutional law took good organizers out of the field and had a dampening affect overall. Then, in late 1934, the Communist Party disbanded the CAWIU in the shift to its new Popular Front strategy, which called for CP labor activists to work within existing unions in order to radicalize them. Unfortunately, in California agriculture there were virtually no other unions interested in organizing farmworkers, and the AFL consistently colluded with growers (Daniel 274). Thus, a heretofore effective statewide union movement was abandoned, not to be seriously resumed until the CIO-affiliated United Cannery, Agricultural, Packing and Allied Workers of America (UCAPAWA) was founded in 1937.

Yet, UCAPAWA was less effective in organizing migrant workers than the CAWIU, because it concentrated its efforts in the canneries and processing plants.[11]

Another development that set back the farmworker cause was the growers' formation of the Associated Farmers in 1934. If they had been a formidable force before then, the AF became the vehicle by which the growers suppressed workers and controlled the countryside even more thoroughly. Under AF auspices, vigilante armies were formed, workers were beaten and killed, law enforcement was more thoroughly co-opted, and growers hesitant to go along were threatened. When contemporary observers like Steinbeck and McWilliams labeled the AF "fascist," the description was justified. Whenever a strike broke out or worker unrest seemed to be on the rise, the AF could quickly mobilize managers, thugs, and hostile townspeople into an armed force. Many groups actually drilled in formal paramilitary units. It was into this extraordinarily hostile situation that the Okie migrants entered. Migrant workers were subjected to some of the worst wage and labor conditions the United States had to offer. Moreover, the Okies—like evicted tenant farmers and the workers who were being deported—were homeless in a hostile land; they had little or no refuge. The white Okies would even find themselves racialized as inferior to other whites as we shall see.

Though the conditions for field workers in California changed little in sixty or seventy years, attention to their suffering was late in coming. When the American Civil Liberties Union tried to get *The Nation* and *The New Republic*—two of the era's leading left-of-center publications—to write articles about the suspension of the constitution during the 1930 lettuce strike in the Imperial Valley, the magazines declined, believing the story minor (Daniel 178). There was more reportage in the liberal press after the middle of the decade—McWilliams, for example, wrote several articles for *The Nation*—but it was not until the white Okies were involved that the story became nationally known. When whites were subjected to fascist conditions, the story became more than just a "labor dispute." Because mythic yeoman farmers were involved, so were the agrarian mythologies of American exceptionalism and their prerequisite white supremacism. If these quintessential Americans could be treated as badly as Mexicans and Filipinos, then Anglo-Saxon white supremacism, an ideological bulwark of US capitalism, was threatened. The worst depredations of California agribusiness had before then been concealed or sanctioned by white supremacism, which effectively blamed non-whites for their own oppression. The Okies thus highlighted the ideological contradiction between the inalienable rights of American whites to freedom and prosperity, and the rights of growers to exploit whomever they could. The Okie mythology became the site on which this struggle played out.

The contradiction the Okies posed to white supremacy was often subsumed by the "dust and drought" explanation, as we have seen in *The Plow That Broke the Plains*. This narrative saved the Okies—and the social order—from blame for their condition, because they could not be expected to control nature. The "pioneer" invocation also tended to erase the social problem by turning the Okies into symbols of America's heritage and then wishing them happily on their way. Yet, Steinbeck (like McWilliams and others) had a lot to do with keeping migrant suffering—not merely the migrant symbol—public. In his October 5-12, 1936, series of articles for the *San Francisco News* (collected as *The Harvest Gypsies*), Steinbeck repeated the "dust and drought" explanation, but did not dwell there, choosing to focus instead on what was happening to the Okies in California. While more nuanced and politically to the left of the mainstream, the analysis in Steinbeck's series seemed to assume Anglo-Saxon white supremacism. As was true with most representations of California agricultural labor after the white workers became a majority, Steinbeck's excluded non-white workers—despite the fact that when the articles were published, the displacement of non-white workers was "by no means total" (Wollenberg xi).[12]

The Harvest Gypsies series articulates, in effect, a rationale for why

Anglo-Saxon whites should dominate accounts of the migrant problem. In the first article, Steinbeck states that his focus will be on the "dust bowl refugees," because they are rapidly replacing deported Mexicans and Filipinos (21). Yet, his analysis does not merely register a quantitative shift in the composition of the workforce, but a qualitative one as well, describing "a new kind of migrant" (20). The Mexican and Filipino workers were "drawn from a peon class" and presumably were "migrants by nature" (22). The Okies, on the other hand, are "Old Americans," "resourceful and intelligent Americans" who have experienced owning their own land (22). "They are the descendants of men who crossed into the middle west, who won their land by fighting," which confirms that "they are gypsies by force of circumstances" rather than birth (22). The nationalities from which they originate are all Nordic: "English, German, and Scandinavian descent" (23).

The reason their racial lineage is important, according to Steinbeck, is because it will prevent the growers from abusing them as they did the "peons." "With this new race, the old methods of repression, of starvation wages, of jailing, beating and intimidation are not going to work: these are American people" (23). (It is little wonder that when the Simon J. Lubin organization—a group of migrants' rights supporters—published the series as a pamphlet in 1938, it was entitled *Their Blood Is Strong*.) On the one hand, Steinbeck seems to be arguing that class exploitation will be exposed for what it really is once the confrontation is clearly between white owners and white workers; on the other hand, he elides the class nature of the problem by arguing implicitly that other races are more amenable to being exploited than whites. And of course, he leaves out the fact that the "peons" had proved militant workers—arguably better unionists than the Okies would become (Wollenberg, xii). One could speculate that Steinbeck refers to a *heritage* of fighting and dissent, rather than a racial *inheritance*. He notes that the new migrants are accustomed to local popular democracies based on the "old agrarian, self-containing farm," where "industrialization never penetrated" (23). When thrust into California agribusiness, they will presumably respond with the independence they are accustomed to. However, he consistently names "race" as the primary agent of this hoped-for migrant militancy.

The second article describes conditions in the makeshift "squatters" camps or "Hoovervilles" common to the roadsides in the agricultural valleys. Steinbeck identifies three categories of Okie families, each in a stage of despair directly correlating with the amount of years they have been in the state. In a pathos-heavy tone, he notes that those having been there the longest are surrounded by "filth," are wearing "foul clothing," and are possessed of a paralyzing resignation. He graphically describes a scene in which fruit flies try to feed on the mucus in a torpid child's eyes (30). The article thus seems to contradict Steinbeck's prediction that the Okies will not stand for their oppression; he depicts no one fighting back.

The third article focuses on the power of the growers over the workers, detailing the existence of armed guards at the company camps, payment in company scrip usable only at high-priced company stores, and the thoroughgoing complicity of legal authorities in these ostensibly private enterprises. He sums up the process of grower control as a "system of terrorism that would be unusual in the fascist nations of the world" (37). In contrast, the fourth article describes the migrant camps run by the federal Resettlement Administration. Prefiguring a similar contrast made in *The Grapes of Wrath*, the "fascism" of the grower camps is countered by the "experiments in natural and democratic self-government" existing in the RA camps. However, as if to be in tune with middle-class morality and propriety, Steinbeck observes that no one is on relief at the camp he visits. In fact, he relates, the self-governing committees have expelled a family who applied for relief; moreover, the reputation of the camp is that its "men are better workers" than average (41). Their hygiene is also excellent: "the people are of good American stock who have proved that they can maintain an American standard of living. The cleanliness and lack of disease in the two experimental camps are proof of this" (43). These observations implicitly divide workers into the good, clean group that will not accept relief, and the unhygienic, lazy, often non-white one that will—in other words, the worthy or unworthy poor. These categories—which were common to representations of the poor in the thirties[13]—inherently create a distance between poor worker and middle-class reader, one from which the middle-class reaction would likely be sympathy, or its repressed other, contempt. In fact, the need to remind readers continually of the worthy qualities of the migrants also keeps alive doubts that they might be unworthy.

Paradoxically, the fifth article in the series demonstrates that the available relief is woefully inadequate. While the previous article never mentions health problems as a possible reason for needing relief, this one chronicles the history of a family in which both parents have been laid up with illness and injury. Steinbeck shifts attention away from the workers' worthiness or unworthiness and onto the outrageous conditions they are suffering. The family trying to get on relief lost a son to a burst appendix after a doctor gave him an incompetent, but expensive, examination (47). As Steinbeck notes of the migrants generally, "even in the flush times the possibility of remaining healthy is very slight"; their diet is so meager as to produce malnutrition and related diseases (49). The analysis here shows that whether or not individual migrants are hard workers is a moot question at best.

The sixth article returns to platitudes about how the growers' methods will not work on "our own people," Anglo-Saxon whites; yet contradictorily, it first recounts the history of resistance among Mexican and Filipino workers. While calling both groups "peons," and the Filipinos "little brown men," he argues that the primary reason they are being replaced in the fields is because they had "attempted to organize" (55). Thus, a contradiction in his evidence looms large; the peons who will accept a miserable lot by nature are being deported for organizing, while the strong-blooded whites are falling into despair. None of the articles resolves this contradiction.

The final installment lists reform proposals for solving the migrant problem. Steinbeck advocates setting aside federal lands in California for subsistence farms for migrant workers, who could buy the land on "long time payments" or rent it cheaply (58). The migrants could work in growers' fields during the harvest, and live off their own produce in the slack seasons. He maintains that farmers' subsistence crops "should be arranged so that they do not conflict with the demand for migratory labor" (59); then their farms can be "managed during the harvest season by women," leaving the men to do the migrant labor (59). The subsistence farms will receive government assistance in health care, sanitation, and "scientific farming." They will be self-governing, giving the farmers experience with "social responsibility" so that they might be "restored to the rank of citizens" (59). Another element of the proposed plan is that farm workers should be "encouraged and helped to organize" into unions to self-advocate, to protect themselves, and to "intelligent[ly]" distribute labor (60). To help insure that unionization can be accomplished, Steinbeck suggests the formation of a "migratory labor board," which would ultimately function like the longshoremen's hiring halls and would also set wage minimums. Simultaneously, the state will begin prosecuting the "deadly fascistic groups"—meaning the Associated Farmers—under the same criminal anti-syndicalism laws used against labor organizing. Finally, Steinbeck argues that to monitor the reforms will require a "militant and watchful organization of middle-class people, workers, teachers, craftsmen, and liberals to fight [the fascistic forces] and . . . to maintain this state in a democratic form" (62). He warns that not undertaking these reforms may cause the Okies to become "an army driven by suffering and hatred to take what they need" (62).

The solutions offered would not have hurt the cause of migrant labor, but they display the middle-class condescension for the poor evident throughout the series. The subsistence farms resemble finishing schools for the rough Okies, who apparently have trouble taking care of themselves—in spite of their ostensible racial advantages. Nor does the solution address the difficulty of arranging crops around agribusiness schedules or of having the older males leave the households for long periods. Moreover, the plan assumes that the family is the requisite—not just normative—unit of labor, which would leave out singles or non-traditional partnering (an example of which would be, ironically, Lennie and George from *Of Mice and Men*). The makeup of the "watchdog" group—a notion that already assumes a middle-class gaze—is heavy with "respectable" types and notably excludes leftists, those who had most closely struggled with migrant workers. The picture painted is not so much one of poor and middle-class workers coming together, but of a paternal stewardship. Despite some vacillations on Steinbeck's part at moments, the analysis in *The Harvest Gypsies* articles is mired in the worthy/unworthy worker ideology, the assumptions of which effectively make fundamental change impossible. Because the plan essentially leaves the growers in control, the watchdogs would essentially be policing a somewhat more benign version of the status quo, with the migrants becoming a kind of managed underclass.

Though public awareness of migrant suffering was growing, it became ubiquitous with the publication of *The Grapes of Wrath* in the spring of 1939. Although Denning asserts that the "racial populism" of *The Harvest Gypsies* "deeply inflects *The Grapes of Wrath* as well," I would argue that the novel does not simply reproduce the articles' racism, as Denning seems to imply (267). On one level, it is undoubtedly true that the novel is inflected by racism; there are no Mexican or Filipino workers in *Grapes*, and Ma's claim that the Joads descend from soldiers in the American Revolution sounds—when read with *The Harvest Gypsies*—like a reference to their Anglo-Saxon pioneer blood. The first point is arguably the more egregious one: there could be no sustainable, whites-only solution to the problem of exploitation; wage competition between racial groups would only play into the growers' hands. Furthermore, the near erasure of non-whites in the novel meant that much of the militant history of farmworker organizing would be forgotten. While Chapter Nineteen in the novel does provide some history of the non-white migrants, they are not included in the story as characters, or even as a presence. However, beyond the racism inherent in this virtual exclusion—a point to which I will return—*Grapes* is otherwise drastically different from *The Harvest Gypsies*. Denning does not account for the novel's critique of the mechanisms of capital accumulation and the brutality those mechanisms visit on the poor and middle class alike.

In fact, I would argue that *The Grapes of Wrath* is a call for solidarity from a middle-class novelist to a similar audience. It attempts—not always successfully—to leave behind the frightened condescension of *The Harvest Gypsies* and to reveal a shared humanity, and, more subtly, a shared condition among members of all non-owning classes. Steinbeck's insight—which Denning misses—is that poor migrants and middle-class readers are both workers and ultimately victims of the same social processes, if in different ways. Thus, what was at stake was not merely sympathy, or even respect for other races, but the possibility of a revolutionary understanding of the mode of production. Doubtless, the novel speaks *for* the migrants, but not in the oddly removed manner, for example, of Erskine Caldwell in *Tobacco Road*. *The Grapes of Wrath* is peopled with thinking working-class characters who are trying to understand the overarching structures that shape their lives and choices. One could argue that there is an inherent condescension in a higher status group speaking for a lower one, which was a point of contention in trying to define proletarian literature in the thirties.[14] Beyond the fact that the distinction between working and middle classes is primarily a matter of degree than kind—both have to sell their labor power in order to sustain themselves—the politics of the novel are a more important issue than the class status of the author. This is especially true of *The Grapes of Wrath*, given that its tremendous popularity meant that it made a powerful intervention in the popular analysis of poverty and of the social structure.

Moreover, there is considerable evidence that the shift from a more distant sympathy in *The Harvest Gypsies* to a call for solidarity in *Grapes* was bound up with Steinbeck's own contact with the migrants in the intervening years between the writing of the articles and the novel. During that time, he saw more strikes, more Associated Farmers atrocities, and most of the migrant experiences depicted in the novel. He was perhaps most radicalized while participating in relief work during the Visalia flood in 1938, which produced tremendous suffering.[15]

At any rate, the novel itself evidences a perspective changed since the newspaper series. Its narrative proceeds not merely with the Joads' journey, but traces the growing awareness of their place in the social structure, particularly in the experiences of Casy, Tom, and Ma. They leave behind not only an irrevocably changed way of life, but also their old ways of understanding. Yet, as Stephen Railton argues, Steinbeck's *readers* also receive a consciousness raising education in the destructiveness of capitalism, one that calls for a new society. The novel is pedagogically structured so that the reader sees the struggle of the Joads placed not just in the context of the Okie migration but also in the larger context of the mode of production. The narrative alternates between the "story"—of the Joads—and the "discourse" of the interchapters, which document general conditions, historicize, and editorialize.[16] This alternation in narrative modes bears an oft-remarked resemblance to Dos Passos's *USA* trilogy, and allows the reader and the Joads different political educations. The Joads become aware of their position near the bottom of the social order by experiencing superexploitation—being forced to work for less than subsistence wages. Their analysis is also deepened by the willingness of Tom, Casy, and Ma to ponder larger forces and to develop the sense of solidarity with others that they already possess. The reader presumably does not have the Joads' experience but is guided by the interchapters, which suggest how to interpret both the story and the social world. While the interchapters have been criticized by some as artless, they steer the reader toward a more radical understanding of the social order than that available to the Joads.[17] True for both the reader and the characters, then, is what the experienced migrant Floyd Knowles repeatedly tells the skeptical Tom: "They's stuff ya gotta learn" (260).

The novel is not just a protest against super-exploitation; its critique is more radical than the reformist argument that capitalism *can* produce terrible conditions. Steinbeck's analysis attacks the logic and consequences of private property itself—including a description of how it damages the psyches of capitalists. This critique begins in earnest in Chapter Five, an interchapter that records a mock exchange between a landlord and a tenant who is being evicted. The tenant wants to fight back, to "shoot" someone, but the owner maintains that the tenant is not being evicted by a person, but by the "monster," which emerges unnamed as capitalism itself (34). The landlord is a company, which is in debt to the banks, which are controlled by bigger banks and companies in "the East." The big companies are not human: "They breathe profits; they eat the interest on money. If they don't get it, they die" (35). Moreover, the monster has to grow to stay alive: "the monster has to have profits all the time. . . . When the monster stops growing, it dies. It can't stay one size" (35). In effect, this passage reproduces Marx's description of capital accumulation: capital cannot rest in equilibrium, but must always be in motion, constantly producing more capital. Therefore, it cannot be reformed into submission, into a system where the mass of peoples' needs are met; as the narrator notes, "Men made it, but they can't control it" (41). Thus, whether or not the landlord feels remorse or anger about having to evict people is immaterial; "all of them were caught in something larger than themselves" (34). Yet, Steinbeck eschews the customary politics of naturalism; the chapter does not end with human powerlessness or hopelessness. The tenant remarks that "We've got a bad thing made by men, and by God that's something we can change" (41). In other words, the system cannot be made humane, because its operations are inherently monstrous; but the system as a whole can be changed because it is social.

Another facet of the novel's critique of capitalism is to document the horrors that result from this drive for capital accumulation, including the increasing impoverishment of "millions" and the obscene waste of resources. The novel frequently depicts simultaneous surplus and want, as this observation typifies: "The fields are fruitful and starving men moved along the roads. The granaries were full and the poor grew up rachitic, and the pustules of pellagra swelled on their sides." In an interchapter late in the novel (Chapter 25), the juxtaposition between waste and want is given its fullest articulation. The chapter is situated at a point in the Joads' story where the family is becoming more desperate; they are out of money and the young children are starting to feel the effects of malnutrition. The narrator notes that fruit is destroyed when its price is not high enough to make it worth harvesting. The prices are low because the largest growing companies—which are vertical operations owning their own processing—decide to squeeze out the smaller growers by taking a profit only on the canning, depressing the unprocessed fruit prices (348). The narrator remarks the deadly irony that technology has enabled the extraordinary production of food, but capitalism causes people to starve. The technologists have not been able to create a "system whereby their fruits may be eaten" (340). Steinbeck then graphically describes the destruction of produce and livestock in the midst of starvation. The outrageousness of this contradiction is underlined by the increasing pitch of the narration, which builds until this judgment is made:

> There is a crime here that goes beyond denunciation. There is a sorrow here that weeping cannot symbolize. There is a failure here that topples all our success. The fertile earth, the straight tree rows, the sturdy trucks, and the ripe fruit. And children dying of pellagra must die because a profit cannot be taken from an orange. And coroners must fill in the certificates—died of malnutrition—because the food must rot, must be forced to rot. (348-9)

The message here is both a critique and an appeal. First, it skewers the popular myth that technology means progress, and further, that technological progress benefits everyone. Instead, Steinbeck shows that technology is in service to profitmaking, and that the needs of humans are subordinate to accumulation. The passage's reference to "our success" also suggests an appeal not to those starving, obviously, but to the sense of justice of those who share *some* of that success. If the reader has a sense of justice and concern for others, then he or she must realize that the system has to change.

The last paragraph of this interchapter—like *The Harvest Gypsies*—refers to the possibility that the dispossessed will revolt if the status quo prevails. But unlike the newspaper series, the novel no longer describes the "wrath" of the people as something that mainly threatens the middle class. Over the shoulders of armed guards, the starving migrants watch the destruction of the food with "growing wrath." The book's title is then invoked: "In the souls of the people the grapes of wrath are filling and growing heavy, growing heavy for the vintage" (349). While the coming vintage sounds potentially ominous, it is not merely the venting of anger, but the harbinger of a better society for all. If *The Harvest Gypsies* implied that revolt would bring chaos, a threat to a nebulous "peace," *The Grapes of Wrath* seems to argue that a change is not only justified, but inevitable. The reader is not so much warned as invited to participate.

The foundation for that invitation depends both on the reader's sense of justice and on a sense that the Joads are worth caring about. Yet, the call for solidarity also appeals to shared interest. The novel describes capitalism as producing super-exploitation, dislocation, and violence for the dispossessed, but it also comments on the alienation experienced by the middle class and by the "great owners" as well. The monster that punishes the Joads simultaneously alienates the more prosperous from a fulfilling sense of their own humanity and from the profound, even spiritual, connection between people. This argument is made in the novel's opposition between the feeling of solidarity that the Joads begin to discover and the alienation felt by the more prosperous and by those workers who betray their class. This is apparent almost from the beginning of the novel, when Tom induces the truck driver to give him a ride by asking him if he wants to be a "good guy" or the tool of "some rich bastard" (11). Although he gives Tom a ride, the driver is implicitly criticized for wanting to become a manager so that he can "tell other guys to drive trucks" (14). We do not know Tom well yet, but his frankness about being in prison and his thoughtfulness contrast with the driver's general nosiness and with his anti-intellectual diatribe against "big words." Soon after, Muley Graves observes that sharing is necessary to human community. He gives rabbit meat to Tom and Casy and says that "if a fella's got somepin' to eat and another fella's hungry—why the first fella ain't got no choice. I mean suppose I pick up the rabbits an' go off somewheres an' eat 'em. See?" Casy answers, "I see," and attributes profound wisdom to the observation (51-2). While a brief scene, moments like this are repeated throughout the novel; those who have little share with those who have even less. The Joads take Casy along with them to California; they share resources with the Wilsons on the road; Ma tries to feed the starving children in the squatters' camp; and truck drivers generously tip a waitress who has undercharged poor migrants for a loaf of bread. The cumulative effect of these stories is to make a communal sense of property normative—and inviting. The reader is encouraged to be "a good guy," not just because it is embarrassing not to be, but because there is a shared reward.

The communal feeling is also preferable to the alternatives of alienation and individualism. In an interchapter (Chapter 17) describing the organic democracies that spring up each night in the migrant camps, the narrative states that there are only two punishments for egregious violations of community rules: "a quick and murderous fight or ostracism; and ostracism was the worst" (195). When deputies under the sway of the "Farmers' Association" send agitators into the dance at the government camp to provoke a riot, the migrants are shocked to discover that the men are fellow Okies. Huston, the camp security committee leader observes, "You're our own folks. . . . You belong with us" (343). He tells them, "Don't knife your own folks. . . . Don't tear all that down. Jes' think about it. You're jes' harmin' yourself" (344). The men are not hurt, but are banished from the camp, and subsequently they "disappeared into the darkness" (344).

Besides the darkness of outright abandonment or ostracism, the rejection of solidarity brings self-objectification. The tractor driver who would take the place of farmers becomes a "machine man, driving a dead tractor on land he doesn't know or love. . . . He is contemptuous of the land and of himself" (117). Connie, who wants to rise out of his class to become a storeowner, flees the family, alienating himself in the process. While the family attributes his flight to a weak character, it is no coincidence that he wants to move to town and take advancement-oriented classes like the nosy truck driver. It is unlikely that Connie could persevere in night school, but this is less ironic than the fact that he derives his materialistic dreams from catalogues and magazines—the false lures of consumer culture (165). The implicitly disapproving judgment upon him exposes some agrarian nostalgia in the novel, associating town life with selfishness, but it also is a critique of the individualism produced by consumerism. Connie's individualist solution to the mass displacement and impoverishment of his people is a hope falsely held out for all, but available only to a few mercenaries. We also see the same impulses working in Al, suggesting that the younger generation is being lured into self-destruction.

Yet the brunt of the novel's judgment does not fall on the working class, but on the "owners." Chapter 14 connects their violent repression of the migrants with the existential wasteland that is the desire to own. Those who exploit the workers, "who hate change and fear revolution," must crush efforts at human understanding in general. When the people who have had their land taken from them begin to feel common cause with one another, the owners feel anxiety and fear. They only feel safe when the oppressed "fear [and] suspect one another" (152). Besides registering moral outrage at profiting from another's suffering, the narrative argues that private ownership stands against the processes of history and nature. Here are combined elements of a thirties Marxist historiography—in which socialist revolution is the inevitable outcome of capitalism—and an evolutionary theory that links that revolution with natural history. The owners' crimes are thus simultaneously against nature and history, as well as morality. The terrible price they pay is that "the quality of owning freezes you forever into 'I,' and cuts you off forever from the 'we,'" a self-imposed ostracism (153). Later, the fearfulness and emptiness of ownership is discussed by the migrant men at a roadside camp. One notes that there is a man in California that owns a millions acres, which mystifies Casy, who wonders what one man could do with that much land. The other answers:

> He's jus' got it. Runs a few cattle. Got guards ever' place to keep folks out. Rides aroun' in a bullet-proof car. I seen pitchers of him. Fat, sof' fella with mean little eyes an' a mouth like a asshole. Scairt he's gonna die. Got a million acres an' scairt of dyin'. (206)

Ownership is thus associated with profound alienation from others and with the delusion that acquisition staves off death. It brings existential, if not material, suffering.

This line of reasoning is also evident in the description of the Farmers' Association vigilantes. They are understood not as evil, but as mistaken or misguided, a sentiment Casy voices before he is murdered. We first see him trying to convince Tom that breaking the pickers' strike will only make the workers more vulnerable and ultimately even hungrier. When Tom argues that his father would never consider more than the immediate interests of his family, Casy tiredly comments, "I wish they could see it. I wish they could see . . ." (384).[18] Then he has to confront a more hardened foe in the vigilantes. He tries to appeal to their senses of justice and shared humanity, telling them, "You fellas don' know what you're doin'. You're helpin' to starve kids. . . . You don' know what you're a-doin'" (386). Casy's appeal obviously does not affect the thugs, but Tom is won over to his position. Even Pa understands after Casy's death that the breaking of the strike will mean a wage cut (390). Simultaneously, the reader is asked not to be complicit with starving kids or to accept the intimidation and killing.

An interchapter (Chapter 21) explains the class position of the vigilante types from what resembles a Marxist perspective. They are "the local people," who have "whipped themselves into a mold of cruelty" mistakenly thinking that they are the owners and that the Okies are a threat to their property:

> The men who were armed did not own the land, but thought they did. And clerks who drilled [in paramilitary units] at night owned nothing, and little storekeepers possessed only a drawerful of debts. . . . The clerk thought, I get fifteen dollars a week. S'pose a goddamn Okie would work for twelve. (283)

Fear in the vigilantes causes them to work against their own interests while enriching the real owners.

In another scene, the more prosperous segment of the middle class struggles with alienation. Two tourists on the way to California, a "business man" and his "sullen" wife, stop at a roadside joint. Although they are well-dressed and drive an expensive car, she seems miserable and he is "worried" (156). They are the Babbittry who are "hungry for security and yet sens[e] its disappearance from the earth":

> In their lapels the insignia of lodges and service clubs, places where they go and, by a weight of numbers of little worried men, reassure themselves that business is noble and not the curious ritualized thievery they know it is; that business men are intelligent in spite of the records of their stupidity; that they are kind and charitable in spite of their principles of sound business; that their lives are rich instead of the thin tiresome routines they know; and that a time is coming when they will not be afraid any more. (156)

Their worry is grounded in two deeper fears: one that a revolutionary change is coming that will end their empty advantages; and two, that the trappings they cling to will never stop making them miserable. The passage argues, in effect, that the prosperous middle class is even more enslaved than the migrants, who are not bogged down in divisive materialism. It is in contrast to this living death—and that of "machine man" and the owner of a million acres—that Ma declares the Okies to be "the people who live." "Rich fellas come up an' they die, an' their kids ain't no good, an' they die. But Tom we keep a-comin'. . . . A different time's comin'" (280-1). The migrants are on the right side of history and nature.

It is worth pausing to note that this attribution of the migration to natural history has long been noted by critics. Recently, Denning has even asserted that the novel is rife with biological determinism, which he associates with Anglo-Saxon white supremacism. Indeed, the narrative makes an analogy between the Okies' movement westward and the behavior of ants and of a turtle. Moreover, the coming revolution is linked to evolution: the owners and their middle-class enablers are resisting the course of natural history. However, one must distinguish this usage of biological metaphors from eugenics or social Darwinism. The novel does not assert that the social hierarchy is natural or even that the current hierarchy will be replaced by a new one based on biology. The owners are not biologically inferior to the migrants; rather, they are *mistaken*. Their problem is one of knowledge, not biology.

In fact, Ma and the other Joads cannot, and do not, wait for history. They have to learn that the old idea of rugged individualism must pass as the conditions that gave rise to it have passed. Of course, the Okies' notion of individualism and that of the owners are different anyway. As the novel is careful to detail, the putative independence of the yeomanry depended on cooperation with neighbors, relative equality, and a reliance on the family as the unit of survival.[19] Yet the industrial quality of California agriculture requires a more organized and encompassing solidarity. Much of the story is taken up with Casy's, and then Ma and Tom's, realization of this fact. This expanded notion of cooperation has to happen not just in the fields, but in what used to be thought of as the sphere of the family. Throughout the story, Ma has nurtured the family as the implicit unit of the coming revolution; what has kept it together has also advanced the revolution, by fighting back against the forces of dissolution. Towards the end of the novel, however, Ma realizes that individualized families will never be strong enough to resist the great owners. She notes, "Use' ta be the fambly was fust. It ain't so now. It's anybody. Worse off we get, the more we got to do" (444). In other words, the sphere of interest must expand from the family to the collective.

Though Ma's realization of the need for class solidarity is no less significant, Tom's "I'll be there" speech a few pages earlier is the more famous articulation. Admitting himself to be Casy's protégé, Tom explicitly makes the connection between labor organizing, socialism, and the concept of a collective soul, while implicitly arguing against individualism. Casy's "great big soul," of which everyone is a "piece," is not simply a transcendentalist religious doctrine as some critics have claimed;[20] it is an attempt to articulate a spiritual expression of the revolution that will take place in society. Even the Biblical passages that Tom remembers Casy reciting concern the strength afforded by sharing and collective action. Though the speech that begins "Wherever they's a fight so hungry people can eat, I'll be there" draws our attention, it is important to note that it comes after Tom plots a more practical course of action. Inspired by the federal camp, with its self-government, democracy, and non-authoritarian discipline, Tom tells Ma "I've been wonderin' why we can't do that all over. . . . All work together for our own thing—all farm our own lan'" (418).[21] The better society Tom imagines carries the trace of the yeoman ideal, but its universalization would nonetheless require a revolutionary change in the social structure. Thus, his immediate plan is to do "what Casy done"—organize workers (419). Only when Ma asks him what will happen if he is killed does he give her the more spiritual "I'll be there" answer. Tom is, therefore, beginning to acquire the more revolutionary analysis evident in the interchapters.

The penultimate scene in the novel is an appeal both to solidarity within the story and to the reader. Rose of Sharon's baby is stillborn during the flood, and Uncle John is given the task of burying it. He decides that the body will bear the message of the migrants to their fellows in the towns. He puts the body in an apple box—two symbols of the products of California agriculture, suffering and fruit—and floats it on the flood towards town. He hopes the body will tell the townspeople a story they have ignored: "Go down and tell 'em. Go down in the street an' rot an' tell 'em that way. . . . Maybe they'll know then" (446). Simultaneously, the novel tells the *reader* a story he or she has ignored. The waste of the fruit is inseparable from the waste of the people.

* * *

While I have read the novel as having a radical critique of capitalism and as calling for a socialist solidarity, there are qualifications and counterarguments that could be raised to such a reading. Denning's argument is that the novel is embedded in the same racial nationalism evident in *The Harvest Gypsies*. In one sense, that argument is impossible to refute: *Grapes* mentions non-white workers only briefly while recounting the history of migrant farming before the Okies. Therefore, the existing non-white workers—while at that moment fewer in number than before—are erased. The anti-capitalist critique thus exists side-by-side with this erasure—a contradiction that goes unresolved. However, I would argue that the novel otherwise implicitly complicates a simple racial nationalism. Foremost, in contrast with the claims of *The Harvest Gypsies*, *Grapes* shows that the Okies' vaunted Anglo-Saxon racial heritage will not save them. It is only through collective action that they can prevail.

Moreover, collective action takes conscious choice and planning and does not happen merely because the Okies are white. All of the characters are white, but they do not all come to this consciousness. Nor do we know what happens to them; the novel ends with the Joads in precarious straits, not in the triumphant climax of Anglo-Saxon pioneering. Furthermore, their race means nothing to the huge growing companies or to the cops and vigilantes who would beat or kill them. This irony is apparent almost as soon as they arrive in California. They are rousted at the river (where Noah leaves the family) by cops who have no respect for their whiteness. Tom and Ma are shocked by the treatment: "we ain't use' ta gettin' shoved aroun' by no cops" (215). It is almost impossible for one to imagine an African-American, or for that matter a Mexican or Filipino worker making such a statement. But the Joads are finding out that they will now be racialized despite their heritage. They hear the cops call them Okies for the first time, and only a few pages later are labeled "gorillas" by gas station attendants (221). At that point, the Joads are setting out across the Mojave Desert in their jalopy, which the reader knows is a brave and stalwart act they have no choice but to undertake. Yet the attendants decide that "They're so goddamn dumb they don't know it's dangerous." Thus, the novel here suggests that what is racialized is not their blood, but their vulnerability to being exploited. The undeniable racism implicit in the erasure of non-white workers exists unresolved alongside an implicit—and perhaps unintended—debunking of white supremacism.

Another political contradiction in the novel arises between its call for class solidarity and its naturalization of gender roles, particularly for women. Ma Joad could be said to be a stereotypically nurturing earth mother. Critic Mimi Gladstein counters that Ma's nurturing of the family is a positive representation because of her great strength and because she takes on masculine responsibilities when necessary. Nor is Ma static, because the journey changes her, and she actively acquires new ways of understanding the situation of the migrants. Furthermore, Gladstein argues, the famous breast-feeding scene at the end of the novel demonstrates that Rose of Sharon is inheriting Ma's legacy by stepping out of her self-centeredness. However, Nellie Y. McKay convincingly argues that although Ma is a force in the Joads' realization that their family-centered world view must change, the roles for women within the "changing society" remain the same: they are nurturers, be it of the family or of the new society. Thus, the novel's comprehension of class solidarity is one that does not adequately take into account gender politics within the working class.

A final question about the novel's political critique concerns possible ambiguity over what constitutes revolutionary change. The novel arguably takes the position that the elimination of capitalism is necessary for a just, democratic, and non-exploitative society. Yet, because we do not see the revolution—even though it is said to be inevitable—there is still doubt as to what it might be. A key moment when this question is broached is when Pa and the men at Weedpatch discuss the change that they feel is coming: "Maybe we won't live to see her. But she's a-comin'. They's a res'less feelin'" (344). In the context of the interchapters, the change would be revolutionary, including the end of private ownership, the redistribution of the land, and presumably more. The incidents that the men cite most admiringly as evidence of the change are the rubber strikes in Akron, Ohio. There, the strikers, "mountain men," armed themselves against reactionary "storekeepers and legioners," and demonstrated their willingness to fight by holding a shooting competition (344). "Five thousan' of 'em jes' marched through town with their rifles. An' they had their turkey shoot, an' then they marched back. An' that's all they done. Well, sir, they ain't been no trouble sence then" (345). On the surface, the story is inspiring because the tire workers realize that they have to fight against the owners—that justice is not to be taken for granted. Yet the notion that the men could show their guns and then there would be no more "trouble" seems both naïve and an outcome that would be far short of revolutionary. In fact, it suggests more that the workers won some concessions from the company, but stopped there, satisfied. But the novel has shown us earlier that capital accumulation never stops, and therefore that the trouble cannot be over. So the scene is perhaps equivocal: it is not clear if the struggle will stop once a somewhat better wage is won or if will it continue until the relations of production themselves change.[22] Nor is it clear if the scene is meant to reflect the limited understanding of the migrants at this point, or if the novel as a whole is endorsing the Akron story as revolutionary.

This ambiguity is not resolved, and neither are the race and class contradictions. However, this open-endedness does not negate the novel's radicalism. *The Grapes of Wrath* offers an appeal to middle-class readers to join forces with the working-class subjects of the story, arguing that the ravages of capital accumulation are felt throughout the social order—if more heavily on the destitute migrant workers. The critique encourages the middle-class reader to move beyond sympathy for those more exploited and to a solidarity based on experiences within the same system. The reader is encouraged to care about the Joads and is simultaneously shown that, as society's unit of economic survival, the family is inadequate, the product of an outmoded social order. The novel relies on the ideological notion of the self-contained family to win the reader's concern for the Joads, and then argues for the necessity of communal, rather than familial, welfare.

Nevertheless, the novel's implicit Anglo-Saxon white supremacism (ambiguous as it may be) cannot be ignored or glossed over. Rather, we need an analysis that is subtle enough to see these contradictions as they are. We are not bound to the interpretive horizons of the 1930s, yet neither should we ignore what writers from that era have to teach us now. At stake, of course, is not the past, but the present and future.

From *Cultural Logic: An Electronic Journal of Marxist Theory and Practice* 5 (2002). Copyright © 2002 by Charles Cunningham. Originally published by *Cultural Logic*. Reprinted with permission of the author.

Notes

I would like to acknowledge the tireless assistance of Greg Meyerson, who offered invaluable suggestions on several versions of this essay. Moreover, his thinking on the race/class relationship has been indispensable to mine.

1. I use the term "Okie" because it names a mythology. It was, of course, a derogatory term in the thirties.

2. I base this claim first on the fact that none of the reviews I have found—even in the leftist press—saw the novel as racist. Moreover, as Greg Meyerson has kindly pointed out to me, even African racial essentialism was just coming to be debunked in the thirties. As late as 1935, Paul Robeson spoke of race as "born, not bred," using such terms as "blood," "stock," and "Negro assets." Only in 1939—the year *The Grapes of Wrath* was published—did Robeson begin to understand race as a "pseudo-scientific" category. (Meyerson notes that this trajectory can be followed by consulting pages 91-131 in *Paul Robeson Speaks* [Philip Foner, ed. New York: Citadel P, 1978].)

3. In general, Denning's book fails to analyze the processes of capitalism as determinants of culture, a major weakness.

4. For example, James N. Vaughn, in *The Commonweal*, states that the "argument" of the novel is that the migrants are being "driven to death by the forces of 'capitalism.'" While his placement of the word capitalism in scare quotes shows that it is not *his* analysis, he nonetheless sees that as a key proposition of the novel. Earle Birney in the *Canadian Forum* makes a similar observation in more sympathetic terms: "These proletarians of the soil are in the bitter process of learning for themselves in their own terms what wage-labor and capital mean, of creating for themselves fire-hardened leaders and cadres for the coming revolution." More conservative critics from publications such as *Newsweek* (Rascoe) and *The Springfield Republican* ("Reviewing Reviews") saw the novel as an incitement to violence and revolution. These reviews are significant because they demonstrate that the novel's anti-capitalist critique was recognizable as such to many mainstream critics in the thirties.

5. For an analysis of *Life*'s depiction of both the Okie migration and of rural poverty during the thirties see Cunningham, "To Watch the Faces."

6. The film's cinematographers disagreed with this emphasis, but Lorentz was unswayed. See Alexander, 93-109, and Denning, 261.

7. I would here invoke Marx's observation in *The Eighteenth Brumaire* that people make history, but not in conditions they choose. For a discussion of the concept of determination, see Williams, *Marxism and Literature*, 83-89.

8. In Steinbeck's *In Dubious Battle*, a smaller farmer is burned out when he contracts with pickers who are striking against the big growers.

9. For this account, I am relying on Daniel and to a lesser extent McWilliams.

10. Following Ruiz, I will use "Mexican" to signify both Mexicans and Mexican-Americans.

11. See Daniel, 280. Daniel's account of UCAPAWA is much less sanguine than Ruiz's, probably because Ruiz focuses on women cannery workers' self-empowerment in Los Angeles-area union locals. Daniel concentrates on migrant field workers, who the UCAPAWA predicted would be harder to organize. He argues, in effect, that the UCAPAWA strategy failed the farmworkers. Interestingly enough, Denning champions Popular Front cultural production about migrant labor, but does not mention—or therefore evaluate—its political strategies.

12. Even the last chapter in McWilliams's *Factories in the Field* drops Mexican and Filipino workers from its narrative—this despite the fact that they are the subject of most of the rest of the book.

13. See Cunningham, "Solidarity."

14. See Foley, 87-97, for debates about the class status of writers, particularly 96-7. In thirties terminology, fetishizing working-class origins was called "workerism."

15. See Benson, DeMott, and Wollenberg. Benson implies that intimate contact with the migrants made Steinbeck realize that he was engaged in a common struggle with them.

16. See Foley for a discussion of the story/discourse interplay in the novel (264-74). In *Grapes*, the interchapters also function to advance the Joads narrative indirectly by describing in detail experiences that are supposed to be common to the migrants, including buying cars, rebuilding roadside communities each night, and others.

17. Foley makes a similar point (417).

18. In the 1950s much of the criticism of the novel focused on its religious allusions, especially statements like Casy's, which were thought to compare him to Christ. Donald Pizer argues convincingly that the Christ-like echo in this speech is about relationships between people, not religious abstractions (92).

19. The extent to which this picture of the past is accurate is less important than the acknowledgment that it no longer existed. See Jones for accounts of the life of the "yeomanry" in earlier times.

20. A good summary of that position is in the "Editors Introduction" to *The Grapes of Wrath*, 552-55.

21. Daniel Aaron argues that because the Weedpatch camp is held up as an ideal, the novel's politics can be summed up simply as pro-New Deal. He also states that the novel is only "radical-sounding." If perhaps Steinbeck personally had naively high hopes for the New Deal, I would argue that in the novel the camp provides an example of how people feel and behave when they are not being exploited. That is why Tom invokes it here, not as a policy endorsement.

22. Sylvia Cook says that this ambiguity results from an unclear definition of the problem (177). I disagree; in the novel the problem is defined clearly enough as the "fruit" of destructive capital accumulation. The ambiguity is over whether or not the solution to the problem will be consistent with the novel's definition of it.

Works Cited

Aaron, Daniel. "Literary Scenes and Movements, 1910-1945." *Columbia Literary History of the United States*. Emory Elliott, ed. New York: Columbia UP, 1988.

Alexander, William. *Film on the Left: American Documentary Film from 1931 to 1942*. Princeton: Princeton UP, 1981.

Benson, Jackson J. "The Background to the Composition of *The Grapes of Wrath*." *Critical Essays on Steinbeck's The Grapes of Wrath*. John Ditsky, ed. Boston: G. K. Hall, 1989: 505-525.

Birney, Earle. "A Must Book." Review of *The Grapes of Wrath*. *Critical Essays on Steinbeck's The Grapes of Wrath*. John Ditsky, ed. Boston: G. K. Hall, 1989: 29-30.

Cook, Sylvia Jenkins. *From Tobacco Road to Route 66: The Poor Southern White in Fiction*. Chapel Hill: University of North Carolina Press, 1976.

Cunningham, Charles D. "Solidarity, Sympathy, Contempt: The Mythology of Rural Poverty in Depression America." Diss. Carnegie Mellon U, 2001.

_____. "'To Watch the Faces of the Poor': *Life* Magazine and the Mythology of Rural Poverty in the Great Depression." *Journal of Narrative Theory* 29.3 (Fall 1999).

Daniel, Cletus E. *Bitter Harvest: A History of California Farmworkers, 1870-1941*. Ithaca: Cornell UP, 1981.

DeMott, Robert. "'Working Days and Hours': Steinbeck's Writing of *The Grapes of Wrath*." *The Grapes of Wrath: Text and Criticism*. Eds. Peter Lisca with Kevin Hearle. New York: Viking, 1997: 526-539.

Denning, Michael. *The Cultural Front: The Laboring of American Culture in the Twentieth Century*. London and New York: Verso, 1996.

Foley, Barbara. *Radical Representations: Politics and Form in U.S. Proletarian Fiction, 1929-1941*. Durham: Duke UP, 1993.

Gladstein, Mimi Reisel. "The Indestructible Women: Ma Joad and Rose of Sharon." *John Steinbeck's The Grapes of Wrath*. Harold Bloom, ed. New York: Chelsea House, 1988: 115-28.

Gregory, James N. *American Exodus: The Dust Bowl Migration and Okie Culture in California*. New York: Oxford UP, 1989.

Hicks, Granville. "Steinbeck's Powerful New Novel." Review of *The Grapes of Wrath*. *New Masses*. 2 May 1939: 22-3.

Jones, Jacqueline. *The Dispossessed: America's Underclass from the Civil War to the Present*. New York: Basic Books, 1992.

Marx, Karl. "The Eighteenth Brumaire of Louis Bonaparte." 1852. *The Marx-Engels Reader*. Ed. Robert C. Tucker. New York: Norton, 1978: 594-617.

McKay, Nellie Y. "Happy [?]-Wife-and-Motherdom: The Portrayal of Ma Joad in John Steinbeck's *The Grapes of Wrath*." *New Essays on The Grapes of Wrath*. David Wyatt, ed. Cambridge: Cambridge UP, 1990: 47-70.

McWilliams, Carey. *Factories in the Field: The Story of Migratory Farm Labor in California*. Boston: Little, Brown, 1939.

Pizer, Donald. "The Enduring Power of the Joads." *John Steinbeck's The Grapes of Wrath*. Harold Bloom, ed. New York: Chelsea House, 1988: 83-98.

The Plow That Broke the Plains. Dir. Pare Lorentz. Prod. Farm Security Administration. 1936.

Railton, Stephen. "Pilgrim's Politics: Steinbeck's Art of Conversion." *New Essays on The Grapes of Wrath*. David Wyatt, ed. Cambridge: Cambridge UP, 1990: 27-46.

Rascoe, B. "But . . . Not . . . Ferdinand." Review of *The Grapes of Wrath*. *Newsweek* 17 Apr. 1939: 46.

_____. "Excuse It Please." Review of *The Grapes of Wrath*. *Newsweek* 1 May 1939: 38.

"Reviewing Reviews." Review of *The Grapes of Wrath*. *The Saturday Review*. 13 May 1939: 18.

Ruiz, Vicki L. *Cannery Women, Cannery Lives: Mexican Women, Unionization, and the California Food Processing Industry, 1930-1950.* Albuquerque: U New Mexico P, 1987.

Steinbeck, John. *The Grapes of Wrath.* 1939. Eds. Peter Lisca with Kevin Hearle. New York: Viking,1997.

_____. *The Harvest Gypsies: On the Road to The Grapes of Wrath.* Charles Wollenberg, ed. Berkeley: Heyday Books, 1988.

Vaughn, James N. Review of *The Grapes of Wrath*. *The Commonweal*. 28 Jul. 1939: 341-2.

Williams, Raymond. *Marxism and Literature.* New York: Oxford UP, 1977.

Wollenberg, Charles. "Introduction." *The Harvest Gypsies.* By John Steinbeck. Berkeley: Heyday Books, 1988: v-xvii.

Of Home-Makers and Home-Breakers:
The *Deserving* and the *Undeserving* Poor Mother in Depression Era Literature_____

Vivyan C. Adair

Americans have long embraced an ethos and a system of classification that separates the poor—in particular poor women—into two categories: those deserving of assistance, compassion, and pity and those undeserving of such sympathies and support. As Michael Katz points out in *The Undeserving Poor: From the War on Poverty to the War on Welfare*, early in our nation's history, public officials "attempted to distinguish between the able-bodied and the impotent poor; a few decades later, officials transmuted these categories into the moral distinction between the worthy and the unworthy, or the deserving and the undeserving poor."[1] In *For Crying Out Loud: Women and Poverty in the United States*, editors Rochelle Lefkowitz and Ann Withorn add that:

> American society, like many others before it, expresses sorrow and responsibility for some poor women—and blames and punishes others. Now, as then, poor women are divided into two categories: good and bad. The worthy widows and their orphaned children, once the deserving poor, are now the truly needy . . . one evil, poor woman remains: the welfare mother, "welfare" being the only adjective since "unwed" that has been able to tarnish motherhood.[2]

Although this dichotomous and hierarchical distinction may have reached its apogee with contemporary rhetoric surrounding 1996 welfare reform and 2002 reform reauthorization debates in the United States, the trope of the undeserving poor women was clarified, honed, invigorated and reified during the nation's Great Depression. For, at its heart Depression era literature reflects and reproduces just such a tidy and dichotomous maternal and marital class paradigm.

An examination of representations of the poor in Depression era literature exposes an often used hierarchy that pits the "deserving" against the "undeserving" poor mother. In this narrative poor mothers of the American Depression are positioned as deserving or undeserving, as good or bad, by virtue of their desire and ability to use their temporary agency to reenact the tenets of a failing patriarchy. Such an examination highlights the degree to which literary representation constructs, patrols, invigorates and reproduces categories of social reality. Further, it allows us to consider and critique the ways in which this ideological construct, marking poor mothers as either deserving or undeserving based on the imprimatur of men and male power, is extant in public representations of poor mothers in contemporary rhetoric.

The stark statistics of the Great Depression are by all accounts scarcely able to convey the distress of the millions of people who lost their jobs, their families, their homes, and their savings. At the depth of the Depression in 1933, one American worker in every four was unemployed, industrial stocks lost much of their value, banks failed, and agricultural distress was extensive and intense. As a result, hundreds of thousands of Americans found themselves hungry and homeless. As Harvey Swados in *The American Writer and the Great Depression* movingly recalls, even those of the Depression generation who were not destitute "had burned into them the dulled and shamed glances of men who were, and who could no longer feed their wives and children."[3] Fred Hobson, in his introduction to *Literature at the Barricades: The American Writer in the 1930s*, expands on the impact that widespread poverty had on Americans during the Depression. Hobson reminds us that:

> The decade of the 1930s embodied one of the major experiences ever to be thrust upon American life and the American mind. The Great Depression was an unprecedented material failure; yet it was more than just material in its consequences and implications. It permeated America's collective consciousness.[4]

Throughout the Depression, the American public had difficulty reconciling the images of poverty that surrounded them on a daily basis with the maxims of upward mobility, social progress, and individual worth that they had internalized as part of the narrative of the "American Dream." As the financial and moral collapse of the Depression called all values into question, a rift developed between cultural narrative and lived spectacle, evoking a profound crisis of meaning. Irving Howe in "The Thirties in Retrospect" theorizes this disjunction by explaining that Americans had believed that we lived under the sign of "provincial destiny." He points out that prior to the Depression the American ideal had been shaped largely by an Emersonian ethos:

> Americans embraced Emerson's call for the self-reliant man, the following of instinct and conscience, and echoes of Romanticism asserting the godly blessedness of human reach. The Emersonian man by virtue of his individuality shared in the universal current of divinity. In the Depression, Emerson's "infinitude of private man" was viewed as a bad joke when one saw millions of private men foundering and lost.[5]

Howe goes on to explain that "what is hard, perhaps impossible, to convey is the sense of social breakdown in the coming apart of those tacit convictions that keep society together."[6] It is the sense that society was falling apart because of the incongruous vision of widespread American poverty that Depression writers responded to with varying styles and degrees of success.

In *Daughters of the Great Depression: Women, Work and Fiction in the American 1930s*, Laura Hapke points out that although traditionally scholars have written and read the Great Depression as the history of "sad, broken or heroic men," writers in this period did not fail to notice that:

... more than two million women ... who faced the specters of homelessness and joblessness gathered in unemployment offices; slept in vacant lots, city subways and Bertha-like in boxcars; wrote pleading letters to the Roosevelts and Labor Secretary Frances Perkins; and hoped for rescue by New Deal agencies.[7]

Of equal concern was the fact that these were white and generationally American mothers, daughters, sisters and wives, and not the racial and ethnic "others" who had unfortunately been so easy to dismiss as deserving of their ill-fate. Embodied in the phenomenon of large numbers of poor, white, American mothers were the fears of a nation; their broken bodies and broken families were viewed as a threat to the most sacrosanct of American beliefs and meaning systems. As a result, a proliferation of stories both allaying and pandering to the fears of a threatened nation was pressed into service.

Hapke reminds us that literature of the period was filled with images of "dutiful daughters and malleable matrons; as well as their flawed (that is, sexually wayward) antitheses." Illustrating the degree to which imagery of the maternal ideal was linked to literary representation, she adds, during this period of hard times "woman, traditionally split into maternal and carnally threatening presence, played an important role in producing this desperate hopefulness" throughout the Great Depression.[8] John Steinbeck and Erskine Caldwell were two widely read and enormously popular writers who addressed these fears by creating enduring archetypes of the "deserving" and the "undeserving" poor American mother that have retained a profound hold on our national imagination and collective consciousness.

The *Good Ma* of Depression Era Literature

Writing during an economic and social depression that called all values into question, John Steinbeck responded to this cultural experience of loss and confusion. In the context of a decade of social upheaval, ideological insecurities, and extreme cultural anomie, Steinbeck found himself in the midst of a culture longing for assurances, for what Swados refers to as "the American desire for an account of their experience that would be both rational and optimistic."[9] Steinbeck's various works were certainly embraced because of their poignant and beautifully written descriptions of the American condition. His work was also enormously popular precisely because it offered just such a "rational and optimistic" account of American poverty, forging narratives that repaired enervated visions of the nation while making sense of the presence of multitudes of poor white mothers in our line of vision. As Sylvia Jenkins Cook points out, Steinbeck provided the American public with "powerful human images around which to crystallize the confused emotions of a turbulent era."[10] Hapke adds that "no writer of his time was more dedicated to the centrality of the mother myth than Steinbeck."[11] Constructing a literary lens through which the American public could read and make sense of the lives of poor white and American mothers, Steinbeck allowed for the perpetuation of underlying traditional beliefs and systems of meaning. In his writing he re-mythologized the poor white mother within the larger context of the Great Depression, allowing Americans to continue to stabilize, embrace, and reproduce highly gendered and racialized ideologies and narratives of agency. In reinforcing foundational dichotomies, Steinbeck's work both covered up and allowed for the reproduction of mainstream ideology and power.

Of all of Steinbeck's writing, the images that most clearly demarcate his culturally invigorating taxonomy of poverty and of poor mothers are found in his best selling novel *The Grapes of Wrath*. This novel was published in 1939, during a period marked by the unsettling presence of a flush of homeless and damaged American men and women—who looked and were, otherwise, "just like us"—whose presence threatened our vision of national identity. Steinbeck's myth of a natural maternal deservedness allowed us to make sense of poverty and instability by portraying male loss and female empowerment as temporary displacements, rather than as evidence of structural flaws. In the process, he revived gendered, raced and classed narratives of progress, individuality, and morality, shoring up frames constituting women as at least potentially deserving mothers, wives, sisters and daughters. In creating a "paean of enduring motherhood" Steinbeck sustained the nation's morale, "rehears[ing] the widespread belief that the return of the wife and mother to her 'natural' sphere [would mean] a sign of the return of 'good times'" in America.[12]

At its heart, *The Grapes of Wrath* yields meaning as a text of libidinal transformation; it is the narrative of a bodily passage towards redemption, a saga of individuation, an oedipal journey. It is the story of the Joads, dispossessed sharecroppers from Oklahoma, who join a great migration of sorrow westward toward the apocryphal promise of work and riches in California. At the level of the mythic, the Joads are excised from the land with which they had been one; expelled, they are destined to move on valiantly, to battle and transgress the forces of chaos that would otherwise destroy them, and ultimately to mature, experience redemption, and thus re-stabilize.

In *The Grapes of Wrath*, as in all oedipal or transformative narratives, the protagonist—Pa, The Joads, The Family of Man—was unwittingly and painfully expelled from his pre-symbolic, pre-cultural unity with the land, wife, and mother. What is left behind is the object of much reflection on the part of the Joads: the dream of an *a priori* maternal unity. Loss becomes the dream remembered. In a highly gendered and metaphoric scenario of paradise lost, the Joads recall with nostalgia that they—and their fathers before them—had colonized, impregnated, cultivated, and regulated the land: the mother. This is the dream of a time when/where the referent was "real" and desire was unmediated.

It is this fantasy of mythic wholeness, this before-the-fall-one-ness and timeless connection to the fertile and regenerative earth that propels the Joads toward the bliss of recuperative unity on their poignant and painful westward migration. The Joads move forward to California with the dream of re-union with the feminized land. They long for a new Californian spring where "the full green hills are round and soft as breasts."[13] Through the novel they painstakingly progress toward the promise of California, the land of milk and honey, and "sweet scented oranges" (443).

Steinbeck employs the metaphor of the earth as both a source of life and a site of displacement in *The Grapes of Wrath*. Mother earth in this foundational myth can be either "good" or "punishing." The metaphor of the gendered land as source of unity and as object of desire also necessarily positions the "garden" as ripe for betrayal. *The Grapes of Wrath* opens with evocative images of the feminized land being raped and colonized by brutish, inhuman, and slippery technology. We are witness to the anathema of a new and competing phallic power:

> . . . its machined surfaces, its surge of power, the roar of its detonating cylinders; but it was not [man's] tractor. Behind the tractor rolled the shining disks, cutting the earth with blades—not plowing but surgery—and pulled behind the disks, the harrows combing with iron teeth so that the little clods broke up and the earth lay smooth. [46]

In the explicit and horror-ridden imagery of an "un-natural" possession, we witness "behind the harrows, the long seeders—twelve curved iron penes erected in the foundry, orgasms set by gears, raping methodically, raping without passion" (46). Now emasculated and powerless, the tenant farmer—the rightful and yet displaced patriarch and authority—"sat in his doorway . . . the driver thundered his engine and started off, tracks falling and curving, harrows combing, and the phalli of the seeder slipping into the ground" (50).

The maternal feminine principle is complicit in its own victimization and man is, as a consequence, both dispossessed and disenfranchised. Betrayed, man the hunter becomes man the hunted. As the literally and figuratively dispossessed Muley tells Tom and Casy: "When you're huntin' somepin you're a hunter an' you're strong . . . but when you get hunted—that's different. Somepin happens to you. I been hunted now for a long time. I ain't a hunter no more. . . . It don't do no good to fool you or me. That's how it is" (74).

As a symbol for the experience of the Depression as a whole, on the now barren farms, the exploiter becomes the exploited; man is divested of sexual, social, and moral power, and as a result the entire meaning system starts to unravel, as the "family stood about like dream walkers" (145). Mother earth becomes infertile and rejects man as cuckold. In violent and twisted imagery, the sun, once a source of life, becomes as "ripe as new blood" (6). The land has spilt its blood, becoming both victim and victimizer. No longer regenerative and fertile, now "the earth dusted down in dry little streams," "the air was thin and the sky more pale; and every day the earth paled" (4).

The product of this unnatural union is multiple and sexualized "dust" coming "so thinly that it could not be seen in the air and it settled like pollen on the chairs and the tables and the dishes" (5). In this apocalyptic vision man too becomes metonymically linked to loss and infertility. The barren earth is crisscrossed with "water cut gullies [where now] the earth dusted down in dry little streams" (1). Like the earth, man's own body is made to bear, indeed it is reduced to, marks of infidelity and infertility: "his cheek bones were high and wide, and strong deep lines cut down his cheeks in furrows, cutting beside the mouth," and "there was a hint of brown pigment in his eyeballs" (9). The "men's sunburned faces were dark and their sunwhipped eyes were light" (44), as in a scarred terrain of profound loss, the family of man is ripped apart. It is this maternal betrayal and subsequent loss that ruptures the naturalized fratriarchal and patriarchal connection of men to the earth and to each other in *The Grapes of Wrath*.

At the level of narrative then, Steinbeck creates an acutely gendered metaphor, positioning the land as feminized, maternal space that "once upon a time" was objectified, colonized, and made to yield (in both senses of the word), but that now betrays man through its sexual "difference." The emasculating land reveals the impoverished feminine as earth or dirt, as innately unstable, corporeal, unfettered, and chaotic. Mother earth becomes paradoxically both naturalized as possession and made unnatural as "other." In this parable she becomes the embodiment of contradiction, disorder, and dis-ease, a negative term of sexual difference as both absence/loss/dream remembered of fertility and unity, and abject and cold body, a site of betrayal.[14]

Through a painful metaphoric scenario, *The Grapes of Wrath* stabilizes a troubling vision of loss, instability, and disconnection. Crucially, the narrative then goes on to allow readers to make sense of their disconcerting vision by giving us hope that despite our deepest fears and suspicions, unlike "Mother Earth," "civilized" real wives and mothers—authorities by default—would neither fail nor betray man, but that on the contrary, the deserving poor woman would willingly lay down her body and her own desire in the service of mankind. In doing so Steinbeck's prescriptive "masterpiece" allayed the nation's most heartfelt fears. As the land was a bearer of sexual difference and thus negation, the female characters in this novel, most notably Ma Joad and her pregnant daughter Rose of Sharon, became—because they were "good" poor mothers and mothers to be—positive bearers of social value. According to Hapke, they were "sanctified" and "home-loving earth mothers" who "offered comfort, a way for men demoralized by Depression indignities to keep their self-respect [as heads of households]."[15]

After they are displaced, the Joads pull up their roots and begin their westward trek toward the dream of transformation and unification with a new, fertile, and compliant land. As many theorists have noted, the journey begins with a loss of male terrain; men's work comes to a halt while the women's work continues. Wagons, horses, plows—all the tools of men's labor and authority—are sold before the journey, and in the process, the men are further emasculated in being robbed and taken advantage of. Yet Ma Joad's kettles and pans are all taken along and become central to the family. Theorists have traditionally read these scenes as a lament for the loss of male power, as what John Timmerman refers to as a disastrous unraveling and "displacement of authority in the novel, from thinking man to spiritual woman."[16] Timmerman adds that in *The Grapes of Wrath* newfound maternal power leaves all of mankind "defeated like a bewildered child" while "the final warfare on male strength ultimately paves the way for [Rose of Sharon and Ma's] ascendancy to a position of authority."[17] Warren Motley similarly claims, in "From Patriarchy to Matriarchy: Ma Joad's Role in *The Grapes of Wrath*," that "as the Joad clan disintegrates under the pressure of dispossession and migration, Ma Joad [dangerously] emerges as a central cohesive force."[18]

Yet, the women in *The Grapes of Wrath* are constructed as archetypes of "good mothers," as deserving poor women. As such, they only assert themselves to the extent that they need to do so to reestablish hegemonic—patriarchal, heterosexual and racist—codes, morals, and concomitant authority. Ma and Rose of Sharon act only in the best interest of the male power structure they hope to reinforce and reestablish.

First the Joad women are "good" because they are white and American citizens. Their children are golden "corn-headed" with "wide eyes the color of pale sky" (40). At least at the beginning of the novel, they are neither "foreign" nor alien/other. Rather, as Grandpa, the senile patriarch, reminds the family with unintended irony, "this is [our] country. My pa took up the land. He had to kill the Indians and drive them away" (43). The women's value as deserving and rights-bearing citizens rests on their heterosexual connection to their white, American men, their ability to generate and maintain male lineage, and their desire to sustain their men's connection to American ancestry and earth. Even in the midst of their own pain and suffering, they "knew deep in themselves that no misfortune was too great to bear if their men were whole" (6). These good poor women knew their place and willingly stood silently behind the squatting men holding council; even when restive they "hold their piece" (129), and they know, accept, and indeed, welcome "their position in life" (96).

Ma Joad as the archetypal good poor woman, as many have noted, is never given a first name. In her role as matriarch she is similarly given no desire of her own. Ma's specific function in this closed circuit of male desire is that of reproduction of the species and maintenance of traditional moral, social, and cultural values. She is tellingly described as "heavy, but not fat; thick with childbearing and work" (80). As the epitome of "high calm and superhuman understanding," Ma Joad is a "goddess" wearing a sex-less "loose Mother Hubbard of gray cloth in which there had once been colored flowers, but the color was washed out now" (95). Ma is only the object of male enunciation—good mother, matronly and obedient wife, dutiful daughter—she is a worn and tattered transcript where generations of men have inscribed their own desire. Body without agency, she is simply a vehicle for bearing, supporting, and nurturing her "fambly of man."

Like Ma, the pregnant Rose of Sharon is imaged as a sign of reproduction and motherhood. Connected to the earth and to nature, for Rose of Sharon "the whole world was pregnant" (111). These good, poor, and "natural" mother-women stand in stark contrast to what Steinbeck in the interchapter of the novel portrays as the unnatural, castrating, wealthy, "languid, heat raddled ladies" who cruise Route 66 in Zephyrs with their effeminate and disempowered husbands. These "little pot-bellied . . . clean, pink men" are ruined by their plastic and sterile wives with "creams, ointments to grease themselves, coloring matter in phials—black, pink, red, green, silver—to change the color of eyes, lips, nail, brows, lashes, lids." Their "bags of bottles, syringes, pills, powders, fluids [and] jellies" made them dangerously Other as "their sexual intercourse [became] safe, odorless, and unproductive" (199).[19]

As good, "deserving" mothers, safely neutralized, naturalized, and confined within the bounds of patriarchy, the poor women in Steinbeck's *The Grapes of Wrath* willingly subject themselves to control and order; their allegedly natural tendencies have been tamed, and they have fully embraced and internalized a rigid masculinist logic as stewards of "social conduct" that remains because of their vigilance, "fixed and rigid" (251). Good poor women, like those who run the government sponsored Weedpatch camp, guard that "the rows were straight and there was no litter about the tents" and assure that "the ground of the street [was] swept and sprinkled" (463). The neatness of the physical camp is an outward manifestation of the internal order and the moral and ethical boundaries that are so sacrosanct to the poor women in this novel. Ma's "nature" is equally tamed and ordered. She is "as remote and faultless in judgment as a Goddess" (96), and her emotions, like her face, were perpetually "controlled" (95). Even when Ma sees her son Tom for the first time in four years, after he has been released from McAlester prison, she maintains her "quiet dignity." Pa was overcome "with excitement" as Tom "shamefacedly stepped over the doorsill" to the mother who had longed to see him for years. Yet the stoic Ma Joad muttered only "thank God." She began to lose control, but recognizing that her joy had caused Tom to bite his lip, immediately "she knew, and her control came back, and her hand dropped" (96).

Ma is the vanguard battling all unlettered emotion. She constantly chides Rose of Sharon for her indecorous and "immature" emotional outbursts. As Ma reminds her pregnant and ill daughter, "how you feel got to be kep' to youself" (192). In initiating Rose of Sharon into what feminist psychoanalyst Nancy Chodorow calls "the sisterhood of mothering the world," she warns her daughter to "git to [her] proper place" (400), to "git ahold on [herself]," and to "not shame [her] folks" by making her inner feelings known (345). Ma even demands that the weak, unsocialized, and somewhat effeminate Uncle John stop bearing his soul to others. When he attempts to confess his sins in an act of catharsis, Ma beseeches him: "Don't go tellin; tell im to God. Don't go burdenin' other people with your sins. That ain't decent" (338).

As a dignified and unsexed mother/matron and a pregnant bride, on a number of levels Ma and Rose of Sharon are "imperturbable" and impenetrable. Ordering their bodies and their subjectivities through patriarchal codes stabilizes and purifies them as both cultural and physical constructs. As a result, their otherwise outlawed feminine bodies are imagined as stabilized, clean, sacrosanct, and closed; they become safe and innocent good women who reassuringly can no longer be penetrated by dirt or colonized by the "other." Although the town's people believe that the "Okies are dirty and ignorant. . . . They bring disease, they're filthy" (363), the migrant women steadfastly maintain and guard their order, discipline, and cleanliness.

It is crucial that in every instance that Ma asserts her will, she does so in order to protect the integrity of the patrilineal family and to hold as sacred its alleged requisite codes; she only asserts her authority in order to keep her husband and her family intact. As Sylvia Jenkins Cook reports in "Steinbeck, the People and the Party,"

> Ma's own primacy in the family, though she is eminently fitted for its leadership, is emphasized as a temporary necessity. The rule of women is as unnatural as the rotting oranges and starving children, and there are frequent hints that when the natural order returns, Ma will retire again from her emergency role to the "great and humble" position she had formerly occupied.[20]

Finally, in the epiphanic closing scenes of *The Grapes of Wrath*, Ma and Rose of Sharon—as good, white, and married poor women—prove their deservedness by making the ultimate maternal sacrifice in order to restore the dominant social/sexual order. The Joads have barely eked out an existence in California, where there is little work and great suffering. Tom, who, battered and bruised, has gone into hiding having avenged Casy's murder at the hands of vigilantes, decides to leave the family to work for the betterment of migrant workers as a whole. His transformation comes as he has evolved from being a silent and introspective son to a "full growed man." His is a journey toward male autonomy and agency, even if it is in the service of all of mankind. In stark contrast to Tom's transformation of male maturation and individuation, Rose of Sharon must learn to subjugate her own desire

---

to the needs of men in order to mature and be transformed. Whereas Tom will use his labor power to experience fulfillment and to express his agency, Rose of Sharon will use her abstract and temporary feminine authority and power to literally revive the symbol of a dying patriarchy with her body. In the final scenes of *The Grapes of Wrath* she will use her regenerative maternal power to force the return of the exiled male subject, and in doing so, to offer a hopeful vision of a return of the center of male authority to the narrative of our cultural identity.

Rose of Sharon begins her transformation, according to most male critics, as a self-absorbed and immature young wife. Consumed with her pregnancy and less concerned with the needs of her new husband Connie, she unacceptably positions him as a vehicle for her own desire. His body, his labor power, his hope for the future had become the screen on which Rose of Sharon projected her own desire for a baby. This symbolic reversal of agency drives Connie from the Joads. He simply walks away one day never to be seen again. In this portrayal, Rose of Sharon's initial "immaturity" is clearly associated with her need to act on her own desire, and thus on her habit of disrupting a traditional and culturally imperative heterosexual expression of male desire.

Yet, in this novel meant to offer hope and reassurance, it is imperative that the young bride/mother transform herself into a "deserving" good woman in order to allow for the perpetuation of a highly gendered, raced, classed—and therapeutic—narrative of patriarchal salvation. The loss of her baby, and its use as sign and sacrifice, mark Rose of Sharon's rapid transformation. When finally the Joads leave their boxcar for the haven of an old dry barn, she is a mature, selfless woman. Inside the barn Ma and Rose of Sharon find a young boy who has stolen bread to feed his dying and aged father. As the father begins to die from starvation, Ma and Rose of Sharon "looked deep into each other" as two mature, selfless, and giving women. Ma looks at Rose of Sharon knowingly, when in an amazing spectacle, Rose of Sharon

. . . hoisted her tired body up and drew the comfort about her. She moved slowly to the corner and stood looking down at the wasted face, into the wide, frightened eyes. . . . Rose of Sharon loosened one side of the blanket and bared her breast. "You got to" she said. . . . "There." . . . She looked up and across the barn, and her lips came together and smiled mysteriously. [581]

John Ditsky in *Steinbeck: Life, Work, and Criticism* claims that "for Rose of Sharon herself, this final action is the personal attainment of maturity" as she "achieves her full womanhood through 'other-commitment'."[21] Ditsky, reading the final scenes of the novel through its Christian imagery and symbolism, refers to the Eucharistic nature of Rose of Sharon's act as a "re-Genesis," as an "epiphany of sorts," as "miracle plus vision." Positioning Rose of Sharon in this re-Genesis as the archetypal Madonna, Ditsky sees her as "a louvre of mixed subjects; a Nativity, a Mona Lisa and an immense and heroic Delacroix," noting that in the final scenes she has achieved "mature" sexuality because finally she is "nursing instead of being nursed, giving instead of taking."[22] Celebrating Rose of Sharon's willing subjugation, Ditsky adds, breathlessly:

> Steinbeck constructs a kind of canopy over this final scene by rendering it as a tableau. . . . Rose of Sharon becomes statuary as worn mother and starving man fuse in lasting composition . . . the perfect stranger finding solace of suck at the breast of the husbandless wife, the childless mother. What a forbidden, what a necessary, nourishment.[23]

Ditsky's passionate analysis of this final scene is revealing. Here, fixed and frozen, Rose of Sharon's body becomes pure spectacle; a safe act of lack and mutilation to be looked at without fear, at once both telos and origin of man's desire. This scene surely represents more than a woman feeding a surrogate child or helping out a neighbor. Note that for Ditsky this is the portrait of a "husbandless wife" and a "childless mother." Here, mother and wife are united as the object of male desire in a masochistic, comforting spectacle of willing lack. With his vocabulary of "tableaus," "statuary," and "canopies," Ditsky also hints at the staged and specular quality of the final scene. This is the reenactment of a scene of great significance to a patriarchy in disarray. Here woman—mother/wife—has willingly positioned herself as sexualized and yet safe spectacle. She has become the stable ground of pure representation, captive as both theoretical and historical body of representation. Rose of Sharon's nursing body becomes what Teresa de Lauretis, in her work on film theorist Laura Mulvey, would call "spectacle-fetish or specular image, in any case obscene, woman is constituted as the [literal] ground of representation, the looking-glass held up to man."[24]

In this final scene, in an elaborate feast of scopophilia, Rose of Sharon's nursing body and the reviving patriarch are fused together as one vision, fixed and indelibly inscribed. In what Mulvey would call her "looked-at-ness," Rose of Sharon poses eternally as castrated and safe mother/wife with man at her breast, bound in man's vision of her sexuality, the Absolute Representation, the Phallic Scenario. Her body is fetishized as memory spectacle, the perpetual and autochthonous reenactment of a "one time" union with the mother, mother earth, daughter and wife; it is a safe, unifying and stable, yet orgasmic fiction of male loss recovered.

What Steinbeck constructs then in this fascinating portrait is the dream of the poor mother and wife as willing midwife to her own oppression—to her own symbolic castration—as she labors only to re-empower man. In their poverty, in their absolute devotion to male authority, and inherent in their naturalized connection to the fertile earth, Steinbeck's poor mothers in *The Grapes of Wrath* allow us as a people to define ourselves by reading, believing, and taking comfort in a feminized classification of humans called the "deserving poor mother." The superior half of this binary of deservedness remains intact in contemporary narratives where "legal" mothers who remain attractive, faithful, subservient, contained, and controlled are heralded as deserving and good. In stark contrast, poor mothers who fail to honor and capitulate to absolute male authority and its allegedly associated codes are marked and punished as undeserving, dangerous and pathological.

Notes

1. Michael B. Katz, *The Undeserving Poor: From the War on Poverty to the War on Welfare* (New York: Pantheon Books, 1989), 5.

2. Rochelle Lefkowitz and Ann Withorn, eds., *For Crying Out Loud: Women and Poverty in the United States* (New York: The Pilgrim Press, 1986), 12.

3. Harvey Swados, ed., *The American Writer and the Great Depression* (New York: Bobbs-Merrill, 1966), xi.

4. Ralph F. Bogardus and Fred C. Hobson, eds., *Literature at the Barricades: The American Writer in the 1930s* (Tuscaloosa: University of Alabama Press, 1982), 12.

5. Irving Howe, "The Thirties in Retrospect" in *Literature at the Barricades*, 19.

6. Ibid., 13.

7. Laura Hapke, *Daughters of the Great Depression: Women, Work and Fiction in the American 1930s* (Athens: University of Georgia Press, 1995), xiii.

8. Ibid., 24.

9. Swados, *The American Writer*, 19

10. Sylvia Jenkins Cook, *Erskine Caldwell and the Fiction of Poverty: The Flesh and the Spirit* (Baton Rouge: Louisiana State University Press, 1991), 60.

11. Hapke, *Daughters of the Great Depression*, 35.

12. Ibid., 222.

13. John Steinbeck, *The Grapes of Wrath* (Portsmouth, NH: Heinemann Press, 1992), 445. Subsequent references will be noted parenthetically in the text.

14. As Hapke notes, "to turn from mothering was to be dangerously oversexed, and paradoxically quintessentially unwomanly . . . even the good wife, if untamed by law giving men, might degenerate into the unregulated woman, threatening to castrate and destroy" (*Daughters of the Great Depression*, 66-67).

15. Ibid., 35.

16. John Timmerman, "The Squatters Circle in *The Grapes of Wrath*," *Studies in American Fiction* 17.2 (1989): 206.

17. Ibid., 210.

18. Warren Motley, "From Patriarchy to Matriarchy: Ma Joad's Role in *The Grapes of Wrath*," *American Literature: A Journal of Literature, History, Criticism, and Bibliography* 54.3 (1982): 397.

19. In Steinbeck's letters he wrote a note expressing his general misogyny and fear/hatred of mothers and wives. An entry from 1958 reads:

> The breed of American woman . . . they have the minds of whores and the vaginas of Presbyterians. They are trained by their mothers in a contempt for men. . . . The American girl makes a servant of her husband and then finds him contemptible for being a servant. American married life is the doormat to the whore house. . . . the impulse of the American woman to geld her husband and castrate her sons is very strong.

Elaine Steinbeck and Robert Wallsten, eds., *John Steinbeck: A Life in Letters* (New York: Viking Adult, 1975), 343.

20. Sylvia Jenkins Cook, "Steinbeck, the People, and the Party," in *Literature at the Barricades: The American Writer in the 1930s*, ed. Ralph F. Bogardus and Fred Hobson (Tuscaloosa: University of Alabama Press, 1982), 84.

21. John Ditsky, *Steinbeck: Life, Work, and Criticism* (Fredericton, N.B., Canada: York Press, 1985), 12.

22. Ibid., 15.

23. Ditsky, *Steinbeck*, 123.

24. Teresa de Lauretis, *Alice Doesn't: Feminism, Semiotics, Cinema* (Bloomington: Indiana University Press, 1984), 15.

Works Cited

Bogardus, Ralph F., and Fred C. Hobson, eds. *Literature at the Barricades: The American Writer in the 1930s*. Tuscaloosa: University of Alabama Press, 1982.

Chodorow, Nancy. *The Reproduction of Mothering: Psychoanalysis and the Sociology of Gender*. Berkeley: University of California Press, 1978.

Cook, Sylvia Jenkins. *Erskine Caldwell and the Fiction of Poverty: The Flesh and the Spirit*. Baton Rouge: Louisiana State University Press, 1991.

_____. "Steinbeck, the People and the Party." In *Literature at the Barricades: The American Writer in the 1930s*, edited by Ralph F. Bogardus and Fred Hobson, 82-95. Tuscaloosa: University of Alabama Press, 1982.

De Lauretis, Teresa. *Alice Doesn't: Feminism, Semiotics, Cinema*. Bloomington: Indiana University Press, 1984.

Ditsky, John. *John Steinbeck: Life, Work, and Criticism*. Fredericton, N.B., Canada: York Press, 1985.

Hapke, Laura. *Daughters of the Great Depression: Women, Work and Fiction in the American 1930s*. Athens: University of Georgia Press, 1995.

Howe, Irving. "The Thirties in Retrospect." In *Literature at the Barricades: The*

American Writer in the 1930s, edited by Ralph F. Bogardus and Fred C. Hobson, 13-28. Tuscaloosa: University of Alabama Press, 1982.

Katz, Michael B. *The Undeserving Poor: From the War on Poverty to the War on Welfare*. New York: Pantheon Books, 1989.

Lefkowitz, Rochelle, and Ann Withorn, eds. *For Crying Out Loud: Women and Poverty in the United States*. New York: The Pilgrim Press, 1986.

Motley, Warren. "From Patriarchy to Matriarchy: Ma Joad's Role in *The Grapes of Wrath*." *American Literature: A Journal of Literature, History, Criticism and Bibliography* 54.3 (1982): 397-412.

Mulvey, Laura. "Visual Pleasure and Narrative Cinema." *Screen* 16.3 (1975): 6-18.

Steinbeck, Elaine, and Robert Wallsten, eds. *Steinbeck: A Life in Letters*. New York: Viking Adult, 1975.

Steinbeck, John. *The Grapes of Wrath*. Portsmouth, NH: Heinemann Press, 1992.

Swados, Harvey, ed. *The American Writer and the Great Depression*. Indianapolis: Bobbs Merrill, 1966.

Timmerman, John. "The Squatters Circle in *The Grapes of Wrath*." *Studies in American Fiction* 17.2 (1989): 203-11.

RESOURCES

1902	John Ernst Steinbeck is born on February 27 in Salinas, California, to John Ernst Steinbeck II and Olive Hamilton Steinbeck.
1919	Steinbeck graduates from Salinas High School.
1920-1925	Steinbeck attends Stanford University while working on and off as a laborer on ranches. His first short stories are published in the *Stanford Spectator.*
1925	Steinbeck drops out of Stanford and moves to New York City, where he works as a construction laborer for Madison Square Garden and reports for the *American* newspaper.
1926	Steinbeck returns to California, where he writes stories and novels.
1929	Steinbeck's first novel, *Cup of Gold*, is published.
1930	Steinbeck marries Carol Henning and moves to the family home in Pacific Grove, in California's Monterey County. He meets Edward F. Ricketts, with whom he begins an important lifelong friendship.
1932	*The Pastures of Heaven* is published. Steinbeck moves to Los Angeles.
1933	*To a God Unknown* is published. Steinbeck returns to Monterey, California. Parts of what will become *The Red Pony* appear in *North American Review.*
1934	Steinbeck's mother dies. His short story "The Murder" is selected as an O. Henry Prize story.
1935	*Tortilla Flat* is published. Steinbeck's father dies.
1936	*In Dubious Battle* is published. Steinbeck travels to Mexico.
1937	*Of Mice and Men* is published and is chosen as a Book-of-the-Month Club selection. The novella *The Red Pony* is published. Steinbeck travels to Europe, then from Oklahoma to California with migrants.

1938	*Their Blood Is Strong*, a collection of articles, is published. A collection of short stories, *The Long Valley*, is published. Steinbeck receives the New York Drama Critics' Circle Award for his stage adaptation of *Of Mice and Men*.
1939	*The Grapes of Wrath* is published and attracts nationwide attention. Steinbeck is elected to the National Institute of Arts and Letters.
1940	*The Grapes of Wrath* wins the Pulitzer Prize. *The Forgotten Village*, a documentary film, is produced. Steinbeck goes on a research trip with Edward Ricketts to the Gulf of Mexico. The film version of *The Grapes of Wrath* is released.
1941	*Sea of Cortez*, a collaboration between Steinbeck and Ricketts, is published.
1942	*The Moon Is Down* is published. Steinbeck and his wife divorce. The nonfiction *Bombs Away*, written for the U.S. Air Force, is published.
1943	Steinbeck moves to New York City and marries Gwyndolyn Conger. He serves as a war correspondent in Europe for the *New York Herald Tribune*.
1944	Director Alfred Hitchcock's film *Lifeboat*, written by Steinbeck, is released. Steinbeck buys his childhood dream house in Monterey, and his first son, Thom, is born.
1945	*Cannery Row* is published. Steinbeck moves to New York.
1946	Steinbeck's second son, John IV, is born.
1947	*The Wayward Bus* and *The Pearl* are published. Steinbeck travels through Russia with photographer Robert Capa.
1948	*A Russian Journal*, an account of Steinbeck's 1947 tour of Russia, is published. Steinbeck and Gwyndolyn Conger divorce. Steinbeck moves from New York to Pacific Grove.
1950	*Burning Bright* is published. Steinbeck marries Elaine Anderson Scott. He writes the script for *Viva Zapata!*

1951	*The Log from the Sea of Cortez*, the narrative part of *Sea of Cortez*, is published.
1952	*East of Eden* is published.
1954	*Sweet Thursday*, a sequel to *Cannery Row*, is published.
1957	*The Short Reign of Pippin IV* is published.
1958	*Once There Was a War,* a collection of Steinbeck's wartime dispatches, is published.
1960	Steinbeck travels around the United States for three months with his dog, Charley.
1961	*The Winter of Our Discontent* is published.
1962	*Travels with Charley*, the journal of Steinbeck's 1960 tour, is published. Steinbeck is awarded the Nobel Prize in Literature.
1963	Steinbeck travels to Scandinavia, Eastern Europe, and Russia on a cultural tour for the U.S. Information Agency.
1964	Steinbeck is awarded the Presidential Medal of Freedom.
1966	Steinbeck becomes a member of the National Arts Council. *America and Americans*, a collection of reflections on contemporary America, is published.
1966-67	Steinbeck reports from Vietnam for *Newsday*.
1968	Steinbeck dies of a heart attack in New York City on December 20. His ashes are buried in the Garden of Memories cemetery in Salinas, California.

Works by John Steinbeck

Long Fiction
Cup of Gold, 1929
The Pastures of Heaven, 1932
To a God Unknown, 1933
Tortilla Flat, 1935
In Dubious Battle, 1936
Of Mice and Men, 1937
The Red Pony, 1937
The Grapes of Wrath, 1939
The Moon Is Down, 1942
Cannery Row, 1945
The Pearl, 1945 (serial), 1947 (book)
The Wayward Bus, 1947
Burning Bright, 1950
East of Eden, 1952
Sweet Thursday, 1954
The Short Reign of Pippin IV, 1957
The Winter of Our Discontent, 1961

Short Fiction
Saint Katy the Virgin, 1936
The Long Valley, 1938

Nonfiction
Their Blood Is Strong, 1938
The Forgotten Village, 1941
Sea of Cortez: A Leisurely Journal of Travel and Research, 1941 (with Edward F. Ricketts)
Bombs Away, 1942
A Russian Journal, 1948 (with Robert Capa)
Once There Was a War, 1958
Travels with Charley: In Search of America, 1962
Letters to Alicia, 1965
America and Americans, 1966
Journal of a Novel: The "East of Eden" Letters, 1969
Steinbeck: A Life in Letters, 1975 (Elaine Steinbeck and Robert Wallsten, editors)

Steinbeck and Covici: The Story of a Friendship, 1979 (Thomas Fensch, editor)

Working Days: The Journals of "The Grapes of Wrath," 1938-1941, 1989 (Robert DeMott, editor)

America and Americans, and Selected Nonfiction, 2002 (Susan Shillinglaw and Jackson J. Benson, editors)

Screenplays

The Forgotten Village, 1941
Lifeboat, 1944
The Pearl, 1945
A Medal for Benny, 1945
The Red Pony, 1949
Viva Zapata!, 1952

Drama

Of Mice and Men, pr., pb. 1937
The Moon Is Down, pr. 1942
Burning Bright, pb. 1951

Translation

The Acts of King Arthur and His Noble Knights, 1976

Bibliography

Astro, Richard, and Tetsumaro Hayashi, eds. *Steinbeck: The Man and His Work.* Corvallis: Oregon State University Press, 1971.

Baskind, Samantha. "The 'True' Story: *Life* Magazine, Horace Bristol, and John Steinbeck's *The Grapes of Wrath.*" *Steinbeck Studies* 15.2 (Winter 2004): 40-74.

Beegel, Susan F., Susan Shillinglaw, and Wesley N. Tiffney, Jr., eds. *Steinbeck and the Environment: Interdisciplinary Approaches.* Tuscaloosa: University of Alabama Press, 1997.

Benson, Jackson J. *Looking for Steinbeck's Ghost.* 1988. Reno: University of Nevada Press, 2002.

_____. "To Tom, Who Lived It: John Steinbeck and the Man from Weedpatch." *Journal of Modern Literature* 5.2 (Apr. 1976): 151-210.

_____. *The True Adventures of John Steinbeck, Writer.* New York: Viking Press, 1984.

_____, ed. *The Short Novels of John Steinbeck: Critical Essays with a Checklist to Steinbeck Criticism.* Durham, NC: Duke University Press, 1990.

Bloom, Harold, ed. *John Steinbeck.* New York: Chelsea House, 2008.

Burkhead, Cynthia. *Student Companion to John Steinbeck.* Westport, CT: Greenwood Press, 2002.

Coers, Donald V. *John Steinbeck Goes to War: "The Moon Is Down" as Propaganda.* Tuscaloosa: University of Alabama Press, 2006.

Crockett, H. Kelly. "The Bible and *The Grapes of Wrath.*" *College English* 24 (1962): 193-99.

Cruz, Frank Eugene. "'In Between a Past and Future Town': Home, the Unhomely, and *The Grapes of Wrath.*" *Steinbeck Review* 4.2 (Fall 2007): 53-75.

Davis, Robert Con, ed. *"The Grapes of Wrath": A Collection of Critical Essays.* Englewood Cliffs, NJ: Prentice-Hall, 1982.

Davis, Robert Murray, ed. *Steinbeck: A Collection of Critical Essays.* Englewood Cliffs, NJ: Prentice-Hall, 1972.

DeMott, Robert. *Steinbeck's Typewriter: Essays on His Art.* Troy, NY: Whitston, 1996.

Ditsky, John. *John Steinbeck and the Critics.* Rochester, NY: Camden House, 2000.

_____, ed. *Critical Essays on Steinbeck's "The Grapes of Wrath."* Boston: G. K. Hall, 1989.

Dunlap, James. "Through the Eyes of Tom Joad: Patterns of American Idealism, Bob Dylan, and the Folk Protest Movement." *Popular Music and Society* 29.5 (Dec. 2006): 549-73.

Fontenrose, Joseph. *John Steinbeck: An Introduction and Interpretation.* New York: Holt, Rinehart and Winston, 1963.

French, Warren. *John Steinbeck.* 2nd rev. ed. Boston: Twayne, 1975.

_____. *John Steinbeck's Fiction Revisited*. New York: Twayne, 1994.

_____, ed. *A Companion to "The Grapes of Wrath."* 1963. New York: Penguin, 1989.

George, Stephen K., ed. *John Steinbeck: A Centennial Tribute*. New York: Praeger, 2002.

_____, ed. *The Moral Philosophy of John Steinbeck*. Lanham, MD: Scarecrow Press, 2005.

George, Stephen K., and Barbara A. Heavilin, eds. *John Steinbeck and His Contemporaries*. Lanham, MD: Scarecrow Press, 2007.

Hayashi, Tetsumaro, ed. *John Steinbeck: The Years of Greatness, 1936-1939*. Tuscaloosa: University of Alabama Press, 1993.

_____, ed. *A New Study Guide to Steinbeck's Major Works, with Critical Explications*. Metuchen, NJ: Scarecrow, 1993.

_____, ed. *Steinbeck's Literary Dimension: A Guide to Comparative Studies*. Metuchen, NJ: Scarecrow Press, 1973.

_____, ed. *Steinbeck's Short Stories in "The Long Valley": Essays in Criticism*. Muncie, IN: Steinbeck Research Institution, 1991.

Heavilin, Barbara A., ed. *The Critical Response to John Steinbeck's "The Grapes of Wrath."* Westport, CT: Greenwood Press, 2000.

Henderson, George. "John Steinbeck's Spatial Imagination in *The Grapes of Wrath*: A Critical Essay." *California History* 68.4 (Winter 1989-90): 210-23.

Hughes, R. S. *John Steinbeck: A Study of the Short Fiction*. New York: Twayne, 1989.

Jain, Sunita. *John Steinbeck's Concept of Man: A Critical Study of His Novels*. New Delhi: New Statesman, 1979.

Johnson, Claudia Durst, ed. *Understanding "Of Mice and Men," "The Red Pony," and "The Pearl": A Student Casebook to Issues, Sources, and Historical Documents*. Westport, CT: Greenwood Press, 1997.

Levant, Howard. *The Novels of John Steinbeck: A Critical Study*. Columbia: University of Missouri Press, 1974.

Lisca, Peter. *John Steinbeck: Nature and Myth*. New York: Crowell, 1978.

_____. *The Wide World of John Steinbeck*. New Brunswick, NJ: Rutgers University Press, 1958.

McCarthy, Paul. *John Steinbeck*. New York: Frederick Ungar, 1980.

McElrath, Joseph R., Jr., Jesse S. Crisler, and Susan Shillinglaw, eds. *John Steinbeck: The Contemporary Reviews*. New York: Cambridge University Press, 1996.

Noble, Donald R., ed. *The Steinbeck Questions: New Essays in Criticism*. Troy, NY: Whitston, 1993.

Owens, Louis. *"The Grapes of Wrath": Trouble in the Promised Land*. Boston: Twayne, 1989.

_____. *John Steinbeck's Re-vision of America*. Athens: University of Georgia Press, 1985.

Parini, Jay. *John Steinbeck: A Biography*. New York: Henry Holt, 1995.

Railsback, Brian E. *Parallel Expeditions: Charles Darwin and the Art of John Steinbeck*. Moscow: University of Idaho Press, 1995.

Schultz, Jeffrey, and Luchen Li. *A Critical Companion to John Steinbeck: A Literary Reference to His Life and Work*. New York: Facts On File, 2005.

Seelye, John "Unlikely Transfusions: Wise Blood and *The Grapes of Wrath*." *Steinbeck Studies* 15.1 (Spring 2004): 41-45.

Shillinglaw, Susan, and Kevin Hearle, eds. *Beyond Boundaries: Rereading John Steinbeck*. Tuscaloosa: University of Alabama Press, 2002.

Tedlock, E. W., Jr., and C. V. Wicker, eds. *Steinbeck and His Critics: A Record of Twenty-five Years*. Albuquerque: University of New Mexico Press, 1957.

Timmerman, John H. *The Dramatic Landscape of Steinbeck's Short Stories*. Norman: University of Oklahoma Press, 1990.

_____. *John Steinbeck's Fiction: The Aesthetics of the Road Taken*. Norman: University of Oklahoma Press, 1986.

Wartzman, Rick. *Obscene in the Extreme: The Burning and Banning of John Steinbeck's "The Grapes of Wrath."* New York: PublicAffairs, 2008.

White, Ray Lewis. "The Grapes of Wrath and the Critics of 1939." *Resources for American Literary Study* 13.2 (1983): 134-64.

Wyatt, David, ed. *New Essays on "The Grapes of Wrath."* New York: Cambridge University Press, 1990.

CRITICAL
INSIGHTS

About the Editor

Keith Newlin is Professor and Chair of the Department of English at the University of North Carolina Wilmington, where he teaches courses in American literary realism and naturalism, American modernism, and American drama. The recipient of a fellowship from the National Endowment for the Humanities, he is the author of *Hamlin Garland: A Life* (2008), coeditor of *The Collected Plays of Theodore Dreiser* (2000) and *Selected Letters of Hamlin Garland* (1998), and editor of *A Summer to Be: A Memoir by the Daughter of Hamlin Garland* (2010), *A Theodore Dreiser Encyclopedia* (2003), *American Plays of the New Woman* (2000), and Hamlin Garland's *Rose of Dutcher's Coolly* (2005) and *The Book of the American Indian* (2005). He is past president of the International Theodore Dreiser Society and the Hamlin Garland Society, and at present he is the coeditor of *Studies in American Naturalism*, distributed by the University of Nebraska Press.

About *The Paris Review*

The Paris Review is America's preeminent literary quarterly, dedicated to discovering and publishing the best new voices in fiction, nonfiction, and poetry. The magazine was founded in Paris in 1953 by the young American writers Peter Matthiessen and Doc Humes, and edited there and in New York for its first fifty years by George Plimpton. Over the decades, the *Review* has introduced readers to the earliest writings of Jack Kerouac, Philip Roth, T. C. Boyle, V. S. Naipaul, Ha Jin, Ann Patchett, Jay McInerney, Mona Simpson, and Edward P. Jones, and published numerous now classic works, including Roth's *Goodbye, Columbus*, Donald Barthelme's *Alice*, Jim Carroll's *Basketball Diaries*, and selections from Samuel Beckett's *Molloy* (his first publication in English). The first chapter of Jeffrey Eugenides's *The Virgin Suicides* appeared in the *Review*'s pages, as well as stories by Rick Moody, David Foster Wallace, Denis Johnson, Jim Crace, Lorrie Moore, and Jeanette Winterson.

The Paris Review's renowned Writers at Work series of interviews, whose early installments include legendary conversations with E. M. Forster, William Faulkner, and Ernest Hemingway, is one of the landmarks of world literature. The interviews received a George Polk Award and were nominated for a Pulitzer Prize. Among the more than three hundred interviewees are Robert Frost, Marianne Moore, W. H. Auden, Elizabeth Bishop, Susan Sontag, and Toni Morrison. Recent issues feature conversations with Salman Rushdie, Joan Didion, Norman Mailer, Kazuo Ishiguro, Marilynne Robinson, Umberto Eco, Annie Proulx, and Gay Talese. In November 2009, Picador published the final volume of a four-volume series of anthologies of *Paris Review* interviews. *The New York Times* called the Writers at Work series "the most remarkable and extensive interviewing project we possess."

The Paris Review is edited by Philip Gourevitch, who was named to the post in 2005, following the death of George Plimpton two years earlier. A new editorial team has published fiction by André Aciman, Colum McCann, Damon Galgut, Mohsin Hamid, Uzodinma Iweala, Gish Jen, Stephen King, James Lasdun, Padgett Powell, Richard Price, and Sam Shepard. Poetry editors Charles Simic, Meghan O'Rourke, and Dan Chiasson have selected works by John Ashbery, Kay Ryan, Billy Collins, Tomaž Šalamun, Mary Jo Bang, Sharon Olds, Charles Wright, and Mary Karr. Writing published in the magazine has been anthologized in *Best American Short Stories* (2006, 2007, and 2008), *Best American Poetry*, *Best Creative Non-Fiction*, the Pushcart Prize anthology, and *O. Henry Prize Stories*.

The magazine presents two annual awards. The Hadada Award for lifelong contribution to literature has recently been given to Joan Didion, Norman Mailer, Peter Matthiessen, and, in 2009, John Ashbery. The Plimpton Prize for Fiction, awarded to a debut or emerging writer brought to national attention in the pages of *The Paris Review*, was presented in 2007 to Benjamin Percy, to Jesse Ball in 2008, and to Alistair Morgan in 2009.

The Paris Review was a finalist for the 2008 and 2009 National Magazine Awards in fiction, and it won the 2007 National Magazine Award in photojournalism. The *Los Angeles Times* recently called *The Paris Review* "an American treasure with true international reach."

Since 1999 *The Paris Review* has been published by The Paris Review Foundation, Inc., a not-for-profit 501(c)(3) organization.

The Paris Review is available in digital form to libraries worldwide in selected academic databases exclusively from EBSCO Publishing. Libraries can contact EBSCO at 1-800-653-2726 for details. For more information on *The Paris Review* or to subscribe, please visit: www.theparisreview.org.

Contributors

Keith Newlin is Professor and Chair of the Department of English at the University of North Carolina Wilmington. He is the author or editor of ten books, and his recent work includes *Hamlin Garland: A Life* (2008) and, as editor, *A Summer to Be: A Memoir by the Daughter of Hamlin Garland* (2008), *A Theodore Dreiser Encyclopedia* (2003), and two reprints of books by Hamlin Garland. At present he is the coeditor of *Studies in American Naturalism*, distributed by the University of Nebraska Press.

Joseph R. Millichap is Professor Emeritus of English at Western Kentucky University. His most recent books include *A Backward Glance: The Southern Renaissance, the Autobiographical Epic, and the Classical Legacy* (2009) and *Robert Penn Warren After "Audubon": The Work of Aging and the Quest for Transcendence in His Later Poetry* (2009).

Ha Jin is the author of five novels, four collections of stories, three collections of poems, and one collection of essays. He has won the National Book Award, two PEN/Faulkner Awards, three Pushcart Prizes, a PEN/Hemingway Award, and a Flannery O'Connor Award. He is a member of the American Academy of Arts and Sciences and has been a Guggenheim fellow and a finalist for the Pulitzer Prize. He was born in Liaoning, China, and came to the United States in 1984. He lives in Foxboro, Massachusetts, and teaches writing at Boston University.

Jennifer Banach is a writer and independent scholar who lives in Connecticut. She has served as the contributing editor of *Bloom's Guides: Heart of Darkness* (2009) and *Bloom's Guides: The Glass Menagerie* (2007) and is the author of *Bloom's How to Write About Tennessee Williams* (2009) and *Understanding Norman Mailer* (2010). She has also composed teaching guides to international literature for Random House's Academic Resources division and has contributed to numerous literary reference books for academic publishers on topics ranging from Romanticism to contemporary literature. Her work has appeared in academic and popular venues alike; her fiction and nonfiction have appeared under the *Esquire* banner. She is a member of the Association of Literary Scholars and Critics.

Matthew J. Bolton is Professor of English at Loyola School in New York City, where he also serves as Dean of Students. He received his doctor of philosophy degree in English from the Graduate Center of the City University of New York (CUNY) in 2005. His dissertation at the university was titled "Transcending the Self in Robert Browning and T. S. Eliot." Prior to attaining his Ph.D. at CUNY, he also earned a master of philosophy degree in English (2004) and a master of science degree in English education (2001). His undergraduate work was done at the State University of New York at Binghamton, where he studied English literature.

Michael Wentworth is Professor of English at the University of North Carolina Wilmington. He has published work in *American Transcendental Quarterly*, *Midwest-*

ern Drama, Connotations: A Journal of Critical Debate, and *MidAmerica: The Yearbook of the Society for the Study of Midwestern Literature*. His research interests include American travel literature, popular-culture studies, and midwestern literature.

Camille-Yvette Welsch is a senior lecturer in English at the Pennsylvania State University. She is the director of Penn State's Summer Creative Writing Conference for high school students and the coordinator of the Red Weather Reading Series. Her work has appeared in *Mid-American Review, Barrow Street, The Writer's Chronicle, The Women's Review of Books,* and *Small Spiral Notebook*.

Frederic I. Carpenter was an authority on Eugene O'Neill, Robinson Jeffers, and Ralph Waldo Emerson. He is the author of *Eugene O'Neill* (1964), *Robinson Jeffers* (1962), *American Literature and the Dream* (1955), and *Emerson Handbook* (1953), among other titles. His correspondence with O'Neill and Jeffers, spanning forty years, is collected in the University of California's Bancroft Library in Berkeley. He taught at the University of Chicago, Harvard University, and the University of California at Berkeley. He died in 1991 at the age of eighty-eight.

Martin Shockley is Professor Emeritus of English at the University of North Texas, where he taught for twenty-four years. He has also taught at the University of Oklahoma, Evansville College, and Carleton College and at the University of Cape Town in South Africa, where he was a Fulbright professor. He has served as president of the Poetry Society of Texas and has published many textbooks, essays, articles, and poems.

Eric W. Carlson is Professor Emeritus of English at the University of Connecticut, Storrs. He is the editor of three major anthologies on Edgar Allan Poe: *Poe: "The Fall of the House of Usher"* (1971), *Introduction to Poe: A Thematic Reader* (1967), and *The Recognition of Edgar Allan Poe* (1966). He is also a founding member and the first president of the Poe Studies Association.

Peter Lisca, who died in 2001, taught at the University of North Carolina, the University of Washington, and the University of Florida. His publications include *John Steinbeck: Nature and Myth* (1978), *The Wide World of John Steinbeck* (1958), and, as editor, *"The Grapes of Wrath": Text and Criticism* (1997).

Warren Motley was Professor of English at Rutgers University and is the author of *The American Abraham: James Fenimore Cooper and the Frontier Patriarch* (1987).

Howard Levant was Professor Emeritus at the Rochester Institute of Technology, where he managed the Photo School's Alumni Database before retiring in 2005. He is the author of *The Novels of John Steinbeck: A Critical Study* (1974), and his poetry has been published in the *Yale Review, Poetry,* and *Sewanee Review.*

Donald Pizer is Pierce Butler Professor Emeritus of English at Tulane University, where he has taught since 1957. His books include *Dos Passos' "U.S.A.": A Critical Study* (1988) and *Twentieth-Century American Literary Naturalism: An Interpretation* (1982). He is the editor of several volumes on the works of Theodore Dreiser, Stephen Crane, Hamlin Garland, and Jack London.

John H. Timmerman is Professor of English at Calvin College. His recent publications include *Woman, Why Are You Weeping? Daily Meditations for Lent* (2007) and *Light of the World: Daily Meditations for Advent* (2007). His scholarly writings focus on the works of Robert Frost, T. S. Eliot, John Steinbeck, and others.

Robert DeMott is the Edwin and Ruth Kennedy Distinguished Professor of American Literature and Writing at Ohio University. He has published more than a dozen books, including *Steinbeck's Typewriter: Essays on His Art* (1996), and has edited John Steinbeck's *Working Days: The Journals of "The Grapes of Wrath"* (1989). His essays have appeared in such journals as *The Georgia Review, The Southern Review*, and *Studies in American Fiction and American Literature.*

Keith Windschuttle is the publisher of Macleay Press and editor of *Quadrant* magazine. An Australian writer and historian, he has published such books as *The White Australia Policy* (2004), *The Killing of History* (1994), and *Unemployment* (1979). He has been a lecturer in Australian history, media, and social policy at various Australian and American universities.

Charles Cunningham is Associate Professor of English Language and Literature at Eastern Michigan University. Lecturing primarily on American literature and culture, he serves as department steward and Bargaining Council representative in the EMU chapter of the American Association of University Professors. Currently, he is researching his next book, which will explore race and individualism during the Great Depression.

Vivyan C. Adair is Elihu Root Peace Fund Chair and Associate Professor of Women's Studies at Hamilton College. In addition to serving as Director of The ACCESS Project at Hamilton, she enjoys teaching nineteenth- and twentieth-century American literature and topics related to race, class, and gender. In 2004, she was named CASE/Carnegie New York State Professor of the Year. Her publications include *Reclaiming Class: Women, Poverty, and the Promise of Education in America* (2003) and *From Good Ma to Welfare Queen: A Genealogy of the Poor Woman in American Literature, Photography, and Culture* (2000).

Acknowledgments

"John Steinbeck" by Joseph R. Millichap. From *Critical Survey of Long Fiction*. 4th ed. Edited by Carl Rollyson. Pasadena, CA: Salem Press, 2010.

"The *Paris Review* Perspective" by Ha Jin. Copyright © 2011 by Ha Jin. Special appreciation goes to Nathaniel Rich, Christopher Cox, and David Wallace-Wells, editors at *The Paris Review*.

"The Philosophical Joads" by Frederic I. Carpenter. From *College English* 2, no. 4 (1941): 315-325. Originally published by the National Council of Teachers of English.

"Christian Symbolism in *The Grapes of Wrath*" by Martin Shockley. From *College English* 18 (1956): 87-90. Originally published by the National Council of Teachers of English.

"Rebuttal: Symbolism in *The Grapes of Wrath*" by Eric W. Carlson. From *College English* 19 (1958): 172-175. Originally published by the National Council of Teachers of English.

"*The Grapes of Wrath* as Fiction" by Peter Lisca. From *PMLA* 72, no. 1 (1957): 296-309. Copyright © 1957 by the Modern Language Association. Reprinted with permission of the Modern Language Association

"From Patriarchy to Matriarchy: Ma Joad's Role in *The Grapes of Wrath*" by Warren Motley. From *American Literature* 54, no. 3 (1982): 397-412. Copyright © 1982 by Duke University Press. All rights reserved. Used by permission of the publisher.

"The Fully Matured Art: *The Grapes of Wrath*" by Howard Levant. From *The Novels of John Steinbeck: A Critical Study* (1974), pp. 93-129. Copyright © 1974 by the Curators of the University of Missouri. Reprinted with permission of the University of Missouri Press.

"John Steinbeck: *The Grapes of Wrath*" by Donald Pizer. From *Twentieth-Century American Literary Naturalism: An Interpretation* (1982), pp. 65-81. Copyright © 1982 by Southern Illinois University Press. Reprinted with permission of Southern Illinois University Press.

"The Wine of God's Wrath: *The Grapes of Wrath*" by John H. Timmerman. From *John Steinbeck's Fiction: The Aesthetics of the Road Taken* (1986), pp. 102-132. Copyright © 1986 by the University of Oklahoma Press. Reprinted with permission of the University of Oklahoma Press.

"'A Truly American Book': Pressing *The Grapes of Wrath*" by Robert DeMott. From *Biographies of Books: The Compositional Histories of Notable American Writings*, edited by James Barbour and Tom Quirk (1996), pp. 187-225. Copyright © 1996 by the Curators of the University of Missouri. Reprinted with permission of the University of Missouri Press.

"Steinbeck's Myth of the Okies" by Keith Windschuttle. From *The New Criterion*

Index

Imagery, 184, 369; animals, 240;
biblical, 94, 124, 196, 377; death, 72,
127, 136, 147, 153, 187, 189, 191,
197, 251, 353; dust, 41, 49, 60, 142,
314, 370; life, 230
In Dubious Battle (Steinbeck), 16, 88,
144, 178, 188, 198, 212, 277, 324, 359
Interchapters, 21, 45, 73, 95, 99, 104,
113, 133, 140-141, 145, 155, 165,
176, 180, 189, 194, 212, 229, 239,
241, 254, 288, 345-346, 349, 357,
360; Route 66, 65, 146; turtle, 136,
142, 183, 239; used cars, 150, 240
Interrante, Joseph, 63

Jackson, Joseph Henry, 91, 260, 307-308
Jain, Sunita, 101
James, William, 121
Jim Casy. *See* Casy, Jim
Jim Rawley. *See* Rawley, Jim
Joad, Al (*The Grapes of Wrath*), 63, 119,
186, 188
Joad, Ma (*The Grapes of Wrath*), 36, 80,
103, 158, 186, 221, 235, 242, 245,
252, 326, 356, 373; leadership role,
166, 193, 254, 375
Joad, Noah (*The Grapes of Wrath*), 73,
129, 132, 187, 212, 300
Joad, Pa (*The Grapes of Wrath*), 76, 103,
168
Joad, Tom (*The Grapes of Wrath*), 34,
60, 101, 173, 203; influence of Casy
on, 118, 185, 298; as Prodigal Son,
130, 132
Joyce, James, 45

Katz, Michael B., 363
Kennedy, William, 304
Kocela, Chris, 104
Krim, Arthur, 65
Kunitz, Stanley, 290

Labor strikes, 30, 38, 88, 121, 178,
225, 277, 283, 309, 322, 336, 345,
357
Labor unions, 30, 32, 75, 174, 185, 225,
322, 336, 342, 359
"L'Affaire Lettuceberg" (Steinbeck), 33,
89, 179, 208, 237, 271, 282
Landownership, 61, 116, 141, 152, 164,
316, 325, 351, 357
Lange, Dorothea, 88, 139, 277, 287,
313, 319
Lawrence, D. H., 264
Lefkowitz, Rochelle, 363
Lewis, C. S., 46
Lewis, R. W. B., 105
Lisca, Peter, 68, 76, 95, 101, 175, 196,
212, 266, 289
Lorentz, Pare, 273, 295, 308, 310, 331,
359
Lubbock, Percy, 140, 144

Ma Joad. *See* Joad, Ma
McCarthy, Paul, 57, 64
McWilliams, Carey, 84, 98, 292, 303,
335, 337, 359
Maine, Barry G., 96
"Manself" concept, 68, 223, 228, 292,
296
Matriarchal values, 159, 252, 373
Meyer, Michael, 95
Minter, David, 38
Modernist literature, 14, 40, 45, 306,
323
Monroe, Elizabeth N., 154
Moore, Harry Thornton, 93, 139, 212,
288
Mothers, 103, 154, 159, 173, 219, 245,
252, 356, 364
Mothers, The (Briffault), 159
Motley, Warren, 372
Muley Graves. *See* Graves, Muley